Learning to Forget

Learning to Forget

**US ARMY COUNTERINSURGENCY DOCTRINE
AND PRACTICE FROM VIETNAM TO IRAQ**

David Fitzgerald

Stanford Security Studies
An Imprint of Stanford University Press
Stanford, California

Stanford University Press
Stanford, California

Special discounts for bulk quantities of Stanford Security Studies are available to corporations, professional associations, and other organizations. For details and discount information, contact the special sales department of Stanford University Press.
Tel: (650) 736-1782, Fax: (650) 725-3457

Printed in the United States of America on acid-free, archival-quality paper

Library of Congress Cataloging-in-Publication Data
Learning to forget : US Army counterinsurgency doctrine and practice from Vietnam to Iraq / David Fitzgerald.
     pages cm
   Includes bibliographical references and index.
   ISBN 978-0-8047-8581-5 (cloth : alk. paper)
   ISBN 978-0-8047-9337-7 (pbk. : alk. paper)
     1. Counterinsurgency—United States—History. 2. United States. Army—History.
3. Vietnam War, 1961–1975—United States. 4. Vietnam War, 1961–1975—Influence.
5. Iraq War, 2003–2011. I. Title.
   U241.F58 2013
   355.02'18097309045—dc23

                                                        2012043943

Typeset by Thompson Type in 10/14 Minion

For Sarah

CONTENTS

Acknowledgments   ix

Introduction: Counterinsurgency and the Uses of History   1

1   The Army's Counterinsurgency War in Vietnam   19

2   "Out of the Rice Paddies": The 1970s and the Decline
of Counterinsurgency   39

3   Low-Intensity Conflict in the Reagan Years   60

4   Peacekeeping and Operations Other Than War in the 1990s   86

5   Mr. Rumsfeld's War: Transformation, Doctrine,
and "Phase IV" Planning for Iraq   109

6   Counterinsurgency and "Vietnam" in Iraq, 2003–2006   134

7   The Return to Counterinsurgency: FM 3-24 and the "Surge"   157

8   A Never-Ending War? The Renegotiation of "Vietnam"
in Afghanistan   181

Conclusion   203

Notes   215

Index   275

ACKNOWLEDGMENTS

IN THE WRITING OF THIS BOOK I have incurred considerable debts of gratitude to a number of people, and I am happy to have the opportunity to thank them, however inadequately, here. First on the list of those to be thanked must be my family—my parents and my sister Claire. It was they more than anyone else who were there—quite literally—from the start and put up with conversations (usually more like monologues) about the "thesis" and then the "book" for what must have seemed like an interminable length of time. Despite all this, their love and support never wavered.

This book began as doctoral dissertation in University College Cork and was finished there when I returned as a staff member. I could not imagine a better home in which to study and work than the School of History. In particular, Sarah-Anne Buckley, Mike Cullinane, James Ryan, and John Borgonovo have provided wonderful friendship and support over the years. Many of the revisions from thesis to book took place during my time at the Clinton Institute for American Studies in University College Dublin, where Liam Kennedy and Catherine Carey have created an extraordinary scholarly community. I owe them a debt of gratitude for welcoming me into that community.

I would also like to recognize the intellectual contribution and support provided by a number of scholars. The two anonymous reviewers helped me sharpen my argument, while John Dumbrell and Geoff Roberts were generous and helpful examiners. Geoff's help in preparing the manuscript for publication was invaluable. Joe Lee was immensely generous to me throughout my time at New York University, and Marilyn Young's wit, passion, and intellect have been (and continue to be) inspirational, while Anders Stephanson's critical rigor strongly enhanced this study at a crucial phase in its development. I have greatly benefitted from conversations with T. X. Hammes, Tim Hoyt, Andrew Mumford, Lydia Walker, Steven Metz, Andrew Birtle, and Conrad Crane. Professor Crane was also instrumental in assisting me in my research at the Military History Institute, while David Keough and Jessica Sheets at the Military History Institute, Richard Boylan at NARA, and Wanda Williams at the Nixon Archive were all helpful in helping me navigate through the vastness of the archives. Funding was provided by the College of Arts, Celtic Studies and Social Sciences and the Department of History at University College Cork, and the Department of Arts, Sports and Tourism of the Irish Government, who funded my fellowship at NYU. Thanks are also due to the National University of Ireland, who generously helped to defray the publication costs of this volume via their "grants toward scholarly publications" scheme. I also want to thank Geoffrey Burn of Stanford University Press, who saw potential in this project and has been extraordinarily professional and supportive throughout the process.

My primary intellectual debt is to David Ryan, my supervisor and mentor, who has been extraordinarily generous with his time, advice, and library. David contributed immensely to my intellectual and professional development and he has been an astute critic, a reader, a counselor, a role model and, most importantly, a friend. Sarah Thelen has commented on and critiqued virtually every draft of every chapter and has given me so much support on this project that words can't express the thanks I owe her. Sarah is not only smarter than I am but a much better writer, and this book would not be nearly as readable without her input. I can't blame her for the errors, though, as she seems to have developed some form of academic Stockholm syndrome along the way and become far more interested in military doctrine and counterinsurgency than I think she ever anticipated. I'm incredibly lucky that she's been there to share this journey, which would not have been possible without her, and it is to her that I dedicate this book.

Learning to Forget

INTRODUCTION

Counterinsurgency and the Uses of History

ON WEDNESDAY MAY 23, 1962, Major General Victor Krulak, special assistant to the Joint Chiefs of Staff for counterinsurgency and special operations, addressed the students and staff of the US Army War College. Krulak's subject was the "Tactics and Techniques of Insurgency and Counterinsurgency," and he began his lecture by quoting a passage from *Alice in Wonderland*, recounting that when Alice asked the White Queen what a word meant, the Queen replied: "What does it mean? Why, it means what I mean it to mean."[1] To Krulak, this illustrated the difficulty of defining *counterinsurgency*: "Each of us has a mental picture of the term, and each picture is different—either as to foreground, background, subject matter, color, or texture. This is one of our real problems."[2] If Krulak admitted that the definition of *counterinsurgency* was complicated, then a similar dilemma soon extended to the lessons of the ongoing war in Vietnam, which proved even more difficult to characterize and harder to simplify into something that could be meaningfully understood as a lesson. This book concerns itself with understanding how the US Army comprehended the lessons of the war in Vietnam and the concept of counterinsurgency that Krulak struggled to define. It is interested in what the US Army meant both *Vietnam* and *counterinsurgency* to mean—that is, the combination of ideology, memory, and identity at work in shaping the Army's constructed understandings of these terms. These various meanings grew out of efforts to process and make sense of the failures in Vietnam.

The lessons of Vietnam have been intensely contested, with disputes over which lessons should be heeded emerging even before the end of American involvement in the war in 1973. Indeed, the struggle over the lessons of Vietnam has been a defining feature of the politics of intervention within the United States, surviving repeated declarations by various presidents that the ghosts of Vietnam had been buried.[3]

This book evolved from an interest in repeated references to Vietnam in narratives of the U.S. war in Iraq. While the analogies could certainly be overwrought and were often overused, the wars in Vietnam and Iraq are linked both through the history of counterinsurgency doctrine within the US Army and the evolving manner in which the US Army understood the Vietnam War in the aftermath of the US retreat from Indochina.[4]

Defeat in Vietnam led the Army to consciously turn away from its experience there and discard what it had learned about counterinsurgency. But the Army could escape neither Vietnam nor counterinsurgency and had to deal with new missions such as low-intensity conflict and peacekeeping that modified its understanding of the lessons of Vietnam. Despite these new missions, the Army's post-Vietnam distaste for counterinsurgency endured. This aversion led to major problems when confronted with insurgency in Iraq. The reasons for both the Army's struggle to deal with this insurgency and its subsequent construction of an entirely new doctrine to address the problems posed by Iraq were deeply rooted in the Vietnam War's competing lessons. The Army's experience in Iraq is a fascinating case study of how an organization can reshape historical memory in an attempt to make it more useful to present challenges.

The use of Vietnam as lesson and analogy, particularly within the US Army, highlights the interplay between military doctrine and the construction of historical narrative. To echo Mikkel Vedby Rassmussen, what is interesting is not necessarily the lessons of history themselves, but rather the "history of the lesson."[5] The Vietnam War not only had a profound effect on Army attitudes toward counterinsurgency, but, as this book will demonstrate, the Army's consensus on the lessons of Vietnam shifted as the needs of contemporary operations dictated: The lessons themselves changed with exigencies of the moment. This book is concerned not only with specific questions of the US Army's relationship with counterinsurgency and the Vietnam War but also with the broader issue of how histories can be constructed and reinterpreted. Historical analogy can influence policy not only in the immediate moment of decision but in setting the broader context for those decisions—the creation of formal and informal doctrine. By studying the evolution of doctrine, this book addresses the question of how these analogies are constructed and used, a question that speaks to how histories are created and why.

By looking at the evolution of doctrine over an extended period, this book will demonstrate that the Army's lessons of Vietnam were fluid, contested, and changeable. It will outline how the construction of lessons is tied to the production of historical memory and describe the interplay between the two processes. It will examine how terms such as *counterinsurgency* and *nation building* have been debated within the US military and describe how agreed-on lessons informed both policy and doctrine and how the realities of war highlighted the malleability of historical memory, how "useful" histories were constructed to serve the needs of the present.

THE US ARMY AND COUNTERINSURGENCY

The US Army's changing understanding of counterinsurgency reflected the processes of collective memory and the evolution of the "lessons of history" in a way that suggests how the past can be used in service of present needs. For while counterinsurgency was and is a malleable concept, the manner in which its meaning and significance within the US Army changed suggests that it was a particularly loaded term within that organization. Russell Weigley's commentary on the matter reflects much of the consensus on the relationship:

> Guerrilla warfare is so incongruous to the natural methods and habits of a stable and well-to-do society that the American Army has tended to regard it as abnormal and to forget about it whenever possible. Each new experience with irregular warfare has required, then, that appropriate techniques be learned all over again.[6]

The literature on the US Army and counterinsurgency indicates that the Army has had a difficult relationship with counterinsurgency; several studies have depicted it as an organization deeply ambivalent toward that form of warfare. Perhaps the most influential work on the US Army and counterinsurgency is John Nagl's *Learning to Eat Soup with a Knife: Counterinsurgency Lessons from Malaya and Vietnam*. Nagl argues that the British Army succeeded in Malaya where the US Army failed in Vietnam because it possessed a learning culture and a flexibility that allowed it to quickly adapt to the realities of counterinsurgency warfare to defeat the communist insurgents.[7] No such learning culture existed in the US Army. According to Nagl, the lessons the

United States drew from Vietnam did nothing to address its shortcomings in counterinsurgency warfare.

This argument appears throughout the literature on the US Army and counterinsurgency. Authors such as Robert Cassidy, Richard Downie, and Conrad Crane all point to a military that retreated from counterinsurgency in the aftermath of the Vietnam War.[8] David Ucko offers an updated version of this thesis in *The New Counterinsurgency Era*,[9] echoing criticism of the US Army's historical attitudes toward counterinsurgency. Ucko, although he is more optimistic about the way in which the post-2003 Army adapted itself to counterinsurgency operations, asserts that the United States suffered from a "counterinsurgency syndrome" whereby they persistently marginalized counterinsurgency operations.

Others argue that the Army has a long history of engagement in counterinsurgency-style operations and never really lost its understanding of counterinsurgency. Andrew J. Birtle's *U.S. Army Counterinsurgency and Contingency Operations Doctrine, 1942–1976*, perhaps the most carefully researched work on the US Army and counterinsurgency, describes the continuity in US doctrine.[10] Birtle contends that the Army *did* in fact pay attention to counterinsurgency historically and that failure in Vietnam and elsewhere had more to do with strategic choices about intervention rather than any operational failures on the part of the US Army. His study traces the evolution of doctrine in impressive detail and questions many of the assumptions behind "hearts and minds" counterinsurgency, instead arguing that coercion and use of force were responsible for most of the US Army's successes and that many of these successes—particularly in Vietnam—were divorced from strategic goals.

Other authors describe a long tradition of American intervention in small wars as a phenomenon rich enough—and important enough—to be considered a major, if often neglected, part of the Army's identity. These authors differ on their attitudes to counterinsurgency and US intervention more broadly; some, like Max Boot and Robert Kaplan, see counterinsurgency as another American way of war, one that needs to be celebrated and promoted.[11] More critical scholars, such as D. Michael Shafer and Michael McClintock, see US involvement in counterinsurgency operations in a more negative light, arguing that optimism about modernization theory and US counterinsurgency capabilities led to disaster in Vietnam and support for repressive regimes throughout the developing world.[12] Both those critical and those supportive of US involvement in counterinsurgency agree that the United States has a long tradition of involvement in small wars—from the conflict with Barbary pirates to the banana wars in Central America to the American war in Vietnam to Reagan's support for the Contras in Nicaragua.

There are, then, two contending narratives of the US Army's relationship with counterinsurgency. One school of thought emphasizes the Army's long involvement in such wars and credits the Army with an enthusiastic embrace of counterinsurgency in the 1960s, while the other calls attention to the Army's constant need to *relearn* counterinsurgency and its habit of forgetting the importance of its fundamental tenets. The disjuncture between the two narratives—the tension between neglect of counterinsurgency and a long tradition of small wars—requires further examination. For although there has been a long tradition within the Army of fighting small wars, it is also true that these wars have not lingered in the organization's historical memory. The experiences of the Civil War, World War I, and World War II have all left a more lasting impact on the Army's identity. This book will explore this process of forgetting counterinsurgency in the post-Vietnam era and show it was closely tied to the Vietnam experience itself. Part of this ability to forget—of which Vietnam is the most compelling example—must be related to aspects of American strategic culture, for which a rich literature already exists.

ORGANIZATIONAL AND STRATEGIC CULTURES

There has been a considerable amount of research on how institutional preferences are formed and the ways in which organizations adapt themselves to change. The first wave of military innovation scholars argued that changes in military doctrine are due to outside pressures, from the insistence of civilian policy makers that the military reorient themselves in a certain way.[13] This school of thought, drawing on Graham Allison's work on bureaucratic politics,[14] argues that military officers are strongly resistant to change, preferring instead to maintain the status quo and to rely on successful past experience as a guide to the future. A dissenting school of thought, led by Samuel Huntington, sees change coming from within the military, not from without.[15] This school privileges military knowledge of warfare over the wisdom of civilian policy makers, contradicting Georges Clemenceau's dictum that war was too important to be left to the generals. Huntington, along with other scholars such as Stephen Peter Rosen and Deborah Avant, argued that military officers, whose first loyalty is to the state, will react to external threats, however imperfectly, rather than institutional prerogatives.

Certainly, the experience of the US Army in Iraq has offered more evidence of innovation coming from within the military. Chad Serena and James Russell have analyzed how midranking and junior Army officers in Iraq were often quick to adapt to their tactical and operational environment.[16] While useful, this focus on tactical innovation ignores the question of how such lessons are institutionalized in both doctrine and education and indeed the ways in which senior officers facilitate or even champion change. For innovation to be meaningful, it must be adapted across an organization. In that sense, these new studies of bottom-up innovation do not necessarily resolve the tension between those who argue that militaries react to external threats and those who see civilian pressure as a more effective driver of change.

There is a third school that balances these two points of view by contending that militaries *do* respond to external threats but often in ways likely to enhance their prestige, status, or funding. In many ways, such a conclusion is obvious: Military leaders are bound to consider the actions of potential adversaries—Kimberly Marten Zisk demonstrates this by observing that Soviet military doctrine was quite responsive to changes in its American counterpart throughout the Cold War—and equally likely to want to maximize institutional prestige wherever possible.[17] However, such simplification obscures a key strength of this literature: its strong focus on cultural explanations for change. At its best, such an approach avoids the mechanistic tendencies of some models and the false dichotomy between interest and culture. As Elizabeth Kier has argued, "One's interest is a function of the cultural context."[18] Certainly, the American treatment of counterinsurgency in the post-Vietnam era was deeply rooted in cultural preferences as well as institutional interests.

This "cultural context" has been another rich area of study, one closely related to the creation of doctrine. For, if doctrine is a repository for the agreed-on lessons of history, it is also created in—and helps shape—the culture of the organization that produced it. The literature on the relationship between strategy and culture has grown exponentially since the cultural turn in academia, and both historians and political scientists have begun to study "strategic culture" in some detail.[19] Colin Gray postulates the existence of an American strategic culture consisting of "modes of thought and action with respect to force, derive[d] from perceptions of the national historical experience, aspirations for cultural conformity . . . and from all of the many distinctively American experiences (of geography, political philosophy and practice [that is, civic culture], and way of life) that determine an American culture."[20]

Jeremy Black, however, makes the vital point that the cultural turn in military history is essentially a reaction to the technological determinism displayed by scholars of the revolution in military affairs. As with any reaction, it is crucial that this pushback does not become an *over*reaction and that cultural determinism does not simply replace technological determinism as the dominant mode of understanding. Black, along with scholars such as Adrian Lewis, is uneasy about any approach to strategic culture that denies agency and contingency.[21] Therefore, if we are to successfully consider not only issues of agency and contingency but also the sometimes contested nature of strategic cultures, we must examine a subfield of strategic culture: that of *organizational* culture, those institutional peculiarities and prerogatives that shape how an organization behaves and what it believes.[22] In the case of the US Army (as opposed to the corporations that are the subjects of much of the literature), it is important to note that its own organizational culture, while certainly narrower in scope and built on long-formed habits and customs, is strongly intertwined with the overall features of American strategic culture. Michael Howard's observation that "the military system of a nation is not an independent section of the social system but an aspect of it in its totality"[23] points to the context in which we should consider military organizational culture.

The notion of a peculiarly American strategic culture is inextricably linked with Russell Weigley's work, *The American Way of War*, which still stands as one of the key works on the subject forty years after its publication.[24] Weigley argues that American military strategy has been characterized by a strategy of overwhelming force and annihilation since the Civil War. The objective was always the destruction of the enemy's main force without much regard for maneuver. During the "Forty Days," General Ulysses S. Grant's Army of the Potomac often attempted to outflank the Confederate Army of Northern Virginia and failed at each attempt. However, the Napoleonic brilliance of General Robert E. Lee could not deal with the overwhelming federal superiority of numbers and material and was decisively defeated by head-on grappling. World War II was the epitome of such an approach, characterized by John Ellis as "brute force."[25] Even General George S. Patton, supposedly the most dashing and maneuver-oriented American commander, stated that:

> Americans as a race are the most adept in the use of machinery of any people on earth, and . . . the most adept at the production of machines on a mass-production basis. It costs about $40,000 for a man to get killed. If we can keep him from getting killed by a few extra dollars, it is cheap expenditure.[26]

This approach to war has shifted substantially since Vietnam, and the literature on the US Army's organizational culture reflects that change. A key work is Richard Lock-Pullan's study of US intervention strategy since the Vietnam War.[27] Focusing on strategic culture and military innovation, Lock-Pullan persuasively argues that the US Army was heavily influenced by Vietnam and shifted away from a culture of a mobilized mass army that was firepower heavy but essentially a blunt instrument to a smaller, professional all-volunteer force that inculcated a previously nonexistent culture of operational excellence embodied in the AirLand battle doctrine.[28]

Many authors, such as Carl Builder in *The Masks of War*, argue that the Army saw itself as the nation's loyal military servant—a notion derived from its origins as a volunteer militia, as a *people's* army.[29] Lock-Pullan sees a rupture caused by defeat, contending that "fundamentally, the social alienation that the Army suffered after the Vietnam War meant that its identity could not be mechanistically determined by the broader national culture which had turned against it."[30] He rightly points to the Army's agency in changing its own organizational culture and shows us that the move toward an all-volunteer force caused senior Army leaders to radically reshape the Army's identity and doctrine. Lock-Pullan's narrative of a post-Vietnam army obsessed with maneuver warfare and operational brilliance is also advanced by Robert Tomes and Stuart Kinross.[31] All three of these works offer valuable insights into the changing nature of the post-Vietnam US Army. But they all start from the premise that, once the Army internalized lessons from that war, those lessons remained fixed, immutable, and unchallenged facts. To understand the evolution of the Army's organizational culture, we must also understand how the lessons themselves evolve and are constantly contested and negotiated.

Interservice rivalries have been well studied, but internal Army struggles over culture and identity have tended to receive comparatively less attention. The value of focusing on these internal tensions is highlighted in Brian McAllister Linn's *The Echo of Battle: The Army's Way of War*. Linn challenges Russell Weigley's notion of a monolithic American strategic culture by carefully outlining the strongly contested nature of the Army's organizational culture. Linn argues that "the wars the United States has actually fought are important less for what happened than for what military intellectuals believed they had learned from them after the shooting stops,"[32] but he identifies some confusion over both these lessons and the definition of some basic terms:

Army officers and military historians, past and present, assume that the service shares a common definition of war. Indeed, this assumption is central
to the regular army's institutional self-identity . . . [but] far from displaying
the rigid organizational unanimity often ascribed to the "military mind," the
army has been engaged in prolonged and often acrimonious debate over the
nature of both war and national defense.[33]

Linn complicates the argument of Weigley's *American Way of War*[34] by demonstrating that there are three distinct intellectual traditions within the Army:
the "guardians," who define the Army's role in a strongly defensive fashion
and rely on technocratic solutions (from the designers of nineteenth-century
coastal defenses to Colin Powell); the "heroes," who emphasize the centrality
of battle and courage on both the physical and moral planes (George Patton
being the classic example); and the "managers," a relatively rare breed who see
war as an outgrowth of political and economic factors and something that
often requires complete national mobilization (George Marshall and Dwight
Eisenhower). These three schools of thought complicate Weigley's notion that
the American way of war has centered on annihilation.

Linn's argument about the contested and fluid nature of American strategic culture echoes a broader point about culture: that we must consider the
phenomenon as a continuing process, constantly being performed and modified, rather than simply an object.[35] *The Echo of Battle* points to potentially
rewarding directions for future scholarship by complicating the idea that the
Army's culture was monolithic in nature and opening up questions about the
contingent and performative qualities of an American "way of war." This book
will build on Linn's description of an Army organizational culture constantly
contested and made anew by considering how historical memory helps to construct that culture and how the Army's changing lessons of Vietnam affected
not only their counterinsurgency doctrine but also their broader institutional
culture.

Nowhere is the fluid and contested nature of culture more apparent than
in American society's long debate over the lessons of Vietnam. The variety
of lessons drawn from that war range from criticisms of the fundamentals
of the American society[36] to Earl Tilford's sarcastic remark that "the United
States must never again become involved in a civil war in support of a na-
tionalist cause against communist insurgents supplied by allies with contiguous borders in a former French colony located in a tropical climate halfway

around the world."[37] There are those who argue for what Earl Ravenal[38] calls the "instrumental" lessons of Vietnam—on how the war was fought and what could be done better next time.[39] There are those who emphasize the "proportional" lesson that Vietnam was a "tragic folly," in which the United States saw interests in Vietnam where it had none and misread the nature of both its opponents and ostensible South Vietnamese allies.[40] Finally, there are those who take what Ravenal calls "strategic" lessons from the war, who argue that Vietnam showed that the United States must adapt to a second-best world, accept that there are limits to its military power, and work within domestic and international constraints by focusing on more limited and achievable foreign policy goals.[41]

What is clear from this disparate set of lessons is that Vietnam shattered what had been a relatively stable foreign policy consensus in the United States. Richard Melanson has characterized much of the history of US foreign policy since then as the attempt to reconstruct the Cold War consensus that unified American society until the 1960s.[42] The "history of the lesson" of Vietnam is as much about attempting to rebuild this consensus as it is about the explicit drawing of lessons from the war. Indeed, Arnold Isaacs, Robert McMahon, David Ryan, Robert D. Schulzinger, and Charles Neu have all explored the way in which Americans reshaped historical memory as they attempted to deal with the fractures caused by the war.[43] These scholars suggest a way of addressing the Army's relationship with the lessons of Vietnam rooted in how memories are constructed. Rather than simply describing the evolution of the Army's lessons of Vietnam, this book will attempt to understand the social and cultural processes that created them; in so doing, it will be possible to understand how the lessons changed as contemporary needs dictated and how they influenced the Army's attitudes toward counterinsurgency.

THE SOCIAL CONSTRUCTION OF HISTORY

Utilizing the past in the service of the present is a problematic concept, raising the issue of how and why histories are created and indeed how they are used by policy makers and strategists. There are a number of processes at work, from the way actors select analogies from which to derive "lessons," to the manner in which collective memories are formed and negotiated, to the broader issue of how institutional culture shapes the construction of those historical lessons and memories. These questions intersect several related fields, including literatures on policy makers and the lessons of history, social constructivism, and organizational culture.

Early work on the "the lessons of history" argued that policy makers and strategists tend to misinterpret lessons and reach for the wrong analogy. Ernest May's groundbreaking work, *"Lessons" of the Past: The Use and Misuse of History in American Foreign Policy*,[44] argued that "framers of foreign policy are often influenced by beliefs about what history teaches or portends" but that they also have a tendency to use history badly. May writes:

> When resorting to an analogy, they tend to seize upon the first that comes to mind. They do not search more widely. Nor do they pause to analyze the case, test its fitness, or even ask in what ways it might be misleading. Seeing a trend running toward the present, they tend to assume that it will continue into the future, not stopping to consider what produced it or why a linear projection might prove to be mistaken.[45]

According to May, policy makers and strategists are notoriously poor historians and have demonstrated this inadequacy through their use of inappropriate analogies in countless crises. Writers such as Alexander George, Richard Neustadt, and Jeffrey Record[46] have all arrived at broadly similar conclusions: that the use of history by decision makers is an area fraught with potential difficulty. In his seminal work *Perception and Misperception in International Politics*, Robert Jervis outlined why analogies, however poorly employed, were popular devices for reasoning among policy makers:

> What one learns from key events in international history is an important factor in determining the images that shape the interpretation of incoming information . . . previous international events provide the statesman with a range of imaginable situations and allow him to detect patterns and causal links that can help him understand his world.[47]

More recent work by Yueng Foong Khong reinforces the importance of analogies as a cognitive shortcut in reasoning.[48] Khong argued that "new events tend to be assimilated into pre-existing structures in the mind [of the receiver] because of the limited cognitive capabilities of human beings." These limited cognitive capacities mean that decision makers, particularly in moments of crisis when they are under pressure and acting with incomplete information, are likely to fall back on past experiences to assist in making decisions. Obviously, the more powerful the experience, the stronger the influence it will have on the decision. For example, Harry Truman perceived strong echoes of Hitler's aggression when contemplating intervention in Korea in 1950, while forty years later George H. W. Bush still saw Hitler when Saddam Hussein invaded Kuwait.

It is possible for decision makers to make good use of history, however severe the pressure—famously, during the 1962 Cuban Missile Crisis, John F. Kennedy was strongly influenced by Barbara Tuchman's account of Europe's 1914 slide into war in *The Guns of August*.[49] Whether they employ them wisely or otherwise, it is indisputable that policy makers do use historical analogies to aid decision making. Michael Howard argues that military strategists are even more liable to rely heavily on historical analogies to inform decision making because the soldier's profession "is almost unique in that he may have to exercise it only once in a lifetime, if indeed that often. It is as if a surgeon had to practice throughout his life on dummies for one real operation, or a barrister appeared only once or twice in court towards the close of his career."[50] Given these limitations, it is no surprise that military leaders rely so heavily on the lessons of the past for guidance or that these lessons are then so strongly contested.

Building on Khong's work, Mikkel Vedby Rasmussen's article "The Social Construction of the Past"[51] looks at the "lessons literature" and its attempts to find the appropriate analogies from a constructivist perspective. Rasmussen is largely dismissive of "self-help books" for "those who govern" on how to use the "right" analogies and instead offers a more limited role for the "lessons of history";[52] he observes that "the present asks us what to do. Perhaps history offers us an answer. According to the lessons literature, a careful study of history provides answers that suit the present; according to constructivism the answer is history itself."[53] Rasmussen, then, is calling for a literature that deals not with the "lesson of history" but rather attempts to examine "the history of the lesson," by looking at the evolution of the lesson in cultural discourse and political use and its changing meaning over time. He argues that a reliance on cognitive psychology undermines the usefulness of the lessons literature because:

Cognitive psychology deals with the way individuals learn lessons and shows how learning lessons fills up the *tabula rasa* of an individual mind. The history of states is different from the history of individuals, and therefore states construct lessons differently from individuals. States do not live lives the way individuals do, and therefore their past is a social product quite different from the psychological product that constitutes individual identity. In other words, governments do not live the results of their state's past the way individuals, trapped in their body, live the results of their past. A state does not have cognition the way individuals do, and therefore cognitive psychology cannot explain the actions of a state.[54]

If we are to take up Rasmussen's challenge to write a "history of the lesson," how can we do so without conflating Harry Truman or Lyndon Johnson's experience of Munich with the broader "lesson of Munich" as internalized by the US national security institutions? The answer must partly lie with the perspectives offered by much of the literature on historical collective memory.[55] David Thelen notes that the process in which collective memories are formed has—like the use of historical analogies by policy makers—as much to do with the present as the past, arguing that "the struggle for possession and interpretation of memory is rooted in the conflict and interplay among social, political, and cultural interests and values in the present."[56] Jay Winter offers both a caution and a potentially useful approach when he argues that "collective memory may be understood as a set of signifying practices linking authorial encoding with audience decoding of messages about the past inscribed in film, or indeed in other sources."[57] When considering collective memory, we must consider both the agency behind the message *and* how multiple audiences receive that same message.

Part of this consideration must involve undoing what Alon Confino has described as the "separation of the construction of memory from either its reception or contestation."[58] While we should certainly trace the construction of a narrative, the "history of the lesson" must include how it is received, disputed, and mediated. After all, even where collective remembrance seems static and uncontested, Jeffrey Olick reminds us of collective memory's fluidity by quoting Montaigne: "Stability is nothing more than a languid motion."[59] Susan Sontag not only argues that collective memories are always contested and contingent but challenges the notion of collective memory itself, claiming instead that "what is called collective memory is not a remembering but a stipulating: that *this* is important." For Sontag, "There is no such thing as collective memory . . . But there is collective instruction."[60] Preferring to talk about "remembrance" rather than "collective memory," Winter has suggested that not only do we need to start thinking more about agency and reception but that we need to move beyond a simple binary of "memory" and "forgetting"; instead he argues that the social construction of silence plays a crucial role in remembrance.[61] Winter calls for a study of "performative" silences that have political and even liturgical importance. Certainly, the US Army's long institutional silence on Vietnam could be regarded as performative.

Even if we accept Sontag's and Winter's strictures on abusing the term *collective memory*, there is still a place for consideration of *lessons*. But if we are to identify who constructs these lessons, how they are contested and received, what they say and where they are silent, then we must identify where such lessons are formed. Theo Farrell, like Rasmussen, argues that a constructivist framework can help to locate these sources.[62] After all, constructivism—the examination of how knowledge is constructed in a social context—is an approach that, in its essence, takes ideas and beliefs very seriously.[63] While acknowledging that "getting inside the heads of actors and knowing their beliefs is a formidable challenge for scholars," Farrell argues that "constructivists are not interested in the beliefs actors hold so much as the beliefs actors share" and that, by definition, "beliefs must be expressed, if not codified and recorded, to be shared. In this way, shared beliefs often leave physical residues."[64] This book will examine those physical residues of memory by exploring how the cultural construction of memory manifested itself in the intersection of counterinsurgency and the lessons of Vietnam.

In the case of the Army, these physical residues are most likely to be found in formal and informal doctrine. After all, historical analogies play a role not only in decision making in crises but in the longer-term formulation of policy. Larry Cable's description is a useful way to illustrate just how important doctrine is to the Army:

> Military doctrine . . . constitute[s] the conceptual skeletons upon which are mounted the sinews of material, the muscles of battalions and brigades and the nervous system of planning and policy decision. At the risk of slight oversimplification, it is useful to understand doctrine as being the officially sanctioned theory of victory outlining the conduct of war on all levels, from the broadest aspects of operational planning down through tactics and standard operating procedures to the most minor details of squad patrolling.[65]

Given how important doctrine is to the Army's mission and identity, it offers a very useful repository of the institution's memory and of historical lessons. Not only that, but doctrine is often one of the key terrains over which battles over identity and memory are fought. Even so, Winter's point about agency and reception still stands. Andrew Krepinevich has demonstrated that the US Army in the 1960s produced a significant quantity of counterinsurgency doctrine without the institution ever internalizing it or taking the concept seriously.[66] Field manuals can be used as a smoke screen to persuade political masters that a military is making desired changes without actually necessitating real change. In an effort to avoid such a trap, this book considers what Keith Bickel defines as formal and informal doctrine.[67] *Formal doctrine* is defined as officially sanctioned documents such as Army strategy statements, field manuals, circulars, and pamphlets and the course curricula at service schools. These strategy statements and field manuals are how the Army defines both its terms of art and its mission and purpose. Indeed, some manuals such as Field Manual (FM) 100-5/FM 3-0 *Operations* effectively contain the Army's conception of war and how it intends to fight war. The ebb and flow—and indeed the constant relabeling—of the Army's manuals on counterinsurgency give some indication of the changing relevance of the concept. The changing course curricula at the Army's various service schools also give us a clear illustration of the institution's shifting priorities; what the Army did and did not teach about Vietnam and counterinsurgency says much about how they perceived both.

Informal doctrine, which relates more to student papers and discourse between more junior officers in professional military journals, is worthy of attention because it is here that lessons are most vibrantly contested. In journals such as *Military Review* and *Parameters*, the issues that most preoccupied the Army were debated and considered in depth, and dissenting articles challenged the consensus. For example, the Army's long institutional silence on Vietnam and counterinsurgency was occasionally broken in the 1970s and early 1980s by articles in *Military Review* by officers dismayed at the lessons the Army was drawing from Vietnam. Similarly, at times where the consensus on the lessons of Vietnam either wavered or changed, there was a rush of articles in these journals by officers seeking to outline new lessons.

This formal and informal doctrine is supplemented by the Army's "lessons learned" literature. These sources include "lessons learned" pamphlets, official historical monographs designed to instruct on the lessons of history, the products of the Combined Arms Center (CAC) and its subordinate organizations such as the Combat Studies Institute (CSI) and, most obviously, the Center for Army Lessons Learned (CALL). Official monographs on the

Army's experiences in various conflicts have been a key source of Army lessons as they effectively write the Army's draft of history. These monographs often contain telling criticisms of how the Army applied the lessons of Vietnam to contemporary situations. Taken together, the processes of doctrinal formulation and lesson learning offer a unique way of looking at both how historical narratives can shape the Army's culture and identity and how that very culture can affect the way in which narratives are constructed.

These sources have been supplemented wherever possible by archival materials. To better understand the Army's performance in Vietnam, this book has used the records of the Vietnam-era organization Civil Operations and Revolutionary Development Support (CORDS), the files of the Army's historical unit in Vietnam, and the oral histories and personal papers of senior officers who served in the war. These personal papers offer an invaluable way of examining what these senior officers, many of whom went on to command and reform the post-Vietnam Army, considered to be the lessons of Vietnam. Lastly, although their availability is only partial, this book has drawn on the unit histories of the various organizations responsible for the development of the Army's doctrine, such as the Combined Arms Center at Fort Leavenworth and the John F. Kennedy Special Warfare School at Fort Bragg. The papers of one of the few organizations for whom complete records are available, the Army–Air Force Center for Low Intensity Conflict, have been a rich source on the internal deliberations behind the publication of doctrine and an indication of just how much more excellent material will be available to scholars once more collections become declassified.

CHAPTER STRUCTURE

Chapter 1 examines the Vietnam War itself, how the Army's attitude toward counterinsurgency evolved throughout the war, and the extent to which Army leaders in both Vietnam and Washington recognized the importance of counterinsurgency. It is particularly concerned with the latter phase of the American involvement, after the Tet Offensive of 1968, when new approaches to the war gained prominence and the pacification of the Vietnamese countryside stepped up. This new campaign was an improvement on what preceded it but one that fell short of its objective and that was full of flaws that postwar counterinsurgency proponents were often slow to acknowledge.

Chapter 2 discusses the post-Vietnam turn away from counterinsurgency and looks at how the Vietnam experience reshaped core aspects of the Army's identity—its operational doctrine and its education system—and how that identity itself affected reception and study of the Vietnam War. Specifically, it examines how the Army's focus shifted toward its NATO mission of confronting Warsaw Pact armies in conventional, armored battles on the plains of Northern Europe and how this new focus meant that the lessons of the Vietnam War were constructed in a way that would not so much improve the Army's ability to conduct counterinsurgency as ensure that the Army would never again be called on to fight such wars.

Chapters 3 and 4 examine how the Army handled the challenges of the 1980s and 1990s respectively, decades in which the major uses of US military power were ones that the Army's preferred model of conventional warfare was ill suited to handle. Chapter 3 looks at how renewed US involvement in counterinsurgency and insurgency in Central America meant that a reconsideration of the Army's preferred way of war was needed, even as the lessons of Vietnam were coalescing around a strong tendency to avoid commitment of Army forces wherever possible. The rise of "low-intensity conflict" (LIC) meant that the debate was reopened to some extent, and the chapter considers how changes in doctrine, education, and force structure reflected both the resurgence of counterinsurgency proponents within the Army and their ultimate failure to overcome the lessons of Vietnam outlined in Chapter 2. Chapter 4 explores the Army's reaction to the end of the Cold War and the growth of ill-defined conflicts that no longer had a superpower rivalry to give them meaning. These conflicts occasionally necessitated US intervention in the form of peacekeeping missions, but the Army's leadership paradoxically both strongly supported the Powell Doctrine as a way of preventing another Vietnam while also recognizing the inevitability, if not the desirability, of Army involvement in what were now termed "operations other than war." The practice of deploying troops on peacekeeping missions but then operating in such a way that the actual accomplishment of the mission had a lower priority than the prevention of American casualties shows just how unimportant (and far from the Army's core role) these missions were to many in the Army.

The second half of the book examines the Army's reconsideration of the importance of counterinsurgency and the lessons of Vietnam in light of the Iraq War. Chapter 5 looks at the initial invasion and the inadequacy of the plans for postwar stabilization in light of not only the lack of counterinsurgency doctrine and understanding within the Army but also the culmination of the technocentric lessons of Vietnam, those that spurred the "revolution in military affairs" of which the Army had become an enthusiastic proponent. Planning for the invasion of Iraq was also refracted through the experience of the peacekeeping operations detailed in Chapter 4, both in terms of the obsession with force protection above all else and the relatively positive measures taken by some to ensure there would be no humanitarian disaster. Chapter 6 considers the period from 2003 to 2006, an awkward transition period in which the Army recognized that its lack of knowledge of counterinsurgency was a severe problem and when narratives of the Vietnam War emerged with full force to influence conduct of the war in Iraq. This period was one in which the lessons of Vietnam were again contested and the Army began to change its consensus on those lessons to create something that was usable in the conflict in which they now found themselves.

This reimagining of the history of the Vietnam War suggested the beginnings of a major change in the Army's institutional culture, one that is further explored in Chapter 7. This chapter examines the profound shift that took place between 2006 and 2008 in the Army's understanding both of counterinsurgency and of the Vietnam War. It looks at how this shift played out both in Iraq—where the 2007–2008 "surge" validated the efficacy of counterinsurgency in Iraq and encouraged a narrative of the US war in Vietnam that redeemed much of the Army's effort there—and in the United States, where new counterinsurgency doctrine, one that drew heavily on the Vietnam experience, was constructed. These new lessons of Vietnam looked on that war not as an example of why the Army should not attempt to conduct counterinsurgency but as a source of lessons as to *how* to conduct such wars. Chapter 8 considers how these lessons were refracted through the experience of the troop "surge" in Afghanistan from 2009 to 2011. This final chapter will look at how the newly established consensus on counterinsurgency was challenged during the McChrystal-Petraeus era in Afghanistan; the limitations of counterinsurgency in Afghanistan led to a reopening of the debate on the lessons of Vietnam. That the debate over the lessons was still taking place over thirty years after the end of US involvement there is testimony not only to the controversy the war still inspires but also to its enduring influence on the American military mind.

1 THE ARMY'S COUNTERINSURGENCY WAR IN VIETNAM

THE AMERICAN WAR IN VIETNAM is one of the most well documented and hotly debated events in the history of the United States. The literature on the war is vast, the historiography strongly contested, the debate never ending. Nancy Tucker argues that Vietnam is "the never-ending war," with the conflict's reverberations being felt long after the end of hostilities.[1]

As John Prados has observed, study of the war has been somewhat atomized, with relatively few grand, overarching works that attempt to tell the story of America's lost war in a single narrative.[2] That atomization diffuses possible "lessons" of the Vietnam War and enables the fashioning of multiple alternative "usable" narratives of the war. In revisionist strands of the literature there is a sense that, if only the particular aspect under discussion had been given more attention, then things might have been different and there might have been a "better war."[3] Indeed, some revisionist scholars argue that there was a better war the United States had in fact won before the vital domino of public opinion gave way.[4] This contention that victory was possible if only something had been done differently has wide repercussions, not only for the historiography of the war but for the lessons that policy makers and strategists draw from it.[5] If the war had been winnable, then arguments about the need to avoid future interventions would lose some of their force, and the Vietnam syndrome would cease to be a key point of concern for policy makers. In short, a "better war" would make military intervention palatable again.

Nowhere is this tendency to offer history as a lesson more prevalent than in the historiography of the US counterinsurgency effort in Vietnam. Gary Hess has divided those who argue that the United States could have prevailed in Vietnam into two groups. There are the "Clausewitzians,"[6] who contend that a less restrained policy, such as increased bombing of North Vietnam or the invasion of Laos, Cambodia, or even North Vietnam, could have led to victory, and there are the "hearts and minders," who believe that better execution of counterinsurgency in South Vietnam could have won the war.[7] The question of whether a better counterinsurgency campaign was possible is at the heart of the tension between those who see Vietnam as "the unwinnable war" and those who perceive a "better war." That tension was a point of conflict throughout the post-Vietnam era, and an improved understanding of the Army's counterinsurgency war in Vietnam can help us better understand the context in which the various factions within the Army constructed their lessons of Vietnam.

THE HISTORIOGRAPHY OF THE ARMY'S COUNTERINSURGENCY WAR IN VIETNAM

The "hearts and minds" revisionist critique of the war argues that had the Army embraced counterinsurgency theory more fully, then a different result would have been possible. Proponents of this view, such as Larry Cable, Guenter Lewy, Andrew Krepinevich, and John Nagl, argue that the Army simply didn't understand counterinsurgency and adhered to an "army concept" and doctrine centered on air mobility and massive use of firepower. General William Westmoreland pursued a costly strategy of attrition and ignored the promises of pacification. For these critics, Westmoreland's opposition to the Marine Corps Combined Action Program, which used joint American-Vietnamese platoons to provide long-term security for hamlets, was a glaring missed opportunity. His focus on destroying the People's Army of Vietnam (PAVN) and National Liberation Front (NLF) "main force" units in the unpopulated highlands rather than securing the Vietnamese population betrayed an adherence to an Army strategic culture that was deeply unsuited to the war in Vietnam.

Westmoreland also has his defenders. Dale Andrade, Andrew Birtle, John M. Carland, and Graham Cosmas have all argued that the "hearts and minds" school is both overly sanguine about the chances of success for a strategy that focused on securing the population of South Vietnam and underplays the sophistication of Westmoreland's understanding of the situation in Vietnam. They frequently cite Westmoreland's description in his memoirs of a "two-handed" strategy, where one (American) hand would keep the PAVN main force units at bay while the other (South Vietnamese) hand would pacify the countryside and secure the rural population from the NLF threat. Further, they argue that the number of American troops needed to pacify South Vietnam would have dwarfed even the 536,000 that eventually deployed there. In those circumstances, Westmoreland was correct to use US forces to "stem the tide" and let the Republic of Vietnam Armed Forces (RVNAF) focus on pacification.

The most comprehensive critique of "hearts and minds" revisionism has not come from those who focus on issues of strategy but rather those who study the *implementation* of pacification at the tactical level. Province-level studies, such as those by David Elliott, Jeffrey Race, James Trullinger, and Eric Bergerud, have been particularly effective in illustrating just how deep the problems with pacification efforts were. These studies all show a resilient NLF, an ineffectual and illegitimate South Vietnamese government, and a US military that was unable to effect change, despite concerted attempts to carry out pacification. Bergerud describes how the 25th Infantry Division in Hau Nghia province employed many of the principles of classic counterinsurgency doctrine yet was unable to make any inroads into the NLF's control of the province. When reading province-level analyses, it is hard to avoid the conclusion that the NLF was far more deeply embedded into rural South Vietnamese society than the South Vietnamese government was and that US efforts at pacification were bound to fail.

A key point of contention between the two schools is the extent to which US pacification efforts improved as the war wore on. Central to this is the status of an internal Army report: Program for the Pacification and Long-Term Development of South Vietnam (or PROVN). PROVN was a 1966 study commissioned by Army Chief of Staff General Harold K. Johnson to reappraise the situation in Vietnam. PROVN identified deep, structural problems with the pacification effort and argued that "the critical actions are those that occur at the village, district and provincial levels. This is where the war must be fought; this is where that war and the object which lies beyond it must be won."[8] Some "hearts and minds" scholars, such as John Nagl and Andrew Krepinevich, argue that PROVN represented both a comprehensive critique of Westmoreland's strategy and a viable counterinsurgency strategy that could have won the war.[9] More recent scholarship by Dale Andrade and Andrew Birtle has pointed out that while PROVN was critical of some aspects of the war and argued that the United States should reorganize its pacification efforts and push harder for Government of Vietnam (GVN) reform, it also firmly endorsed Westmoreland's strategy of attrition and the US forces' focus on the main unit war in the highlands.[10] According to Birtle and Andrade, while the document criticized elements of US performance, it was nowhere near the transformative, revolutionary document that "better war" advocates claimed. In fact it endorsed the central points of Westmoreland's approach and supported his conventional campaign.

After PROVN, there was a reorganization of the pacification effort and a new organization, Civil Operations and Revolutionary Development Support (or CORDS), that placed all civilian and military pacification activities under a civilian—Robert W. Komer—and then made the head of CORDS deputy commander of MACV (Military Assistance Command, Vietnam). This new agency would centrally plan all pacification activities and replace the chaos of multiple programs from multiple agencies. Further, in 1967, the Central Intelligence Agency (CIA), together with Army Special Forces and the South Vietnamese government, launched the Phoenix Program, a controversial operation to target the "Viet Cong infrastructure," the political and support apparatus of the NLF in the villages, and to disrupt it by killing or capturing NLF cadre. These initiatives, together with the replacement of Westmoreland with General Creighton Abrams, were, some revisionists claim, a sign of long-overdue progress in the war. As Lloyd Gardner has noted, the "hearts and minds" revisionists claim that "when General Westmoreland was replaced, a better war was fought and the light at the end of the tunnel [was] relit." It is this alleged rekindling of the "light at the end of the tunnel" that we must concern ourselves with, for although the orthodox historiography has strongly criticized any contention that the war was winnable, much of that criticism revolves around the strategic choices that Westmoreland faced or the viability of the PROVN report. The contention that General Abrams fought a "better war," one primarily made by Lewis Sorley, garnered very favorable coverage at times in the postwar era, and the claim deserves closer examination.

THE BETTER WAR? ABRAMS'S STRATEGY

Abrams took over as commander, US Military Assistance Command Vietnam, in June 1968. Abrams, with his often-rumpled appearance, ever-present cigar, and abrupt manner, was a stark contrast to his predecessor, General William Westmoreland, the one-time superintendent of West Point. He was also more popular among journalists, so much so that the *New York Times* ran an article declaring that "General Abrams deserves a better war." It is from this article that the "better war" narrative derives its name. Abrams, so the narrative goes, was responsible for a dramatic turnaround in US fortunes by finally implementing a strategy that emphasized securing the population of South Vietnam from attack rather than chasing after the wraithlike North Vietnamese Army in the unpopulated highland jungles near the Cambodian border. This school of thought, which strongly challenges the orthodox view of Vietnam as an unmitigated failure, takes advantage of the fact that the Vietnam historiography has overwhelmingly focused on the pre-1968 era, before Abrams took over.[11] This "better war" narrative was at the core of the version of "Vietnam" advanced by counterinsurgency advocates in the wake of the US invasion of Iraq in 2003 and is therefore central to postwar contentions over the lessons.

Certainly, Abrams made some significant changes on taking command. Rather than pursue Westmoreland's strategy of attrition, he preferred to emphasize his "One War" concept—that there was not one war against enemy main forces units, one war to pacify the countryside, and one war in the air against North Vietnam, but that all these operations were deeply intertwined and would be treated as such in future. Abrams explained,

> We preach it as "one war," just one war . . . we mean the province chief and the district chief, the RF [Regional Forces] and the PF [Popular Forces] and the Provincial Reconnaissance Units and the Police. Everybody in here has got to work together . . . the Americans shouldn't do anything, really, in the way of operating that the district advisor isn't in on, doesn't know about . . . this is really a complex environment to work in.[12]

The three-month-long Accelerated Pacification Campaign, launched in November 1968, was the epitome of this "one war" concept. Known to the US military as the APC, its objective was to reestablish the South Vietnamese government's (or GVN) presence in the countryside in the wake of the Tet Offensive through a three-month special effort. Conceptually, there was little new to the APC. It employed the same pacification tools as previous campaigns: emphasis on the use of Regional Forces and Popular Forces (RF/PF) to secure hamlets, the establishment of a part-time militia (the People's Self-Defense Force/PSDF) to provide extra personnel, the *Chieu Hoi* (or Open Arms) program for encouraging NLF desertions, and the nascent *Phuong Hoang*/Phoenix program for targeting the NLF infrastructure (political cadres and supporters) in the hamlets.[13] What was new was the firm support of the US Army in executing it. Abrams was not only instrumental in securing Vietnamese backing of the plan, but he also directed that population security be the primary operational objective for US and Vietnamese forces over the three months of the campaign.

Territorial security was the centerpiece of the APC, and it is worth noting, as some critics do,[14] the emphasis on the coercive elements of counterinsurgency, rather than the "hearts and minds" aspects of doctrine that had been emphasized by counterinsurgency advocates earlier in the 1960s. A briefer made the point explicit when he noted, "There's no question that pacification is either 90 percent or 10 percent security, depending on which expert you talk to. But there isn't any expert in the world that will doubt that it's the first 10 percent or the first 90 percent. You just can't conduct pacification in the face of an NVA [North Vietnamese Army] division."[15] Without security, a necessary but not sufficient condition, development work and good governance programs would be impossible. As Robert Komer explained, the objective was to quickly spread a thin "security blanket" over the countryside, which he argued would "achieve greater results more quickly by seeking to expand a diluted form of government control while destroying enemy forces and infrastructure than by seeking a high degree of security and efficient administration." The focus therefore would not be on improving GVN governance but on gaining as much territory as possible in advance of any possible cease-fire.

On its own terms, the APC was a major success. US and RVNAF forces moved into and secured over a thousand hamlets, the number of *Hoi Chanh* (NLF deserters under the *Chieu Hoi* program) greatly exceeded the plan's goal, and the number of hamlets rated "secure" under the Hamlet Evaluation Survey (HES)[16] jumped from 70 percent to 86 percent between November 1968 and June 1969.[17] The APC set the pattern for future operations: The GVN's Central Pacification and Development Council developed a comprehensive and ambitious Pacification and Development Plan for 1969 while Abrams—although never explicitly disavowing Westmoreland's attrition strategy—placed heavy emphasis on population security in his 1969 Combined Campaign Plan.[18] Not only did the planning follow the pattern of the APC, but so did the results, at least for a time: The period from 1969 through 1971 marked the high point of GVN control over the countryside, with HES indications showing almost total control over the countryside by mid-1971.[19]

The statistics that measured control were not uncontroversial. Richard Hunt notes the problems that creep in when such data become an end in themselves: "Rather than merely being a means to identify trends and collect uniform data on the countryside, HES became, in the absence of any other clear and universally accepted standard, one of the principal yardsticks of progress and inferentially a measure of individual performance."[20] If this happened, then HES figures were just as liable to be inflated as the notorious "body count" was earlier in the war. William Colby—head of the pacification effort—though generally supportive of HES as an indicator of trends, offered the important qualifier: "Some of the statistics, though, we thought were fairly soft, to put it mildly."[21] As noted in a July 1969 talk by Brian Jenkins at the RAND Corporation, the focus on statistics, accurate or otherwise, was often counterproductive:

> Frequently, increases in the amount of our own military efforts are measured and this is called progress. On this basis, if twice as many bombs per month are dropped in 1969 as were dropped per month in 1967, we are doing better. The same with leaflets, battalion days of operations, and so on. If we ignore the scores and statistics, as the enemy seems to have done, then we are left with a different question: *what is different about Vietnam today from two or three years ago and what is still the same?* I have had to ask myself that question frequently. What impresses me is the remarkable degree to which things remain the same [emphasis in the original].[22]

By June 1969, there were in fact indications that the impressive results of the Accelerated Pacification Campaign were more ephemeral than permanent. Craig Johnstone, chief of CORDS's Pacification Studies Group, reported that "on the balance the efforts at improving territorial security received a great stimulus during the Accelerated Pacification Campaign but have slowed perceptibly as a result of troop shortages and increased enemy terrorist activity." More ominously, Johnstone also argued that "little qualitative improvements in RF/PF forces or in ARVN units in their role of providing a security shield have been noted" and that "practical control of either PF or RD cadre is still mythical."[23] Given that the Accelerated Pacification Campaign was designed to provide breathing space for reform of the GVN and ARVN, such inertia was worrying. Johnstone's concerns were echoed a year later by General Arthur S. Collins, commander of I Field Force Vietnam. In a memorandum written after inspecting his area of operations, Collins observed:

It is a different war than when I was here in 1966–67, particularly in II Corps. At that time we were constantly running into strong NVA and VC [Vietcong] units, well equipped, well armed, well organized and always from regimental to division strength. This no longer pertains, and we do not meet the main enemy units. . . . At the same time, and spotted like measles throughout the country, you consistently find that the VC come right into the village and are not caught or bothered . . . This indicates either very good intelligence from the VCI [Vietcong Infrastructure] structure in the villages or some sort of an accommodation . . . I sometimes get the feeling that the government forces do not have the will to win, and in the long run that may decide the issue.[24]

This lack of main force units does much to explain the ability of Abrams to break his forces into small pieces and to focus so much on population security, but the continued health of the guerrilla pockets "spotted like measles throughout the country" indicates the shallowness of GVN control. The NLF's July 1969 strategy document, COSVN [Central Office for South Vietnam] Resolution no. 9, reflected this change in the nature of the war by calling for a shift from large-scale attacks to protracted guerrilla action in anticipation of US withdrawal.

Even so, the Accelerated Pacification Campaign and the NLF strategy of protracted warfare did not mean that Abrams stopped focusing on those PAVN and NLF main force units that were operating in South Vietnam. As Graham Cosmas notes, as late as 1971 "in all four corps areas, U.S. and South Vietnamese units devoted much effort to what formerly were called search-and-destroy missions." This included the large-scale 1970 incursion into Cambodia and the bloody "main force" battles in the A Shau Valley (most infamously at "Hamburger Hill"). Indeed, analysis by Andrew Birtle has shown that, in quantitative terms, Abrams's approach to the war, even during the Accelerated Pacification Campaign, did not differ significantly from that of Westmoreland.[25] The number of battalion days spent on large-unit operations actually increased, and spending priorities, which emphasized the main force war over security and development, remained the same.

The literature that directly challenges the "better war" thesis makes two pertinent claims: that pacification, even when it was apparently successful, was a shallow, temporary measure; and that any difference between Abrams and Westmoreland was one of emphasis rather than substance. By considering the experiences of two units during and after the Accelerated Pacification

Campaign, we can gain further understanding of these key points. The two units, the 9th Infantry Division operating in the Mekong Delta and the 173rd Airborne Brigade in Binh Dinh province, took very different approaches to pacification, but the experiences of both strongly validate the central criticisms of the "better war" thesis.

OPERATION SPEEDY EXPRESS AND FIREPOWER IN ABRAMS'S WAR

In the same speech in which Brian Jenkins worried about things remaining the same in Vietnam, he argued that "[General Abrams] has only partly succeeded in making his own ideas prevail over the traditional doctrine."[26] Given the practices of some American units, Jenkins's concerns would appear well founded. Perhaps the most egregious example of firepower-oriented pacification tactics under Abrams was Operation Speedy Express, launched by the 9th Infantry Division in the Mekong Delta during the first half of 1969. Based on tactics that entailed the use of helicopters for reconnaissance before rapidly piling available troops and firepower onto enemy targets, the operation seemed as heavily driven by the old "body count" criteria as by population security and drew opprobrium from John Paul Vann, senior pacification advisor in the Delta and key figure in the American war effort.[27] In 1972, Kevin Buckley of *Newsweek* reported that the 9th Division claimed 10,899 "enemy" dead while recovering only 748 weapons in that time. One estimate put the amount of civilian dead during this effort to pacify Kien Hoa province at 5,000, a figure that would be unsurprising given that there were 3,381 tactical air strikes carried out during Speedy Express.[28] Julian J. Ewell, former commander of 9th and later a commander of II Field Force Vietnam, explained his rule:

> Military operations would be given first priority in every case. That doesn't mean you wouldn't do pacification, but this gets at what you might call winning the hearts and minds of the people. I'm all for that. It's a nice concept, but in fighting the Viet Cong and NVA, if you didn't break their military machine you might as well forget winning the hearts and minds of the people.[29]

Ewell was quite proud of his unit's record, recalling, "I think the last month I had the Division—either March or April 1969—we killed something like 2,300 VC and NVA and captured maybe five, ten or fifteen . . . As a result, the skill level just kept going up and up and up. Very successful. In fact, so successful that many people in Vietnam thought we were cheating or something. They didn't believe the results."[30] What the 9th Infantry Division was practicing was the "body count" as applied to pacification. Lt. Gen. Orwin C. Talbott— who had tried Lt. William Calley for the My Lai massacre—complained that "the 9th Division insisted on a body count. They didn't care what body. I heard about Americal and 9th Division all the time. The 9th was worse, all on the body count basis."[31] Similarly, according to Nick Turse, a 1972 inspector general's report on Speedy Express found:

> While there appears to be no means of determining the precise number of civilian casualties incurred by US forces during Operation Speedy Express, it would appear that the extent of these casualties was in fact substantial, and that a fairly solid case can be constructed to show that civilian casualties may have amounted to several thousand (between 5,000 and 7,000).[32]

Ewell, while denying that he was overly focused on the body count, wrote a postwar study on the use of such metrics in combat and concluded that an approach that attempted to maximize the number of enemy dead "did not lead to a brutalizing of the conflict. In fact, the reverse was true." According to Ewell, "It resulted in fewer friendly casualties in both killed and wounded. More importantly, pacification progressed more rapidly. Thus we see a system which entailed maximum force and higher enemy casualties initially, but, in the long run, wound the war down and facilitated all the developments necessary to defeat the enemy and protect the people."[33]

Such a continuing emphasis on the 'body count' runs completely against the grain of the narrative advanced in the "better war" thesis and illustrated the Army's continuing reluctance to embrace counterinsurgency. On taking command, Abrams had introduced more restrictive rules of engagement; had ordered a drastic reduction of artillery ammunition expenditure, effectively banning speculative "harassment and interdiction fire"; and was quick to praise units that emphasized small unit, intelligence-led operations.[34] Yet Abrams strongly praised Ewell and the 9th Division, telling assembled 9th Division troops at a change of command ceremony in April 1969, "The performance of this Division has been magnificent and I would say that in the last three months, it's an unparalleled and unequaled performance." Abrams singled out Ewell as someone who in "a little more than a year has proven to be a brilliant and sensitive commander. His tactical concepts have been characterized by imagination, sensitivity to the kind of situation that you all are in, and he plays hard."[35]

Abrams's praise of Ewell at the height of Operation Speedy Express indicates a commander who had not ruled out the heavy use of force in the pursuit of pacification. Certainly, he was not averse to massing firepower when he felt it was called for: Abrams considered the B-52 "Arc Light" tactical strikes his strategic reserve and one of his greatest assets[36] and stated, "If he [the American soldier] hasn't got enough stuff there, you've got to give it to him. You've got to bring in air there . . . he expects you to do certain things. And one of them is that when he's getting shot at, by god you'll bring everything to bear."[37] Bringing everything to bear was certainly a skill US force in Vietnam had perfected by 1968–1969. A postwar study on Army tactics noted just how firepower heavy these operations were:

> Attacks were usually conducted by fire rather than by ground assault. Under normal circumstances, an infantry assault was avoided or it was delayed until after the enemy had been virtually destroyed by supporting fires. The high density of automatic weapons among the enemy caused high loss rates in assaulting and exposed allied troops. The function of ground forces (especially the infantry) thus became the "finding" and "fixing" of the enemy, but the "fighting" and "finishing" were most often accomplished by massive artillery and air firepower . . . These "pile on" tactics represented a new high in the US Army's emphasis on firepower and enemy attrition.[38]

This devastating use of firepower led some critics, such as the historian David Elliott, to charge that the increased GVN control of the countryside was not due to any great American acumen at counterinsurgency but could be credited to this massive firepower causing equally massive rural depopulation and a move by refugees into "secure" GVN areas. Certainly, some commanders, such as Ewell, were more impressed by the coercive aspects of counterinsurgency than by any ideas about civic action or good governance.[39] Referring to acts of pilfering from an oil pipeline, he advocated a harsh line:

> You can get a sapper unit mining the road, and you kill two or three and they'll knock it off. It may be that a month later they'll come back. These people can count. And, boy when you line them up [bodies] and they count one, two, three, four, their enthusiasm is highly reduced. That's the way we opened up Highway 4—just killing them. It doesn't take many.[40]

Operation Speedy Express was the American way of war carried out to its logical extreme. What makes its indiscriminate use of firepower and focus on the body count even more surprising was that the operation was not supposed to focus conventional warfare but on pacification and population security.

THE 173RD AIRBORNE BRIGADE AND OPERATION WASHINGTON GREEN, 1969

In contrast to the 9th Infantry Division, some units *were* conducting pacification operations that mirrored classic counterinsurgency doctrine. Some, like the 199th Separate Light Infantry Brigade, were effectively emulating the US Marine Corps Combined Action Program, where units broke down into platoons that mentored and collaborated with local militia forces, living and fighting alongside them in the hamlets. On a larger scale, as part of Vietnamization, advisory efforts became much more central to the mission of US combat forces. A classic example of how these operations could be conducted was Operation Washington Green, carried out by the 173rd Airborne Brigade. Their commander, Brigadier General John W. Barnes, outlined his objectives thus:

> No longer would we be chasing and killing the VC/NVA in the unpopulated jungle and mountainous areas. Even more important, body count would no longer be the criteria for success. Instead, we henceforth would be securing the people and their homes and farms. Our aim would be to deny the VC their support from their hamlets, without which they could not survive.[41]

To this end, his brigade was completely integrated with local RF/PF and became, in the words of its commander "in effect . . . a big mobile advisory team." According to Barnes, the brigade's efforts at securing the population were successful due to "the absence of threat by large, well-trained, well-equipped NVA forces" and the "integrated US/GVN effort at district, village and hamlet level, in response to a single plan—the District Pacification Plan." Barnes also pointed to the "increased effectiveness of RF/PF through constant daily association with similar US elements" and their success in "convincing the people that security forces are there to stay for as long as the job takes."[42] The CORDS Pacification Studies Group approvingly noted that the "173rd AB has boldly but sensibly deployed their forces in small units (sometimes as small as squads)," and that (in stark contrast to the 9th Infantry Division) the "number of kills and number of operations are not adequate parameters of progress."[43] HES data during their deployment showed marked improvement, with GVN control of hamlets increasing from 67 percent to 86 percent and NLF-controlled hamlets correspondingly decreasing from 18 percent to o percent between March and October 1969.[44] So successful did the Nixon administration consider the operation that they adopted Barnes as an unofficial spokesperson for Vietnamization (see the following discussion); at the urging of Secretary of Defense Melvyn Laird he briefed the White House press corps on October 11, 1969, before being sent on the road with his briefing.[45] Therefore, it would seem that Washington Green represented something of a model for both Vietnamization and pacification.

Despite this success, the brigade's tactics did not meet with universal approval. Major General Charles P. Brown, commander of I Field Force Vietnam and Barnes's immediate superior, strongly disapproved of their methods. In his oral history, he recounted:

> When I got there . . . the 173rd Airborne Brigade, which had a good reputation and had done well earlier, had been given the job of holding hands with the regional forces along the coast. Frankly, the unit had become basically ineffective, as a fighting organization . . . Later, I made the 173rd go back to work and put them back into the field operationally. They had gotten used to sitting on their ass holding hands with RF'ers and the PF'ers; it was damn hard to get them aggressive again.[46]

Brown's attitude illustrates the fundamental cultural difficulty in getting a force as technology- and firepower-intensive as the US Army in adapting to the different requirements of a counterinsurgency war. While Barnes and Laird saw Washington Green as a model for the future, Brown—the Army's senior commander in the area—essentially saw the 173rd Airborne as a failed unit. Such disagreements were indicative of the way in which contrasting memories of the war would lead to different factions constructing competing lessons of Vietnam.

While Brown's disapproval of the 173rd Airborne's tactics was a harbinger of the future of counterinsurgency in the US Army in the post-Vietnam era, it would also appear that some of the 173rd Airborne's own troopers had similar (if more serious) difficulties in adapting to the demands of counterinsurgency. A CORDS field evaluator reported incidences of troopers throwing rocks from their trucks onto Vietnamese Lambrettas, "taxation" by American troops guarding bridges, and, more seriously, allegations that US troops were killing animals and people indiscriminately. The evaluator, John S. Figueira, was unable to find any firm evidence for this but heard from villagers that at least four civilians had been shot and killed by US troops on patrol or in firebases.[47]

The field evaluator's description of abuses was not an isolated report; Samuel Popkins, a social scientist and counterinsurgency theorist, visited Binh Dinh province in 1969, and he reported that "he witnessed incidents where soldiers threw sandbags from moving trucks onto passing Lambrettas and other taxi-like vehicles. He reported cases where soldiers tossed candy to children and then followed with a smoke grenade."[48] Such abuses evidently had a negative effect on the 173rd Airborne's operations. Reports from CORDS field evaluators were similarly pessimistic about Vietnamese public opinion:

> Despite generally well-thought-of friendly security forces, enemy cadre were reported regularly entering parts of highly "secured" villages to conduct extended propaganda and supply missions. Except for an instance in which enemy forces deliberately took foodstuffs and livestock from a village, village opinion seemed most frequently to be weighted against friendly forces.[49]

This pessimism was well founded, as the 173rd Airborne's withdrawal coincided with a decline in HES statistics, an increase in terrorist incidents in Binh Dinh, and a decline in the performance of GVN forces. While the 173rd Airborne's partnering with local force increased RVNAF performance in the short run, it also led to dependency and, once American fire support and logistics were withdrawn, the Vietnamese units became increasingly ineffectual. While the APC (and Washington Green) succeeded in seizing and securing vast amounts of the South Vietnamese countryside, the GVN was left with huge new areas to administer, when they had not been doing a particularly good job of administering the areas that were *already* under their control. Kevin Boylan's study of the operation noted that, without a commensurate increase in resources, "there were simply not nearly enough trained and qualified village, hamlet, and higher-echelon officials, health care providers, teachers, and police to keep up with the extremely rapid pace of expansion."[50]

Washington Green is an interesting example of both the potential and limits of counterinsurgency in Vietnam, as it demonstrated that American units *could* be trained to conduct counterinsurgency operations that focused on population security; it was a far more effective operation than the firepower-intensive, body count–focused Operation Speedy Express. And yet, despite being well resourced, well led, and well executed, it ultimately did not succeed, as the old problem of how to get the GVN to govern effectively and to take over the burden of combat was a limitation that the Army never overcame. Such an outcome demonstrates not only the extraordinarily difficult nature of the task the United States had set for itself in Vietnam but also the limitations of even the best counterinsurgency plans when dealing with a foreign population. The way the Nixon administration—which had taken office in January 1969, after Abrams's launch of the Accelerated Pacification Campaign but before Speedy Express and Washington Green—understood that these limitations would do much to shape the post-Vietnam fortunes of counterinsurgency.

THE NIXON ADMINISTRATION AND COUNTERINSURGENCY

The limitations of Operation Washington Green were apparent not only in Binh Dinh province but also in Washington, D.C. Binh Dinh had been selected for special study as part of a National Security Council effort to take a fresh look at pacification in the Vietnamese countryside. A new ad hoc group formed by National Security Advisor Henry Kissinger—the Vietnam Special Studies Group, or VSSG—carried out the study. The VSSG stemmed from Kissinger's skepticism about the analysis coming out of MACV headquarters in Saigon. In his September 5, 1969, memorandum to President Nixon recommending that the group be formed, he wrote, "Looking back on our experience over the last few years, it is remarkable how frequently officials have let their preconceptions about Vietnam lead them astray even though a careful and objective analysis of readily available facts would have told them differently."[51] The VSSG's study on pacification, "The Situation in the Countryside," bore that skepticism out. While the report highly praised the 173rd Airborne's operations in Binh Dinh, crediting them with "spectacular security and control gains,"[52] it also recognized the fleeting nature of this control and just how reliant it was on US support, arguing that "when the shield is removed and enemy main forces are allowed to operate in populated areas . . . GVN control is erased."[53] Even more ominously, there was little evidence that South Vietnamese forces were ready to take on the challenge of providing security: "From the Allied point of view, progress in achieving security gains is attributable primarily to the presence of U.S. and Korean forces; the role of ARVN [Army of the Republic of Vietnam] in improving security is less clear."[54]

Interestingly, the VSSG study attributed much of the pacification progress to *conventional* operations, not sophisticated counterinsurgency techniques, another incidence of the way in which studies of the war—even contemporary ones—could complicate the transmission of counterinsurgency lessons. If the 173rd Airborne received praise, so too did the 9th Infantry Division and Operation Speedy Express. According to the "Situation in the Countryside" report, security in Dinh Tuong rapidly improved once US forces arrived: "Using fast-paced, sophisticated air-mobile tactics, it [a brigade of the 9th Infantry Division] was able to inflict severe casualties on four of the seven VC main force battalions, particularly in June and July." More broadly, the study also argued that many of the gains in pacification came from progress in the main force war, contending, "It was the vigorous offensive activity of US forces more than ARVN forces which gave the Allies the upper hand in the main force war during 1968."[55] The VSSG study, then, while pessimistic about the prospects of Vietnamization, did not see a redoubled counterinsurgency effort as an adequate solution to the problem.

The study was remarkably clear on the extent of the problem and much more pessimistic than MACV estimates, claiming that the "GVN now controls some six million rural inhabitants; but there are still five million rural inhabitants whom it does not control and who are thus subject to some degree of enemy influence."[56] This finding was an affirmation of Kissinger's skepticism of the figures coming out of Saigon, particularly the HES data. Kissinger had noted that when he had visited Vietnam and questioned those entrusted with gathering HES data and had "asked these people their criteria for judgment of village security, their answers ranged from the highly sophisticated to the appallingly crude."[57] This mistrust of the HES figures was rooted in the Nixon administration's deeper uncertainty in the prospects for success in Vietnam and indeed its ambivalence toward counterinsurgency in general. One of Nixon's first acts in office was the drafting of a National Security Study Memorandum (NSSM 1) on the situation in Vietnam.[58] Opinions were sought from MACV, the American Embassy in Saigon, CINCPAC (the Commander in Chief, Pacific Command), the Joint Chiefs of Staff, the State Department, the CIA, and the Office of the Secretary for Defense (OSD). The replies on pacification showed two divergent views of its success. The military and the American Embassy in Saigon were quite optimistic about the situation, arguing that "at the present time, the security situation is better than any time during period in question, i.e., 1961–1968." The civilians at OSD and the State Department were far less sanguine, arguing that at least 50 percent of the Vietnamese population was subject to some NLF influence or control.[59] This standpoint is perhaps best illustrated by the contents of a Special National Intelligence Estimate (NIE) of January 16, 1969 on the pacification effort:

> Thus far the GVN's principal success has been in expanding its presence into the countryside. Providing permanent security for these gains has been more

difficult . . . A large part of the countryside is still contested and subject to the continuing control of neither side. As for gaining the allegiance of the people, this is almost impossible to measure . . . Saigon now seems finally to have accepted the need for a vigorous pacification effort. However, progress may still be hampered by the political situation in Saigon, continuing inefficiency, corruption, and the parochial concerns of the GVN.[60]

Even the recommendations of optimists about US prospects in the war served, if unintentionally, to underline just how big a challenge counterinsurgency in Vietnam was. Robert Thompson, one of the classic theorists of counterinsurgency, who had some record of success in Malaya and rather less with the Diem regime in the early 1960s, had been strongly critical of the American conduct of the war up to 1968.[61] However, having been sent by Nixon to examine the situation in Vietnam in 1970, 1971, and 1972, Thompson came back with unfailingly glowing reports of the prospects for pacification, a sign that Abrams was at least conforming to classical counterinsurgency theory in his strategy, even if some of his subordinates were not.[62] However, amid this cheeriness and optimism, Thompson noted that, although the situation was under control, he saw the war continuing for another twenty-five years, albeit at a lower intensity than in 1965 through 1968.[63] According to Thompson, South Vietnam would manage to "win" sometime around the mid-1990s. Such an assessment, though completely at odds with the goals of the Nixon administration and the strategic climate in which the war was being conducted,[64] was probably a relatively accurate best-case scenario, given the history of counterinsurgency campaigns being long, tedious, and indecisive. Given such a perspective from an avowed optimist on the war, it is easy to see why the Nixon administration was less than wholehearted about the concept of counterinsurgency, something that complicated the postwar future of the doctrine.

A persistently pessimistic streak ran through the Nixon administration's prognoses of the condition of pacification in Vietnam, and there was little belief at high levels that South Vietnamese control of the countryside was durable, either under US auspices or following withdrawal. Reporting to President Nixon after a visit to Saigon, Secretary of Defense Melvyn Laird noted that he had informed US military leaders:

. . . that the American people expect the new Administration to bring the war to a satisfactory conclusion. The people will not be satisfied with less. A satisfactory conclusion, I emphasized, means to most Americans the eventual

> disengagement of American men from combat . . . The presentation given to me by the MACV staff was based on the premise that no reduction in US personnel would be possible in the absence of total withdrawal of South [sic: North?] Vietnamese troops. I do not believe that our national interests, in the light of our military commitments worldwide, permit us to indulge in this assumption. Nor do I feel that true pacification and GVN control over its own population can ever be achieved while our own forces continue such a pervasive presence in South Vietnam.[65]

Success, then, was not military victory but the disengagement of US troops from combat. Abrams was to conduct pacification as a means to help extract his troops rather than win the war in any conventional sense. Nixon, in a remarkable 1969 memorandum to Kissinger, wrote, "In reading Abrams' analysis of the military situation in South Vietnam I get the rather uneasy impression that the military are still thinking in terms of a long war and eventual military solution. I also have the impression that deep down they realize the war can't be won militarily, even over the long haul."[66] This memorandum is instructive not only in the context of Vietnam but also in the wider context of the Nixon administration's view of counterinsurgency. It seems that Nixon viewed the Army's efforts in Vietnam as doomed to failure. Nixon also worried that the Army lacked imagination and was constrained by conventional thinking; in a note scribbled to himself during a National Security Council (NSC) meeting, he mused on the nature of the war and the inability of senior commanders to adapt to it—"Lincoln appointed Grant and Sherman (in early 40's). We need a man of this war—(Abrams and Westmoreland = WWII)."[67] In an even more remarkable 1972 memorandum to Kissinger and Alexander Haig, Nixon voiced his deep dissatisfaction with how the military had conducted the war:

> I do not pretend to have any knowledge or experience whatever in military matters. But I do know that military men are generally noted for the courage and loyalty of their character and notorious for the plodding mediocrity of their strategy and tactics. Particularly where American military men are concerned, all they seem obsessed with is superior numbers (with even quality a secondary consideration) and with doing things the way they have been taught to do them in the book . . . our military leadership [in Vietnam] has been a sad chapter in the proud military history of this country . . . during the past three and a half years when we have begged them to come up with new initiatives, they have dragged their feet or even openly blocked them.[68]

While this may sound similar to the arguments of counterinsurgency advocates like Andrew Krepinevich and John Nagl, the main thrust of Nixon's memorandum was an inquiry as to whether a massed tank attack could turn the war's fortunes around. The idea that Nixon's dissatisfaction with the military's performance in Vietnam reflected passion on his part for counterinsurgency can be safely discounted.

It is not surprising that it was Nixon who ended presidential interest in counterinsurgency, given the persistent doubt expressed by various reports on pacification, the unrealistically lengthy paths to victory sketched out by counterinsurgency advocates such as Robert Thompson, and his own evident disbelief in the prospects for military victory and dissatisfaction with the way the Army fought the war in Vietnam. If President Kennedy opened what Douglas Blaufarb called the "counterinsurgency era"[69] with his speech about "a new kind of war" to the cadets at West Point on June 6, 1962, then Nixon surely ended it with his July 25, 1969, remarks at Guam, where he declared that:

> As problems of internal security are concerned, as far as the problem of military defense, except for the threat of a major power involving nuclear weapons, that the United States is going to encourage and has a right to expect that this problem will be increasingly handled by, and the responsibility for it taken by, the Asian nations themselves.[70]

With this statement Nixon effectively foreswore direct US involvement in future counterinsurgency campaigns and enunciated what became known as the Nixon Doctrine. In the context of a failed counterinsurgency campaign in Vietnam, the decision was an understandable one.

CONCLUSION

Much of the debate between the orthodox and revisionist schools on the Vietnam War centers on the question of whether the war could have been won. A subset of that debate is the dispute between orthodox scholars who maintain the counterinsurgency war was unwinnable and revisionists who claim that if the US Army had better understood how to prosecute a counterinsurgency campaign, then victory would have been within reach. This chapter has argued that orthodox scholarship is correct: The war *was* unwinnable, but this chapter also recognizes a key insight of the "hearts and minds" revisionist school—that the Army could have done a much better job at conducting the counterinsurgency war. But even where the Army applied classic counterinsurgency techniques, such as Operation Washington Green, they still lacked success, as the problem of what would happen when American troops left was unresolved.

Given the strategic choices available to Generals Westmoreland and Abrams, it is difficult to see what action they could have taken that would have led to success. The enemy was too well supported, the South Vietnamese government too weak and corrupt, and US forces were too ill adapted for the war they fought. Those who argue that General Abrams turned a failing war around overlook both the similarities between his campaigns and those of Westmoreland and the limitations he faced in prosecuting his "better war." Westmoreland was not as ignorant of counterinsurgency or the importance of pacification as critics have argued, nor was Abrams as strong an advocate of counterinsurgency as some have contended.

The successes and failures of the Accelerated Pacification Campaign showed that many of the fundamental problems of counterinsurgency, apparent since the Kennedy administration, had not been resolved. Abrams, in a conversation with General Cao Van Vien, chairman of the South Vietnamese Joint General Staff, remarked on the problems soldiers had in understanding these difficulties:

> It doesn't get any easier. It just gets kind of different. And here's this—us poor soldiers. You know, we've been to Leavenworth or something, and had all those lessons and books. And I don't remember anybody talking about the stuff you and I are talking about today. They didn't have any lectures on that—anything! And they don't have F.M.s [field manuals] about that. And here we are, we're all mixed up in it, supposed to be helping. I don't think any of us could graduate now. They'd probably have to expose us—too dumb. Can't understand it.[71]

Abrams (and to a lesser extent, Westmoreland) made a strong effort to understand the type of war he confronted, but his failure to find solutions to the challenges he faced meant the post-Vietnam army would not spend time trying to perfect its understanding of counterinsurgency warfare. The failure of counterinsurgency in Vietnam meant that the Army of the 1970s would not seek to build on the innovations that had occurred but would rather turn away from them in an effort to rebuild and redefine an institution that had been shattered by the war in Vietnam.

2 "OUT OF THE RICE PADDIES"

The 1970s and the Decline of Counterinsurgency

IN A 1975 REPORT on the "lessons of Vietnam," the US State Department observed, "Having been badly burned in Vietnam, the American people now appear to have quite different, and more limited visions of our proper role in the world and our ability to influence events." The authors of the report argued, "In a sense, a control mechanism has evolved within our society which is likely to prevent for the foreseeable future any repetition of a Vietnam style involvement."[1] This "control mechanism" did not exist just in the form of public opinion but also in the way in which the post-Vietnam Army rebuilt itself and its doctrine. Crucially, the way the Army chose to interpret the lessons of the Vietnam War meant that internal constraints on intervention in such wars were just as powerful as public sentiment against involvement. Senior leaders responsible for the rehabilitation of the post-Vietnam Army created a force that was cautious about intervention,[2] skeptical about the promises of nation building and, above all else, anxious to avoid repeating the Vietnam experience.

During the 1970s, officers commanding the newly formed Training and Doctrine Command (TRADOC) reasserted a "war-fighting" identity while asserting that fighting conventional wars in Europe was a more fitting mission for the Army than getting lost in unconventional and quasi-conventional conflicts in Southeast Asia and elsewhere. This choice reflected both the political realities of the time and the capabilities of a highly mechanized, technology-centric Army. However it was also rooted in something deeper, in a sense of self that meant that certain types of warfare—such as counterinsurgency—were defined as outside the Army's purview, regardless of circumstance. In its strategic planning, its doctrine, and its education system and in various studies of the lessons of Vietnam—from the tactical to the operational to the strategic—the institutional Army moved not only to erase memories of Vietnam but also to reassert its identity as a "war-fighting" force that did not get involved in counterinsurgency campaigns.

THE ARMY OF THE 1970S

The Army of the 1970s was one that suffered deep-seated problems with morale and discipline. Junior officers regarded the Army's ethical system to be a charade, while bases in both the United States and Europe had endemic problems with drugs and race relations. A 1970 study on professionalism by the US Army War College found that most junior and midlevel officers perceived a climate where there was strong tension between the traditional values of "Duty, Honor, Country" and the prevailing institutional pressures of careerism and incompetence.[3] This pessimism was deeply rooted in the Vietnam experience and the moral compromises made there. Ironically, this dissatisfaction was at its most intense well before the Saigon regime collapsed in April 1975 and indeed during a period where most Americans, including the leaders of the Army, believed the South Vietnamese regime was going to survive.[4] Defeat, then, was not the cause of this malaise. Rather, discomfort with US objectives and methods in Vietnam was far more important. The authors of the War College's professionalism study noted some of the more egregious ethical problems encountered by junior officers in Vietnam:

> Nobody out there believes the body count. They couldn't possibly believe it. This is probably the most damning thing the Army has used recently . . . we had one lad even tell us of an experience where he almost had to get in a fist fight with an ARVN adviser over an arm, to see who would get the credit for the body, because they were sorting out pieces . . . it just made him sick to the stomach.[5]

Such complaints were symptomatic of a wider discontent with Army leadership. The study, which drew on the elite section of the officer corps (those attending service schools), found that officers believed that "military personnel, primarily career types, are too concerned with promotions, efficiency reports, and conforming to the wishes of their commander . . . Many times a good soldier is . . . treated unfairly by his superiors for maintaining high standards of professional military competence."[6] Rates of resignations by West Point graduates who had served as junior officers in Vietnam were far above the norm,[7] and there was a flurry of critical works[8] on the Army's institutional breakdown. In surveying this state of affairs, Ronald Spector commented, "If the Army's experience in Vietnam teaches any lesson it is that no armed service no matter how well trained, equipped, and led can continue indefinitely to fight a meaningless war for which it can perceive neither compelling necessity nor hope of success."[9] The price of fighting this "meaningless war" was apparently institutional near-breakdown, and so the prevention of any such interventions in the future became a central part of the Army's response to Vietnam.[10]

Structural reforms in the immediate post-Vietnam era included the 1973 ending of the draft (an initiative that came from outside the military) and Army Chief of Staff General Creighton Abrams's "Total Force Concept." Abrams's expansion of the Army to sixteen divisions by integrating reserve and active duty units meant that presidents could no longer go to war without calling up the reserves, something President Lyndon B. Johnson had refused to do in Vietnam.[11] Such reforms were also at least partially intended to restore some sense that the Army was indeed "America's Army"; that it was, in the words of General Fred Weyand, "an Army that had the support of the American people, an Army that merited that support."[12] Indeed, Weyand (with Harry Summers) argued that the withdrawal from Vietnam was not necessarily due to military defeat but rather simply a reflection of the wishes of the people. Weyand and Summers contended: "The American military withdrew from Vietnam in good order in accordance with the wishes of the American people—a fact that should enhance, not diminish, our prestige as servants of the American people."[13] By integrating reserve forces into the active Army, the connection between the Army and the people—disrupted by an unequal draft system and by a president who did not call up the reserves and thus call the nation to arms—could be reestablished.

These structural reforms were not just about restoring Army morale and its ties to the nation but also about the need to refocus on the NATO mission in Europe. The Army's institutional collapse meant that force readiness had plummeted. The Army's Historical Summary for 1971 reported: "Personnel shortages and turbulence, along with austere funding, precluded any substantial improvement in training readiness in fiscal year 1971." Personnel turnover mean that training frequently had to be recycled at lower levels to "insure basic proficiency in primary skills," and "major commands were not able to conduct effective exercise programs in the year because of congressional reductions of $3.7 million in field exercise funds from the Army's operation and maintenance budget."[14] Senior leaders such as General Donn Starry worried about the effect that Vietnam had on Army modernization and doctrine. Starry later recalled that "on the other side of the inter-German border, it was apparent that the Soviets understood what was happening in U.S. Army Europe and elected to take advantage of the situation" by fielding new operational doctrine and a new generation of armored vehicles and artillery systems.[15] Even as late as 1980, he worried about this state of affairs, declaring that "Vietnam is over, and I don't have to make the obvious point that the world conditions have changed. We no longer enjoy any advantages, conventional or integrated."[16] In later years, Starry reflected how the deterioration of the Army led to a clear choice for Army leaders:

> One of General Abrams' first challenges as Chief of Staff, having redeployed from Vietnam early in 1972 and been confirmed as Army Chief of Staff later that year, was to resolve the issue of "back to Europe first" versus the pressing need for counterinsurgency doctrine. The best advice was, while we did know a lot about counterinsurgency, we had not yet digested what we knew to the point from which we were ready to write doctrine and spell out equipment requirements, organizations, and related requirements; hence, the decision to fix the U.S. Army in Europe first.[17]

In truth, the "pressing need for counterinsurgency" did not seem apparent to Army planners at the time. Army strategic planning reflected that "Europe first" decision and emphasized a return to a traditional role, focused on NATO operations and on the alliance with Japan.[18] The structural reforms of the 1970s were about affirming a traditional understanding of the Army's purpose. General Frederick Weyand noted that the primary thrust of these moves was to legitimize the Army's post-Vietnam return to what they saw as a more traditional role, quoting T. S. Eliot: "At the end of all our exploring / Will be to arrive where we started / and know the place for the first time."[19] That strategy was as much about reasserting a limited mission for the Army as it was about adapting the Army to work with the Nixon Doctrine. As Richard Lock-Pullan argues, "What was militarily achievable was defined by the Army's professional identity, rather than the demands of policy." This (to use Lock-Pullan's phrase) "inward-looking time" was the result of an institution that had been shaken to the core by Vietnam and defeat.[20]

DOCTRINE

The reimagining of the force as "America's Army" was part of an effort to return to a more traditional role. The key shifts took place not in senior officer speeches about the future of the Army or even strategy documents but in the core sources of knowledge for the Army's formal collective memory: its doctrine and education curricula. The Army's institutional response to this crisis involved a reaction to Vietnam that embedded itself in both its doctrine and its training and education system.[21] Under the leadership of General William E. DePuy, the new Training and Doctrine Command (TRADOC) addressed itself to an era beyond Vietnam, but the manner in which it did so necessitated reshaping the past.[22] For throughout this time of doctrinal and educational ferment, Vietnam and counterinsurgency were strangely absent from the discourse.

In July 1976, the US Army published its first post-Vietnam edition of FM 100-5 *Operations*, its capstone manual describing both the Army's view of war and its preferred methods of waging it. In a letter to the Army Chief of Staff General Fred C. Weyand, primary author General William DePuy commented, "It [the manual] is written in recognition of the fact that the entire United States Army, from Private to General needs to focus on a form of combat in which the Army of today has had no battlefield experience. In a sense, this manual takes the Army out of the rice paddies of Vietnam and places it on the Western European battlefield against the Warsaw Pact."[23] In many ways, the 1976 edition of FM 100-5 and the intellectual and institutional tumult that surrounded it were signs that the Army desperately wanted to move beyond the Vietnam era. DePuy's stated desire to shift the Army's focus meant the construction and acceptance of a set of lessons of Vietnam that were less an attempt at historical analysis than an effort to ensure that an event like Vietnam could never happen again. Furthermore, even before the Army's lessons crystallized into a definitive set of principles, Army leaders began to implement them, essentially acting on its preferred version of Vietnam long before coming to formal conclusions about the war.

This edition, commonly known as "Active Defense," was a curious document. Ordinarily, this field manual expresses the Army's vision of war and principles it would adhere to as it conducted operations. However, DePuy had a much more elementary focus. He believed that the manual should "teach the Army how to fight wars again." DePuy explained this decision: "We wanted to change the whole tone of the manual to what I would almost call, an operator's manual for the division level and below . . . We were trying to . . . retrain the United States Army after Vietnam."[24] From the content of the manual, it was clear that DePuy wanted to retrain the army for a very specific type of combat. Clearly, Vietnam-style conflict was not what he had in mind. DePuy realized the oddity of an operational-level manual discussing things as basic as digging trenches: "I was a four star general. I was talking about platoon and company mechanized and armored tactics to an Army which, in general, knew nothing about it. At the low tactical level."[25] This focus on "the low tactical level" was indicative of just how thoroughly DePuy believed the Army needed retraining after its Vietnam experience.

Not only did much of the manual spend time discussing *battles*, the affairs of battalions and companies, rather than how larger units—such as corps and armies—would conduct operations, but the Vietnam experience was entirely absent from the document. The writing team, led by DePuy and Major General Don Starry, ignored the conflict that had just ended and instead focused on the possibility of war with the Soviets in Northern Europe. The preface baldly stated: "Battle in Central Europe against the forces of the Warsaw Pact is the most demanding mission the US Army could be assigned. Because the US Army is structured primarily for that contingency and has large forces deployed in that area, this manual is designed mainly to deal with the realities of such operations."[26] The focus on Europe was so explicit that the manual contained detailed meteorological data for Germany, and the chapter on urban operations included a map showing urban density from the Ruhr to the Oder Rivers.

Starry illustrated where TRADOC's priorities lay when he discussed the writing team's assumption that while war with the Warsaw Pact in Europe "while probably least likely, was certainly the most important from the standpoint of our national survival and the well-being of Western civilization. Contingency operations with light forces, while perhaps less important to our national survival, were still probably likely although perhaps less so than in former times."[27] Indeed, the likelihood of US involvement in such contingency operations would have been politically unpalatable; the Clark Amendment to the Arms Export Act of 1976 blocking covert US activity in Angola hinted at how intolerant Congress was of such interventions. The writing team were nonetheless quite conscious of the relative likelihood of contingency operations versus war with the Soviets. It would appear that much of the focus on the Soviet Union was more about reaffirming a core Army identity than about fighting the next war, especially given the fact that détente was still intact when the manual was written. DePuy later recalled:

> I think the whole American Army after the Viet Nam war was in some state of disarray, certainly had lost some of its confidence. More importantly, of course, it wasn't oriented on European type combat against very large enemy armored forces. Much of my effort was to try and get the Army reoriented from a light infantry war to its main mission in Europe which was an entirely different kind of a war.[28]

One Command and General Staff College department director stated it even more clearly: "The Army had its tail between its legs in 1975. The morale was terrible. DePuy gave it a mission and gave it back its self-respect."[29] DePuy's achievement in giving the Army back its self-respect was at least partially grounded in the fact that—despite his own service there—he steadfastly ignored the conflict that took away so much of the Army's confidence; the Vietnam War barely featured in the pages of the 1976 edition of FM 100-5.

Not only was the Vietnam War absent from the manual, but the type of warfare that had so dominated that war—counterinsurgency—was largely missing. In keeping with the new mission DePuy gave it (or rather, an old mission reaffirmed), the references to the Army's mission to provide stability in Third World countries that had featured so prominently in the 1968 edition of FM 100-5 were completely excised. Contingency operations did not feature in the 1976 manual except for purely technical references to the more difficult terrain—such as jungle or mountains—in which the Army might need to fight. DePuy, who had served two tours in Vietnam,[30] strongly concurred with Col. Harry Summers's belief that counterinsurgency had been an unproductive dogma in Vietnam and that resolute execution of a thoroughly conventional strategy of invading Laos and Cambodia to cut off the Ho Chi Minh Trail could have brought victory.[31] He was critical of units that conducted "counterinsurgency of the deliberate, mild sort" in Vietnam, and he believed that the United States never suffered any tactical failures in Southeast Asia and that counterinsurgency itself was the problem.[32] In short, DePuy internalized the same lessons as had many senior officers who served in Vietnam. His skepticism about counterinsurgency in some ways reflected a belief in the limits of American power:

The whole thing [counterinsurgency], of course, was eventually sucked into the maw of Vietnam, but it was a very activist philosophy. It was premised on the assumptions that if you were smart enough at all those things you could somehow thwart the efforts of the communists to subvert the third world. You could bring up some disadvantaged country in the image of America. Well, now after all these years we know better. We have a much more modest view of our capabilities.[33]

In this set of lessons from Vietnam, American capabilities were also limited by technology. What haunted DePuy and the other authors of *Active Defense* was the notion that the United States had fallen behind its rivals in terms of force modernization. Later DePuy recalled, "What we were really pre-occupied with was the fact that we had a light infantry Army because of Vietnam. The experience of that Army was fighting VC, which wasn't easy. But it was low tech."[34] However, "because of the cost of and preoccupation with the Vietnam War the Army lost a generation of modernization."[35] This meant that the United States would need to look outside its own recent experience for lessons on how new technology was shaping the battlefield. Despite his service in Vietnam, the key conflict for DePuy was the 1973 Yom Kippur War between Israel and Egypt and Syria, which, according to DePuy, provided a "marvelous excuse or springboard if you will" for revising and updating doctrine.[36] The Yom Kippur War displaced Vietnam as a source of tactical lessons for the US Army with astounding rapidity, with the Army producing a comprehensive "lessons learned" report for the Yom Kippur War before they ever produced something similar for Vietnam.[37]

This turn away from the tactical lessons of counterinsurgency in Vietnam extended not only to high-level operational doctrine: *Infantry in Battle*, the Command and General Staff College's 1975 primer for infantry tactics, contained sixty-two historical case studies. Of these, over half were from World War II, a quarter from Korea and only 10 percent from Vietnam. Furthermore, the only non-American example cited, the 1973 Yom Kippur War, received as much attention as the Vietnam War.[38] The Army's manual on counterguerrilla tactics, FM 31-16, which was published in 1967, was not updated until 1981 when it was withdrawn from service without a replacement.[39] The counterinsurgency doctrine that survived actively reflected the Nixon Doctrine and the preference for security assistance to Third World allies over direct intervention. The 1972 edition of FM 31-23 *Stability Operations*, which dealt with counterinsurgency at brigade and higher levels, was a major change from the 1960s editions of that manual. It stated that "the US role in any counterinsurgency mission must be primarily advisory" and that "assistance is predicated upon the requirement that any country whose security is threatened and who requests assistance must assume primary responsibility for providing the manpower needed for its own defense."[40] In 1974, the term *stability operations* disappeared, too, with the new manual—FM 100-20—referring instead to "Internal Defense and Development."[41] Such changes were both a clear reflection of Army priorities and a recognition that Army intervention, at least in the immediate post-Vietnam era, was highly unlikely. In its deletion of references to Vietnam and counterinsurgency, Army doctrine of the 1970s reflected (and encouraged) this state of affairs.

SPECIAL FORCES AND THE EDUCATION SYSTEM

Even the home of counterinsurgency itself, the JFK School for Special Warfare, did not escape the drawdown. The year 1972 was the first since 1962 that did not see the deployment of any military advisory training teams to anywhere in the world.[42] It operated under severe personnel and financial restrictions throughout the 1970s, its command language school was ordered to close, and, as early as 1973, the Special Forces Officers Course at Fort Bragg was devoting only ten of its 704 academic hours to counterinsurgency, preferring instead to focus on its unconventional warfare mission of raiding and operating behind enemy lines.[43] Meanwhile, the Army deactivated four Special Forces groups—the units responsible for advising foreign militaries on counterinsurgency—between 1969 and 1974.

This shift in emphasis followed the lead of the Special Forces officers who wrote in *Military Review* that "we have accepted that the Army will not change the thrust of its preparation, therefore, special operations forces must be applied within that context or be labeled 'not applicable' which, we feel, is the first step in an institutional process that ultimately will do away with the forces."[44] The effects of this policy were clear in the mid-1980s, when there was a resurgence of interest in counterinsurgency due to involvement in El Salvador. An instructor from the Command and General Staff College, preparing to deliver a course on low-intensity conflict to the officers of an Asian nation, traveled to Fort Bragg to review the Special Warfare School's files on counterinsurgency and found that staff there had been ordered to throw them out in the 1970s.[45] Not only were courses on counterinsurgency discontinued, but the physical residue of those courses was also destroyed. This discovery led one of the CGSC instructors to comment: "We don't do dishes, we don't do windows, and we don't do insurgencies."[46] It was extraordinary that such a remark could be made less than twenty years after President John F. Kennedy had predicted that "shadow wars" would be a prominent future mission for the Army and that the Special Forces would play a hugely important role in such wars. Now the Special Forces branch of the service was reduced to accommodating itself to the Army's conventional mission by training for unconventional raids behind Warsaw Pact lines and minimizing instruction on counterinsurgency.

Meanwhile, other service schools either drastically reduced or eliminated the hours devoted to counterinsurgency. Between 1972 and 1976, the Armor and Artillery Schools both eliminated instruction on counterinsurgency, while the Intelligence School devoted only four hours on its Officer Basic Course to the topic.[47] Likewise, the Command and General Staff College saw a steady decrease in the hours that it dedicated to counterinsurgency, reaching a nadir in 1981–1982 when only eight of 482 academic hours were devoted to the subject.[48] The Army War College also drastically reduced the time spent on counterinsurgency. In 1972, it eliminated its course on Internal Defense and Development, while cutting the number of counterinsurgency-related topics available to students from sixteen to six, over the strong objections of both instructors and students. The faculty expressed concern that "the Army was running away from wars of national liberation and back towards conventional warfare and massive retaliation."[49] Given that the Army *was* in fact consciously moving away from counterinsurgency at the time, it is striking to see dissent to such an important policy from some of the Army's most important thinkers. The final course report reflected both student and faculty opinion when it complained that "in the new curriculum, there apparently will be little or no coverage of the new Security Assistance Program, impact of military assistance in developing countries, country team operations, Vietnam lessons, and future trends in IDD [internal defense and development]— all critical in understanding the Nixon Doctrine."[50] The students' protest that "there is both a great importance and interest in the politico-military lessons to be drawn from the Vietnam experience and their applicability in applying the Nixon Doctrine in the future" went unheeded. Counterinsurgency's place in the Army's education system was virtually erased even before the end of the Vietnam War.

This too could at least be partially traced to General DePuy's relentless drive to use TRADOC as a means with which to reorient the Army back toward a more predictable, conventional form of war. Just as his edition of FM 100-5 concentrated on basic tactical methods, DePuy worried that a focus on abstract topics at service schools was detrimental to what he saw as core warfighting skills:

> Thus, over the years, we have loaded into our school system many peripheral quasi-military subjects. When I arrived in TRADOC and first visited Fort Benning, I was told that there was no time on the curriculum for the Officer Basic Course to teach the construction of defensive positions for the individual soldier because such subjects as leadership, management, and motivation had taken precedence. In other words, we did not teach platoon leaders, but rather we taught "officers."[51]

DePuy and his deputy chief of staff for training, Major General Paul Gorman, swung the pendulum heavily away from education and back toward training as the primary mission for all Army schools. The service schools were pushed away from the "military-political" level of discourse and back toward the more functional aspects of military training. In a May 1977 letter to the Army chief of staff, General Bernard Rogers, DePuy outlined an approach that would move away from what he called the "whole man concept" in vogue in the early sixties.[52] Although this had salutary effects on the tactical capabilities of the Army in conventional war, it did not bode well for its ability to handle more complex counterinsurgency operations, where officers at all levels would need a broader set of skills than "war fighting."

With the deletion of Vietnam and counterinsurgency from the War College syllabus at its commandant's behest, the Army educational system's silence on the experience of Indochina was now almost complete, even though the war was still ongoing. While doctrine could be, and often was, radically changed in a short period of time, the absence of Vietnam from service schools meant that a generation of officers, those who were too young to serve in Vietnam, had neither personal experience of counterinsurgency nor any understanding of it through Army schools. One dissident officer was still critical of this approach in 1989:

> Both inside and outside the Army, to talk about Vietnam is much like discussing AIDS; it has been, and continues to be, a subject far too delicate, and

something to which there is no known solution. In a way, the Army's conscious avoidance speaks to how deeply the war's trauma continues to be felt by those senior officers now leading the Army. They fought the war at the platoon, company, and battalion level. They saw their profession almost destroyed by the war. To them fell the unenviable task of rebuilding a badly damaged Army. A professional contract of silence on Vietnam descended upon the Army during the mid-1970s, and endured well into the late 1980s.[53]

DePuy's attempt to refocus the Army on more traditional forms of warfare, ones that fit more comfortably with its self-image, was strongly rooted in the trauma of Vietnam. The "professional contract of silence" on the war was a result of an understandable wish to minimize this trauma of Vietnam by forgetting it. However, the act of forgetting was itself a way of legitimating certain lessons from the Vietnam War, lessons that were not about a desire to "do better next time" but rather to prevent something like it from ever happening again. DePuy's body of reform was ultimately successful because it was a change the Army eagerly desired in the wake of Vietnam. Nevertheless, such a reshaping of priorities would be incomplete without at least some accounting for what happened in Vietnam. It is instructive to observe the contrasting fortunes of the various studies commissioned by the Army on the lessons of Vietnam.

THE ARMY'S "LESSONS" OF VIETNAM

Interestingly, one of the first attempts to define the lessons of Vietnam, a May 10, 1975, paper prepared for National Security Advisor Henry Kissinger, was deeply pessimistic about the prospects for the Army to learn from Vietnam. The authors, W. R. Smyser and W. L. Stearman, argued that "there has been no whole-hearted effort for reform within our military structure and we are not optimistic that any will be made"[54] and were equally critical of the Army's performance in the war:

> On the military side, it is clear that the US Armed Forces are not suited to this kind of effort. The one-year tour, the career attitude, the bloated structure and unimaginative tactics, all contributed to the undoing of our effort and of the South Vietnamese. When we thought it was "our war," we would not let the South Vietnamese fight it; when we no longer thought it was "our war," we would not support them in fighting.[55]

Ironically, while William DePuy and many senior Army officers would have agreed that the United States was not suited to that kind of war, they were working assiduously to reform the Army, but in such a manner as to *prevent* involvement in such future conflicts, not to improve their efforts. Smyser and Stearman, however, had a different view of the uses of force, arguing that "it is tempting to say, as many do, that we should either use our power totally or not use it at all . . . but this converts every military engagement into a total exercise."[56] This observation foreshadowed later critiques of the reticence of the Army to contemplate intervention but was made in a vacuum, as there was no contemporaneous Army effort to match the Ford administration's study of the lessons of Vietnam. While the Army's eventual consensus on the lessons of Vietnam would arrive at a starkly different conclusion to Smyser and Steadman, the institution would not begin to formally consider the lessons of Vietnam until the end of the decade, late in the Carter presidency.

The Army War College's Strategic Studies Institute undertook the Army's first (and only) official study of the Vietnam experience as a whole,[57] initiating its "Vietnam Lessons Learned Study" in 1975.[58] Commandant of the War College Major General DeWitt Smith believed that it was "absolutely imperative that we study how it is that you win so frequently, and so well, in a war-fighting sense, and yet lose a war in a strategic or political sense."[59] However, the scale of the task threatened to overwhelm the resources of the institution and a private contractor, the BDM Corporation, completed the work with the publication of an eight-volume report in December 1979.[60] Among other things, the authors of the BDM study questioned the notion that Vietnam was a war of tactical victories and strategic defeat, making the point "for the sake of historical accuracy and for future analysis" that "the US lost more battles, both large and small, in Vietnam than it admitted or possibly even comprehended at the time."[61] However, their principal criticism of the Army took issue with what Russell Weigley called the "American Way of War," the technology-focused and firepower-intensive tactics that the Army indiscriminately deployed in Vietnam.[62] In effect, the authors argued, overwhelming firepower, although it saved American lives, was in fact counterproductive to US goals in Vietnam— to the extent that those goals were ever defined—and ran counter to classic counterinsurgency theory. The omnibus summary concluded:

> The US approach to military strategy is basically a direct and unsubtle one which is heavily biased towards the materiel and technological end of the scale

and slights the psychological and political elements; a serious, comprehensive and continuing reappraisal of the basis for future US political-military strategy is overdue.[63]

This conclusion echoed not only the Smyser and Steadman report on "the lessons of Vietnam" but much of the orthodox historiography on the war.[64]

Like Smyser and Steadman, the authors of the BDM study were not overly optimistic about the prospects for such a reappraisal. The authors asked whether the Army had "zealously over-trained for one type of conflict" and concluded that "the answers to these questions are intimately entwined with the US perception of limited (non-nuclear) war, shaped (and perhaps altered) as a result of Vietnam."[65] Strongly implied throughout the study was the answer that the Army *had* overtrained for conventional warfare and continued to do so. The authors recognized that the US Army's commissioning of their study meant that the idea of "deriving lessons from the extremely traumatic experience in Vietnam is regaining respectability—at least in some quarters." Nonetheless, the fact remained that, within the US Army,

Counterinsurgency was, and still is, seldom mentioned and study of any low intensity or unconventional war was relegated to the environs of limbo. National planners realized that funds would not be made available for anything which remotely resembled preparation for anything like another Vietnam.[66]

Interestingly though, the BDM study, despite its criticism of the Army's performance in Vietnam and its advocacy of CORDS as a model for civic action programs of the future, expressed some skepticism about the utility of US intervention in what the authors termed "banana wars." The study recognized that there were limits to US power and that democracy was not an easily exported commodity, the authors concluding that "the US should help, not substitute for, the government of its ally. To the extent that the US takes charge, we postpone (and may even jeopardize) the achievement of the US's ultimate objectives."[67] According to the BDM study, future interventions would have to be based on a clear-eyed understanding of the nature of the regime the United States was supporting and a realization that "external aid and advice, especially when based on misconceptions, cannot provide a client state with the requisite leadership, determination, and cohesion to defeat a pervasive and sophisticated insurgency."[68] Nonetheless, the authors of the study also argued that such limitations did "not provide policy makers with a built-in rationale for inaction or vacillation when vital issues or interests are at stake."[69] There was, therefore, an unresolved internal tension within the BDM study: on the one hand, strong criticism of the Army's inability to conduct counterinsurgency in Vietnam and, on the other hand, real doubt as to whether or not US-led counterinsurgency could achieve its goals in any case. The solution, it appeared, was to argue for an enhanced counterinsurgency capability not because it was something the Army could do well but simply because it was unlikely to be able to avoid such conflicts in future.

While the BDM lessons learned study did not provide a clear alternative to the focus on conventional warfare, the eventual Army War College–commissioned book ostensibly based on its findings provided a strong validation for that very focus. When the Army War College's hoped-for publication based on the BDM study never materialized, the commandant tasked a member of the Strategic Studies Institute, Colonel Harry Summers, with drawing on this study and synthesizing its findings into a book.[70] Summers, however, entirely ignored the BDM Corporation's conclusions, and his book *On Strategy: The Vietnam War in Context* took a diametrically opposite view of the war.[71] In a sense, he was seeking to revise both the memories and the lessons of the Vietnam War at once.

Summers cast his study as an application of the principles of the Prussian military theorist, Carl von Clausewitz, to US decision making in Vietnam and found that both policy makers and strategists came up short. Dismissing counterinsurgency as a "fad" and a "dogma," he argued that the insurgency in Vietnam was merely a sideshow to the main force war, reminding readers, "There are those who would blame our failure in Vietnam on the forces of history or the tide of human events. But . . . it was four North Vietnamese Army corps, not 'dialectical materialism' that eventually conquered South Vietnam."[72] Summers was ironically ignoring the question of *Vietnamese* will and resilience, something that was strongly linked to the actions of US forces. Summers argued that the Army's troubles in Vietnam stemmed from a failure to heed Clausewitz: "Cut off from the foundation of military art . . . the Army's basic confidence in itself was shaken."[73] For Summers, the war was winnable. All that was required was that the United States fight the war full throttle, ignoring faddish counterinsurgency doctrines and paying heed to Clausewitz, particularly his idea that war must be conducted by a harmonious trinity of the state, the military, and the people.[74] One of the major themes of the book is the disregard for Clausewitz and for military advice in general shown by civilian strategists. Summers complained that "our civilian leadership in the Pentagon, the White House, and in Congress evidently believed the military professionals had no worthwhile advice to give."[75] This breakdown in civil–military relations was evidence of Clausewitzian friction, as were such problems as Johnson's refusal to declare war or call up the reserves, thereby failing to mobilize the "national will." This then led to another instance of friction: the antiwar movement. A fear of Soviet or Chinese intervention and possible nuclear escalation, together with a very un-Clausewitzian confusion over the definition of victory and of how "limited" the war really was, also contributed to defeat.[76] To Summers, refusal to intensify or expand the war by a more devastating, decisive bombing campaign against North Vietnam or by extending the demilitarized zone (DMZ) across the 17th parallel as far as the Mekong in Thailand was a major strategic mistake and indicative of a muddled approach to the war in both Washington and Saigon.[77]

Summers reserved most of his disdain for the Army's doctrine of counterinsurgency, arguing that defeat "did not grow out of the degree to which we pursued counterinsurgency doctrine, but out of the doctrine itself." He noted that the 1968 edition of FM 100-5 *Operations* contained woolly definitions of the purpose of the Army centered on notions of providing stability and development throughout the world, whereas the North Vietnamese General Van Tien Dung stated simply that "the basic law of war was to destroy the enemy's armed forces."[78] According to Summers, this American refusal to see the true nature of war contributed directly to defeat. Of the final collapse of the South Vietnamese government, Summers wrote, "Everyone, it seemed, [was] enamored with counterinsurgency but the North Vietnamese, and as the decisive battles in the spring of 1975 clearly illustrated, they were still playing by the old rules."[79]

The problem, according to Summers, was that, thanks to intervention from President John F. Kennedy and the Army's need to find a role in a world with nuclear weapons, "Counterinsurgency became not so much the Army's doctrine as the Army's dogma and . . . stultified military thinking for the next decade."[80] In Summers's narrative, Vietnam should have been a reprise of Korea, where the US forces oriented themselves on the external threat and left the minor task of cleaning up guerrilla pockets to local forces, who knew the terrain and the people better. Even Westmoreland's widely derided "search and destroy" tactics are somewhat redeemed in Summers's account. According to Summers, America's firepower-heavy conventional tactics were so effective that the North Vietnamese themselves not only used them during their successful campaign to overrun South Vietnam in 1975 but employed them while putting down an insurgency in Cambodia a few years later.[81]

However, Summers's importance lies not in his contribution to the historiography of the Vietnam War but the manner in which the US Army adopted his arguments. The foreword from the commandant of the Army War College, Major General DeWitt C. Smith, was at times lukewarm. Smith noted that this is "one man's critical analysis of American strategy in the Vietnam War . . . this work has become somewhat controversial even before its publication" and that "this book by no means represents the ultimate judgment, nor is it without flaws. But it exists, it is good and it begins something."[82] However, the Army as a whole did not share Smith's gentle skepticism. In 1982, Smith's successor as commandant, Jack N. Merritt, described *On Strategy* to be "firmly on the mark." Merritt, who later became director of the Joint Staff and eventually retired as a four-star general, also wrote that the War College had received overwhelmingly favorable comments about *On Strategy*, including responses from active Army leadership.[83] A young defense reformer called Newt Gingrich sent copies of the book to every member of Congress, it was put on the Army chief of staff's recommended reading list (and stayed there until 2004), and it became required reading at the Command and General Staff College, the Naval War College, and the National Defense University.[84] Not only that, but Summers himself used it as a teaching aid in his course on the Vietnam War at the Army War College. An entire class of that course was devoted to the "dogma" of counterinsurgency and its ills.[85] The course description succinctly described Summers's ideas on Vietnam and how he would teach those lessons at the War College:

> Our most recent war, Vietnam, is too often seen as an aberration outside the norms of 'traditional' wars such as World War II. Through the classic treatise on the dynamics of conflict, Clausewitz's *On War*, and our own principles of war, this course will put Vietnam in its proper context and allow us to draw strategic lessons for future application.[86]

The reception of those ideas would be a crucial indicator of how the Army applied the lessons of Vietnam to its doctrine, its education system, and its force structure.

Articles on Clausewitz began to feature heavily in the Army's professional journal *Military Review* while articles on Vietnam or counterinsurgency, with the notable exception of Donald Vought's 1976 protest "Preparing for the Wrong War?," did not.[87] *Military Review* did not devote an issue to Vietnam until 1989.[88] The memoirs of senior US leaders in Vietnam, such as Generals William Westmoreland and Bruce Palmer and Admiral Grant Sharp, echoed Summers's thesis.[89] For all the criticism directed at the generals who led the US Army in Vietnam, it is worth noting that essentially the very same officers led the post-Vietnam restructuring of the Army. William Westmoreland, Creighton Abrams, and Fred Weyand, all senior generals during the Vietnam War, served as chiefs of staff in the crucial years of rebuilding from Vietnam. Therefore, it is instructive to see an endorsement of Summers in the oral histories of senior officers; General Art Collins noted that "certainly that book on Strategy in Vietnam that Colonel Harry Summers wrote is a wholesome effort, and it's good that we are addressing Vietnam in that context."[90] General Charles P. Brown echoed the view of many general officers when he argued that "if we undertake to do something about it, we need to go in with purpose—our country, our people need to be convinced that there is a reason and it is necessary."[91] This emphasis on the need for public and congressional backing was one heard throughout the military in the post-Vietnam era, an emphasis that also echoed Fred Weyand's attempts to recast the Army as "a servant of the people."

There is, however, a more systematic source than the oral histories for studying senior officers' interpretations of the lessons of Vietnam. Brigadier General Douglas Kinnard's survey of his fellow generals from Vietnam revealed that 91 percent agreed with Summers's contention that the war could have been prosecuted with clearer objectives, with one respondent complaining that "the US was committed to a military solution, without a firm military objective—the policy was attrition—killing VC—this offered no solution—it was senseless." Of the group, 32 percent also thought that the concept of "search and destroy" was unsound, and 58 percent considered its execution to be inadequate, while 42 percent felt that large-scale set-piece battles had been overdone from the beginning.[92] However, one respondent showed that skepticism about search and destroy in South Vietnam did not mean lack of sympathy for Harry Summers's interpretation of the lessons of Vietnam. He commented that "large-scale operations were correct but should have been employed against specific objectives in North Vietnam and not against a will o' the wisp enemy in some un-strategic jungle."[93] If the generals were split on the utility of search and destroy, a firm majority deplored the "body count," with 55 percent considering kill ratios as misleading devices for measuring progress while 61 percent believed the body counts were wildly inflated. The responses included such comments as "the immensity of false reporting is a blot on the honor of the Army," "a fake—totally worthless," and "a great crime and a cancer in the Army in the eyes of young officers in 1969–1971."[94] Therefore, although there was broad sympathy for Summers's lessons of Vietnam among these general officers, there was still a sense that certain things could have been done better, that the United States could have fought the war with more sophistication.

A similar survey taken years later showed a contradictory divide in the officer corps's ideas of Vietnam. In a 1989 MA thesis at the School of Advanced Military Studies, Major Michael Brady surveyed his peers' attitude toward the legacy of Vietnam.[95] Brady's analysis, which focused on the then-current class at the Army's Command and General Staff College, showed some interesting results. *On Strategy* emerged as the book on Vietnam most widely read by junior and middle-ranking officers, while it was also "overwhelmingly singled out as the most influential book in the survey's sample," whereas only six out of 392 officers had read the BDM study.[96] However, the officers did not actually echo Summers's views on counterinsurgency or on the conduct of the war in Vietnam; less than 2.5 percent considered Vietnam to be a conventional war, and most respondents were critical of the *lack*—not surfeit—of adequate counterinsurgency doctrine, both during Vietnam and in their own time.[97] Ironically, then, even though the BDM study was apparently rarely read, its arguments about the Army's unpreparedness for counterinsurgency resonated quite strongly with another generation of officers, including those who counted El Salvador as just as central an experience as Vietnam had been for an earlier generation.

CONCLUSION

Such a paradoxical attitude can be partly attributed to the timing of the survey (coming as it did after involvement in counterinsurgency in El Salvador throughout the 1980s), but it also came from a recognition that the Army did not in fact acquit itself very well in Southeast Asia. These officers, most of whom were too young to serve in Vietnam, appeared to differentiate between Vietnam as history and Vietnam as lesson. As history, Vietnam was an example of poor understanding and misapplication of counterinsurgency, a dark time for the Army in terms of both morale and ethics. As lesson, however,

Vietnam meant not improving the Army's ability to fight such wars but restructuring the Army so that it could not be called on to fight them. Summers was fundamentally important to the Army's post-Vietnam outlook. While his work confirmed the wisdom of the reforms of the 1970s, it also laid the foundations for a generation of senior Army leaders who displayed an ever-greater caution about intervention. *On Strategy* served as the default parable about Vietnam for this cohort of generals, and its warnings about counterinsurgency were largely heeded. This meant that, for all the challenges the Army faced throughout the 1980s and 1990s, counterinsurgency could never return to the heart of the Army's identity.

Summers's narrative was a perfect fit for such an approach and strongly validated that set of lessons that urged that the Army abandon counterinsurgency and focus instead on conventional missions. Indeed, we can see how *On Strategy* served as validation rather than instruction for the Army by looking at the reforms of the 1970s, all of which were in place before either the BDM Corporation's lessons learned survey or Summers's pithy and influential rebuttal were published. DePuy and his associates, partly in reaction to the challenges of a new volunteer military, recast the Army's doctrine and education system in a way that decisively turned it away from the challenges of counterinsurgency and toward an old and familiar role. The 1976 edition of FM 100-5 deliberately emphasized armored warfare and the role on NATO's central front as a means of returning to that old role and a more comfortable identity for the Army. Meanwhile, the neglect of counterinsurgency manuals and the deletion of counterinsurgency from the syllabi of the various service schools, coupled with the striking absence of discussion of the Vietnam War in either the Army's field manuals or education system, signaled that the Army would rather move on from its traumatic experience in Vietnam. In this sense, perhaps the most salient lesson of Vietnam for the Army of the 1970s was that it should not speak of its experience of defeat in Indochina.

Thus, the Army's lessons of Vietnam, embodied in its doctrine, education, and training system, were also a site for the contestation of the *memory* of the Vietnam War. The silences in the various field manuals and course curricula were a way of limiting the discourse on the lessons of Vietnam, of privileging a certain narrative of the war. This led to a self-reinforcing phenomenon, whereby the Army's institutional identity as it related to the "American way of war" led the Army to construct narratives and lessons from Vietnam that emphasized the need to not let the Army's focus stray from conventional operations, and those narratives and lessons in turn further reinforced the Army's conventionally-focused identity. These actions reflected and reinforced the Army's institutional preference for conventional conflict, but the rapid and near-total elimination of counterinsurgency from Army doctrine suggests an almost-universal reaction to the traumas of Vietnam. The Army aggressively turned away from the strategies it associated with the humiliating defeat in Vietnam, and Army leaders were almost uniformly cautious in advocating military intervention. Not only that, but the Army's force structure and doctrine were amended with the intention of making policy makers more reluctant to call on the military to intervene. Army reticence was just as much a crucial constraint on interventionist impulses in the post-Vietnam era as the public reticence traditionally associated with the Vietnam syndrome.

3 LOW-INTENSITY CONFLICT IN THE REAGAN YEARS

WHILE THE REFORMS of the immediate post-Vietnam years meant that the Army reoriented itself almost entirely toward its conventional mission in Northwest Europe and effectively erased counterinsurgency from its institutional memory, it did not follow that American policy makers would remain convinced of the limits of US power for long. In 1981, the new president, Ronald Reagan, was eager to demonstrate US resolve and dispel any perceived notions of post-Vietnam weakness. In Central America, this stance, while consistent with the Nixon Doctrine's wariness of direct intervention, meant that the United States became embroiled in several insurgencies there, as supporters both of insurgency in Nicaragua and of counterinsurgency in El Salvador and Guatemala. The specter of a leftist insurgency threatening a corrupt, repressive, but US-backed regime, together with attendant issues of US prestige and credibility, presented the United States with a chance to demonstrate that it had learned from the mistakes of Vietnam. The crises in Central America meant that the Army was involved in a counterinsurgency campaign, despite a decade of active neglect of the attendant doctrine.

When counterinsurgency reemerged, it did so as part of the new concept of "low-intensity conflict," which described a range of problems that the military could face: from peacekeeping, to peace enforcement, to support for insurgency, to counterinsurgency, to counterterrorism. The elasticity of the term meant that attempts to define low-intensity conflict (LIC) and how it should affect the Army's doctrine and force structure became a major preoccupation for the Army's doctrinal thinkers throughout the 1980s. The contested nature of LIC illuminated the evolution of attitudes toward counterinsurgency and the lessons of Vietnam as well as how consensus on those lessons was shaped by contemporary events as much as the Vietnam experience. This reemergence of both counterinsurgency and the specter of "Vietnam" illustrated that the lessons of Vietnam were still fluid, contested topics within the Army as the meaning of those lessons were again debated in both Fort Leavenworth and El Salvador.

REDISCOVERING COUNTERINSURGENCY— AND VIETNAM—IN EL SALVADOR

As a presidential candidate, Ronald Reagan had argued that "for too long, we have lived with the 'Vietnam Syndrome'" and that "it is time we recognized that ours was, in truth, a noble cause." Reagan's embrace of the "noble cause" also meant an acceptance of a set of lessons from Vietnam that decried lack of US resolve in prosecuting such wars:

> There is a lesson for all of us in Vietnam. If we are forced to fight, we must have the means and the determination to prevail or we will not have what it takes to secure the peace. And while we are at it, let us tell those who fought in that war that we will never again ask young men to fight and possibly die in a war our government is afraid to let them win.[1]

However, in practice, Reagan's foreign policy was just as proscribed by the Vietnam syndrome as that of his predecessors. Reagan's policy of covert and overt support for anticommunist right-wing groups throughout the Third World relied on the assumption that US intervention with combat troops would not be possible, given domestic constraints.[2] In that sense, while this "Reagan Doctrine" was more aggressively anticommunist and focused more on the support of anticommunist *insurgents*, it still conformed to the Nixon Doctrine's injunction against direct military intervention in Third World conflicts.

US support for the various Salvadoran governments in their civil war with the Frente Farabundo Martí para la Liberación Nacional (FMLN) leftist guerrillas, then, denotes a place where the Reagan Doctrine resided comfortably within the broader framework of the Nixon Doctrine. While the Reagan Doctrine tended to focus on support for anticommunist insurgents, in El Salvador the anticommunists were the *counter*insurgents.[3] US involvement in counterinsurgency in El Salvador indicated a more aggressive stance toward Third

World insurgencies than the Carter administration had displayed but one that was confined to financial assistance and military aid in the form of arms and advisors. President Reagan's support for the Salvadoran military regime was a policy he inherited from his predecessor, but, due to his ideological leanings, he was much quicker to militarize that support and frame the conflict in Cold War terms. Reagan eventually declared (in 1984) that "Central America is America; it's at our doorstep, and it has become a stage for a bold attempt, by the Soviet Union, Cuba, and Nicaragua, to install Communism by force throughout the hemisphere."[4] The Reagan administration's response to this perceived threat "on their doorstep" was to increase financial aid to the Salvadoran military and to send more US military advisors.[5] This military aid created a new mission for the US Army: to advise and support the Salvadoran government in its counterinsurgency campaign against the FMLN. This mission, although never more than fifty-five strong (at least officially), meant that the Army could no longer afford to ignore counterinsurgency. Not only that, but the Army could not ignore the parallels with and the danger of repeating the mistakes of Vietnam.

Indeed, the irony of this fear of repeating the mistakes of Vietnam was that, on one level, Reagan's interest in El Salvador, and in Central America in general, was based on a desire to restore the credibility the United States lost in Vietnam by winning an easy victory against communist forces. Secretary of State Alexander Haig assured Reagan: "Mr. President, this is one you can win."[6] If there was a parallel with Vietnam that supporters of Reagan's policy accepted, it was that Congressional vacillation and weakness could again prevent US victory. For instance, Richard Nixon, while observing that "Vietnam was far away and El Salvador is only five missile minutes away" argued that "when the red tide of blood and steel rolls over the 4.5 million people of El Salvador," then Congress would have no one to blame but themselves for the tragedy.[7] El Salvador, then, was to be Vietnam, but Vietnam as it should have been. However, in the popular discourse, the Vietnam analogy was not helpful to the administration. Critics charged that the US support for an obviously corrupt and repressive government under the guise of anticommunism was a clear echo of what had happened in Southeast Asia. Reagan himself dismissed the analogy, arguing that "there is no parallel whatsoever with Vietnam" and that "only Salvadorans can fight this war."[8] Closer to the ground, however, the shadows of Vietnam were clearly visible; one diplomat in San Salvador complained, "The Vietnam analogy is tearing at the guts of our policy here. Every time you try to do something here, you come up against it."[9] Indeed, many of the diplomats and military advisors in El Salvador were veterans of the war in Vietnam and strongly conscious of the parallels between the two wars and the need to avoid repeating their Indochina experience.[10]

Certainly, many in the military were cautious about repeating the mistakes of Vietnam. In 1983, retiring Army Chief of Staff General Edward C. Meyer not only urged that the United States should focus more on the political aspect of the problem but that the United States should not contemplate increased involvement in the absence of strong public support, a clear echo of Vietnam. Meyer argued:

> Guerrilla warfare is based on the legitimate concerns of the people . . . Having been involved in guerrilla warfare, in Vietnam, I realize that, unless you have the commitment of the people or the indigenous forces . . . you're not going to solve guerrilla warfare. I think that's one of the great lessons that comes out of Vietnam.[11]

According to Meyer, it would be wrong to send combat troops "without the support of the American people" to a country that "isn't fully committed to the resolution of its internal problem."[12] Meyer cautioned against direct involvement, noting: "I wouldn't even know how to design, right now, a US military solution . . . If I thought the 82nd Airborne going in there would be a solution to the problem. I'd probably recommend that right now. I don't think it would be."[13]

Meyer's caution, and indeed the fact that intervention with US combat troops was being contemplated at all was rooted in both the poor performance of the Salvadoran military in counterinsurgency campaigns and the apparent ineffectiveness of the US advisory effort there. Certainly, critics deplored an approach that seemed to repeat many of the same mistakes of the earlier war in Southeast Asia. Max Manwaring, a counterinsurgency theorist working for US Southern Command (SOUTHCOM), argued that US Army advisors in El Salvador had essentially created their mirror image in Central America, a conventional force "comfortable operating in battalion-sized formations, dependent on heavy, indirect firepower, and reliant on helicopters and trucks for mobility. Indeed, they would probably be comfortable in the Fulda Gap; certainly they would be comfortable in the Choluteca Gap."[14] Internal Army analysis in the early stages of US involvement echoed many of the criticisms heard in Vietnam. The FMLN very nearly succeeded in its 1981 "final offensive" attempt to overthrow the Salvadoran regime before Reagan took office, illustrating just how serious the problems of the Salvadoran government were. In response to this and a successful August 1981 rebel offensive, the Pentagon commissioned a report into what it would take to win the war. The "Report of the El Salvador Military Strategy Assistance Team" (commonly known as the Woerner Report) heavily criticized the corruption of the Salvadorian officer corps and contended that US assistance had yet to make any material difference in changing this mind-set, noting:

> An assessment of the MTT [Military Training Teams] impact on Salvadoran internal defense capabilities clearly demonstrates that we have barely begun to scratch the surface . . . functional training requirements of tactical proficiency, command control, combat support below Armed Force level, maintenance other than the UH-1H helicopter, leadership, and intelligence have been addressed only in rudimentary form and to a limited number of military personnel. There is much more to be done.[15]

Similarly, the report noted, "There is no national level civic action program. Presently, civic action activities and their effectiveness are primarily a function of the interest of local commanders which is quite minimal, if not zero"[16] and that there was no coordinated communications program aimed at the general population; neither was there any population control system in place or any effort to implement one. The lack of such basic counterinsurgency practices suggested that US advice could significantly alter the outcome of the war. However, many of the criticisms contained in the Woerner report were aimed at the Salvadoran government, not those running the US advisory effort. In fact, Woerner—who went on to command the US Army Security Assistance Agency, Latin America from 1982 through 1986 and commanded SOUTHCOM from 1987 to 1989—would help play a major role in shaping the overall US approach in El Salvador.

Indeed, those involved in SOUTHCOM claimed that they had indeed learned the lessons of Vietnam and were acting accordingly. General Paul Gorman, commander of SOUTHCOM from 1983 to 1985, later recalled that "one of the difficulties I had all the time I was down there was the idea of many in Congress that we were on a slippery slope to another Vietnam—that we were going to hit the Salvador tar baby and get ourselves immersed in yet one more of those unwinnable wars." Gorman was doing his "damnedest in the meantime to convince the House Armed Services Committee (HASC), particularly, that to the contrary, everything that was going on down there was being done by people who, if anybody knew the lessons of Vietnam, they did." He argued that, among the key US players in Central America, "there was probably more knowledge of what really happened in Southeast Asia than you would find in any other part of the US government. Those Congressmen didn't have the foggiest idea what they were talking about."[17]

Certainly, the US approach under the Reagan doctrine was to emphasize the importance of reform and civic action–oriented counterinsurgency, while supplying weapons, equipment, funds, and intelligence. President Reagan eventually outlined the overall approach in December 1983 by emphasizing the four *Ds*—democratization, development, dialogue, and defense.[18] Similarly, the President's National Bipartisan Commission on Central America (popularly known as the Kissinger Commission) reported in January 1984 that democracy and the emphasis on human rights were essential for the region as a whole and yet recommended a significant increase in US military aid in El Salvador.[19] This approach was similar on one level to that taken during the Diem years (1954 through 1963) in South Vietnam, only this time there was never any real possibility of US escalation to include ground troops. The Army's vice chief of staff, General Maxwell R. Thurman, commissioned a study in 1984 on the "correlates of success" in counterinsurgency, based on the El Salvador experience. Unsurprisingly, the authors of the study concluded that "the primary focus of the H[ost] G[overnment] in an insurgency must be to defend and expand its legitimacy. This means providing security to the people first and foremost. It means being accountable and perceived, within the culture, as non-corrupt. And, it means being able to deliver the normal government services at an acceptable level."[20]

It is clear, then, that few on the US side really saw a strictly military solution to the conflict in El Salvador, and even fewer wanted to repeat the mistakes of Vietnam, either in terms of overemphasizing military measures or in getting US troops committed. There was still plenty of criticism of ineffective Salvadoran Army tactics, with Manwaring as late as 1991 criticizing the "unwieldy conventional-type government battalions" that still focused on search and destroy missions "supported by fixed-wing aircraft, attack helicopters, artillery, and anti-tank weapons." He also argued, "The force established between 1981 and 1986 has become largely irrelevant to the conduct of the present wars of legitimacy, subversion, and external support."[21] Indeed, the repressive and murderous tactics of the death squads associated with the

Salvadoran military directly impeded both the legitimacy of and the external support for the Salvadoran regime. However, few would conflate these tactics with American preferences. Indeed, even the fifty-five-troop limit on US advisors had its defenders. Col. James Steele, commander of US military advisors in El Salvador from 1984 to 1986, argued:

> Nobody has cursed the 55-man limit more than I probably have in the last two and a half years, but I just have to tell you that doing it with a low US profile is the only way to go. If you don't, you immediately get yourself into trouble, because there is a tendency for Americans to want to do things quickly, to do them efficiently—and the third step in that process is to do it yourself. If you take that third step here, you have lost the battle.[22]

The problem, however, was not that US advisors did not understand the tenets of counterinsurgency—although the lack of clear published doctrine did cause some frustration among advisors in El Salvador—but rather that this understanding did not or could not translate into increased effectiveness in the Salvadoran armed forces or government. The institutional interests of the Salvadoran government and military in preserving their repressive, oligarchic way of government were too strong, and the United States faced the same problems of leverage as it did in Vietnam.[23] Brigadier General Fred Woerner wrote in his report on the Salvadoran military that "the team was unable to persuade the Armed Force General Staff to identify specifically extreme rightist terrorism as a threat."[24] Woerner cautioned that "unabated terror from the right and continued tolerance of institutional violence could dangerously erode popular support to the point wherein the Armed Forces would be viewed not as the protector of society, but as an army of occupation."[25] Yet while the general clearly understood the problems caused by government acquiescence in the activities of right-wing death squads, the killings continued. It took the 1984 visit of Vice President George H. W. Bush to El Salvador, where he personally chastised the Salvadoran military, to see any decrease in violence, and even that was partial.[26] Loyalties within the Salvadoran military meant that prosecuting those responsible for the killing was rarely an option, and real social reform would have undermined the power and position of the governing class.

It was clear that American military advisors, many of whom were veterans of Vietnam, largely *did* understand both the dangers of an overly conventional approach and of the unrestrained use of violence against civilians and *did* understand the tenets of classic counterinsurgency doctrine, yet the situation still did not markedly improve.[27] Indeed, a critical study by the RAND Corporation noted, "Those involved in the American effort appreciated from the start that Salvadoran society was truly one of the sickest in Latin America and that the rebels had ample cause to lead a revolution."[28] The human rights record of the regime remained abominable,[29] and economic inequality remained widespread. The various Salvadoran regimes simply did not have incentives to change that. To be sure, the FMLN never managed to overthrow the government, but ever-increasing American support for the Salvadoran regime could only bring stalemate, not victory. With varying degrees of sincerity, American advisors consistently suggested improving the human rights situation and implementing democratization, yet little was done, and the war ground on.[30] The RAND report summed up the problem:

> American officials once again allowed their efforts to be influenced by an assumption that had proved to be a principal source of our frustration in Vietnam: namely, that it is relatively easy to ensure that an ally does what American policymakers deem necessary to eliminate insurgency. This assumption has once again proved false. There are inherent limits on the ability of one nation, no matter how powerful, to influence the direction and character of another. It is not self-evident whether the interests of America's instrument and necessary reforms are reconcilable. In El Salvador, as in Vietnam, our help has been welcome, but our advice spurned, and for very good reason. That advice—to reform radically—threatens to alter fundamentally the position and prerogatives of those in power.[31]

The core problem then was the limits of American leverage. Despite the recognition on the part of US advisors that the war was ultimately up to the Salvadoran government to win, there was still an assumption of the utility of American agency, that the United States could make a difference and had the ability to do so. However, a decade of conflict in El Salvador vividly illustrated the difficulties of involvement, even at advisory level, in someone else's war. The Army's involvement in El Salvador paradoxically demonstrated that its advisors did understand some of the fundamental tenets of counterinsurgency and could limit US involvement in the conflict but also that this understanding did not necessarily translate into effectiveness.

Nonetheless, given that the problems inherent in the limits of US power and leverage essentially lay outside the Army's purview, institutionalizing the lessons of El Salvador overwhelmingly focused on tactical or operational concerns. As the limits of American leverage in San Salvador were made apparent, the El Salvador experience did raise more fundamental questions about the utility of counterinsurgency doctrine and about the wisdom of backing such regimes, but such concerns were subsumed by both narrower discussions of tactical and operational lessons and the broader debate over defining the exact nature of this type of conflict. The deeper concerns played surprisingly little role in this broader debate. This was partly because so much of the debate revolved around the classification of such missions and more significantly because the Army largely defined its operations in El Salvador as successful—both in that the Salvadoran regime survived and, crucially, that it survived without the introduction of US ground troops to the conflict. This narrow definition of success was evidence of the limited expectations even counterinsurgency advocates within the Army had for the US ability to successfully prosecute this type of warfare.

The Army's advisory role in El Salvador, limited though it was, highlighted many of the same problems as its much more traumatic experience of Vietnam had. It was just as difficult as ever to push a corrupt, repressive government to reform, and firepower was again overused, albeit this time largely by the Salvadorans themselves. However, these similarities did not reinforce the caution and conventional mind-set of the Army of 1970s but rather opened some space for a debate within the Army as to what the lessons of Vietnam should be and what role counterinsurgency should play in the Army's institutional culture. The debate was rarely explicitly about counterinsurgency—the post-Vietnam burial of that concept had made it a loaded term—but rather about a relatively new phrase, one that seemed to describe the US experience in El Salvador well; this was the concept of low-intensity conflict.

DEFINING LOW-INTENSITY CONFLICT

Given Reagan's difficulties with securing public and Congressional support for his policies in Central America, "low-intensity conflict" (LIC) became a useful way to describe conflicts such as that in El Salvador. It was less controversial than counterinsurgency in that it encompassed missions other than Vietnam-style warfare: Although it included "*support* to insurgency and counterinsurgency," it also involved peacekeeping, combating terrorism, and "peacetime contingency operations." The Reagan administration's 1987 *National Security Strategy* (NSS) (written long after US involvement in El Salvador had intensified) outlined US policy toward low-intensity conflict. The

National Security Strategy declared that "when it is in the US interest to do so, the United States will take measures to strengthen friendly nations facing internal or external threats to their independence and stability by systematically employing . . . the full range of political, economic, informational, and military instruments of power."[32] However, military instruments of power did not necessarily mean combat forces, as the NSS also stated that "the fundamental tenet of US strategy for dealing with Low Intensity Conflict directed against our friends and allies is that military institutions in threatened states must become able to provide security for their citizens and governments." The authors also argued that "US Low Intensity Conflict policy, therefore, recognizes that indirect—rather than direct—applications of US military power are the most appropriate and cost effective ways to achieve national goals."[33] This indirect approach, given the post-Vietnam constraints on intervention, was essentially as far as Reagan could go.[34]

Indeed, one of the enduring features of the Reagan administration's policy in Central America was a continuing battle with Congress over funding for both the Contra insurgents in Nicaragua and the regime in El Salvador. Much of the congressional reluctance to fund US military aid to El Salvador was based on fears of a repeat of the Vietnam experience.[35] When Senator Daniel K. Inouye broke with US policy in 1983, he explicitly invoked the war in Indochina as a reason, stating that "one cannot easily forget Vietnam, especially if you had to live through that experience, realizing that your decisions would have affected the lives of many young people." For Inouye, "History was repeating itself. I've been conditioned by Vietnam."[36] In this vein, the National Security Council's 1987 report to the Congress on low-intensity conflict noted: "The instruments we have at our disposal are of little use without US public support for our engagement in protracted struggles that may not appear imminent to threaten vital US interests. We cannot persevere if there is a sharp asymmetry of wills—if our adversaries' determination is greater and more enduring than our own."[37] One critic argued that "Americans want to be the good guys. The government and military are closely identified with the people and must, therefore, fight the good fight or lose popular support. In America, that which does not have popular support is not paid for and dies."[38] Reagan's indirect approach was a way of maintaining popular support by keeping the costs of any intervention—at least when measured in terms of American boots on the ground—low enough to prevent any mass dissatisfaction. The Reagan Doctrine, although it involved rhetorical bluster, was inherently cautious when it came to military intervention. This meant that low-intensity conflict occupied a central place in the application of the doctrine.

However, the issue of maintaining popular support was not the only problem inherent in the concept of low-intensity conflict; defining the very nature of LIC was itself deeply problematic. Given the issues raised by renewed US military involvement in Central America, it became more and more important to define this concept and what US policy toward it would be.[39] As late as 1987, the full meaning of the term was not clear. The National Security Council's 1987 report to the Congress on LIC noted:

> At times, the discussion and debate on the subject of Low Intensity Conflict has been characterized by confusion. For example, some equate Low Intensity Conflict with terrorism, some with trade sanctions, and others see it as all conflict short of direct engagement between the US and the Soviet Union. This lack of clear focus has complicated development of effective policy to deal with Low Intensity Conflict in the past.[40]

The profusion of tasks and missions associated with LIC meant that, as a doctrinal term, it lacked coherence. Indeed, it was not even fully clear that LIC *was* war. The 1991 edition of FM 100-20, *Low Intensity Conflict*, seemed to think of it as something different, stating, "Low Intensity Conflict, more than war, will often present the United States and its armed forces with difficult ethical and moral challenges. The type of aggression encountered in LIC is not as blatant as that in war. Combat operations in LIC are conducted primarily for their psychological effects."[41] Even proponents of LIC had difficulty in defining the concept at times. Colonel Albert M. Barnes, commander of the Army–Air Force Center for Low Intensity Conflict (see the following discussion), an organization whose stated area of expertise was LIC, briefed the secretary of the Army that "Low Intensity Conflict does appear to be a lot of Jell-O—you can shoot into the blob and not hit anything."[42] Lt. Col. John S. Fulton charged that LIC was, in effect, a "doctrinal foster home for orphaned warfare concepts, including counterinsurgency, antiterrorism, peacekeeping, contingency operations, rescue and foreign military assistance. LIC's definition is too broad, and the category is too large."[43] Certainly, LIC encompassed a very broad category of activities, each with its own imperatives and peculiarities. Writing in *Military Review*, Fulton remarked that these differences meant that it was foolhardy to assume that LIC either had any coherence as a category or was capable of offering solutions to those problems:

Each occurrence, when examined individually, has its own causes and effects. Coups, tribal hatred, land reform, sectarian violence, civil war, the reestablishment or preservation of the old order, the narcotics trade and religious and racial strife have been the root causes of individual conflicts. This does not lend itself to a neat Western strategy for dealing with this phenomenon.[44]

The problems the United States encountered when attempting to influence elements of the Salvadoran military to stop supporting the death squads was a vivid illustration of the difficulties of a "neat Western strategy." Similarly, another *Military Review* correspondent, Major Michael W. Symanski, expressed some skepticism about the wisdom of taking on such missions and echoed Harry Summers's concerns about counterinsurgency's effect on the Army's institutional health when he argued:

> The US military will be the likely loser in a LIC operation. Even if the Army wins a victory in the field and the outcome serves immediate national interests, the struggle will degrade the military institution, squander its combat power and alienate it from its parent society. Outright tactical defeat would not be worse than the strategic defeat of losing public support.[45]

Undoubtedly, some of this skepticism came—like the countervailing effort to promote LIC—from the US experience in Central America. One of the best examples of skepticism about LIC flowing from the Central America experience was a 1988 study by four US Army colonels, "American Military Policy in Small Wars: The Case of El Salvador,"[46] which listed the many problem with the war in El Salvador. These included lack of real interest on the part of the institutional Army (claiming that the Army had, in effect sent its third team)[47] and the need to overhaul organizational responsibilities and security assistance procedures. The authors understood the difficulties US advisors had in terms of leverage with their Salvadoran counterparts but were still unimpressed with the Army's performance. However, what was noteworthy about this report was not the criticism of the Army's effort in El Salvador but the authors' overriding pessimism that much could be done to change things. Regarding the report's own recommended measures, the authors stated:

> Yet, on the printed page, these points seem axiomatic. Had the United States not botched them in El Salvador, they would hardly merit consideration. The self-evident nature of such conclusions recalls for us the views of the

CINCSOUTH who, when asked to reflect on the lessons of the Salvadoran insurgency, replied, "my gut feeling is that there is nothing new."[48]

Ironically, though, the very officer Bacevich quotes was one of the driving forces in trying to improve the Army's ability to conduct counterinsurgency. General John R. Galvin, commander of US Southern Command from 1985 to 1987 (and therefore responsible for directly overseeing US military activities in Central America), was one of a group of senior officers with experience in SOUTHCOM—others included General Paul Gorman[49] and General Fred Woerner—who were strong proponents of LIC. Galvin argued forcefully (in a speech allegedly written by his aide, a young captain named David Petraeus)[50] that "military men . . . feel uncomfortable with warfare's societal dimension and tend to ignore its implications . . . At the same time internal war—in which the societal dimension takes on crucial importance—has become a dominant form of conflict throughout the world."[51] By seeking to define LIC in such a manner, Galvin *was* drawing lessons from El Salvador, and those lessons were in direct contradiction of the Army's post-Vietnam caution about counterinsurgency.

Such sentiments led to a renewed focus on what Galvin called "uncomfortable wars," with the Pentagon organizing a high-level LIC conference in 1986 while the 1986 edition of FM 100-5 paid attention to the problems of LIC, the first time this capstone manual had done so since Vietnam. This new edition stated that while "the overriding mission of US forces is to deter war," the Army must be prepared to act "on the unique battlefields of Low Intensity Conflict (LIC). This form of warfare falls below the level of high- and mid-intensity operations and will pit Army forces against irregular or unconventional forces, enemy special operations forces, and terrorists."[52] While the manual was still very much focused on conventional operations, the fact that it even mentioned LIC as a possible mission illustrated the growing prominence of the concept and the possibility that the lessons of Vietnam could be rethought. Indeed, the tactical lessons of Vietnam became subject to new scrutiny when the Army collaborated with the Air Force to establish a joint institution, the Army–Air Force Center for Low Intensity Conflict, which was explicitly intended to "retain the lessons learned from Vietnam" and to explore ways to use US forces in LIC.

The Army also began to think about which combat forces might be appropriate for LIC when they revisited the concept of the Light Infantry Division, reversing previous plans to mechanize all the remaining active light infantry divisions, apart from one airborne and one air assault division.[53] With the "Army 86" and then the "Army of Excellence" study, the Army began to look at light forces again. Initially, the study intended Light Divisions for purely conventional roles—seizing beachheads and landing zones, repelling counterattacks, readying an area for the arrival of heavy forces, and reinforcing those heavy forces in urban and difficult terrain in Europe.[54] Soon, however, the planned role changed, when General John C. Wickham replaced General Edward S. Meyer as Army chief of staff. Wickham's 1984 White Paper on the Light Infantry Division defined the Light Division's primary role as operating in LICs. While the division was to be capable of operations (when augmented) in mid- and high-intensity conflict, it was to be an austere, rapidly deployable force, focused primarily on potential missions in the Pacific, Latin America, and Africa. Its mission statement read, "Rapidly deploys to defeat enemy forces in Low Intensity Conflict and, when properly augmented, reinforces US forces committed to a mid–high intensity conflict."[55] Wickham was always eager to emphasize the centrality of LIC to the Light Infantry Division's mission, writing to the commander of the 25th Infantry Division, one of the first to convert to light status, to inform him that the division's primary role would be LIC and that training should be oriented toward LIC.[56]

Army doctrine began to reflect this new orientation as the Army's major doctrinal publication on LIC, FM 100-20 *Low Intensity Conflict*, was updated twice in the next five years, first in interim form in 1986 as FC (Field Circular) 100-20, then as FM 100-20, again in a joint publication with the Air Force in 1990.[57] FC 100-20's approach to the counterinsurgency element of LIC was to emphasize the importance of low-key assistance at the early stages of insurgency and the use of security assistance programs to improve indigenous capabilities for counterinsurgency operations. It also recognized that the reality was that "the host nation, however, is unlikely to request the presence of US troops, even in small numbers, unless the threat has reached serious proportions."[58] FC 100-20, however, did not rule out a bigger US military commitment, stating: "Should the insurgency continue to escalate to a war of movement, expanded US assistance may include selected and specially tailored US combat forces." Conditions, however, would be imposed on any introduction of combat forces to counter an insurgency:

US combat forces are used only when and where they have a high probability of decisively altering the situation. Combat forces are not committed where the effect would be irrelevant or counterproductive to US interests and national prestige. The objective of committing US forces to a combat role is to effect a decisive change in the conflict, preserve US interests that are in serious jeopardy, or provide the time and space for local forces to regain the initiative and resume control of tactical operations.[59]

Despite the limitations of US interests and prestige, this declaration marked a much stronger commitment to direct involvement in counterinsurgency than had been present since the end of the Vietnam War. Indeed, in many ways, FC 100-20 was ahead of both the mainstream Army and the Reagan administration in its willingness to consider the use of combat troops. Certainly, caveats that "the nations directly threatened will assume the primary responsibility for providing the manpower for their own defense, will devote a fair share of their other resources to their defense effort, and will make the best possible use of their resources"[60] ostensibly limited US involvement. Nonetheless, this manual went far beyond the caution of Nixon and even Reagan to contemplate a much more serious Army commitment to counterinsurgency.

FC 100-20's willingness to consider intervention in a counterinsurgency scenario, even if only under limited circumstances, did not fit in with the Army's still-prevailing caution on such operations; outside all this discussion of the merits of LIC, the Weinberger Doctrine's restrictive criteria for such interventions (see Chapter 4) was very much the prevailing consensus within the Army.[61] Nonetheless, both FC 100-20 and the widespread and lengthy Army discourse on LIC hinted at a broader struggle to redefine what "Vietnam" now meant, in light of experience in Central America.

THE PUSH TO INSTITUTIONALIZE
LOW-INTENSITY CONFLICT

FC 100-20's description of American combat forces being used in an LIC environment, however, proscribed the circumstances, was part of a growing confidence on the part of certain sections of the Army that US forces could actually win a counterinsurgency campaign, that successful intervention in the Third World was possible. This confidence derived in part from the experience of El Salvador. US involvement there, however problematic, was held up as an example of successful prosecution of LIC, as the FMLN never succeeded in coming to power. However, the resurgence of counterinsurgency advocacy was also tied to a reconsideration of the lessons of Vietnam. Some relatively junior officers began to challenge the consensus of the 1970s, so strongly embedded in the Army's institutions and doctrine. Writing in *Military Review*, Col. Cecil B. Currey argued:

> The reason for the failure of American efforts in Vietnam is clear. The military managers of that era did not understand the kind of war facing them. They believed conventional approaches to combat, so successful in all theatres of operations during World War II and in which they were trained and prepared, could easily subdue an ill-equipped and ill-trained guerrilla force in Vietnam."[62]

If the United States had fought the wrong war in Vietnam, then it followed that its preparations for war in the 1980s should reflect the unlearned lessons of counterinsurgency from Indochina.

Lt. Col. Rudolph C. Barnes disagreed, arguing that the United States had in fact been successful at counterinsurgency before, that "in contrast to the Vietnam experience, US LIC (counterinsurgency) doctrine was successfully applied elsewhere in Southeast Asia, Africa and Latin America until the capability was dismantled in the early 1970s."[63] Barnes was describing a history of US military intervention that both privileged US intervention in "small wars" and decried the Army's habit of forgetting the lessons of those small wars. Similarly, writing in 1985, John Waghelstein, commander of the US Military Group in El Salvador from 1982 to 1983, complained that "in the post-Vietnam era, counterinsurgency has virtually become a non-subject in the US military educational system."[64] For Waghelstein and others, the lesson of Vietnam was not that the Army should not have allowed itself to become immersed in the war, or that it should have pushed harder for a freer hand, but that it did not fight the war particularly well in the first place.[65] Andrew Krepinevich's 1986 book, *The Army and Vietnam*,[66] was effectively a codification of those new lessons and served as a direct rejoinder to Harry Summers's lessons of the war (see Chapter 2). Krepinevich argued that the "Army concept" of high-tech conventional war meant that the United States never fully adapted to the war in Vietnam as it should have, and—despite the intentions of the Kennedy administration—never quite embraced counterinsurgency as a way of war.

Krepinevich never secured the institutional backing that Summers did; indeed, his career in the Army ended relatively soon after the publication of his book, and *The Army and Vietnam* was heavily criticized in review articles in the Army's major journals.[67] However, he certainly managed to influence some senior officers with his critique of the Army's failure to adapt to counterinsurgency in Indochina. In a 1988 memorandum, Major General Gordon R. Sullivan, then the deputy commandant of the Command and General Staff College (CGSC), wrote that "I think I agree in general . . . with Major Krepinevich who wrote in his book *The Army and Vietnam* about our experience in Vietnam that our approach was wrong." Sullivan agreed that "this has been so true since the end of WW II, that we easily rationalize our focus on mid to high as the worst case and most 'preferred' focus of our organizational intellectual interest." Interestingly, Sullivan also saw events in Central America as evidence that the Army needed to focus heavily on LIC. He argued that "we must find a way to devote as much organizational intellectual and analytical energy on the less conventional aspects of LATAM [Latin America], and other places or I fear we are in danger of travelling a well worn trail with predictable consequences."[68] Sullivan's perspective on Vietnam then was much more critical of the Army's organizational culture and much less willing to reinforce traditional roles than DePuy and Summers had been. He was in effect directly disputing the Army's consensus of the lessons of Vietnam. Krepinevich's lessons emphasized not only the importance of learning counterinsurgency but also of the need for institutions that could adapt to the challenges they faced. Sullivan was in a unique position to help the Army adapt to what he saw as its most important future challenges.

Given Sullivan's position as deputy commandant of the CGSC, where he had significant influence over both Army doctrine and education, his reconsideration of both the lessons of Vietnam and the importance of counterinsurgency were potentially of major importance for the Army. Prior to his arrival at the CGSC, instruction there on low-intensity conflict had grown 250 percent between 1983 and 1986, from thirteen to thirty-two hours of instruction. Not only that, but 45 percent of students requested even more hours on the topic, and the College would have accommodated them had the post-Vietnam nadir in counterinsurgency's fortunes not meant that there was a sheer lack of subject matter experts for assignment to the college.[69] However, instructors at the School of Advanced Military Studies (SAMS), a graduate-level offshoot of the CGSC, found that their course on LIC actually "provoked more disputes than it resolved."[70] The instructors concluded that the reason for this discord was that the doctrine itself lacked coherence, and the concept of LIC lacked a unifying theme. This spurred debate within SAMS on how to redefine the concept and better fit it with the Army's overall doctrine.

Sullivan's arrival led to an explicit questioning of the linkage between LIC and the Army's core concept, the technology-focused "AirLand Battle," which was focused on defeating Soviet armored thrusts in Northwestern Europe. For although the 1986 edition of FM 100-5 mentioned LIC, its primary focus was still unashamedly on conventional conflict and the "AirLand Battle" concept.[71] Sullivan conducted a series of discussions with the School of Advanced Military Studies and the Department of Joint and Combined Operations, which resulted in a consensus questioning the suitability of the basic logic of AirLand Battle for LIC. General Sullivan wryly "granted [that] the tenants of AirLand Battle—initiative, synchronization, and depth—were applicable in both types of contingencies. But . . . they were also useful for buying a house."[72] One seminar leader declared that "war planning, as described in FM 100-5, was inapplicable to Low Intensity Conflicts. He reasoned that most of the components in the concept of LIC simply were not war."[73] While the principles of AirLand Battle were supposed to apply across all types of war, TRADOC's guidance on the matter, PAM 525-44 *US Operational Concept for Low Intensity Conflict*, noted that "for Low Intensity Conflict, the basic tenets of AirLand Battle doctrine . . . will frequently have a broader meaning . . . and application . . . will be different."[74] This vague turn of phrase essentially glossed over the many inconsistencies between the technocratic warfare intended for use against the Soviets in Europe and the imperatives of LIC. The commander of the Army–Air Force Center for Low Intensity Conflict, Colonel Thomas E. Swain, argued that "only a limited correlation can be made between operations in the LIC environment and the ALB-F [AirLand Battle Future] battlefield cycle because . . . actual combat operations make up only a small portion of potential operations conducted in the LIC environment."[75]

Remarkably, this led to a situation where the CGSC recommended a major change in how the Army defined their doctrine in a way that would have elevated LIC to a level it had not achieved even during the Vietnam War. Instead of a continuum of conflict, from high to mid- to low intensity, there would instead be two distinct categories, each of which would have its own field manual. FM 100-5 would no longer be the Army's capstone field manual, defining its approach to war, but would instead be recast as FM 100-5 *Combat Operations*, where it would deal only with conventional and nuclear operations. FM 100-20 would no longer be a subordinate manual but would be elevated to coequal status and would be rechristened *Military Operations in Conflicts Short of War* rather than the ambiguous "low-intensity conflict."[76] The Army would then have not one but two capstone doctrines. This would have been a huge development, given that even at the height of the 1960s interest in counterinsurgency the Army had never seen the need for more than one capstone manual to define all operations. That the CGSC attempted to change this speaks to just how important the intellectual interest in LIC was throughout the 1980s and how interpretations of the lessons of Vietnam could change. If LIC was not counterinsurgency, then it certainly encompassed the concept, and much of the doctrine and instruction on LIC were devoted to studying insurgency and counterinsurgency. For the Army to return to counterinsurgency just over a decade after abandoning it would have been a remarkable development.

The chief of staff of the Army, General Carl Vuono, however, did not support the idea of coequal capstone manuals, and the commander of TRADOC— General Maxwell Thurman—refused to accept the notion of replacing "low-intensity conflict" with "conflict short of war," and the idea died.[77] Indeed, as the Combined Arms Center official history notes, not everybody at the CGSC supported the idea, either: Colonel John Landry worried that the Army might undertake an LIC mission but still find itself in a war, as it had done in Vietnam. In this case, Landry asked, which doctrine would the Army use: its doctrine for war or its doctrine for operations other than war?[78] The problem posed by this question was solved by a reemphasis on more restrictive criteria for intervention. Writing to Vuono on the subject of the new edition of FM 100-20 *Low Intensity Conflict*, Thurman wrote that "a genuine concern has been expressed to ensure our military forces sent to assist in counterinsurgency operations do not relieve the host nation of their sovereign responsibility for resolving those issues which often prompt the insurgency at its beginning. Of course, we agree with this concern."[79] Thurman was echoing the Nixon Doctrine's perspective on intervention and its doubts over the utility of introducing US troops into a Third World insurgency scenario.

Thurman was also responding to the concerns of Lieutenant General John W. Foss, commander of the XVIII Airborne Corps, who complained of an earlier draft of the manual that "US combat units should not be given a direct combat role in another nation's counterinsurgency, as a matter of basic doctrine. US units could be directed to fight an overt incursion of a third country's forces into a nation with an insurgency problem." Foss argued that, contrary to the consensus among LIC theorists, "our doctrine should also be to apply overwhelming combat power as rapidly as possible to bring the contingency operation to a close on favorable terms as soon as possible."[80] Foss's comments were instructive, as not only was he due to succeed Thurman at TRADOC— and therefore take overall charge of the Army's doctrine, training, and education—but his emphasis on overwhelming combat power in all situations very much fit the Army's concept of war. For all the production of doctrine and reports that emphasized the importance of counterinsurgency capabilities and their criticism of AirLand Battle, LIC reformers were ultimately neither able to dislodge the centrality of AirLand Battle in the Army's concept of war, nor reorient the Army toward unconventional challenges like El Salvador. The reaction among senior officers to the prospect of reorienting the Army's doctrine so strongly toward LIC was a palpable indication of the difficulties those who wished to change the Army's organizational culture faced. For an even clearer illustration of these difficulties, we can turn to the attempts to change the Army's force structure to suit the demands of LIC.

ATTEMPTS TO REMODEL THE ARMY
FOR LOW-INTENSITY CONFLICT

Nowhere were these difficulties more apparent than in the way the Army remodeled its force structure throughout the 1980s. For while doctrine is a hugely important source of both institutional memory and direction on how to conduct war, it is the type of forces the Army maintains that gives the clearest indication of the wars it expects to fight. Writing in 1989, General Fred Woerner, commander of SOUTHCOM, argued that the wars in both El Salvador and Nicaragua were not only low intensity in nature but "high probability," in that the United States was likely to encounter far more of it in the future, not less.[81] Woerner argued that this had significant implications for Army force structure:

> Abrams tanks, B-1 bombers and cruise missiles have limited utility in the low-intensity/high-probability environment that characterizes this [Western] hemisphere. At the lower end of the conflict spectrum, the set of relevant deterrent force options is far more likely to consist of activities encompassing security assistance, combined training exercises, intelligence support, officer exchanges, civic action, psychological operations, engineer construction, medical exercises and infrastructure development.[82]

Remarkably, it was not the Army but the Congress that pushed for a reorientation toward forces appropriate for LIC. The same Congress that had fought Reagan over funding for his operations in Central America was broadly sympathetic to the goal of restructuring the Army so that the noncombat activities described by Woerner got more emphasis. Even Senator Ted Kennedy, who had strongly opposed Reagan on El Salvador, signed a 1989 letter to Lt. Gen. Brent Scowcroft, incoming national security advisor, urging him to do more to make the NSC focus on low-intensity warfare.[83] Congress was also instrumental in forcing the Pentagon to accept both a new unified command—Special Operations Command, or SOCOM—and a new civilian proponent for LIC—the assistant secretary for low-intensity conflict and special operations—when it passed the Nunn-Cohen amendment to the Goldwater-Nichols Defense Reorganization Act in 1987.[84] Pentagon resistance to this was strong, with Secretary of Defense Caspar Weinberger stalling on naming both the new assistant secretary and the commander of SOCOM,[85] while the recently retired General Paul Gorman called the amendment "one of its worst pieces of legislation in recent history," saying that "it ranked together with tax reform in its ill-conception" and that the last thing the Pentagon needed was another assistant secretary for defense.[86] The Army was particularly reluctant to hand any of its forces over to SOCOM and refused to do so wherever there was a gray area in the law.[87] While this was undoubtedly parochial bureaucratic politics, it was bureaucratic politics grounded in the continuing wariness of Special Forces in the wake of Vietnam. The institutionalization of LIC would mean the introduction of forces and doctrine that would make another Vietnam more likely, not less.

According to one military critic, the tragedy of this was that "US reaction to defeat in Vietnam was to throw the baby out with the bathwater. Rather than learn from that experience, US leaders bowed to antimilitary sentiment in the early 1970s and discarded the strategy, doctrine and fledgling capability for SO [Special Operations] in LIC, only to reinvent them 10 years later."[88] While any notion that Fred Weyand, William DePuy, and Donn Starry "bowed to antimilitary sentiment" was misplaced, it was certainly true that Special Operations capabilities had been neglected. However, Special Operations were revisited in the 1980s, with the Army adding a fourth Special Forces Group (by reactivating the 1st Special Forces Group), a third Ranger battalion, and a fourth psychological operations battalion, while spending on Special Forces (including those of the other services) increased from $441 million in 1981 to

$1.7 billion in 1987.[89] However, even this buildup, closely linked to events in Central America, did not mean the full redemption of counterinsurgency in the eyes of the Army. As late as 1987, the LIC branch (responsible for managing LIC and counterinsurgency doctrine at the school) of the JFK School for Special Warfare consisted of only one person.[90] Furthermore, as they had been in the 1970s, the Special Forces were deeply concerned with how they would fit into the Army's conventional operations. The school's commandant discussed how important it was to "show the SOF [Special Operations Forces] community and the Army as a whole how Special Operations Forces fit into the Army's plans for current and future battlefields."[91] An article in *Military Review* was even more direct; Major Glenn M. Harned, a Special Forces officer, wrote that:

> The implications are clear. The Army and Air Force are fully committed to the AirLand Battle. If SOF doctrine fails to demonstrate how to employ SOF as part of the AirLand Battle, the doctrine fails to integrate SOF into the mainstream of Army and Air Force doctrinal thinking. This failure will adversely affect SOF efforts to reorganize and modernize and to educate conventional commanders and staff officers about SOF capabilities, requirements and operational considerations.[92]

AirLand battle would mean conventional operations, a surprising focus for Special Forces given that the United States was deeply immersed in insurgency and counterinsurgency in Central America at the time. This worry about how Special Forces could relate to AirLand Battle was an illustration of the branch's memory of being severely downgraded in the 1970s; the focus on complementing conventional operations indicated the branch's own reiteration of the lessons of Vietnam.

The results of this focus, at least in the eyes of the Special Forces themselves, were apparent as early as 1991. According to the Special Warfare School's annual historical review, a "Foreign Internal Defense" exercise in Thailand, Operation Cobra Gold, illustrated that both conventional and Special Forces planners were deeply ignorant of psychological operations and civil affairs, key tenets of counterinsurgency, and that interagency cooperation was still poor. Not only that, but the exercise illustrated that the Special Warfare School's own regional studies course "still did not contain enough material on Low Intensity Conflict, support to SF [Special Forces] in Foreign Internal Defense (FID)/Unconventional Warfare (UW) and the actual planning and implementation of Civic Action."[93] Special Forces rapidly increased in number throughout the 1980s, but, despite the doctrinal ferment on low-intensity conflict and the Army's recalibrating some of the lessons of Vietnam, this branch was apparently no more effective at counterinsurgency at the decade's end than it had been at the beginning.

While Special Forces were essential to counterinsurgency, the major change in force structure to adapt the Army for LIC was the formation of new Light Infantry Divisions, which were to make up six of the Army's sixteen active duty divisions.[94] As we have seen, these were central to the Army's reconsideration of LIC missions. However, even as the new divisions were forming, there was some criticism of the focus on LIC. William DePuy, now retired but still active, visited one of the new units, the 7th Infantry Division (Light), in training and then sent a letter to Wickham to express his concerns:

> The division takes it as given—given by you—that their mission is to prepare for Low Intensity Warfare as a first priority and for mid- to high-intensity second. The problem is that they do not know exactly what they are to do in LIW [low-intensity warfare]. I suspect this confusion is not confined to the 7th Division. As a consequence they are loyally trying to carve out a niche which generally lies at the nexus where Ranger techniques, anti-guerrilla warfare and deep raids come together. At the other end of their mission (mid intensity war) they see the NTC [National Training Center] as a guide . . . I suspect we may have to disarm Nicaragua some day and the 7th will be needed. It won't be LIW. Someday they may be sent to seize Wheelers field in Libya or stop the Revolutionary Guards on the approaches to Kuwait City.[95]

Ironically, DePuy's concerns about light divisions not understanding their role in LIC were shared not only by critics of light forces but by their proponents as well. Writing in *Military Review*, Major Peter N. Kafkalas argued:

> It is as if we assume the light divisions will automatically know how to fight in an unconventional low-intensity environment. This assumption may not be valid, considering the lack of historical perspective in LIC doctrine and how the light infantry could best be used in a LIC scenario. As negative as Vietnam was to our psyche, there is a wealth of lessons from that conflict applicable in a LIC scenario today.[96]

Certainly, the Army's specific doctrine for light infantry divisions, Field Circular 71-101 *Light Infantry Division Operations*, did not really address LIC to any degree, despite the primary mission of those divisions. Although FM

100-5 and AirLand battle were cited as the core doctrinal basis for FC 71-101, there was no mention of FM 100-20 *Low Intensity Conflict* as a reference manual, a startling omission given the ostensible purpose of these light divisions.[97] Similarly, the training scenario for light forces at the Joint Readiness Training Center involved the Light Divisions fighting a Soviet-style motorized rifle division. While guerrilla warfare was part of the exercise, the scenario stated, "Operations against guerrilla forces will include only those necessary for local security."[98] The focus, then, was self-evidently not on preparing the divisions for what was supposed to be their primary role.

Other traits of the light divisions militated against their utilization in LIC. The very focus on rapid deployability betrayed a focus on sharp, short operations rather than long, drawn-out counterinsurgencies. In some ways, as with the introduction of more special forces, the Light Infantry Division was supposed to be used in Grenada-like[99] conventional scenarios. Even Wickham's introduction to the White Paper on the light infantry division specifically referenced conventional operations such as the Falklands, Israeli operations in Lebanon, and Grenada as positive examples to follow.[100] "Low-intensity conflict" then meant something entirely different in this context. Also, each of these new divisions (apart from the 7th Infantry Division, which was tasked with deployment to Europe) was to only have two active brigades, with the third being a National Guard unit that would mobilize on call. Given that the reserve was highly unlikely to be mobilized for anything but all-out war, this meant the light divisions were even less useful for LIC.

Unsurprisingly, the imperatives of potential war in Europe began to assert themselves as well, with planners devoting more and more thought to how light forces could fight on the European battlefield, despite the fact that they had been designed for Third World contingencies. Maj. Louis D. Huddleston complained that "many military thinkers of today have difficulty accepting light forces because they grew up preparing to fight in Europe. Thus, a force is not considered credible if it cannot stand alone when deployed to fight in Europe."[101] Ironically, one of those involved in focusing on a European role for the light divisions was one of those who would later be essential in focusing the Army on counterinsurgency: Captain David H. Petraeus. Writing in *Military Review*, he argued that:

> The question should no longer be whether light forces have a place on a high-intensity Central European battlefield. Rather, the question we should seek to

answer is what the balance between heavies and lights in Europe ought to be and how that balance can be achieved . . . the new light infantry units could provide a way to strengthen the US conventional deterrent in Europe while, at the same time, enhancing the strategic flexibility of the Army as a whole.[102]

Given this confusion over roles, it was no surprise that light divisions were among the first victims of post–Cold War budget cuts. To maintain as many of its heavy forces as possible, the Army cut four of six light divisions; Army planners reasoned that they could simply use mechanized infantry units as light infantry in peace operations—no other missions requiring light forces were envisaged.[103] By 1992, when the Army started deactivating light units, their role had already shifted far away from their original focus on LIC.

Given their rapid shift in role, from Low Intensity Conflict to conventional operations, the light infantry divisions were in many ways emblematic of the Army's approach toward nonconventional operations in the 1980s. The Army ostensibly recognized the need to deal with such missions and took steps toward addressing this need. Nonetheless, through a process of institutional inertia and a still-prevalent focus on conventional warfare, units originally designed for LIC, be they Special Forces or light infantry divisions, found themselves merely serving as adjuncts in the Army's primary task of mid- and high-intensity warfare. Such a development highlighted just how strongly entrenched the post-Vietnam focus on Europe was and how much more work advocates of different priorities faced if the Army's institutional culture was to change.

CONCLUSION

The Army's experience of LIC in Central America somewhat resuscitated the concept of counterinsurgency within the Army. Certainly, Army officers engaged in supporting the counterinsurgency in El Salvador displayed a solid understanding of the fundamental tenets of counterinsurgency. Nonetheless, if El Salvador posed some unanswered questions about the utility of counterinsurgency, it also demonstrated that LIC was something both US policy and Army doctrine needed to address. Indeed, to begin with, the Army needed to delineate exactly what this hazy term meant. The assortment of activities contained within the concept encompassed far more than counterinsurgency, but few if any fit within the Army's traditional concept of its mission. The issue, therefore, was not only how best to define LIC but also how to make it fit with the Army's overall doctrine and strategic culture.

The struggle to define not only what the term meant but also where it fit in the Army's overall doctrine and how the Army would need to adapt to accommodate it highlighted some paradoxical qualities. For while some elements within the Army's doctrinal community displayed a surprising willingness to recast fundamental tenets of operational doctrine that did not change even during the Vietnam War, there was also a marked institutional reluctance to accommodate these elements. Therefore, the emergence of LIC did see genuine discourse within the Army on institutional imperatives, but the result of that debate was preordained. The designation of the new light infantry divisions as forces designed for LIC did not last long in the face of broader interpretations of what their role in "contingencies" meant. If a contingency was taken to mean reinforcing NATO forces in Europe or rapidly deploying to Saudi Arabia, then they were far more likely to be involved in midintensity conflict, and they trained for that role accordingly.

The Army *did* effectively erase institutional memory of Vietnam and counterinsurgency; however, when circumstances dictated, they were willing to revisit the ghosts of both, if in a halting and reluctant fashion. This willingness to revisit historical consensus and to rethink lessons indicated not only a degree of intellectual openness but also a tendency to reconstruct histories and lessons as the needs of the contemporary environment dictated. For the Vietnam discussed by those advocating LIC in Central America was not the same Vietnam as that of William DePuy or Harry Summers. Ultimately, however, the DePuy and Summers view of Vietnam prevailed. There was a new debate on counterinsurgency and some dissent on what the lessons of Vietnam should be, but the results of that debate ultimately led back to the same consensus that the Army had at the start of the decade. The emergence of LIC may have shaken the Army's aversion to counterinsurgency, but, as the distortion of attempted reforms showed, that aversion—and the lessons of Vietnam that accompanied it—survived. The Army at the close of the Cold War still overwhelmingly focused on its conventional role, and the counterinsurgency mission remained sidelined, its brief resurgence in the guise of low-intensity conflict notwithstanding.

4 PEACEKEEPING AND OPERATIONS OTHER THAN WAR IN THE 1990S

THE END OF THE COLD WAR presented the Army with a new challenge: how best to adapt to a world without the certainty provided by the familiar mission of deterring (and therefore preparing to fight) a Soviet invasion of Western Europe. The collapse of the Soviet Union, the unification of Germany, and the "velvet revolutions" that swept Eastern Europe in 1989 fundamentally reordered the security challenges facing the United States. Policy makers struggled to understand this new era and gauge the appropriate strategy for it, searching for a concept that would define their approach much as Kennan's model of containment provided a guiding light for US strategy throughout the Cold War. This search ranged from official declarations of principles, such as George H. W. Bush's short-lived "New World Order" and Bill Clinton's economically driven strategy of "engagement and enlargement," to more explicit attempts to provide a "Mr. X" article, such as the competing theses of Francis Fukuyama's "end of history" and Samuel Huntington's "clash of civilizations."[1]

In the midst of this debate, the Army's intellectual culture was remarkably stable. Low-intensity conflict, the subject of so much debate in the 1980s, had shaken, but not broken, the Army's focus on conventional operations, and the triumph of the US military in the 1991 Gulf War did much to underline both the Army's conventional superiority and the potential for technology to revolutionize how war was fought. The massive armored operations against the Iraqi military served only to reinforce the Army's preference for conventional operations. Nonetheless, given the ongoing debate over American strategy for the post–Cold War world, the Army did adapt itself to this "new world order" in two ways.

First, the set of lessons of Vietnam, as described by Reagan's Secretary of Defense Casper Weinberger and Chairman of the Joint Chiefs of Staff General Colin Powell, were elevated almost to the level of formal doctrine within the Army. Second, and somewhat paradoxically, given the reticence toward intervention contained in Powell and Weinberger's lessons of Vietnam (see the following discussion), the Army began to formulate a new doctrine for the peacekeeping interventions it expected to embark on throughout the 1990s. This doctrine, with its emphasis on restraint, legitimacy, and improving relations with the local populations in general, in many ways owed a debt to classical counterinsurgency doctrine. The tensions between these two approaches, both derived from different sets of lessons from Vietnam, never really affected the broader institutional identity of the Army, as the imperative to "fight and win the nation's wars" was always too strong, but they did influence the actual conduct of peacekeeping operations. How these tensions resolved themselves, or failed to do so, speaks not only to the particular difficulties the United States faced when undertaking peacekeeping or peace enforcement missions but to the way in which the ghosts of Vietnam continued to haunt the Army.

THE POWELL DOCTRINE

Speaking of Vietnam during his inaugural address in January 1989, President George H. W. Bush declared, "That war cleaves us still. But, friends, that war began in earnest a quarter of a century ago; and surely the statute of limitations has been reached. This is a fact: The final lesson of Vietnam is that no great nation can long afford to be sundered by a memory."[2] US victory over Iraq in the 1991 Gulf War seemed to vindicate this approach and to restore the utility of US military power; a jubilant Bush declared that "the specter of Vietnam has been buried forever in the desert sands of the Arabian Peninsula."[3] The Army's swift destruction of Saddam Hussein's military within just over 100 hours was a vivid illustration of how different this force was from the one that had fought in Vietnam.[4] In a sense, the Army's contribution to victory in the Gulf War[5] was the culmination of the rebuilding effort that had taken place since Vietnam, starting with DePuy's early reforms in the mid-1970s and continued by AirLand Battle doctrine in the 1980s. Indeed, Major General Barry McCaffrey declared, "This war didn't take 100 hours to win, it took 15 years."[6]

This triumphant narrative informed many accounts of the Army's performance in the war, some of which presented the Vietnam experience as a "Valley Forge"[7] from which a better, stronger army emerged. The Gulf War, then, was a validation of the Army's preferred interpretation of the lessons of Vietnam.

However, what marked that war as an example of the successful implementation of the lessons of Vietnam were not just improvements in technology, training, and tactics but changes in how the United States approached the war on the strategic level. Retired General Donn Starry argued that while the Gulf War was a limited war like Korea and Vietnam, there were "significant differences, differences that reflected our determination to not relearn the hard lessons of those earlier limited wars." The differences were that "the political goal of the operation was made clear at the outset." Crucially for Starry, "success of the operation was contingent on joint operations by US forces as well as extensive participation by coalition allies and on public support among US and allied 'people at home' . . . [and] when the agreed-upon political aim had been accomplished, forces were redeployed."[8] In the aftermath of the war, General Colin Powell, chairman of the Joint Chiefs of Staff and himself a Vietnam veteran, was quick to emphasize that those lessons had been reinforced by the successes of Desert Storm; in a 1992 article in *Foreign Affairs*, he wrote: "When the political objective is important, clearly defined and understood, when the risks are acceptable, and when the use of force can be effectively combined with diplomatic and economic policies, then clear and unambiguous objectives must be given to the armed forces."[9]

Powell's focus on decisive means and results was the product not only of intensely held personal beliefs about the reasons for US failure in Vietnam but also of his association with former Secretary for Defense Caspar Weinberger. In November 1984, in a speech to the National Press Club entitled "The Uses of Military Power," Weinberger had outlined six "tests" that he believed needed to be applied when the United States considered the use of force abroad:

1. The United States should not commit forces to combat overseas unless the particular engagement or occasion is deemed vital to our national interest or that of our allies.

2. If we decide it is necessary to put combat troops into a given situation, we should do so wholeheartedly, and with the clear intention of winning. If we are unwilling to commit the forces or resources necessary to achieve our objectives, we should not commit them at all.

3. If we do decide to commit forces to combat overseas, we should have clearly defined political and military objectives.
4. The relationship between our objectives and the forces we have committed—their size, composition and disposition—must be continually reassessed and adjusted if necessary.
5. Before the United States commits forces abroad, there must be some reasonable assurance we will have the support of the American people and their elected representatives in Congress.
6. The commitment of US forces to combat should be a last resort.[10]

This speech was delivered in the aftermath of the 1983 bombing of the Marine barracks in Beirut that led to the loss of 241 US lives and in the context of the Reagan administration increasing its military involvement in Central America. Weinberger was deeply uneasy about the open-ended commitment of such missions. However, the speech did not represent a consensus within that administration on the use of force; Reagan's Secretary of State George Shultz later described it as "the Vietnam syndrome in spades, carried to an absurd level, and a complete abdication of the duties of leadership."[11] For Shultz, coordination of military and diplomatic efforts, and the availability of military force as a tool of coercive diplomacy, was more important than avoiding what he saw as a spurious Vietnam analogy. However, even if, as Arnold Isaacs has pointed out, Weinberger's caution may not have reflected a consensus in the White House,[12] it certainly did articulate the lessons of Vietnam, not only for the Pentagon but for Congress as well. Even if interventionists wanted to commit US forces overseas, the congressional support simply was not there.[13] Certainly, Powell strongly rejected any hint of a gradualist approach to the use of force that Shultz and other critics of Weinberger advocated. In his 1992 *Foreign Affairs* article, "US Forces: The Challenges Ahead," he made his views (and his reluctance to intervene in the growing crisis in the Balkans) abundantly clear: "We should always be skeptical when so-called experts suggest that all a particular crisis calls for is a little surgical bombing or a limited attack . . . History has not been kind to this approach to war-making."[14]

In this way, Powell essentially restated and simplified the Weinberger Doctrine. If there were to be an explicitly stated Powell Doctrine, then its central tenets would be that military action is the last resort, to be used only when national interests are clearly at stake; force, if used, must be overwhelming; strong support from Congress and the general public is necessary; and a clear exit strategy is essential. Certainly, the aftermath of the Gulf War reinforced Powell's notions about what was and was not an appropriate mission for the Armed Forces. In a 1993 press briefing on the new Clinton administration's "bottom-up review" of the Pentagon, Powell started by giving the assembled journalists a "little bit of a tutorial about what an armed force is all about." Powell argued that "notwithstanding all of the changes that have taken place in the world, notwithstanding the new emphasis on peacekeeping, peace enforcement, peace engagement, preventive diplomacy, we have a value system and a culture system within the armed forces of the United States. We have this mission: to fight and win the Nation's wars."[15]

While the United States did militarily intervene several times in the 1990s—in northern Iraq, Somalia, Haiti, Bosnia, and Kosovo—it did so with a largely reluctant military, wary of entanglements and unnecessary loss of American lives. Indeed, military reluctance to intervene prompted Clinton's UN ambassador (and later Secretary of State) Madeline Albright to ask Powell, "What's the point of having this superb military you're always talking about if we can't use it?"[16] Clinton's Secretary for Defense Les Aspin was also critical of the Powell Doctrine, describing it as the "'all-or-nothing' school [which] says if you aren't willing to put the pedal to the floor, don't start the engine."[17] This tension between reluctant military leaders and interventionist civilians, already seen in the dispute between Weinberger and Shultz, would in many ways severely strain civil–military relations throughout the 1990s.[18] The Army's lessons of Vietnam as contained in the Powell Doctrine were now more rigid than ever, and Army leaders invoked them frequently. Later on in the decade, Chairman of the Joint Chiefs of Staff General Hugh Shelton summarized the military's reaction to international crises in a 1999 speech:

> If you're going to threaten force, you better be prepared to go all the way to whatever capital you want to go to achieve it if in fact your political objectives may require you to do that. . . . So I think that's the first thing that you want to look at is: what are your objectives and can the military achieve that objective? . . . Is it in our national interest? Our vital national interest? Is it going to pass, as I say, the Dover test?[19] You know, let's don't go through Somalia again where we commit our great men and women in uniform and then the first time we suffer casualties decide it's not worth it. Let's decide up front that our national interest is at stake, and we're willing to pay the cost to win. And then when we do that, then use the force overwhelmingly. Go for the jugular vein . . . don't dally around.[20]

Shelton was echoing the Powell Doctrine, but he was also deeply concerned with the lessons of Vietnam. While chairman of the Joint Chiefs of Staff, Shelton sent a copy of H. R. McMaster's *Dereliction of Duty: Lyndon Johnson, Robert McNamara, the Joint Chiefs of Staff and the Lies that Led to Vietnam*[21] to each of the service chiefs and the regional CINCs (commanders in chief).[22] McMaster's work examined the "five silent men"—the Joint Chiefs of Staff—who acquiesced in the escalation of the war in Vietnam and failed in their duty as military advisors. Shelton invited all seventeen of the military's four-star generals (and naval equivalents) to a breakfast meeting in January 1998 so McMaster could brief them on the book personally.[23] The need to speak truth to civilian power was McMaster's foremost message, but his version of "Vietnam" was very similar to the one seen in the Powell Doctrine.[24]

The Powell Doctrine was perhaps the ultimate culmination of the debate on the lessons of Vietnam and is certainly the only articulation of lessons that has seen any semblance of consensus on its merits. For Powell, the avoidance of another Vietnam was his life's mission,[25] and his doctrine was perhaps his greatest accomplishment. There was an emotional core to Powell's caution, one that drew heavily and directly on his Vietnam experience:

> Many of my generation, the career captains, majors and lieutenant colonels seasoned in that war, vowed that when our turn came to call the shots, we would not quietly acquiesce in half-hearted warfare for half-baked reasons that the American public could not understand or support. If we could make good that promise to ourselves, to the civilian leadership, and to the country, then the sacrifices of Vietnam would not have been in vain.[26]

Here Powell was certainly echoing the thoughts of a generation of Army officers and drawing on the ideas of those who had gone before. Previous Army leaders had expressed similar sentiments even if they never formulated them as a foreign policy doctrine. General Donn Starry—whose AirLand Battle doctrine was so instrumental to Operation Desert Storm—expressed such sentiments as early as 1975, at a dedication of a Vietnam War memorial in Valley Station, Kentucky. In this address, Starry foreshadowed not only Weinberger and Powell, but Reagan-era revisionism as well, declaring that "it would be a shame if it were all in vain. . . . It would be even more tragic if we didn't learn the lesson that history so clearly tells us time and again—that is, if you're really not sure how serious you are about something, don't send your military forces to deal with it until you are."[27] Starry, however, unlike Powell, was pessimistic as to whether such a lesson would ever be learned outside the military. Writing to a fellow Vietnam veteran in 1979, he complained:

> As a professional skeptic, which I suppose most Army officers turn out to be in the end, I doubt seriously that our country will heed the lessons of Vietnam. We certainly didn't heed the lessons of Korea, and so were destined to repeat many of them in Vietnam. Don't forget that Vietnam really started just as Korea was ending. One would think, therefore, that someone smart enough to do so would have figured out what we learned in Korea, then had it engraved on the walls of the Oval Office for Presidents to read and heed. But it was not to be so. Like you, I am proud to have served, and angry at the way we let it all turn out. Most angry am I if once again we fail to heed the lessons of history, for which the nation pays so dearly in the treasure it can least afford to waste away—the lives of its young men. That indeed would be the ultimate tragedy.[28]

The Weinberger/Powell Doctrine represented a concerted attempt to avoid such a tragedy. Powell's success (at least within the military) in enshrining his principles as a doctrine speaks not only to Gulf War's galvanizing effect on Army confidence but also to the Army's abiding fear of repeating another Vietnam. Certainly, the Weinberger/Powell Doctrine offered the most succinct and clear reiteration of the Army's lessons of Vietnam since debate on the subject had started. The Powell Doctrine in many ways was an end point in that debate; while the military's caution about intervention had been apparent since even before the end of the Vietnam War, the lessons seem to have crystallized with Powell. While there were dissenting voices within the military throughout the 1990s, the Weinberger/Powell Doctrine was the dominant way of approaching questions of intervention.

ARMY DOCTRINE FOR PEACEKEEPING

Yet, despite Powell's and the Army's misgivings, the United States did intervene throughout the decade. Even at the height of the popularity of the Powell Doctrine, the Army found itself in places like Somalia, Haiti, Bosnia, and Kosovo, conducting the very missions that Harry Summers feared would degrade their "war-fighting" capabilities. Indeed, a 1994 study by the Army's Training and Doctrine Command (TRADOC) showed that between January 1989 and December 1993 the US military participated in no fewer than forty-eight "named military operations." These operations ranged from war with Iraq (operations Desert Shield and Desert Storm), to hurricane relief (Task

Force Hurricane Andrew), to peacekeeping and peace enforcement (operations Provide Comfort in northern Iraq from 1991 through 1996 and Restore Hope in Somalia in 1992 and 1993).[29] With such a heavy involvement in a variety of missions, there was a clear need to modify doctrine to define how the Army would operate in such environments. Not only that, but national strategic level doctrine would also have to be adjusted accordingly. Here was a potential source of tension between Powell's lessons of Vietnam and an interventionist foreign policy driven by the imperatives of the CNN effect and the uncertainties of the post–Cold War world.

The Army published their first post–Cold War version of their capstone manual FM 100-5 *Operations* in 1993; this manual also reflected this unresolved paradox in that it largely stuck to the same principles that had animated other post-Vietnam editions of FM 100-5 while also trying to adjust Army doctrine so that it might be relevant for the post–Cold War world. This edition largely marked an evolution from the AirLand Battle concept, rather than a revolutionary approach to reflect the similarly revolutionary change in the international environment.[30] Even so, there was a general recognition among TRADOC planners from an early stage that the manual needed to go beyond the operational level of war to engage more strategic issues. This meant that doctrine, like Army military actions in general, was now more directly linked to broad strategic planning documents, such as the National Security Strategy and National Military Strategy.[31] Given the more strategic focus of this edition, the manual's authors reconsidered the nature of the tasks the Army would have to undertake and the milieu in which they would operate. This meant doing away with the old high-, medium-, low-intensity conflict categories in favor of a continuum of three overlapping environments—peacetime operations, conflict, and war—as well as recognizing that "often the Army will operate in all three environments at once."[32] However, appreciation of the differing environments the Army would operate in did not result in equal focus on these different situations; FM 100-5's introduction stated that "winning wars is the primary purpose of the doctrine in this manual."[33] Indeed, the manual's position on military intervention not only reflected this focus on war fighting (something that had been present since the end of the Vietnam War) but linked to broader strategy by strongly echoing the tenets of the Powell Doctrine, which were by now virtually conventional wisdom among foreign policy and defense elites. The manual defined the "American view of war" thus:

The people of the United States do not take the commitment of their armed forces lightly. They charge the government to commit forces only after due consideration of the range of options and likely outcomes. Moreover, the people expect the military to accomplish its missions in compliance with national values. The American people expect decisive victory and abhor unnecessary casualties. They prefer quick resolution of conflicts and reserve the right to reconsider their support should any of these conditions not be met. They demand timely and accurate information on the conduct of military operations.[34]

This commitment to decisive victory and quick resolution of conflict manifested itself not only in the American view of war but also in defining what was *not* war: strikes and raids (such as the 1983 intervention in Grenada), peacekeeping, peace enforcement, antiterrorism, and support for insurgency and counterinsurgency were all awkwardly defined as "operations other than war" (OOTW). This term, first used in debates over low-intensity conflict at Fort Leavenworth in the late 1980s (see the previous chapter) provided a way to maintain an "American way of war" while simultaneously recognizing that the Army would have to deal with other missions. Thus, the Army would no longer have to shoehorn these missions into a concept where they did not fit. Operations other than war (as defined by the 1993 FM 100-5) had a different set of principles to the principles of war, and these—focusing on the need for clear objectives, unity of effort, legitimacy, perseverance, restraint, and security—could easily be applied to counterinsurgency as well.[35] Nonetheless, the fact that they were defined in such a way to separate them from war in an Army that so strongly believed that its core mission was and always should be to "fight and win the nation's wars" meant that no matter how well thought out those principles were, it was highly unlikely that they would form a key part of the Army's institutional identity. This distinction between "war" and "peace" not only meant that OOTW would always find themselves underresourced compared to conventional operations but spelled the end for the doctrinal buzzword of the 1980s—low-intensity conflict— whose very point was to emphasize the ambiguity between states of peace and war.[36] Even the assistant secretary for defense for special operations and low intensity conflict felt the term "was counterproductive, because it has too much emphasis on violence and ignores nation building."[37] One author in *Military Review* argued that the decline in the popularity of LIC was due to its association with Vietnam:

LIC began life as a euphemism. The term reflects our failure in Vietnam and our long dislike (not entirely dissipated) of discussing it. We had used counter revolutionary, counterinsurgency, stability operations, internal defense and development and maybe other terms. Whenever their coded meaning was discovered and the government was suspected of planning for another Vietnam, the name was changed.[38]

While *operations other than war* became the new catchall term, the phrase *peacetime engagement* was also more and more popular in the early 1990s. Peacetime engagement, a term that described President George H. W. Bush's overall national security strategy,[39] was essentially all US security policy in an environment short of war. It included such things as diplomatic measures, economic aid, security assistance, conflict resolution, forward presence of deterrent forces, and nation building. Peacetime engagement was a much broader category than low-intensity conflict, if only because it was less focused on the military means to achieve national security goals. This policy was closely tied to President Bush's "new world order" and his optimism, following the end of the Cold War and the victory in the Gulf War, that this new era could be ushered in via a concerted effort by the United States and its allies. Building on this concept, Bush spelled out his ambition for future US involvement in UN peacekeeping operations and the steps he was taking to ensure that the US military would be prepared for such operations in a September 1992 address to the General Assembly of the United Nations. Bush told the General Assembly that "because of peacekeeping's growing importance as a mission for the United States military, we will emphasize training of combat, engineering, and logistical units for the full range of peacekeeping and humanitarian activities." More important, he declared that he had "further directed the establishment of a permanent peacekeeping curriculum in US military schools."[40]

Both Bush and his successor, President William J. Clinton, were initially enthusiastic about US involvement in peacekeeping operations. Clinton ordered a review of peacekeeping operations—Presidential Review Directive (PRD) 13—that envisaged a greater US role in peacekeeping missions than prior policies had allowed. Previously, the United States would commit significant troops to peacekeeping operations only if it could make a unique contribution that could not come from elsewhere. PRD-13 envisaged that the United States could take part if its participation "would catalyze involvement by other nations or more generally advance US interests" while still taking care to secure public support for the mission and ensuring that any commitment was not open ended.[41] Clinton, while essentially concerned with domestic issues and mostly interested in foreign policy as a means of complementing economic policy, was just as supportive as his predecessor of US involvement in peacekeeping and, more broadly, "peacetime engagement."

Its institutional focus on the core mission of war fighting notwithstanding, elements of the Army did push doctrine that lived up to Bush's promise to the United Nations of a US military more attuned to peace operations. FM 100-23 *Peace Operations*—intended as a foundation for further development of peacekeeping doctrine, training plans, and service school curricula—was heavily based on recent US experiences in northern Iraq and Somalia and on international best practices and norms.[42] Unusually, for an Army manual, it took a broad view of where the use of force fit into overall strategy. FM 100-23 emphasized that military operations could only complement diplomatic, humanitarian, and economic efforts and that "a force's security is significantly enhanced by its perceived legitimacy and impartiality, the mutual respect built between the force and the other parties involved in the peace operation, and the force's credibility in the international arena."[43] The manual provided a sophisticated set of instructions for support to diplomacy, peacekeeping, and peace enforcement. Many of the principles contained in the manual would have been familiar as critiques of how the Army had conducted itself in Vietnam. For instance:

> An overemphasis on firepower may be counterproductive. Because of the potential linkages between combatants and non-combatants, the political and cultural dimensions of the battlefield become more critical to the conflict. When force must be used, its purpose is to protect life or compel, not to destroy unnecessarily; the conflict, not the belligerent parties, is the enemy.[44]

The emphasis on legitimacy, interagency cooperation and on subordinating military actions to the overall effort would also fit very well in any of the typical works on counterinsurgency (however, peace operations are governed far more by the principles of consent and impartiality, crucial differences from counterinsurgency) and marked quite a different emphasis than the Army's core doctrine. FM 100-23 may have been unlike most Army doctrine in many ways, and it may have been underused (given the subsequent US reluctance to take part in UN peacekeeping operations), but its very existence symbolized the Army's evolving attitude toward the post–Cold War world.

In addition to FM 100-23, there were other signs of an Army that was taking peacekeeping and stability operations more seriously. Army Chief of Staff General Gordon R. Sullivan established a Peacekeeping Institute at the Army War College in Fort Carlisle in 1993; this was to be the main source for peacekeeping doctrine, training, and education within the Army.[45] However, given the small budget and staff of the Peacekeeping Institute, education on peacekeeping was primarily delivered as part of courses on operations other than war. The Command and General Staff College, in particular, began to deliver instruction on OOTW, with the core curriculum (which was required for all students) devoting a thirty-six-hour course to the concept in the 1994–1995 academic year (out of 523 core curriculum hours), which increased to forty-five hours in 1996–1997.[46] Thirty-six to forty-five out of 523 hours, although an upward trend, was indicative of the low base from which the Army was starting in relation education on OOTW. Certainly, figures like Sullivan seemed to recognize the problem, resisting the urge to categorize "war" as separate from all other military uses of force and arguing that "we will no longer be able to understand war simply as the armies of one nation-state or group of nation-states fighting one another. Somalia again demonstrates that this understanding is too narrow—it always has been." Sullivan even recognized that "we must learn to deal with reality as it is, not as we want it to be . . . in not facing reality as it is, we could prepare the Army for the wrong war."[47]

Yet, if it was the case that the Army now understood the importance of LIC/OOTW, there was no significant reorganization of US forces to reflect this new emphasis, as Force XXI, the Army's 1994 modernization plan, focused almost exclusively on conventional forces. TRADOC Pamphlet 525-5 *Force XXI Operations* (1995), which described this modernization plan, recognized that "most of the conflicts involving the US Army will be OOTW or low-intensity conflicts, as few states will risk open war with the US"[48] but actually spent little time considering how the Army should change itself to adapt to these conflicts, claiming that "well-trained and disciplined units, provided with sufficient time and resources to train, can transition to OOTW missions as required."[49] The issue of OOTW was essentially an afterthought tacked on to Force XXI, which focused heavily on new technologies and "lethality," a concept that would be of little use in OOTW.[50] Even the project director on Force XXI, Maj. Gen. Garret, admitted that the document "lacked a clear conceptual path to meet challenges of MOOTW [Military Operations Other than War]" and that the document "failed to address the complexities of achieving MOOTW desired end states." Garret conceded that the Army might need "a separate effort to better define its role in MOOTW," but no such effort appeared.[51]

Force XXI's neglect of OOTW was reinforced by a 1995 research report for the Army on force structure that concluded that "it makes most sense to conduct military operations other than war with existing forces, [and] forces should not be earmarked for peace operations nor should new forces be created."[52] The conference report of a 1995 TRADOC conference on OOTW found:

> Front-line troops well versed in war-fighting skills were almost unanimously viewed as the preferred forces for OOTW. Again considering that an OOTW environment may quickly change to a combat setting, commanders felt it essential to have troops in place who could respond effectively to threats if needed. Once war-fighting skills are in place, the mission-specific specialties necessary for a given peace support operation can be overlaid on a seasoned force; the opposite, it was said, is not true.[53]

If the Army was fundamentally unwilling to revisit its force structure, which was optimized for conventional conflict, then operations other than war were never likely to occupy more than a niche role in Army capabilities. Doctrine existed for peacekeeping, but, so long as the Army's structure and culture emphasized conventional capabilities, then that doctrine was unlikely to be fully internalized by US troops. A major institutional source for the advocacy of this new doctrine, the Center for Low Intensity Conflict, was shut down in 1996, when the Army withdrew its support, claiming that it had now learned enough about low-intensity conflict/operations other than war and "understood their principles well."[54] Lt. Col. David A. Fastabend suspected that this inability to focus on missions beyond conventional conflict was due to a broader problem with organizational inertia, arguing, "We digitize tanks. We slash force structure. We revise our doctrine. But we do not reorganize."[55]

Even the School of the Americas, which trained the officers and noncommissioned officers (NCOs) of Latin American allies, continued to emphasize "large unit AirLand Battle studies" over OOTW in its curriculum. This was at least partly due to practical concerns: Because the School of the Americas got their training materials from the CGSC at Fort Leavenworth, and the vast majority of CGSC courses dealt with conventional operations, then it was inevitable that the courses the School of the Americas offered would be skewed toward such operations.[56] Here was a case of the Army's success in the Gulf War drowning out lessons from other recent conflicts. The 1993 edition of FM 100-5 may have included more discussion of OOTW than previous editions, but it remained fundamentally attached to the tenets of AirLand Battle, and although FM 100-23 *Peace Operations* contained sophisticated guidance that was in tune with the political and diplomatic imperatives of strategy, it was not replaced or updated as the years went by, and the Peacekeeping Institute, which had been charged with maintaining peacekeeping doctrine, suffered from a chronic lack of funding and personnel from 1998 onward.

Part of the reason the Peacekeeping Institute faced such problems was that senior leaders, such as Secretary of Defense William Cohen (1997–2001) and Chairman of the Joint Chiefs of Staff Hugh Shelton, were deeply skeptical of the utility of peacekeeping operations. Cohen, a Republican, had been strongly critical of Clinton's intervention in Bosnia when he was a senator, and he expressed a similar reticence about intervention even in the aftermath of overseeing NATO's bombing campaign and subsequent introduction of peacekeepers to Kosovo:

> Everything else has to fail before you turn to the military. And if you do turn to the military, you must be very clear on what the objectives are . . . and how military action can be consistent with carrying out and furthering those goals. I want to be very clear that we have domestic support before we ever commit our forces to combat. It's always important to get the support domestically before you go into battle, rather than trying to seek it afterwards. Also, we must have the support of the allies.[57]

Meanwhile, Shelton, who had proposed a "Dover test" to gauge public support for military interventions (see the discussion in the preceding pages), rejected suggestions that the Army create specialized peacekeeping units, reasoning that "the most effective peacekeepers are those highly trained in war-fighting skills" and that the military should not lose sight of its fundamental purpose: "to fight and win our nation's wars."[58] Shelton's focus on "fighting and winning the nation's wars" was very much in keeping with the Army's post-Vietnam dislike of anything that hinted at counterinsurgency. Given such high-level lack of interest in peacekeeping and acceptance of Powell's lessons of Vietnam, then it is not the decline in funding for the Army's Peacekeeping Institute or the neglect of FM 100-23 that seems remarkable but the fact that the institute was established and the manual published in the first place.

The doctrinal innovations contained in FM 100-23 and even in FM 100-5 showed that the Army was thinking about the post–Cold War world, where the monolithic Soviet threat no longer existed and battle could no longer be expected to be joined on the plains of Northwestern Europe. However, the focus on war fighting persisted, even as the Army recognized that, just as with LIC, OOTW (or at least the various missions contained within those two concepts) would occupy a significant amount of the Army's operational attention for the foreseeable future. That the focus on war fighting continued despite this recognition speaks to just how strong the post-Vietnam aversion to counterinsurgency (and, generally to all forms of limited wars and conflicts) was.

"VIETMALIA," HAITI, BOSNIA, AND FORCE PROTECTION

There was a fundamental tension between the caution espoused by Powell, Cohen, and Shelton and the fact that the American military was heavily involved in peacekeeping and humanitarian intervention throughout the 1990s, an indication that perhaps Powell's lessons of Vietnam were not as influential in the White House as they were within the military and defense establishment. Nonetheless, the actual operational experience of US forces on peacekeeping missions provided another vivid demonstration of how deeply certain lessons of Vietnam were engrained within the Army's culture. For if Army doctrine on peacekeeping and OOTW was flawed and its institutional response to the concepts sluggish, interpretation of that doctrine on the ground was even more conservative than national policy on peacekeeping. Lt. Gen. Barry McCaffrey, assistant to the chairman of the Joint Chiefs of Staff, explicitly invoked Vietnam as a caution against sending a peacekeeping force to Bosnia in Congressional testimony in 1992:

> The country of Bosnia is about the size of South Vietnam. And I spent three combat tours, pieces of them, in that operation. So we have considerable experience in trying to hold open roads and lines of communication against a guerrilla force. This mountainous terrain and forested area and the weaponry involved would be tougher than that situation.[59]

Unsurprisingly, his concerns were echoed by Col. Harry Summers who, in congressional testimony on peacekeeping operations, worried that such "peripheral missions" would badly damage the Army's effectiveness in carrying out its conventional tasks claiming that "that rifle company [on UN peacekeeping duty] in Somalia is degrading its wartime skills. We need to understand that. We need to understand that, as we saw in the Gulf War, the training of maneuver units today is a full-time job."[60] Summers's worry about the harmful effects of peacekeeping duty on readiness for conventional war was rooted in a deep skepticism about the efficacy of nation building in any form, be it counterinsurgency or peacekeeping. He described such missions as "growing out of civilian academic conceits that one can change the world with the tools of social science." Summers argued that "this wrong-headed notion that political, social, and economic institutions can be built with the sword, flies in the face of not only of our Vietnam experience but also the centuries-old American model of civil-military relations."[61]

The popularity of Summers's conservative approach was even more pronounced after the US peacekeeping mission in Somalia (1992 through 1994) ended in failure; US forces withdrew after the death of eighteen soldiers in a day-long running firefight in downtown Mogadishu and the subsequent TV images of one of the dead soldiers being dragged through the streets by a mob.[62] This experience led to a renewed reticence on peacekeeping among both the administration and the military, something Richard Holbrooke (ambassador to Germany during the operations in Somalia and later Clinton's Balkans envoy) dubbed the "Vietmalia syndrome."[63] Failure in Somalia, illustrated the dangers of what Maj. Gen. S. L. Arnold, commander of Army forces during Operation Restore Hope, called "mission creep."[64] Indeed, the mission had morphed from securing food supplies for the Somali populace to a broader nation-building role to the hunt for Somali warlord, Mohammed Farrah Adid. Senator Richard Lugar, of the Senate Foreign Relations Committee, argued that "the Mogadishu incident dramatically indicated that Americans were not tolerant of losing American lives, and grossly intolerant if it appeared that American leadership had no idea of what we were doing, and why they were lost and what sort of control we had."[65]

Reacting to this humiliation, Clinton's National Security Council produced a national security strategy that strongly echoed the Powell Doctrine while backing away from commitment to peacekeeping operations.[66] In the 1994 National Security Strategy (NSS), the Clinton administration declared that "in those specific areas where our vital or survival interests are at stake, our use of force will be decisive and, if necessary, unilateral. In other situations posing a less immediate threat, our military engagement must be targeted selectively on those areas that most affect our national interests."[67] Furthermore, the authors of the NSS asserted that "when we send American troops abroad, we will send them with a clear mission and, for those operations that are likely to involve combat, the means to achieve their objectives decisively."[68] This emphasis on vital interests and a clear mission were explicit invocations of the caution of Colin Powell and Casper Weinberger and, as such, were not conducive to open-ended peacekeeping commitments. Indeed, the NSS stated that "in order to maximize the benefits of UN peace operations, the United States must make highly disciplined choices about when and under what circumstances to support or participate in them."[69] This did not mean an absolute ban on US involvement in peacekeeping operations but a much more restrictive interpretation of when it would be in US interests to get involved than had prevailed in the earlier part of the decade and than Clinton had supported during his campaign for the presidency.

Clinton laid out his approach in much more detail in his May 1994 Presidential Decision Directive "PDD 25: Reforming Multilateral Peace Operations"; he ordered that US forces would not participate in multilateral peacekeeping operations unless:

- Participation advances US interests and both the unique and general risks to American personnel have been weighed and are considered acceptable.
- US participation is necessary for the operation's success.
- The role of US forces is tied to clear objectives and an endpoint for US participation can be identified.
- Domestic and congressional support exists or can be marshaled.
- There exists a determination to commit sufficient forces to achieve clearly defined objectives.[70]

PDD 25 therefore marked a deliberate approach toward peacekeeping that was wary of "mission creep," overreliance on US participation, and a lack of a clear end point. Such caution not only reflected the lessons of failure in Somalia and the worry that intervention in the Balkans would see similarly disappointing results but the deep internalization of the Army's cautious lessons of Vietnam. These lessons, which had crystallized with Weinberger and Powell, adapted to take account of the changing global security environment and the inevitably different nature of the challenges the United States faced after the demise of the USSR, but they remained at the core of US policy on intervention. That Clinton stepped back from campaign commitments toward greater involvement in humanitarian and peacekeeping operations is unsurprising, given this broader institutional reluctance to intervene. Moreover, this sentiment was not limited to the National Security Council and the Joint Chiefs of Staff; it permeated virtually every aspect of the Army's actual performance in peacekeeping operations, certainly after Somalia. For despite attempted institutional and doctrinal reforms to adapt the Army for peacekeeping, this caution strongly manifested itself throughout the military.

This caution was more than an aversion to casualties as it also reflected a broad distaste for counterinsurgency. Counterinsurgency was as unpopular in an era of peacekeeping operations as it had been in the immediate post-Vietnam era. If anything, the Somalia experience strengthened this institutional bias. Although the soon-to-be-closed Center for Low Intensity Conflict organized a 1995 conference on counterinsurgency because they felt that the Army's counterinsurgency doctrine was badly outdated and that "in operations as those in Somalia and Rwanda, military units faced situations strongly akin to counterinsurgency environment in many respects,"[71] others saw Somalia as a reason *not* to relearn counterinsurgency. The National Defense University's "Somalia: Lessons Learned" report concluded that the US mission in Somalia had become a combat mission rather than a peacekeeping one, citing commander of US forces in Somalia Maj. Gen. Thomas Montgomery's remark that "if this isn't combat, then I'm sure having a helluva nightmare."[72] Unsurprisingly, then, many of the Army's "lessons learned" conclusions centered on the efficacy or otherwise of small unit infantry tactics or on command and control issues related to combat; the Center for Army Lessons Learned report on Somalia maintained:

> It is essential that the Army maintains its focus on war fighting and adapts as necessary to meet requirements during OOTW. With operational tempos continuing to increase in the face of diminishing resources, units cannot afford OOTW requirements creeping into unit METLs [mission essential task lists]. Allowing OOTW requirements to distract Army training or equipment acquisition programs would degrade combat readiness and eventually lead to another "Task Force Smith." As lessons are reviewed from Somalia, the Army must be vigilant and analyze the issues with respect to war-fighting capabilities rather than performing OOTW.[73]

This focus on combat overshadowed other insights that directly related to counterinsurgency doctrine such as the Center for Army Lessons Learned's (CALL's) criticism of the lack of a coherent political-economic-military plan. This lack of a plan meant that "rather than taking advantage of the large amounts of aid that was pouring into Somalia to influence political actions, reward positive activities, and to help suffering Somalis, the military was forced to raid its dispensaries and mess halls for medicine and food to distribute as part of its Civil Affairs and Psyop efforts."[74] However pertinent this lesson was, it was lost in the overall focus on combat and on the question of whether the US forces involved in the fatal "Black Hawk Down" mission could have been provided with better protection in terms of fire support and armor. This focus on better protection soon manifested itself with the notion of "force protection" and a focus on minimizing US casualties above virtually all other considerations.

The experience of US forces in Haiti in 1994 through 1995 illustrated the point vividly. The first attempt to land troops in Port-au-Prince ended in humiliation when the troopship, USS *Harlan County*, failed to disembark its Army engineers as a large, angry mob filled the docks and threatened to turn Haiti into the "next Somalia," a stark reminder of the limits of US capabilities.[75] Once US Army forces did deploy to Haiti, they prioritized the avoidance of casualties to such an extent that all other matters, such as reconstruction or peacekeeping, took second place. A later Combat Studies Institute study of Army operations in Somalia and its aftermath depicted a situation where force protection had become the de facto mission of Army forces in Haiti. The authors of the study claimed that "fearing that Port-au-Prince might in fact be another Mogadishu, the Army's conventional forces maintained a posture of maximum vigilance while assuming minimum risk to its personnel." This meant that US troops were constantly making displays of force in what was in fact a relatively peaceful environment, given that the populace of Port-au-Prince largely viewed US soldiers as a liberating force. The Mogadishu experience was inescapable in Haiti:

> The memory of Somalia hung over the Haiti mission like a dark cloud. Selecting the 10th Mountain Division, including many personnel fresh from the Somali ordeal, as the lead force in Haiti all but ensured comparisons in the minds of both participants and observers . . . Most 10th Mountain Division personnel in Port-au-Prince remained permanently locked down in well-

bunkered compounds. Direct engagement of the populace was minimal, at least within the limits of the Haitian capital.[76]

This same attitude carried over to Bosnia, not only in terms of the lengthy debate on whether the United States should intervene and in what form but also in the posture of Army forces once they deployed there. Given the Army task force's mandate, this is unsurprising. Secretary of Defense William J. Perry (1994–1997) had ordered the 1st Armored Division, preparing to deploy to Bosnia, to posture itself for midintensity conflict, personally telling officers of the division on December 19, 1995, to be "the meanest dog on the block." The division's own movement order heavily emphasized the need to protect the force, even elevating this to the task force's mission statement: "On order, TF *Eagle* deploys to SECTOR TUZLA, Bosnia-Herzegovina, and conducts peace enforcement operations to compel compliance with the peace accord; *ensures force protection* [added emphasis]."[77] The Army in Bosnia was evidently trying to implement aspects of the Powell Doctrine by displaying the capability for overwhelming force and by ensuring that they would do as much as possible to avoid the casualties that would sap public support. If the *mission* was force protection, though, then clear, achievable objectives were inherently lacking.

US V Corps, the headquarters responsible for the Army deployment to Bosnia, even set up a "force protection working group" to oversee all aspects of the force protection posture. This led to a situation where US forces acted in a manner consistent with the sentiment of one senior Army commander that "all commanders must believe they are always only a heartbeat away from a gunfight." This meant that American soldiers effectively cut themselves off from the local population to better protect themselves. One officer complained:

> US troops wear helmets and body armor—hence their nickname, "ninja turtles." They travel in convoys with guns manned and ready. When they stop, they disperse to over watch positions, ready to apply defensive force. At night, most retire to fortified camps or outposts as Romans did on campaigns, cut off from the people they came to protect.[78]

US soldiers had to wear body armor even while on their own bases. This led to the ludicrous situation where American Special Forces working in local communities, who dispensed with body armor and helmets so as not to create unnecessary barriers between themselves and the local population, had to put on full body armor to *enter* American bases.[79] Less comically, the rule that vehicles could not leave their base unless they were traveling in a convoy of at least four vehicles meant that Civil Affairs soldiers, whose job it was to engage with the civilian population, were often stranded on base as they had difficulty acquiring the necessary escort vehicles.[80] General George Joulwan, commander of NATO forces in Europe at the time, stated that this force protection policy was based on military necessity due to the increased threat of terrorist attack that US forces faced compared to their NATO allies (who usually dispensed with body armor and wore soft hats in place of helmets). Interestingly, Joulwan also cited a belief that a lack of professionalism contributed heavily to US failures in Vietnam and that lax uniform standards were part of this loss of professionalism.[81] American forces in Bosnia, therefore, would wear their helmets and body armor at all times in a show of discipline and readiness.

This force protection approach, however, should not obscure the valuable lessons some in the Army took from Bosnia. Lt. Col. Joseph Anderson[82] published an article in *Military Review* about priorities in peacekeeping operations that included the need to "establish a positive relationship with the civilian population and influence adversaries not to use force," and "defining and restoring some sense of normalcy in the region as part of the mission's post-conflict resolution phase."[83] Anderson even approvingly used the phrase "winning hearts and minds." Meanwhile, other US forces pioneered such techniques as weekly meetings with local power brokers to kick-start reconstruction projects and to deal with any potential grievances and establish protected marketplaces, where different ethnicities could intermingle and trade without fear of violence.[84] The Army, then, did innovate in Bosnia and learn some tactical lessons about how to engage with a local population. Considering the fact that tens of thousands of troops served in Bosnia between 1996 and 2002, this was not an inconsiderable amount of experience; general officers who would later play important roles in the counterinsurgency campaign in Iraq, from Ricardo Sanchez to George Casey to David Petraeus, spent time on peacekeeping missions in the Balkans. However, these tactical innovations were of a similar nature to those made in Vietnam. Stability operations doctrine of the 1990s and the early 2000s may have been better at capturing the lessons of Bosnia than the Army's counterinsurgency doctrine of the 1960s had been at internalizing the lessons of Vietnam, but neither ever seemed to affect the Army as deeply as the broader lessons about force protection.

One commander who served a tour in Bosnia complained that "successful command has come to mean, in large part, returning home with no casualties. Commanders are pressured, unconsciously or consciously, into taking a short-range approach to their assignment and therefore are reluctant to take risks. Exit strategy becomes personalized—don't get anyone killed."[85] This understandable reluctance to risk American lives for what some commanders considered to be unclear goals had transformed into a force of its own where the possibility arose of force protection becoming the mission of any unit engaged in peacekeeping or operations other than war.[86] If units adopted such a low level of activity that they were seeking only to preserve their forces for future use, then force protection would be the de facto mission of the unit, a situation that occurred both in Haiti and Bosnia at various times. If preventing casualties was to be the mission, then surely that could be accomplished just as well in Fort Benning as in Bosnia. One Army critic decried the belief that force protection needed to be based on a zero-casualties policy as a "myth," but one "so widely accepted that it has become folklore and changed US military bureaucracy. As an example, force protection is being institutionalized in formal structures, which underscores its importance, provides additional legitimacy to the myth and enhances its usefulness in explaining the world."[87] This zero-casualties approach was in many ways an awkward solution to the tension between the Powell Doctrine's reluctance to risk US troops for less than vital interests and the American imperative to intervene: The United States would use its military in these situations but in such a way that there would be little or no risk to its troops. Force protection was, in effect, a way to prosecute an interventionist foreign policy while still staying within the constraints of the Vietnam syndrome.

CONCLUSION

This awkward solution to the problems posed by participation in peacekeeping missions was a direct product of an institutional culture that strongly supported the Powell Doctrine as a way of preventing another Vietnam but also recognized the inevitability, if not the desirability, of Army involvement in "operations other than war." The practice of deploying troops on peacekeeping missions but then in operating in such a way that the actual accomplishment of the mission had a lower priority than the prevention of American casualties shows just how irrelevant (and far from the Army's core role) many in the

Army considered these missions to be. The disaster in Somalia and the rise of a "Vietmalia syndrome" only strengthened these tendencies. Casualties, particularly casualties taken on missions that were only vaguely understood and with no clear end point, were unacceptable. This meant that doctrine, from the 1993 edition of FM 100-5 to the Clinton administration's PDD-25, heavily emphasized the need for clear, limited objectives while operational practice was strongly focused on force protection above all other imperatives.

What is particularly interesting, however, about the debate over peacekeeping operations throughout the 1990s was not only the continuing strength of the lessons of Vietnam but the even more pronounced waning of counterinsurgency doctrine. While the debates around low-intensity conflict in the 1980s often explicitly invoked lessons from Vietnam that emphasized the importance of good counterinsurgency doctrine, few of the advocates of peacekeeping acknowledged their intellectual debt to counterinsurgency and field manuals produced in the 1990s, from FM 100-5 to FM 100-23, made little or no mention of the subject. With the codification of the lessons of Vietnam into the Powell Doctrine, interest in counterinsurgency was the lowest it had been since the immediate aftermath of the Vietnam War. This was so even though aspects of counterinsurgency doctrine were well suited to the new international situation, one where the bipolar organization of the world had definitively ended and security threats came from what Clinton's National Security Advisor Anthony Lake called "backlash states," more so than they had been to the height of Reagan's Cold War.[88]

Crucially, given the fact that peacekeeping missions formed the vast bulk of the Army's operational experience in the aftermath of the Gulf War, the norms the Army developed on these missions were to have a heavy influence on the way the Army conducted the occupation of Iraq, especially in its earlier years. However, these norms—particularly the emphasis on force protection—themselves came not necessarily from the operational experience of peacekeeping itself (for there were relatively few violent incidents involving American troops in either Haiti or the Balkans) but rather from a fear of the consequences of casualties and of another Vietnam. The irony was that this emphasis on force protection and neglect of other aspects of stability operations would later be a contributing factor to the early failures in what was to be the closest the United States had ever come to repeating the Vietnam experience—the war in Iraq.

5 MR. RUMSFELD'S WAR

Transformation, Doctrine, and "Phase IV"
Planning for Iraq

IN A JANUARY 2002 ADDRESS to the staff and students of the National Defense University, Secretary of Defense Donald Rumsfeld told a story about recent operations in Afghanistan[1] that he felt was emblematic of the transformation he wanted to bring about in the Pentagon. Rumsfeld exulted in this tale of horse-mounted US Special Forces calling in precision air strikes on Taliban positions; it was, as he put it, "the first US cavalry attack of the 21st century."[2] However, the lesson "was not that the Army should begin stockpiling saddles" but that future forces should be flexible, adaptable, and, above all, light.[3] For Rumsfeld, these would be "rapidly deployable, fully integrated joint forces, capable of reaching distant theatres quickly and working with our air and sea forces to strike adversaries swiftly, successfully and with devastating effect." They would "need improved intelligence, long-range precision strike, and sea-based platforms to help counter the 'access-denial' capabilities of adversaries." Such a force could only come about through a complete change in both the mind-set and capabilities of the US military, particularly the Army.

The purpose of this chapter is to examine how this top-down quest for transformation affected Army approaches to counterinsurgency and the broader family of stability operations and how these considerations informed the planning and execution of what was to be the largest stability operation attempted since Vietnam—the invasion of Iraq. By examining both the doctrine in place prior to the war and the specific planning and execution of the war, we can see how thirty years of accumulated doctrinal neglect of counterinsurgency and the broader family of stability operations affected operations in Iraq in the spring of 2003.

Vietnam, as ever, was present as a cautionary tale, but it is worth noting that the operations of the 1990s were much more recent, and relevant, historical analogies. How the Army related—or failed to relate—its experience in places like Northern Iraq, Somalia, and the Balkans to the planned operation in Iraq says much about the interplay between history and doctrine. On a related theme, it is also worth examining how an approach rooted in technological hubris rather than historical lessons—that of "transformation"—influenced both Pentagon attitudes toward an intervention in Iraq and Army doctrine. This chapter will first outline some of the intellectual origins of "the Revolution in Military Affairs" (and how they too related to a particular set of lessons of Vietnam) and the major studies that influenced Rumsfeld. It will then examine how Rumsfeld's vision of defense "transformation" interacted with the Army's ideas on war before considering how the tension between these two ideas manifested itself in the planning for the invasion of Iraq.

THE TRANSFORMATION AGENDA: INTELLECTUAL ORIGINS

Speaking to the Association of the United States Army in October 1969, Chief of Staff of the Army General William Westmoreland described his vision of the future battlefield:

> On the battlefield of the future, enemy forces will be located, tracked, and targeted almost instantaneously through the use of data links, computer assisted intelligence evaluation, and automated fire control. With first round kill probabilities approaching certainty and with surveillance devices that can continually track the enemy, the need for large forces to fix the opponent becomes less important. I see battlefields that are under 24-hour real or near real time surveillance of all types. I see battlefields on which we can destroy anything we can locate through instant communications and almost instantaneous application of highly lethal firepower . . . With cooperative effort, no more than 10 years should separate us from the automated battlefield.[4]

For Westmoreland, it seemed as if computers could take the inherent confusion—Clausewitz's "friction"—out of the battlefield, something that was no doubt immensely desirable given his Vietnam experience. Technological developments toward the end of American involvement in the war, such as precision-guided munitions and advanced sensors, hinted at a way to project American power more forcefully and make it possible to overcome the limitations seen in Vietnam. While the Army's most important lessons from

Vietnam centered on strategic questions about intervention and on the avoidance of counterinsurgency campaigns, the technological advances of the war fascinated the military establishment as a whole, as well as many within the Army. Advanced sensors—such as those used in the "McNamara Line" in an attempt to interdict the Ho Chi Minh Trail—and laser-guided bombs played a more and more prominent role as the war ground on.[5] While advances such as "people sniffers" proved ineffective in combating the insurgency, they were part of a broader history of US military obsession with technology, which the sociologist James Gibson critiqued in his *The Perfect War: TechnoWar in Vietnam*.[6] Gibson focused on the role that "managerial science," in both the Pentagon and Vietnam, played in the war and on how faith in technology was a key to how the United States pursued the war in Indochina. Certainly, Westmoreland's vision of an "automated battlefield" fit comfortably in the narrative of technological determinism on the battlefield (even if the Vietnam experience did not), and that narrative gained strength with the precision munitions-based "AirLand Battle" doctrine of the 1980s and its vindication in the 1991 Gulf War. By the mid-1990s, the narrative turned to technological triumphalism, and some writers proclaimed an imminent "revolution in military affairs" that would revolutionize how war was fought.

The epitome of the potentially revolutionary nature of this "transformation" was a 1996 National Defense University Study entitled *Shock and Awe: Achieving Rapid Dominance*,[7] by Harold Ullman and James Wade Jr. Ullman and Wade argued for what they called a "rapid dominance" force that would defeat its enemies not by physical destruction alone but by managing to "paralyze or so overload an adversary's perceptions and understanding of events so that the enemy would be incapable of resistance at tactical and strategic levels."[8] Thus, rather than relying on the overwhelming force advocated by Powell, the military would attempt to create "the non-nuclear equivalent of the impact that the atomic weapons dropped on Hiroshima and Nagasaki had on the Japanese." The psychological shock caused by the inability of the "average Japanese citizen" to comprehend "the destructive power carried by a single airplane . . . produced a state of awe."[9] Ironically (and in keeping with the broader silence on Vietnam in doctrine and military theory) Ullman or Wade did not consider the psychological shock that the Vietnamese Tet Offensive had inflicted on US culture. Nevertheless, *Shock and Awe* was to be a new departure in military doctrine. The psychological effect of an action would be just as important as the action itself; the rapid destruction of a few key nodes could cause a whole system to collapse. Moreover, this approach would not be limited, as it had been in the past, to strategic air forces: All forces—air, sea, and land—would be oriented toward this end. This concept of "rapid dominance" through "shock and awe" shaped basic assumptions of Iraq War planners.[10]

However, as befitting a study drafted at a time when the 1st US Armored Division was deployed in its entirety to Bosnia, the study recognized that there was still ambiguity in the world and that technological and tactical brilliance could not provide the absolute clarity that futurists sometimes wished for. The authors acknowledged that "the formidable nature and huge technological lead of American military capability could induce an adversary to move to a strategy that attempted to circumvent all this fighting power through other clever or agile means." Invoking the Vietnam War as "a grim reminder of the political nature of conflict and how our power was once outflanked," Ullman and Wade pointed out that "the greatest constraints today to retaining the most dominant military force in the world, paradoxically, may be in overcoming the inertia of this success. We may be our own worst enemy."[11] In this case, the authors posed more questions than they answered about how rapid dominance would apply to complex scenarios, noting that "the German Blitzkrieg would have performed with the greatest difficulty in the Vietnam war, where enemy forces had relatively few lines to be penetrated or selectively savaged by this type of warfare."[12] The authors repeatedly referenced "operations other than war," but how *Shock and Awe* could be utilized in these multifarious scenarios was an open question, left unanswered. The limits of American power were only hinted at, amid all the technological optimism.

Shock and Awe's role as an intellectual seed for much of the defense establishment's thinking on "transformation" was evident in *Joint Vision 2020* (JV 2020),[13] a planning document prepared by the Joint Chiefs of Staff. Published in May 2000, it predated Rumsfeld's tenure at the Pentagon, but the publication certainly broadly fitted with his view of future warfare. From "maneuver dominance" to "precision strike" to "information operations,"[14] the document focused almost exclusively on types of high-tech conventional war, essentially more sophisticated and complex variations on Donn Starry's 1980s "AirLand Battle" doctrine, which had been successfully employed in Kuwait and Iraq in 1991. Technological and technical innovation feature so predominantly in *JV 2020* that it would seem that *JV2020*'s talk of "full spectrum dominance" was referring to the electromagnetic spectrum rather than the continuum of possible military operations.[15] In many ways, *JV 2020* was little more than an updated vision of Westmoreland's "automated battlefield"; the technology had changed, but the basic aspiration had not.

What is surprising about Westmoreland's speech, *Shock and Awe*, and *JV 2020* is their essentially optimistic view of future warfare, an optimism untarnished by previous failures. The hard lessons on the limitations of technology, seen so clearly in Vietnam, seemingly remained unlearned. Indeed, in one sense, the optimism of *JV 2020* in particular partly seemed to obviate history itself, in that technological prowess would make warfare clean, logical, and therefore usable; that somehow technocratic and technological innovation would erase lessons related to time, place, space, and context. The experience of the Balkans and Somalia, despite being so recent, had very little influence on *JV 2020*.[16] The authors of *JV 2020* understood that warfare was changing but ignored changes that did not suit the American way of war. Vietnam, El Salvador, Bosnia, and Somalia, all of which offered their own lessons about the transformation of war, were not referred to at any stage.

Even consideration of the potential strategies of US opponents, precisely those who could surely be expected to employ "low-intensity" or nonconventional strategies, was cast in technological terms in *JV 2020*. *JV 2020* may have recognized "asymmetric warfare" as a threat, but the unrelenting focus on conventional operations seemed to suggest some sort of cognitive dissonance or unclear definition of what *asymmetric* might mean. In fact, one of the major asymmetric threats listed was that of long-range ballistic missiles from rogue states, the response to which was the suggestion to enhance large-scale investment in missile defense technology. The authors argued that "the potential of such asymmetric approaches is perhaps the most serious danger the United States faces in the immediate future—and this danger includes long-range ballistic missiles and other direct threats to US citizens and territory."[17] This definition of *asymmetry* focused on the technological means that opponents could use to defeat the United States, not the strategies, such as insurgency, that attacked American will. In echoing Westmoreland's earlier buoyancy about the capabilities of American arms, the authors were subscribing, if only implicitly, to an extraordinarily narrow set of lessons from Vietnam. These lessons recalled precision-guided munitions and electronic sensors but not the Vietnamese insurgents that defeated them. *JV 2020*, for all its mention of *dominance*, a term loaded with connotations of overwhelming force, focused on the idea of overwhelming *capabilities* and technological innovation rather than sheer weight of numbers or firepower. However, by seeking a way around the Powell Doctrine by lowering the numbers of troops needed—which would result in less public controversy over the costs of intervention—*JV 2020* failed to address problems that might not be amenable to technology-heavy, personnel-light solutions.

TRANSFORMATION: RUMSFELD AND THE ARMY

Despite these problems, the Bush administration wholeheartedly endorsed *JV 2020*'s view of warfare, with President George W. Bush defining "a revolution in the technology of war, [with] powers increasingly defined not by size, but by mobility and swiftness." In such a climate, "safety is gained in stealth and forces projected on the long arc of precision-guided weapons." Therefore, the US goal would be "to move beyond marginal improvements to harness new technologies that will support a new strategy."[18] Indeed, the whole point of "transformation" was to take advantage of the "revolution in military affairs" to effectively skip ahead a generation of weapons development to give the United States an unassailable lead in military capabilities. This very ambitious goal meant that marginal improvements would not be enough. Rumsfeld's intent on returning to the post of secretary of defense (a position he had also held under President Gerald Ford) was to push this "transformation" through the Pentagon, and he began by ordering a series of sweeping reviews intended to convert the US military into a lighter, more lethal force. These reviews, led by Andrew Marshall of the Office of Net Assessment,[19] aimed to challenge the military service's prevailing assumptions.[20] In a Pentagon "town hall" meeting on September 10, 2001, Rumsfeld outlined just how seriously he took transformation and the extent to which he viewed it as a bureaucratic battle against institutional inertia:

> The topic today is an adversary that poses a threat, a serious threat, to the security of the United States of America. This adversary is one of the world's last bastions of central planning. It governs by dictating five-year plans. From a single capital, it attempts to impose its demands across time zones, continents, oceans and beyond. With brutal consistency, it stifles free thought and crushes new ideas. It disrupts the defense of the United States and places the lives of men and women in uniform at risk. Perhaps this adversary sounds like the former Soviet Union, but that enemy is gone: our foes are more subtle and implacable today. You may think I'm describing one of the last decrepit

dictators of the world. But their day, too, is almost past, and they cannot match the strength and size of this adversary. The adversary's closer to home. It's the Pentagon bureaucracy.[21]

Rumsfeld's evident frustration was the result of a long summer of disagreement with the military services over the nature of transformation. Increased lethality and precision targeting capabilities were welcome additions, but not if it meant the Navy losing an aircraft carrier or the Army an armored division; while institutional imperatives did much to prevent counterinsurgency from ever gaining much importance in the post-Vietnam era, they were similarly well positioned to oppose civilian initiatives such as force transformation. Rumsfeld's initial reviews were entirely civilian led, and he began to meet with the Joint Chiefs on the issue, in several bad-tempered meetings, only in May 2001, with one service chief complaining that he had not even received a copy of Marshall's strategy paper before the meeting.[22] By September, it was clear to him that if he wished to transform the military he would have to do so in an aggressive fashion.

In support of this policy, Rumsfeld created an office whose mandate was explicitly to help promote transformation: the Office of Force Transformation, whose focus on technological solutions was apparent in their emphasis of the importance of lasers and space-based weapons as the wave of the future. Under the leadership of long-time "transformation" advocate, retired Admiral Art Cebrowksi, this office strove to promote "network-centric warfare," a way of war deeply dependent on sensor platforms, communications systems, and remote weapons. Rumsfeld also pushed his transformation agenda in the 2001 Quadrennial Defense Review (QDR 2001). In his introduction, written in the immediate aftermath of 9/11, he called for flexibility, as "we can identify threats, but cannot know when or where America or its friends might be attacked."[23] Rumsfeld's introduction was a further endorsement of the transition toward a "capabilities-based" strategy as opposed to a threat-based strategy. The review also called for joint forces that "must be lighter, more lethal and maneuverable, survivable, and more readily deployed and employed in an integrated fashion." The revolutionary potential of this doctrine, made possible by new technologies, was clear to Pentagon planners:

> For the United States, the revolution in military affairs holds the potential to confer enormous advantages and to extend the current period of US military superiority . . . Moving to a capabilities-based force also requires the United

States to focus on emerging opportunities that certain capabilities, including advanced remote sensing, long-range precision strike, transformed maneuver and expeditionary forces and systems, to overcome anti-access and area denial threats, can confer on the US military over time.[24]

What was particularly noteworthy about this "capabilities-based" approach was that it shifted the emphasis from reaction to preventative intervention, much as had George W. Bush's expansive National Security Strategy of 2002. Not only that, but it also emphasized dominance; the emphasis on "capabilities" rather than "threats" seemed to indicate that the United States would spend less time worrying about what its opponents could do to it and more time thinking about what it could do to them. This emphasis on dominance echoed the 1992 Draft Defense Planning Guidance, which sought to maintain the "mechanisms for deterring potential competitors from even aspiring to a larger regional or global role."[25] Given that Andrew Marshall, the defense analyst chosen by Rumsfeld to lead the most important review of the Pentagon's priorities, had been consulted by Paul Wolfowitz for the 1992 Defense Planning Guidance[26] and was heavily involved in the 2001 QDR, this echo was not surprising. Despite the timing of its publication (in October 2001), the QDR contained much of the technological optimism of the 1990s. This "capabilities-based" approach also meant lighter forces with less troops on the ground and (it was hoped) shorter wars, which could overcome the problem of ensuring public support for such conflicts. This was the core of the "Rumsfeld Doctrine": High-technology combat systems heavily reliant on air power, with nimble, light ground forces would have both a smaller supply chain and fewer soldiers exposed to danger. As such, the force described in the QDR ideally suited neoconservative interventionist politics.

Army leaders had an ambivalent relationship with "transformation," with Army Chief of Staff General Eric Shinseki at one point telling a gathering of senior officers, "If you don't like change, you're going to like irrelevance even less."[27] Shinseki himself was a vocal advocate for transformation, insisting that Army Transformation be spelt with a capital *T* to reflect institutional emphasis.[28] He pushed the Army toward a lighter, more deployable force, emphasizing an "expeditionary culture," and he began the process of restructuring the Army around modular brigades, rather than the larger, less deployable division. These brigades would be heavily reliant on lighter, faster, wheeled Stryker armed fighting vehicles and would be rapidly deployable to crisis points. The Army's plan for "Army 2010" was centered on "dominant maneuver," "precision engagement," "full dimensional protection," and "information superiority."[29] Steven Metz has argued that, despite its misgivings about transformation, the Army had made more of an effort than any of the other services to adjust its structure since the 1990s.[30] However, senior Army officers were just as quick to dismiss elements of the "revolution in military affairs" that discomfited them as they were to dismiss counterinsurgency in the wake of Vietnam. As Metz pointed out, "transformation" was something that made sense to the Air Force and Navy, who saw their primary job as destroying targets, but it was a much more problematic term for the Army and the Marines, whose missions tended to be far more nuanced.[31] Given the personnel-intensive and complex nature of these missions, transformation was a much less obvious fit for the land warfare services. As John Sloan Brown has noted, Shinseki's major contribution to transformation, the Stryker Brigade, was also the most personnel intensive.[32]

Shinseki then (and others within the Army) saw the limitations and pitfalls of transformation. Retired Army Chief of Staff General Gordon R. Sullivan decried "the easy but erroneous conclusion that by spending hundreds of billions of dollars weaponizing space, developing national missile defense, and buying long-range precision weapons, we can avoid the ugly realities of conflict."[33] Another Army critic complained that transformation enthusiasts were advocating "'immaculate warfare' whereby the United States can stand secure behind high-tech missile defenses and space systems and smite enemies from afar without fear of suffering casualties."[34] In testimony to the Senate Armed Forces Committee in March 2000, Shinseki supported the broad goals of transformation, sounding the common refrain of flexibility and lightness. However, he also insisted that the Army be allowed to continue funding programs that better fit the Army's self-image, such as the Crusader heavy artillery system and the Comanche attack helicopter, both holdovers from the Cold War.[35]

Despite the Army leadership's ambivalent support for the concept, Army doctrine was essentially as untouched by "transformation" as it was by counterinsurgency; the Army's doctrine in the Rumsfeld era was probably as conservative as it had been at any time following the Vietnam War. The Army's capstone manuals, FM 1 *The Army* and FM 3-0 *Operations* (both 2001), still saw the Army's core mission in unambiguous terms as, respectively "to fight and win our Nation's wars"[36] and "rapid, decisive victory."[37] However, the peacekeeping and peace enforcement missions of the 1990s, now termed "stability operations" (as a less hazy construct than "operations other than war"), did leave their mark on Army thinking, as can be seen in the contents of FM 3-0 (renumbered from FM 100-5 to fit with the numbering system for joint doctrinal publications). In the typology of operations, FM 3-0 placed stability operations (along with support operations, those nonmilitary missions that covered such things as disaster relief and aid to the civil power) alongside offensive and defensive operations as the Army's core missions. However, it noted that "Army forces cannot train for every possible mission; they usually train for war and prepare for specific missions as time and circumstances permit."[38] In practice, this would mean that conventional warfare would remain the prime focus of the Army. The manual's coauthor, Lt. Col. Michael D. Burke, noted: "There is a larger impetus evident in the manual's tone. The US Army is now the premier land force in the world; its capabilities present almost insuperable challenges to any opponent. Consequently, this is a fundamentally offensive doctrine."[39] This was an echo of Rumsfeld's preference for a "capabilities-based approach" that could make military force easier to use and therefore less restricted by Powell's caution.

Nonetheless, FM 3-0 certainly had considered both the necessity and difficulty of stability operations. Primarily, the Army was to provide and promote a stable environment through "a combination of peacetime developmental, cooperative activities and coercive actions"[40] and be prepared for a potential shift in missions "from promoting peace to deterring war and from resolving conflict to war itself."[41] Flexibility was crucial, and small unit leaders were expected to "develop interpersonal skills—such as cultural awareness, negotiating techniques, and critical language phrases—while maintaining warfighting skills,"[42] which required great mental agility. The Army internalized the lessons of the Balkans and Somalia, even if only partially, in a way that Rumsfeld and his civilian reformers did not. The Army may have had a rough consensus around Powell's lessons of Vietnam, but there was also an understanding that the Army could not avoid Bosnia-type stability operations in the future. Donald Rose argues that FM 3-0 demonstrated that "resistance to OOTW as a viable mission for the Army has been overcome by a combination of the Army's own lessons learned process and the cumulative experience of the early 1990s."[43]

However, there was still a note of Vietnam-influenced caution present in the manual. The use of US combat forces in counterinsurgency or foreign internal defense (FID) was discouraged:

> Normally, using US forces in combat operations is a temporary measure. FID operations are closely scrutinized by a variety of audiences, to include the American public, international organizations, and the host nation populace. Hostile propaganda will attempt to exploit the presence of foreign troops to discredit the host government and the US. Poorly executed, direct involvement by the US military can damage the legitimacy and credibility of the host government and host nation security forces.[44]

Eventually, host nation forces must stabilize the situation and provide security for the populace. According to the authors, the success of Task Force Eagle in Bosnia was due to a Powell-like "credible, overwhelming force coupled with extensive planning, liaison, leadership, and discipline."[45] Vietnam was present in more explicit ways, as the manual cautioned commanders that they "must not allow stability issue solutions to become a US responsibility . . . In any successful stability operation, the host nation—not the US forces supporting it—must ultimately prevail."[46] Indeed, Vietnam was invoked as an example to prove this particular point, with the FM 3-0 authors noting:

> The majority of South Vietnamese people came to rely on US forces for their protection, eroding their confidence in their own government to provide for their security. US forces intended to support the South Vietnamese, but by significantly increasing their role in defending Vietnam, they undermined Vietnamese government authority and ARVN credibility.[47]

However, caution meant more than just referencing the pitfalls of the past. There was a recognition that stability operations did not just occur in isolation, that they belonged to the same continuum as more conventional forms of war (something that the previous moniker of MOOTW—military operations other than war—had essentially denied). In perhaps its most prescient passage, FM 3-0 stated:

> A period of post-conflict activities exists between the end of a conflict and redeployment of the last US soldier. Army forces are vital in this period. As a sequel to decisive major operations, Army forces conduct stability operations and support operations to sustain the results achieved by the campaign. These

operations ensure that the threat does not resurrect itself and that the conditions that generated the conflict do not recur. Post-conflict stability operations and support operations—conducted by Army forces—transform temporary battlefield successes into lasting strategic results.[48]

As a capstone manual, whose task was to provide an overall concept for the operations the Army could be called on to conduct, FM 3-0 did not have the time or space to get into exactly how lasting strategic results would be achieved through stability operations. However, a more detailed manual, FM 3-07 *Stability Operations*, published on the eve of war with Iraq in February 2003, described the "nuts and bolts" of such operations.[49]

FM 3-07 was wary of the risk of mission creep, another Vietnam echo, noting that "in stability operations and support operations, the military objective usually supports another agency,"[50] as opposed to conventional war, when the military had undisputed control over their area of operations. Therefore, not only was there a danger of the Army being asked to do things that it was not equipped for, but—in the absence of unity of command in the area of operations—there must be a unity of effort among all agencies. Interestingly, the Vietnam experience of CORDS was referenced as a successful, albeit unusual, example of how this might be brought about.[51] Given the experience of complex peacekeeping operations in the 1990s, it seemed that certain counterinsurgency lessons from Vietnam, such as the importance of interagency cooperation and unity of effort, were slowly making their way back into the Army's collective consciousness.

Even so, FM 3-07's chapter on counterinsurgency, largely drawn from FM 90-8 *Counter-Guerrilla Operations*, a publication that had not been updated since 1986, echoed the type of counterinsurgency campaigns supported by Nixon and Reagan. Essentially, wherever possible, the Army's role would be restricted to assisting local forces, through training and logistical support. Direct combat should be avoided, as "the threat to American interests does not support that degree of involvement, even if it were effective." Additionally, "an American combat role tends to undermine the legitimacy of the host government and risks converting the conflict into an American war."[52] While FM 3-07 (like FM 3-0) recognized that stability operations were to play a major part in the Army's future, the authors apparently hoped that these operations would be conducted with sufficient competence (or that national decision makers would be cognizant of the Army's reluctance) to make direct involvement in counterinsurgency operations unnecessary. Army doctrine, then, was very slowly adapting itself to a world where stability operations were inevitable, even if it retained Powell's core lessons from Vietnam. In the same testimony to Congress where he defended heavy weapons system such as Crusader and Comanche, Gen. Shinseki also described a force that was significantly influenced by the operations of the 1990s. Shinseki noted that as small-scale contingency operations (that is, Bosnia and Kosovo) became long-term national commitments, the Army became more and more organizationally adapted to these missions, with units rotating in and out of theater for the long haul.[53]

This, however, was anathema to the Bush administration in general and to Rumsfeld in particular: The scaling back of US commitment to such missions had been a central part of Bush's foreign policy platform during the 2000 election. Candidate Bush had promised "a more humble foreign policy"[54] on the campaign trail and, in an article in *Foreign Affairs*, Condoleezza Rice spelled out what the foreign policy of a Bush Administration would be. Rice decried military involvement in peace keeping and nation building, arguing: "It [the military] is not a civilian police force. It is not a political referee. And it is most certainly not designed to build a civilian society. Military force is best used to support clear political goals."[55] Rice later quipped that "we don't need to have the 82nd Airborne escorting kids to kindergarten."[56] Rumsfeld told Pentagon reporters that "I think that we organize, train, and equip, and recruit for people to come in and serve in the military in military functions . . . and to the extent we can have as few people in uniform doing nonmilitary functions, I think we better serve ourselves, our country and our personnel."[57] To this end, he attempted to close down the Army's Peacekeeping Institute, which only survived because of events in Afghanistan and Iraq.[58] Indeed, Rumsfeld initially felt that events in Afghanistan had validated his disdain for peacekeeping operations. In a speech entitled "Beyond Nation-Building" delivered in New York in February 2003, on the eve of war with Iraq, he outlined why Afghanistan would be a model for Iraq:

> The objective is not for us to engage in "nation building"—it is to help Afghans, so they can build their own nation. That is an important distinction. In some "nation building" exercises, well-intentioned foreigners arrive on the scene, look at the problems, and say, "let's go fix it for them." This can be a disservice. Because when foreigners come in with international solutions to local problems, it can create a dependency.[59]

This illustrates not only a worldview informed by classic conservative wariness of government involvement in society but also a reluctance to commit to nation-building tasks in any substantive form. However, despite the fact that Rumsfeld shared the Army's general dislike of peacekeeping and nation building, this conservatism was of a different nature from the one that marked the Army's approach to transformation. Rumsfeld essentially wanted to *use* this lighter, more agile force, whereas Army leaders were much more inclined to observe the principles of Colin Powell's cautious lessons of Vietnam. Indeed, Shinseki's disagreements with Rumsfeld about transformation and about the Iraq war were eventually to cost him his job. In his final memorandum to the secretary of defense, he complained about Rumsfeld's risk taking:

> There has been a lack of explicit discussion on risk in most decisions. Without this explicit discussion, there is opportunity to miscalculate with unacceptable consequences. For those of us who consider risk assessment to be part of our core responsibilities, it is much easier to execute decisions aggressively once risk has been quantified.[60]

This was the most crucial distinction between the Army's approach and Rumsfeld's. While technology had always played a large part in the Army's way of war, what Rumsfeld was proposing to do was to radically enhance the role of technology to make war cleaner and to make intervention possible again in the age of the Vietnam syndrome.

PLANNING FOR POSTINVASION IRAQ: WARNINGS FROM THE OUTSIDE

Nothing better illustrates the tension between both the Army's caution and Rumsfeld's recklessness and the Army's conventional focus and its slow accretion of knowledge of peacekeeping than the planning process for the invasion of Iraq in 2002 and 2003. The narrative of the Iraq War often presumes that there was a complete absence of planning for the postinvasion phase.[61] Some, such as Retired Special Forces Lt. Col. Kalev Sepp, have criticized attitudes toward Phase IV (the postcombat stabilization phase) as "when you put everything in the sea, air and land containers and ship it back to Fort Stewart, Georgia,"[62] and they have argued that there was a shared assumption among soldiers that civilians would be running postwar Iraq. However, just as with the planning process itself, such a narrative overlooks several important studies on postwar planning and presupposes the Army to be a much more monolithic institution than was the case. These studies were all based on the lessons of peacekeeping operations in the 1990s and were much more grounded in historical reality than Rumsfeld's technocentric hubris.

Certainly, those who had experience of stability operations in the 1990s were under no illusion as to the difficulties any invasion of Iraq would pose, the most high-profile example being Army Chief of Staff General Eric Shinseki's February 2003 congressional testimony on the force levels that would be required to stabilize Iraq. Shinseki estimated that an occupation force would require "something on the order of several hundred thousand soldiers" as the army would have to maintain "post-hostilities control over a piece of geography that's fairly significant, with the kinds of ethnic tensions that could lead to other problems." In such a potentially unstable environment, Shinseki reminded Congress that "it takes a significant ground-force presence to maintain a safe and secure environment, to ensure that people are fed, that water is distributed, all the normal responsibilities that go along with administering a situation like this."[63]

Shinseki's was certainly no voice in the wilderness: CENTCOM's 1999 contingency plan for stabilizing a post-Saddam Iraq, codenamed *Desert Crossing*,[64] assumed that 400,000 troops would be needed and that the mission would be exceedingly complex.[65] Indeed, many throughout the National Security establishment held similar views. "Force Security in Seven Recent Stability Operations," an NSC study completed for Condoleezza Rice and her deputy Stephen Hadley, noted that the numbers of troops required to stabilize a country were completely unrelated to the numbers required to defeat that country's military. According to the briefing, "If the United States and its allies wanted to maintain the same ratio of peacekeepers to population as it had in Kosovo . . . they would have to station 480,000 troops in Iraq. If Bosnia was used as a benchmark, 364,000 troops would be needed. If Afghanistan served as the model, only 13,900 would be needed in Iraq."[66] Whether the Army would choose Kosovo or Afghanistan as a model was not, of course, a decision it would get to make by itself, as seen in Rumsfeld's "Beyond Nation-Building" speech. Rumsfeld's fondness for an extremely light footprint and minimal substantive involvement in postwar reconstruction efforts would heavily influence planning for Iraq. Rumsfeld had pushed back on initial Army estimates that 385,000 troops would be needed for the operation, at one stage seeming to favor a plan that would begin the invasion with only 18,000 troops.[67] Rumsfeld even sent the CENTCOM commander, General Tommy

Franks, a note in December 2002 suggesting that he and his planners review Ullman and Wade's *Shock and Awe* study for inspiration.[68]

However, Rumsfeld's thinking found little traction elsewhere. The State Department's "Future of Iraq" study noted that "Iraq is not Afghanistan" and advocated a commitment on a scale similar to that of Germany or Japan after World War II.[69] Like "Desert Crossing," the "Future of Iraq" project posed more questions than it answered, but the thirteen-volume study offered similar cautions about the need for a fully integrated, well-funded interagency political-military effort to stabilize post-Saddam Iraq. Nonetheless, none of these studies constituted a viable plan for postinvasion Iraq. "Desert Crossing" was essentially a war game that looked at what might happen, while "The Future of Iraq Project," though voluminous, was disjointed and did not finish its work until after the occupation had begun. What these reports do show, however, is that significant elements of the National Security establishment were not nearly as sanguine as Rumsfeld was about the prospects for postinvasion Iraq. These studies all essentially heeded some of the central tenets of the Powell Doctrine—the need for overwhelming force and a clear exit strategy— that did not fit with Rumsfeld's vision of transformation or with the short-lived "Rumsfeld Doctrine."

Much as "Desert Crossing" was condemned once Rumsfeld began issuing directives about troop levels and Tommy Franks began implementing them, the "Future of Iraq" project was rendered irrelevant when President Bush issued National Security Presidential Directive (NSPD) 24 *Post-War Iraq Reconstruction* in December 2002. This directive placed the Department of Defense in charge of all postconflict activity in Iraq.[70] Secretary of State Colin Powell acquiesced to this, given his department's lack of resources,[71] but the directive essentially created a policy environment in which Pentagon war planners could safely ignore outside studies from the NSC and State Department. Given this situation, as well as Rumsfeld's habit of reaching deep into the bureaucracy to push his agenda, it was inevitable that any war plan would strongly bear his mark. In fact, Rumsfeld even interfered with the Army's intricate time-phased forces-deployment list (TPFDL), the complex plan that dictated what units would arrive in the Gulf and in what order, to emphasize his preferred "light footprint."[72]

Rumsfeld's preferences for this "light footprint" meant that CENTCOM rejected a study from the Army War College's Strategic Studies Institute. Conrad Crane and Andrew Terrill coauthored the monograph *Reconstructing Iraq:*

Challenges and Missions for Military Forces in a Post-Conflict Scenario, which explored both historical examples and Iraqi history to contemplate what type of missions the US military might face in Iraq.[73] Its breakdown of missions into a matrix evaluating "critical," "essential," and "important" tasks across twenty different areas, from security to fisheries, was as lucid and comprehensive a summary available for planners as any. Furthermore, the study broke down these tasks over the phases from initial occupation to handover and detailed which agencies, whether Iraqi or US, should be responsible for them. Such comprehensiveness should not be surprising, as the matrix was based on the interagency reconstruction plan for Operation "Restore Hope" in Haiti.

Crane and Terrill also realized that "recent American experiences with post-conflict operations have generally featured poor planning, problems with relevant military force structure, and difficulties with a handover from military to civilian responsibility" and that this history of confusion further emphasized the need to do better this time. The task would be extremely challenging; anticipating future developments, the study noted that "military forces will be severely taxed in military police, civil affairs, engineer, and transportation units, in addition to possible severe security difficulties." Crane and Terrill warned that "an exit strategy will require the establishment of political stability, which will be difficult to achieve given Iraq's fragmented population, weak political institutions, and propensity for rule by violence."[74] They also realized how lengthy and taxing a commitment an occupation would be, warning of "detailed interagency planning, many forces, multi-year military commitment, and a national commitment to nation-building." In many ways, the study offered a way to apply the lessons of 1990s stability operations to Iraq.

Although such warnings did not constitute a plan, they do demonstrate that at least part of the Army did not see an invasion of Iraq as being anything like a "cakewalk"; the transformation agenda did not completely obliterate the lessons of the 1990s, nor did it mean that the doctrine written to reflect those lessons was entirely ignored. Studies from NSC to the State Department to CENTCOM and to the Army War College had described both the vast complexity of any occupation and the several hundred thousand troops needed to run it. More importantly, Army Chief of Staff General Eric Shinseki essentially agreed with these studies in congressional testimony. That planners ignored both him and the various studies is testimony to the extent to which Donald Rumsfeld had overridden the Army's lessons of Vietnam. The problem was that the Army's preferred focus on conventional warfare as a means of avoiding Vietnam-like commitments was logical if the Army itself could dictate when and where it could be committed. When policy makers like Bush and Rumsfeld, aided by "transformation" advocates, overrode not only the military but also much of the National Security apparatus to commit US forces to an invasion of Iraq, the Army found itself without the institutional knowledge on how to stabilize a country like Iraq. When the president and the secretary of defense ignored their preferred lessons of Vietnam, the Army did not have a backup available.

PHASE IV PLANNING: ASSUMPTIONS VERSUS DOCTRINE

Staff at levels ranging from the National Security Council and the Department of Defense, to CENTCOM, to Coalition Land Forces Component Command (CFLCC) to V Corps (the Army Corps that provided the main Army contribution to the Iraq invasion force), with varying levels of competence, were involved in planning for the postwar occupation. The manner in which they carried out that planning illustrates the problems inherent both in Rumsfeld's obsession with "lightness" and the Army's lack of institutional knowledge of counterinsurgency. For, despite misgivings on the part of Army planners about the state of the occupation plan (known as "phase IV"), they never imagined the possibility of an insurgency emerging in postinvasion Iraq.

Much of the criticism and debate over prewar planning (or lack thereof) focuses on the civilian level, from the wrangling over whether the Pentagon or the State Department would be responsible for postwar stabilization to Rumsfeld's insistence on as low a troop footprint as possible, to the late January 2003 creation of the Office of Reconstruction and Humanitarian Assistance. There was also a clear disconnect between civilian and military planners at the DoD-CENTCOM level, as seen in General Tommy Franks belief that "while we at CENTCOM were executing the war plan, Washington should focus on policy-level issues." Franks was happy to know that "the President and Don Rumsfeld would back me up, so I felt free to pass the message along to the bureaucracy beneath them: *You pay attention to the day after* and *I'll pay attention to the day of*" [emphasis in the original].[75]

Such a clear and unambiguous division of responsibilities suited Franks, as it left him free to plan a campaign of conventional combined-arms tactics, executed in the blitzkrieg style so popular with the authors of *Shock and Awe*. However, this approach betrayed a fascination with operations, not strategy.

As Andrew Bacevich observed, Franks's "operational matrix," was not so much a strategy as a collection of tactics. This matrix contained seven "lines of operation" representing American capabilities and nine "slices" representing Iraqi centers of gravity and thirty-six intersections between the two where the Americans would focus their efforts. Rather than, as Franks termed it, "your basic grand strategy," the plan was nothing like strategy; it had so many "centers" of gravity that there was no real center to speak of, while it focused relentlessly on operational matters without any clear vision about what an end state would look like.[76] Franks, then, was repeating many of the same mistakes as "transformation" advocates. In his obsession with targets to "service," he missed broader problems with the war plan. Unlike many of his subordinates, Franks had no experience of peacekeeping operations in the Balkans or elsewhere; even though others involved in the planning process did, the result was still the same. Indeed, then Army Vice Chief of Staff General Jack Keane pointed out that the Army as an institution must take its share of the blame for what went wrong:

> The Joint Chiefs asked questions, but when Phase III, Major Combat Operations went to the President it had the thumbprints of the Joint Chiefs on it, as well as Phase IV. That is another thing that is not fully understood. People attacked it as Rumsfeld's troop list and he kept the size of the force down. It was Tommy's [Franks] plan and the Army supported it. That is the truth of it.[77]

Although the overall planning effort for Phase IV may have been disjointed, there was at least some substantial and realistic planning taking place within Coalition Land Forces Component Command (CFLCC). The C5 (plans) cell tasked Col. Kevin Benson to come up with CFLCC's plan for postwar stabilization. Unlike many in the Bush administration, Benson's planners did not expect US troops to be greeted by Iraqis as liberators. In fact, Benson, who had been the lead planner for XVIII Airborne Corps operations in Haiti, recalled that he and his staff wondered if "maybe the guys in Washington know something we either don't know or can't know because it's that protected of a source."[78] Benson's plan, named Operation Eclipse II (in reference to the original Operation Eclipse—the post–World War II occupation of Germany), called for some twenty brigades and a total troop number of 300,000 to secure Iraq in the aftermath of invasion. These numbers were both far above the numbers that Rumsfeld found acceptable and based much more on experience of stability operations in the 1990s than on ideas about "transformation."

While CFLCC's phase IV planners did anticipate a very complex and challenging postinvasion stability operation (indeed, these operations were judged so complex as to merit their own separate plan, Eclipse II as distinct from the invasion plan, Cobra II), they did not anticipate the possibility of an insurgency emerging. Benson recalls: "We were prisoners of our education. The model we used to analyze that was the Maoist model and we did not see external safe havens, a competing political ideology or vast support."[79] The phrase *prisoners of our education* is apt, as these planners were not the product of Rumsfeld's "transformed" military but rather veterans of the many stability and peacekeeping operations of the 1990s. Consequently, their personal experience of the complexities inherent in trying to stabilize a country informed their plans, but the long neglect of counterinsurgency doctrine took its toll, as outdated assumptions on what could constitute an insurgency constrained the thinking of even those with the most clear-eyed view of the situation.

While the relative foresight of Benson's group was certainly due to their individual and collective experience, it is also important to note that they had access to Crane and Terrill's study, with its clear warnings about the potential for postwar chaos, which almost certainly informed their recommendations. However, the disjointed nature of postwar planning meant that the study was ignored where it mattered, at the higher levels. At a 2004 symposium on postconflict stability, Crane remarked that, despite the fact that Ambassador George Woods, a top civilian at ORHA, "made the point of standing up and saying 'This [study] is not our plan,'" Crane knew that the "study got around" and pointed out that, despite rejection of the study at the upper levels, "a number of people who have come back from the theatre and said, 'We saw your stuff. We tried to implement some of it, but we just either didn't have the resources or weren't allowed to do all the things we wanted to do.'" Additionally, although "the study was not as important as we hoped it would be," Crane "concluded that General Shinseki's opinions about the number of US troops it was going to take to occupy Iraq were shaped, to some extent, by the study."[80] Indeed, there was strong after-the-fact consensus among postwar planners about the accuracy of General Shinseki's predictions. General (retired) Jay Garner, head of ORHA, after seeing the need for troops for himself in Baghdad, recognized that "the force was just not sufficient to do what it had to do . . . You can go back in time and say Shinseki was right. You know, they beat up Shinseki, but he was right."[81]

Right he may have been, but Rumsfeld and Franks did not share Shin-seki's prescience, nor, more importantly, was there adequate pressure coming up the chain of command. Benson faults the Army as much as anybody for this, arguing that their focus on operational matters blinded them to what neoconservatism actually entailed, meaning that the Army were "reduced—as General Franks said in his book—to calling Undersecretary of Defense for Policy Douglas Feith [who directed the Pentagon's post-war planning effort] the 'dumbest m———f——— in government.' He's not dumb; we just didn't understand."[82] What Benson and Army thinkers failed to understand was the expansive nature of the neoconservative project. "Rapid dominance" was a workable concept when the mission was narrowly defined and the objectives were clear, but when the end result entailed occupying and governing another country, Army doctrine and planning fell far short of what would be required.

During war-gaming of plans, the gap between the optimistic assumptions that informed planning and the actual requirements of phase IV were evident. Col. Thomas Torrance, artillery commander of 3rd Infantry Division, recalls "asking the question during our war gaming and the development of our plan, 'Okay, we are now in Baghdad, what next?' No real good answers came forth." Torrance remembers that others were asking, "Who is responsible for eco-nomic development? Who is responsible for a judicial system? Who is respon-sible for a monetary system? Who is responsible for health care?" even as he was "always sort of personally questioning, 'what next? What now? Now that we are here, what now?'"[83] Despite these questions and misgivings, prewar planning neglected to address these issues and provide answers. Benson simi-larly noted that planners did voice discontent about decisions made at a higher level. Referring to the decision to stop the flow of extra forces into Iraq after Baghdad fell, he noted:

> CFLCC C5 and CENTCOM J5 planners argued strongly for a continuation of the force flow and for the position that no one goes home until 1 September . . . Subsequent decisions made later on in April and May 2003 concerning the battle handover and the stopping of the flow of combat forces were made based on information other than that which was provided by either the CFLCC C5 or the CENTCOM J5.[84]

Benson recognized that the planning rested on three major assumptions— that there would be significant numbers of Iraqi soldiers and police available to help provide security, that there would be significant foreign assistance in the way of peacekeepers, and that an Iraqi government would quickly spring back into being. These optimistic sentiments may have come from a higher level, but planners accepted them (and the limitations imposed by Rumsfeld) and let them define prewar planning, without taking into account worst-case scenarios. Troop levels were pared to the bone to achieve Rumsfeld's light footprint—designed to minimize antagonizing the American public—with no regard to previous experience. Condoleezza Rice described the Bush administration consensus on the postwar situation when she said that "you would be able to bring in new leadership, but we were going to keep the body in place."[85] Rice's optimistic prognosis demonstrated how easy higher-level planners thought the occupation would be. Evaluating the results of that optimism, General Scott Wallace, V Corps commander during the invasion, argued, "The military did their job in three weeks. I give no credit to the politicians for detailed Phase Four (the reconstruction of Iraq) planning. But . . . I don't think any of us could have or did anticipate the total collapse of this regime and the psychological impact it had on the entire nation."[86] Wallace recalled:

> When we arrived in Baghdad, everybody had gone home. The regime officials were gone; the folks that provided security of the ministry buildings had gone; the folks that operated the water treatment plants and the electricity grid and the water purification plants were gone. There were no bus drivers, no taxi drivers; everybody just went home. I for one did not anticipate our presence being such a traumatic influence on the entire population. We expected there to be some degree of infrastructure left in the city, in terms of intellectual infrastructure, in terms of running the city infrastructure, in terms of running the government infrastructure. But what in fact happened, which was unanticipated at least in [my mind], is that when [we] decapitated the regime, everything below it fell apart. I'm not sure that we could have anticipated that.[87]

The realities of the invasion and occupation of Iraq betray a contradiction between the "shock and awe" doctrine and the "transformational force" envisioned by Rumsfeld and extant Army stability operations doctrine. The war plan constructed within the strict limits defined by Rumsfeld—its Phase IV planning apart—emphasized lightness, speed, and technology. Indeed, Rumsfeld and Franks's "lessons learned" briefing to Senate Armed Services Committee emphasized that "overmatching power" had now replaced "overwhelming force" as the key planning factor.[88] To Rumsfeld, the invasion of Iraq provided vindication of his vision of how the Army should fight.

However, this very vision clashes with the optimistic assumptions about the postwar scenario. A doctrine that emphasizes paralyzing an entire system through psychological shock (although it did eschew physical destruction of most infrastructure) leaves itself open to the possibility that this systemic shock will cause not just paralysis but the collapse of the very system war planners assumed would remain in place. Unfortunately, such contradictions were inherent in the war plan: For instance, planning to skirt around major cities rather than occupying them was understandable in terms of wishing to avoid the house-to-house fighting and the type of casualties seen in Somalia, but it made little sense in terms of attempting to secure the population. Additionally, speed made sense in terms of blitzkrieg warfare, but not when the enemy was inept and the goal was to occupy a country. The one exception was Baghdad, where V Corps conducted detailed planning on urban operations there. However, their efforts to identify the key nodes used to control the city focused on their destruction and the consequent paralysis of the entire system so troops could avoid house-to-house fighting—rather than on the need to secure them.[89] The eventual armored "thunder runs" into the city and the haphazard occupation of the huge city testified to this continued focus on the problems of conventional war rather than the end state.

CONCLUSION

The invasion and occupation of Iraq, and the chaos and dysfunction that it entailed, were symptomatic of the problems masked or overlooked by "transformation." In a March 2004 study decrying the "new American way of war" as more a "way of battle than a way of war," Lt. Col. Antulio Echevarria of the Strategic Studies Institute observed that "the assumptions underpinning Defense Transformation . . . appear to have more to do with developing an ever exquisite grammar than they do with serving war's logic. However, this new grammar—which focuses on achieving rapid military victories—was equipped only to win battles, not wars."[90] Transformation, as applied in Iraq, bore little relation to the counterinsurgency war the Army was required to fight there. Echevarria's study continued:

> The current American way of war focuses principally on defeating the enemy in battle. Its underlying concepts—a polyglot of information-centric theories

such as network-centric warfare, rapid decisive operations, and shock and awe—center on "taking down" an opponent quickly, rather than finding ways to apply military force in the pursuit of broader political aims. Moreover, the characteristics of the US style of warfare—speed, jointness, knowledge, and precision—are better suited for strike operations than for translating such operations into strategic successes.[91]

However, despite this disconnect between the more aspirational elements of doctrine and realities on the ground, doctrine did exist to deal with the world as the Army found it, rather than how they wished it were. "Full spectrum operations" did recognize the complexity with which armies now had to deal, and FM 3-07's guidance on how to conduct stability operations was nuanced and relatively well informed by the lessons of the 1990s, even if that doctrine lacked flexibility. FM 3-07 presented stability operations as either something that followed a major conflict, or (as was popular in Army training centers) as something that gradually gave way to conventional war. The authors of the official Army history of the invasion, while generally quite sympathetic to Army efforts at planning for postwar stabilization, note how this doctrinal gap shaped commanders' expectations. Even though Army planners "realized that a successful engagement in a city or town had to be followed by successful transition to post-combat operations . . . Few anticipated the frequent transitions from major combat to support operations and back again."[92]

This uneasiness with complex stability operations was compounded by the fact that just because doctrine had been written and taught did not mean it had been absorbed. In one of the most telling chapters of Thomas Ricks's book *Fiasco*, he recounted a conversation between Brigadier General David Fastabend (who had been involved in writing the 2001 edition of FM 3-0) and another Army general who had written that Army doctrine had not prepared him for what he encountered in Iraq in spring 2003. Fastabend responded: "Look, in 1993, we introduced military operations other than war, and then we introduced the idea of full-spectrum operations. From '97 to 2001, we introduced the ideas that operations are a seamless combination of offense, defense, stability, and support. How could you say that your doctrine did not prepare you for what you experienced in Baghdad?" The response was telling: "He said, yeah, Dave, I know. I read all that stuff. Read it many times, and I thought about it. But I can remember quite clearly, I was on a street corner in Baghdad smoking a cigar, watching some guys carry a sofa by and it never occurred to me that I was going to be the guy to go get that sofa back."[93]

The chaos of spring 2003 revealed an Army caught in the middle, between its experience of peacekeeping and stability operations and the 1990s, and the ultralight, technology-driven, conventional operations–focused force Rumsfeld embraced. This tension between high-technology warfare and the low-technology, personnel-intensive imperatives of securing a population manifested themselves in a disjointed war plan for Iraq that was, in turns, sober and realistic, shallow, and far too optimistic. Army attempts to deal with these failures, and the insurgency that resulted from them, involved the return of Vietnam to discourse on doctrine, both within the Army and outside it.

6 COUNTERINSURGENCY AND "VIETNAM" IN IRAQ, 2003–2006

THE OCCUPATION OF IRAQ starkly illustrated the absence of knowledge about how to conduct counterinsurgency operations within the Army. One of the most revealing periods was the immediate aftermath of the invasion, when the US Army found itself effectively without a plan.[1] The growing insurgency highlighted the inadequacies of preinvasion planning, shattering assumptions about the Army's capabilities and doctrine. In this vacuum, commanders and commentators alike turned to the past to make sense of the present, employing analogies from postwar Germany to Vietnam to Lebanon to explain the situation. The differences among various units' performances illustrate the dearth of counterinsurgency doctrine or training within the Army and how that absence led commanders to adopt disparate lessons from their own experiences. The question then is: How did the US Army comprehend the war in terms of past experience? Specifically, how did narratives of Vietnam affect how the Army understood Iraq? Additionally, how did the prolonged absence of counterinsurgency from the Army's collective memory (and certainly its doctrine and curriculum) affect its ability to deal with the insurgency in Iraq?

These are crucial questions, but this chapter is not only concerned with the absence of collective memory—of both Vietnam and counterinsurgency—as it also examines attempts to fill that void, both by reaching back for old lessons and by constructing new ones. The reemergence of counterinsurgency in 2004 through 2006 is inextricably tied to the rise of an alternative set of lessons from Vietnam than the ones that the Army brought with it to Iraq. These old and new lessons from Vietnam shaped the occupation, from the early tension between peacekeeping imperatives and inclinations toward conventional warfare to later arguments over whether the priority for counterinsurgency should be training Iraqis and preparing for withdrawal or securing the population and further embedding into Iraq. This chapter will explore how analogy interacted with reality in Iraq and how those interactions led to the construction of new lessons and the dismissal of old ones.

THE OCCUPATION: COMBAT AND PEACEKEEPING AMID CHAOS

Historical analogy strongly influenced Ambassador L. Paul Bremer as he took charge of the new Coalition Provisional Authority (CPA) and, by extension, Iraq on May 11, 2003. Bremer's first measures—particularly his decisions to disband the Iraqi Army and introduce "de-Baathification," the removal of Baath Party members from public positions—were directly and consciously modeled on the US occupation of Germany and Japan. In his memoirs, Bremer recalled that he held impromptu history seminars with his aides, the subject of which was often comparing Iraq to post–World War II occupations.[2] Bremer later argued:

> The concept behind the de-Baathification decree was that the Baath Party had been one of the primary instruments of Saddam's control and tyranny over the Iraqi people for decades. Saddam Hussein himself openly acknowledged that he modeled the Baath Party on the Nazi Party because he admired the way in which Hitler was able to use the Nazi Party to control the German people. Just as in our occupation of Germany we had passed what were called "de-Nazification decrees" and prosecuted senior Nazi officials, the model for the de-Baathification was to look back at that de-Nazification.[3]

While Bremer favored such World War II analogies, another parallel may have been more relevant to the situation. In the summer of 2003, the Pentagon sent retired Marine Col. Gary Anderson—an expert in counterinsurgency—to Baghdad to advise on how to deal with the emerging insurgency and he met with Bremer in early July. Tom Ricks recounted the meeting: "'Mr. Ambassador, here are some programs that worked in Vietnam,' Anderson said. It was the wrong word to put in front of Bremer. 'Vietnam' Bremer exploded, according to Anderson. 'Vietnam! I don't want to talk about Vietnam. This is not Vietnam. This is Iraq!'"[4] Ironically, Bremer's senior aide and closest advisor,

Clayton McManaway, had spent five years in wartime South Vietnam working for USAID and CORDS, so there was at least someone in the CPA who knew how the war in Vietnam had been run.[5] Despite this, Bremer refused to recognize that Vietnam had anything to teach him; not surprising, considering that the Iraq war, in a sense, represented an attempt to overcome the limitations of the Vietnam syndrome.

Bremer was not alone in his optimistic vision of Iraq as postwar Germany. Despite the controversy over the appropriate US troop levels for occupation, there was little formal dissent from senior Army leaders about Bremer's decision to disband the Iraqi military—a decision that more junior officers protested and virtually all later agreed was a mistake.[6] Unlike the Army, which expected those Iraqi soldiers to be recalled to service quickly, the CPA envisioned a much slower, more deliberate rebuilding of the Iraqi Army. Even as Bremer's plans found favor in Washington, they were completely divorced from the situation on the ground. De-Baathification and a lack of Iraqi troops to help provide security and personnel for reconstruction (something that Army planners had counted on and local commanders had already started to use) severely increased the Army's difficulties. For instance, the engineer brigade of the 1st Armored Division, after struggling to reestablish basic sewer and electrical services in Baghdad in May 2003, eventually had to find the ex-Baathist bureaucrats and technicians and place them back in their jobs.[7] Col. Michael Tucker, who commanded the 1st Brigade Combat Team, 1st Armored Division, in eastern Baghdad, found problems with the lack of reliable Iraqi personnel. He recalled that "everything you fixed, to include pumps for sewage and the incinerator for the hospital, you ended up having to guard . . . Of course, the guards often became corrupt as well, so we found ourselves 'guarding the guards.'"[8] The problems faced by the Army that summer overwhelmed anything they were expecting. Although there were plans in place for postinvasion stabilization (see Chapter 5), those plans were either ignored by higher headquarters or proved to be completely inadequate to cope with the scale of problems encountered. Those difficulties stemmed partly from the very act of invasion itself, partly from the already existing problems of Iraq, and partly from the incompetence of the Bush administration's planning. The Army itself, however, cannot be absolved from blame. Even as the chaos of postinvasion Iraq unfolded, the Army took actions that showed that it still did not comprehend the seriousness of the situation.

General Franks's decision to pull out the Army-level headquarters Coalition Land Forces Combat Command (CFLCC) and upgrade the V Corps headquarters to a Combined Joint Task Force further exacerbated these problems. This change meant that those personnel responsible for postwar stabilization planning would be rotating home, while being replaced by a much smaller headquarters staffed by people who hitherto had been focused on the tactical situation. Essentially, by withdrawing CLFCC, Franks was assuming that—as President Bush had declared—major combat operations were now over. General Wallace, the departing commander of V Corps, later complained that this move in itself damaged the effectiveness of US forces in Iraq:

> You can't take a tactical headquarters [V Corps] and change it into an operational [level] headquarters [CJTF-7] at the snap of your fingers. It just doesn't happen. Your focus changes completely, and you are either going to take your eye off the tactical fight in order to deal with the operational issues, or you are going to ignore the operational issues and stay involved in the tactical fight.[9]

The downgrading of the importance of Iraq was also evident in the fact that the commander of this new Task Force, Lt. Gen. Ricardo Sanchez, was the most junior three-star general in the Army. Unlike Franks, Sanchez was not an unreconstructed Cold Warrior but rather a veteran of peacekeeping operations in Kosovo (where he commanded a brigade from 1999 to 2000) and served on the staff of the joint headquarters with the most experience of dealing with complex interagency operations and small wars: SOUTHCOM.[10] Sanchez *had* experience of stability operations. This experience however, did not translate into a plan to deal with the growing insurgency.

Indeed, there was some debate throughout the summer of 2003 within the Army on whether to call the evolving situation in Iraq an insurgency. General John Abizaid, the new commander of CENTCOM, acknowledged as early as July 2003 that the Army was seeing "classic signs of insurgency" in Iraq and in his memoirs, Sanchez recalls supporting the definition, even arguing that the Army were occupiers in Iraq, not liberators.[11] Conversely, Maj. Gen. Steve Whitcomb, a planner on the CENTCOM staff, later recalled:

> There was a lot of discussion during the fall time period about using the term counterinsurgency or insurgency, or however you wanted to coin it, and a lot of work was done . . . on what are the classic signs of an insurgency and what are the characteristics. As we looked at those, we didn't necessarily think it was an insurgency.[12]

This failure to either recognize or correctly categorize the situation was symptomatic of an Army that no longer understood counterinsurgency. Certainly, there were political imperatives at play, not least Secretary of Defense Donald Rumsfeld's consistent downplaying of the extent of the crisis, but the Army in Iraq also displayed a marked reluctance to acknowledge the situation it faced.

By late June, the CPA, in cooperation with Sanchez's planners, developed a plan that reflected classic stability operations doctrine: security, essential services, governance, economy and strategic communications.[13] Meanwhile, Gen. Abizaid, after taking command of CENTCOM in July 2003, introduced what he called the "Five I's" to guide US military operations: Iraqization, improvement of intelligence, development of infrastructure, internationalization, and information operations.[14] On the one hand, this would indicate, on a broad level, familiarity with the key concepts of counterinsurgency. But on the other hand, CJTF-7's concept of operations was to "conduct offensive operations to defeat remaining noncompliant forces and neutralize destabilizing influences in the A[rea of] O[perations] in order to create a secure environment in direct support of the Coalition Provisional Authority."[15] The focus on the "defeat of remaining noncompliant forces" betrayed a focus on the military destruction of the enemy, the very thing the US Army was criticized for doing in Vietnam. Indeed, the conflict between CJTF-7's campaign plan that included all the elements of classic counterinsurgency and its concept of operations that emphasized destroying the enemy highlighted a problem that also appeared in Vietnam. It was easy for senior leaders to say the right things about how campaigns would be conducted, but much more difficult to carry out these plans when they clashed with broader Army culture. To further complicate this situation, Sanchez had a hands-off approach to command, leaving commanders free to interpret this campaign plan as they saw fit—essentially pushing the weight of decision making on how best to deal with the insurgency downward. While it was problematic for the Army, this state of affairs does offer us an opportunity to more closely examine how the Army as a whole understood counterinsurgency, as a lack of guidance from above meant that commanders fell back on doctrine, training, and education. How commanders adapted to this situation demonstrates some of the major strengths and weaknesses of the post-Vietnam Army.

Unquestionably, the Army tried to adapt to the situation on the ground, particularly at brigade and battalion level. Field artillery and armor battalions were rapidly converted into infantry or military police, and staffs were assigned new roles that involved governance and civil affairs. Much of this low-level adaptation was due to previous experience in the Balkans and elsewhere. Major Daryl Rupp recalled that the 3rd Infantry Division "had done that mission [in SFOR in Bosnia] and they knew what it meant to do a 'presence patrol' . . . They knew what it was to go in and do a bilateral meeting with a councilman or a tribal leader."[16] Similarly, Colonel Joseph Anderson, commander of the 2nd Brigade Combat Team, 101st Airborne Division, relied on experience when conducting operations to stabilize Mosul in 2003. According to Anderson, he "did the same in Panama; did the same in Kosovo; did a little bit in Haiti; and now [in Iraq]."[17] Indeed, Anderson's division commander, Maj. Gen. David Petraeus, had served as chief operations officer of the UN Mission in Haiti and had served a ten-month tour in Bosnia just prior to the Iraq War. Even more importantly, Petraeus had written his PhD dissertation on the Army's lessons of Vietnam (see Chapter 7) and had questioned the Army's neglect of counterinsurgency in the 1980s.

In many ways, the 101st Airborne operated in a way that went beyond the experience of limited peacekeeping operations, with Petraeus enthusiastically pushing his commanders to stabilize Mosul by providing security for the local population, jump-starting the economy and training Iraqi security forces to take over. His division artillery commander found that his primary role was to run Mosul's employment center before handing it over to the Iraqis.[18] Petraeus's explicit priority was nation building, a phrase that, in many ways, was anathema to the post-Vietnam Army. He explained that there were "two or three infantry battalion commanders [in the 101st] who were either not that comfortable with the nation-building aspect of things, or really weren't that enthusiastic about it," which resulted in Petraeus briefing his immediate subordinates on the central importance of civil affairs: "So they got it. Everybody did it. Even aviation battalion commanders were given civil-military areas of responsibility."[19] This resulted in a reconstituted police force, a functioning city council, and even a reopened border with Syria.[20]

The situation was very different in other areas of Iraq, however. Maj. Gen. Raymond Odierno's 4th Infantry Division, facing a more organized and active enemy in the groups of former Baathists, chose to emphasize more traditional combat roles. To be sure, Odierno's forces faced a more difficult situation than did others (for example, Petraeus's 101st Airborne in Mosul); they were clearly not operating in an environment conducive to peacekeeping. However, in the absence of doctrinal guidance they were forced to improvise. Those improvisations revealed the predispositions of Odierno and his subordinates to think in terms of applying firepower, not providing security. Dexter Filkins described tactics that mirrored Israeli approaches in Gaza and the West Bank: "In selective cases, American soldiers are demolishing buildings thought to be used by Iraqi attackers. They have begun imprisoning the relatives of suspected guerrillas, in hopes of pressing the insurgents to turn themselves in."[21] While the US Army claimed they were not purposefully copying Israeli tactics, they acknowledged that they "studied closely the Israeli experience in urban fighting."[22]

Throughout the summer of 2003, the 4th Infantry Division conducted a series of massive sweeps of their area of operations and adopted a much more aggressive posture than the Marine unit they replaced. An inspector general report on their handling of detainees noted that the Division had a habit of "grabbing whole villages, because combat soldiers [were] unable to figure out who was of value and who was not" and the practice of detaining all military-age males practically overwhelmed the facilities at Abu Ghraib prison.[23] The 4th Infantry Division even reinstituted a version of the body count, with CENTCOM press releases enumerating the 400 people detained on sweeps such as Operation Peninsula Strike and Operation Ivy Serpent.[24] Furthermore, the division aggressively used heavy firepower to fight the insurgents. According to Filkins, Odierno's order to his subordinates after a spike in insurgent activity was to "increase lethality."[25] This included Vietnam-era practices such as "harassment and interdiction fires"—the practice of firing unobserved artillery at likely points of enemy concentration, such as crossroads.[26] Taken together, such actions were reminiscent of the worst American practices in Vietnam, with media commentators beginning to employ the analogy.[27] The 4th Infantry Division's focus on firepower may have been the natural by-product of an Army culture that sought to avoid future Vietnams, but in Iraq these tactics only served to remind people of the similarities. They were also deeply counterproductive; retired Colonel Douglas McGregor complained:

> Most of the generals and politicians did not think through the consequences of compelling American soldiers with no knowledge of Arabic or Arab culture to implement intrusive measures inside an Islamic society. We arrested people in front of their families, dragging them away in handcuffs with bags over their heads, and then provided no information to the families of those we

incarcerated. In the end, our soldiers killed, maimed and incarcerated thousands of Arabs, 90 percent of whom were not the enemy. But they are now.[28]

One proponent of this "increased lethality" was Lt. Col. Nathan Sassaman, a battalion commander in the 4th Infantry Division. Sassaman's attitude toward the insurgency was very much focused on force. On one occasion he responded to a single insurgent mortar round by firing twenty-eight 155-millimeter artillery shells and forty-two mortar rounds and calling in two airstrikes, one with a 500-pound bomb and the other with a 2,000-pound bomb.[29] When his men came under fire from a wheat field, Sassaman would routinely burn it down with white phosphorus shells. One of Sassaman's company commanders, Captain Todd S. Brown, later justified this use of firepower as a force protection measure:

> Prior to the arrival of our bullish tactics, we had multiple shots and reloads from the enemy in this city. Now they shoot and run . . . fast. Shoot as much as fast as you can at the enemy regardless of straight-up target acquisition—if you saw him there before, shoot there and continue to look for him. Recon by fire—this is not a surgical operation.[30]

In his memoirs, Sassaman recalls numerous run-ins with his brigade commander about his tactics, which would suggest that, even within the 4th Infantry Division, such emphasis on force was not uncontroversial.[31] In fact, Sassaman's downfall came when he was prosecuted for helping to cover up the alleged drowning of two detainees by his men. That he was able to pursue the tactics he did speaks to the damage the doctrinal vacuum on counterinsurgency and what the post-Vietnam retrenchment of "the American way of war" did to the Army's operations in Iraq. Sassaman may not have been typical of US commanders in Iraq—after all, few were charged with covering up detainee abuse and murder—but he operated under orders that were favorable toward heavy use of firepower and indiscriminate treatment of Iraqis. Such orders were indicative of a culture that was firmly focused on conventional, mechanized warfare and completely unsuited to counterinsurgency campaigns.

The contrasting approaches taken by various units in Iraq in 2003 through 2004 reveal an uncertain and ambivalent approach to counterinsurgency, unsurprising given the lack of institutional knowledge of this type of conflict. Certainly, some units—most notably David Petraeus's 101st Airborne—performed admirably and drew heavily on their experience of peacekeeping and stability operations in the 1990s. However, given that the challenge of Iraq was much greater than anything seen in the Balkans, the Army simply did not have the doctrine to deal with anything more violent than what they encountered in post-Dayton (1995) Bosnia, nor did they have a culture that was suited to such war. What they did have was a culture of tactical innovation. Even when the US Army's tactics were counterproductive, they were still genuine attempts by commanders on the ground to respond to the problem. Petraeus in Mosul drew on his experience in Haiti and the Balkans, whereas Odierno in Tikrit instead drew on more conventional doctrine. Such a patchwork approach to the war—due to differing conditions, different commanders, and a lack of overall guidance—meant that there was a need to focus US efforts and to give a clear sense of the type of war they were fighting.

A NEW APPROACH AND A RETURN OF
THE VIETNAM ANALOGY

General George Casey replaced Sanchez in Iraq in June 2004 by, just as CJTF-7 was wound down and replaced by a four-star command, Multi-National Force Iraq (MNF-I). This change marked a transition not only in commanders but also in approach. Initially, Casey was as cautious as Sanchez in describing the situation, and Kalev Sepp criticized his August 2004 Campaign Plan as too timid:

> It was a product that seemed to be toning itself down. It was written as if there were knowledge of this bad thing, an insurgency, that was coming up underfoot, and you had to deal with it, but you had to be careful about being too direct in calling it an insurgency and dealing with it that way, because then you would be admitting that it had always been there but you had ignored it up to that point. It did not talk about what you had to do to defeat an insurgency. It was not a counterinsurgency plan.[32]

Within a few months, though, Casey recognized the problem with this approach. He enlisted Sepp (a retired Special Forces colonel and a lecturer on counterinsurgency in the Naval Postgraduate School) in September 2004 to help form a group he called "doctors without orders," a collection of officers and civilians with PhDs who were to reassess the conduct of the war and come up with an explicit counterinsurgency plan.[33] At that point, Casey had no qualms about describing the situation in Iraq as an insurgency and emphasized counterinsurgency as the way to prosecute the war. Casey later recalled: "I had two objectives. The first was to instill a philosophy of counterinsurgency. Our army was built for kinetics—shooting the enemy and winning battles. In Iraq, that wasn't the way to go. Second, we had to partner with the ambassador and the embassy, not fight with them. I gave the guidance and let the colonels write the plans and the assessments."[34] Indeed, Casey lectured each incoming battalion commander on the fact that Iraq was a counterinsurgency war and opened a "counterinsurgency academy" in Taji that he made mandatory for all incoming commanders.[35] Although the academy was mostly focused on hands-on, practical training, students there also looked at case studies of insurgencies in Malaya, Algeria, and Latin America.[36] Under Casey, the Army in Iraq began to open up to historical lessons that did not necessarily suit its self-image.

Even as it did so, Powell's lessons of Vietnam still deeply influenced Army efforts in Iraq. Casey's June 2005 Campaign Review specified the campaign's "center of gravity" as US public opinion, rather than increased security in Iraq per se.[37] His deputy, Lieutenant General Thomas Metz, declared, "[I] don't think we will put much energy into trying the old saying, 'win the hearts and minds.' I don't look at it as one of the metrics of success."[38] Certainly, conditions in Iraq and security were central to the plan, but these were framed within the larger problem of declining US domestic support for the war. The intent was to withdraw most coalition forces from Iraq by the end of 2006 by getting Iraqi security forces to take over the fighting and ensuring that Iraqi political structures were functional enough for the United States to withdraw without Iraq collapsing into chaos. Casey explained:

> The easy thing to say is, in counterinsurgency, the center of gravity must be the population. I took a little different view in saying that yes, the population is ultimately the one that has to be brought around, but it's the perception of a sovereign Iraqi Government that is more likely to bring the population around than [were] our forces. . . . Throughout this whole campaign, demonstrating to the Iraqi people that this was a sovereign Iraqi Government was critically important.[39]

Casey's worry about public opinion, both US and Iraqi, stemmed directly from a certain set of lessons from Vietnam. Remembering the political aftershocks of the 1968 Tet Offensive, he and Metz convinced the interim Iraqi government to cancel all leave for Iraq Security Forces during the January 2005 elections, lest the insurgents attempt an attention-grabbing offensive.[40]

At the same time some military and civilian leaders forgot the consequences of optimistic statements about progress from policy makers and US commanders. A Marine officer was quoted after the seizure of Fallujah saying that the US military had "broken the back of the insurgency." Vice President Dick Cheney declared in May 2005 that the insurgency was in its "last throes,"[41] and, in an even more explicit echo of Westmoreland in 1967, President Bush declared that there was "light at the end of the tunnel" in Iraq. Ironically, such optimism engendered pessimism in those who had not forgotten Vietnam. According to Bob Woodward, incoming ambassador to Iraq John Negroponte (who had served in Vietnam with CORDS) "was not surprised that the Pentagon would put out optimistic reports. It was natural. He had seen it in Vietnam. The generals and civilians would sugarcoat things, praising their people and insisting there was light at the end of the tunnel."[42] Colonel Derek Harvey was even more critical of such optimism:

> We've constantly heard that we've "reached a tipping point," or we've "broken the back of the insurgency," or we've heard things similar to "There's light at the end of the tunnel," which harkens back to Vietnam, if you will. Dates and things that are important for us—for example, getting through a transition to an Iraqi interim government—are not as important to them [the Iraqis]. Squashing the insurgents in Fallujah and eliminating the city as a sanctuary is a very important event for us, but maybe not as critical to them operationally and definitely not strategically.[43]

Such echoes of Vietnam seemed only to reinforce the urgency of a strategy that would withdraw American troops from Iraq before US domestic support for the war completely collapsed. While President George W. Bush refused to accept the analogy on the basis that it "sends the wrong message to our troops, and sends the wrong message to the enemy"[44] and promised to "stay the course" in Iraq, the US military was adopting a posture that focused on preparing American forces for withdrawal from Iraq.

IRAQIFICATION: "VIETNAMIZING" THE WAR

In 2004 through 2006, the dominant lesson of Vietnam was one of withdrawal. In an echo of "Vietnamization," "Iraqification" became the centerpiece of American strategy in Iraq.[45] Handing affairs over to Iraqis had always been US policy, from initial hopes for quick occupation in 2003, to the first references to "Iraqification," in November of that year, to Bush's June 2005 promise that

"as Iraqis stand up, we will stand down." However, this took on added importance with the 2005 campaign plan's focus on US public opinion as a "center
of gravity." "Iraqizing" the war would help bolster public support for the war
by reducing US exposure to combat and thus casualties. This policy was supported by Vietnamization's architect, Nixon's Secretary of Defense Melvyn
Laird, who argued in *Foreign Affairs* that Vietnamization could offer many
positive lessons for Iraq. Laird's view of Vietnam was unsurprisingly revisionist, claiming that he presided over a "four-year withdrawal from Vietnam that,
in retrospect, became the textbook description of how the US military should
decamp."[46] He advocated a gradual withdrawal of US troops as a sign of confidence in the Iraqis and as a means of removing fuel from the insurgency. The
National Security Council's November 2005 *National Strategy for Victory in
Iraq* echoed Laird, claiming that "as security conditions improve and as Iraqi
Security Forces become increasingly capable of securing their own country,
our forces will increasingly move out of the cities, reduce the number of bases
from which we operate, and conduct fewer patrols and convoy missions."[47]
This was essentially describing the plan that Casey was already putting into
action. Following from CENTCOM commander General John Abizaid's observation that US troops were an "antibody in Iraqi society," Casey intended
to slowly withdraw US troops from combat operations, replacing them with
Iraqis. Simultaneously, he would add ten-person advisor teams to each Iraqi
brigade in an effort to improve Iraqi combat capabilities.

The first element of this campaign plan—the slow withdrawal of US forces
from combat—led to the consolidation and expansion of huge Forward Operating Bases (or FOBs), another echo of Vietnam. Present in Iraq since the first
signs of danger to occupying American troops in the summer of 2003, these
bases became even bigger and troops more centralized under Casey. These
FOBs were "self-contained cities with basketball courts, gyms, movie theatres,
Internet connections, snack bars, pizza parlors, video games, and beds instead
of cots."[48] As in Vietnam, it appeared that resources and energy were being
poured into creature comforts, and therefore troops' exposure to Iraqi society
suffered.[49] Col. Peter Mansoor, discussing the early implementation of this
policy in 2003, argued that "although I supported the decision [to move to
larger bases], it turned out to be a double-edged sword and in retrospect, the
wrong call." Mansoor contended that "although forward operating bases en-
abled the combat team to mass combat power in surge operations, we lost con-
tinuous contact with Iraqi citizens in those parts of the zone where companies

used to live and work in smaller outposts."[50] The use of FOBs can partly be related to concerns over casualties and force protection; the imperatives of force protection in Iraq were just as prevalent as they had been throughout the 1990s. However, the focus on minimizing casualties was indicative of the continuing relevance of the lessons of Vietnam. In a war where progress was not readily evident to the American public, a continuing stream of US casualties would be especially damaging to public support for the war. Given that whatever progress US commanders were claiming in Iraq was very hard to detect, then the move to minimize these casualties, even at the expense of combat effectiveness, was unsurprising.

If Vietnamization was to be the solution to the US problem in Iraq, then the US Army soon found itself facing many of the same problems with the advisory effort as it had in Vietnam. The second part of Casey's plan was an increased emphasis on Iraqi combat capabilities, something that, hitherto, had been sorely lacking. As early as January 2004, CENTCOM had recognized that the Iraqi Security Forces (ISF) were not building capacity nearly fast enough, despite consistently optimistic prognoses from Secretary of Defense Donald Rumsfeld. The Army's official history later argued that "the inability of the ISF to take the lead in combating the insurgency in 2003 and 2004 was one of the greatest shortcomings of the overall Coalition and Iraqi campaign" and that:

> US advisors [to Iraqi forces] frequently found themselves without critical aspects of support despite operating near or with US and Coalition forces. These problems were not unprecedented and could have been foreseen. Indeed, these deficiencies in supplies and coordination would have been familiar to Soldiers and Marines who served as military advisors in Vietnam in the 1960s.[51]

The formation of a new headquarters to run the advisory effort (Multi-National Security Transition Command-Iraq or MNSTC-I) and the return of Lt. Gen. David Petraeus to Iraq had some positive effect, but deep structural and cultural problems remained. When the Army formed advisor teams for Iraq—Military Transition Teams (MiTTs)—in autumn 2005, it looked for a list of officers available to head brigade level advisory teams. This list, described by retired Colonel Kevin P. Reynolds as a "cattle call of the Army's colonels," specified only that the officer be a colonel, be from a combat arms branch, and have been back from a previous tour for at least a year.[52] Notable in their absence were proficiency in Arabic, combat experience, and experience with counterinsurgency operations. Reynolds also noted that "as with Vietnam, the priority of quality officer fill in Iraq goes to US combat units. Most officers view their chances for school selection, promotion, and command assignment as directly tied to their performance in US units leading and commanding US soldiers."[53] The advisors who did deploy received a six-week training course, but, as much of this was taken up in validating essential skills such as weapons proficiency, first aid training, and nuclear, biological, and chemical drills, most of the advisor's training for his or her role was received on the job. Indeed, many of the advisors deployed were reservists, who had fewer disincentives in terms of career progression but also needed even more predeployment training, eating into the time spent on skills specific to the advisor mission.[54] One officer who went through the training recalled, "They really didn't know what they were doing. They weren't well resourced for it either. The training was very generic . . . There were about 160 of us . . . A lot of them had no idea what they were going to do or where they were going. They had all just been identified as individual replacements."[55] These problems, which, as the Army's official history rightly argued, would have been familiar to anyone who had served as a military advisor in Vietnam, are again indicative of just how much the Army had forgotten about counterinsurgency since the end of the war in Indochina.

In this sense, the reemergence of the Vietnam analogy stemmed in large part from frustrations with how the war in Iraq was progressing. Just as the difficulties advisors encountered would have been familiar to American veterans of Vietnam, the frustrations of combat commanders also echoed the Indochina experience. Lt. Col. Ross Brown, who commanded a cavalry squadron in South Baghdad in 2005 through 2006, recalls reading Andrew Krepinevich's argument for adopting a "clear, hold, build" strategy in Iraq and attempting to implement it in his area. However, Brown was not impressed with the "hearts and minds" approach to counterinsurgency, arguing that "some [counterinsurgency] thinkers believe that civil-military projects can influence the loyalty of the people. I concluded that while the Iraqis in my AO would accept gifts, money, and projects, such perks did little to sway them to our side."[56] Similarly, Col. Ralph O. Baker, a brigade combat team leader in Baghdad in 2004 through 2005, argued that "we have all heard about 'winning hearts and minds.' I do not like this phrase, and I liked it less and less as experience taught me its impracticality. The reality is that it will be a long, long time before we can truly win the hearts and minds of Arabs in the Middle East."[57] Brown was equally pessimistic about the ability of Iraqi forces to take over, observing: "When I left Iraq, the ISF in my area were clearly incapable of providing security or conducting operations without our support and guidance. I often wondered whether they were as interested in winning the war as we were or whether they just needed a paycheck."[58]

Colonel Joseph DiSalvo commanded the 3rd Infantry Division's 2nd Brigade Combat Team in the Rasafah district of Baghdad from January 2005 to January 2006 and was deeply unimpressed with the assistance given by other agencies in the reconstruction effort. DiSalvo remembered: "This is where I sort of looked to see if the State Department had anybody who could help out. I'll just tell you: they work hard but they brought nothing to the fight. They were vastly inexperienced, not aggressive; they didn't like coming out of the Green Zone into our area, and that was disappointing."[59] This dissatisfaction with the war was all too common among Army officers. It was partly rooted in an understanding of just how difficult conducting counterinsurgency was in reality. These officers all appeared to understand the intellectual tenets of counterinsurgency doctrine but were also deeply conscious of the challenges inherent in its practice.

Throughout 2005 and 2006, the ghosts of Vietnam in Iraq became ever more visible, both for soldiers serving there and for outside commentators.[60] The Army was retreating into vast "super-FOBs" that recalled Vietnam-era excess, while "Iraqification" revealed commanders' frustrations with both the ability and motivations of their Iraqi counterparts and with the difficulty of an underresourced advisor mission. However, such dissatisfaction with the way the war was progressing also meant that the Army's previous lessons of Vietnam, which had little to say about how to conduct counterinsurgency, were beginning to lose their force. While Vietnamization offered one potential way to reinterpret the Vietnam experience in a way that was useful to the situation the Army found itself in Vietnam, its ultimate past failure offered little guidance to US commanders and advisors seeking to transition their sectors to Iraqi government control.

COUNTERINSURGENCY INNOVATIONS IN 2003–2006

If Vietnamization was only a partially useful analogy for the Army in Iraq, then there was also tension over the usefulness of classic counterinsurgency as a guiding concept for commanders. Lt. Col. Gian Gentile, later one of the few prominent dissenters to the growing dominance of counterinsurgency within the Army, strongly objected to the notion that the US Army in Iraq of 2003 through 2006 somehow did not "get" counterinsurgency and was repeating the same mistakes as they had made in Vietnam. Gentile argued:

> When I was in Tikrit . . . in mid-2003, my unit was already executing coun-terinsurgency operations, rebuilding the area's economic infrastructure, re-storing essential services, and establishing governance projects. When I was training my cavalry squadron a year later, we focused nearly exclusively on counterinsurgency.[61]

As noted earlier, many commanders expressed skepticism that Iraqi "hearts and minds" could be so easily won and some, such as Lt. Col. Gentile, were still supportive of combat operations as the most effective way to win against an insurgency. Gentile recalled:

> The high points for my squadron in 2006 were when we achieved tactical suc-cess by conducting a small ambush team operation that resulted in killing either Shiite militia or Sunni insurgents who demonstrated hostile acts or intent. Those times were few, but they meant a lot and they guaranteed, at least for a time, the regaining of the initiative and increased morale among my soldiers.[62]

Gentile's reaction to "nonkinetic" approaches, which later became part of his broader critique of counterinsurgency doctrine, illustrates the continuing tensions between different cultures within the US Army. Some units still dis-played a strong cultural preference for conventional operations, even in what General Casey and others recognized as a counterinsurgency campaign. Col. Michael D. Steele—who, as a captain, commanded US Army Rangers in the "Black Hawk Down" battle in Mogadishu in 1993—exemplified this approach. Steele, whose 3rd Brigade Combat Team of the 101st Airborne Division de-ployed to Samarra in 2006, told his commanders that his intent was to "kill insurgents and focus on bringing every soldier home." While forming up for deployment, he refused "to waste precious collective training time" on non-kinetic stability and support operations and promised a specially made coin to each soldier that killed an insurgent on operations.[63] This approach meant large-scale air assaults such as Operation Swarmer in Samarra in March 2006[64] and led to the deaths of four unarmed Iraqi men in a May 2006 raid.[65] Steele's approach to counterinsurgency, which so strongly resembled that of Lt. Col. Nathan Sassaman in 2004, was all the more surprising, given how late in the war it occurred. While Sassaman made his mistakes in an early phase of the war, Steele served his tour in Iraq long after the Army as a whole had begun to recognize the importance of population-centric counterinsurgency. That a brigade of the 101st Airborne, which had effectively pacified Mosul under Maj. Gen. David Petraeus in 2003, could operate in such a way in 2006 speaks to the abiding strength of the Army's cultural preference for overwhelming force. Steele's aggressiveness was a product of the thirty years the post-Vietnam Army had spent emphasizing conventional operations and the destruction of the enemy.

While Steele's actions were rooted in the Army's culture of firepower, the evident shortcomings of such tactics when applied to Iraq led to an increased willingness to revisit the lessons of Vietnam and assumptions about counterinsurgency. Zalmay Khalilzad, Negroponte's replacement as ambassador in Baghdad, invited Andrew Krepinevich, a strong advocate of "doing better" at counterinsurgency in Vietnam, to advise him on the war effort,[66] which resulted in the publication of this advice as a *Foreign Affairs* article entitled "How to Win in Iraq."[67] He advocated an "oil spot" strategy of slowly extending security from key areas to the whole of Iraq, something that, according to Krepinevich, should have been done in Vietnam but never was. Similarly, the US Army Center of Military History sent General Casey's headquarters "a number of papers on CORDS . . . in the hope that they'll fall on fertile ground."[68] Kalev Sepp endorsed this approach, telling Casey that he should follow Creighton Abrams's example from Vietnam and merge the civilian and military elements of the campaign under his own direction[69] (betraying a flawed understanding of the history of Vietnam, as CORDS was actually set up under Westmoreland, not Abrams). Meanwhile John Nagl's *Learning to Eat Soup with a Knife: Counterinsurgency Lessons from Malaya and Vietnam*,[70] which heavily critiqued US methods in Vietnam while praising the British approach in Malaya, became popular reading for officers deploying to Iraq. Army Chief of Staff General Peter Schoomaker echoed Nagl's views in his foreword to the paperback edition of *Learning to Eat Soup with a Knife*:

> The US Army [in Vietnam], predisposed to fight a conventional enemy that fought using conventional tactics, overpowered innovative ideas from within the Army and from outside it. As a result, the US Army was not as effective at learning as it should have been, and its failures in Vietnam had grave implications for both the Army and the nation.[71]

Schoomaker's endorsement of Nagl's critique demonstrated a growing acceptance within the Army of that revisionist strand of Vietnam history that emphasized how much better the United States could have done there, if only it had applied counterinsurgency doctrine properly.[72] Schoomaker also gave a copy of Nagl's work to Gen. George Casey before he deployed to Iraq.[73]

These developments, although disparate, all suggested that Vietnam did have lessons to offer on how to deal with the insurgency itself, rather than just public perceptions about the war. However, not all counterinsurgency innovation stemmed from old ideas; there were some new measures and new approaches in the Casey era. Firstly, the Commander's Emergency Response Program (or CERP) offered commanders a way to get funding to important reconstruction projects without having to go through peacetime bureaucratic procedures. Petraeus observed that, during the invasion of Iraq, he could expend a $500,000 missile with just a call on the radio, whereas getting money for reconstruction projects, at least in the early stages of the occupation, required mountains of paperwork and red tape. CERP, initially using funds captured from Saddam and later funded by the United States, offered commanders an effective means to undertake projects in their areas.[74] In a war where "money is ammunition," such an innovation was useful in aiding operations. CERP was predicated on the idea that "good governance" could in itself enhance security in a way that raids and checkpoints could not.

Similarly, Gen. Peter Chiarelli, who commanded the 1st Cavalry Division in Baghdad throughout 2004 (and later commanded Multinational Corps-Iraq, effectively taking operational command of all coalition forces in Iraq), took a similar approach to counterinsurgency, arguing:

> It is no longer sufficient to think in purely kinetic terms. Executing traditionally focused combat operations and concentrating on training local security forces works, but only for the short term. In the long term, doing so hinders true progress and, in reality, promotes the growth of insurgent forces working against campaign objectives. It is a lopsided approach.[75]

Chiarelli mapped violence in Sadr City and found that it directly correlated with those areas where services were poorest. His solution was SWET (sewage, water, electricity, trash) teams, who helped restore essential services to neighborhoods in the hope that it would induce cooperation from the residents of Sadr City. Chiarelli believed that emphasizing physical security before projects, economic incentives, and governance was a wrong-headed approach.

Col. Robert Abrams (the son of General Creighton Abrams) went further than Chiarelli and envisioned economic support as a sort of artillery support for counterinsurgency. Abrams described how his unit "would focus non-lethal fires in the form of money to help get that place better and then we would reap the non-lethal effects from it, versus having to go in there and conduct kinetic operations and just kill everybody."[76] These innovative approaches were rooted in the experiences of the 1990s as much as in the lessons of Vietnam. Between its lived experience of peacekeeping in the Balkans and an emerging discourse on what lessons the Army should have drawn from the Vietnam experience (see Chapter 7), new approaches emerged.

THE INSTITUTION REACTS

Much of the change in approach in Iraq was coming from the bottom up, with colonels and majors adapting their tactics to local circumstances. However, the US Army's doctrine, education, and personnel systems were also reacting to the challenges of counterinsurgency, if slowly. Vice Chief of Staff of the Army General Richard A. Cody issued a memorandum that the advisor mission—key in counterinsurgency campaigns—was the most important one the Army had and that it should be resourced accordingly. According to Petraeus, "The idea is to professionally reward them for doing this, and not do what, in some cases, we did in Vietnam, which was send the message that advising was not an important assignment. We certainly don't want that kind of impression created."[77] This meant giving those who served as advisors for foreign forces in counterinsurgency campaigns as much credit as those who commanded US combat forces when it came to promotions. This innovation of changing the personnel system to facilitate focus on counterinsurgency was an indication that what had previously been a strong institutional bias against such missions was beginning to change.

The Army's training centers also adapted to the new mission. Whereas units deploying to Iraq in 2003 and 2004 trained for high-intensity conflict before deploying, by 2005–2006 the emphasis in predeployment training had fundamentally shifted. The National Training Center at Fort Irwin, California—which had been set up to train units for conventional, mechanized warfare and as a means of testing doctrinal concepts for AirLand Battle—now emphasized counterinsurgency. According to its director, Brigadier General Robert W. Cone, training at the NTC now placed "more emphasis on full-spectrum combat operations, especially counterinsurgency training involving both kinetic and non-kinetic means. Cultural awareness training is a central feature of all phases of the rotation."[78] The NTC constructed thirteen different towns and villages across its training area and populated them with 1,600 role players, including 250 Iraqi-Americans. The NTC also attempted to reconstruct the complexity of operations in Iraq. According to Cone, "Each role player is influenced by respective tribal and religious leaders and maintains familial, social, and business relationships throughout the rotation. Some role players have businesses and jobs; others are unemployed and disenfranchised, ripe for insurgent recruitment."[79] However, while such training was undoubtedly necessary, it still was not sufficient. US forces heading to Vietnam had also trained in clearing "villages" and interacting with "Asian peasants" before deployment, but it took a lot more to shift the Army's culture.[80]

For instance, the Army's education system appeared to be slower to change. Given that the service schools' mission was not overwhelmingly focused on current contingencies, as the training centers were, it is not surprising that this would be so. A study of the US Army War College's 2006 and 2007 curricula by retired Colonel Kevin P. Reynolds found that counterinsurgency, either as the subject or a major subsection, appeared in only eight lessons in the core curriculum, or only 4.8 percent of the hours in that curriculum, and that only 6.2 percent of all courses offered formally addressed counterinsurgency. Furthermore, of the ninety elective offerings to students in the 2007 academic year, only two of those directly addressed counterinsurgency. These meant that only thirty to forty students out of a student body of 350 would benefit from these courses. Adding the elective courses to the core curriculum, the number of hours dedicated to counterinsurgency in the total curriculum totaled only 0.5 percent of all hours.[81] Reynolds argued, "It appears that the Army War College is devoting a relatively small amount of its curriculum to the study of a type of warfare that for the past four years has taken up nearly 100 percent of the Army's resources, energy, and effort."[82] Although the War College was the pinnacle of Army education and had been a source of criticism for Rumsfeld's ideas on transformation, it appeared to be disconnected from the problems and challenges of contemporary operations, an indication of just how strong the fixation with conventional operations had been. That the school that trained the Army's future generals was downplaying the importance of counterinsurgency at a time when the Army was completely immersed in counterinsurgency operations in Iraq, demonstrated how deeply William DePuy's 1970s efforts to move the Army away from its Vietnam experience had embedded themselves in the Army's organizational culture.

While the service schools' reluctance to address counterinsurgency indicated a continuing hesitation to include these types of operations as central to the Army's role, the publication of a new interim Field Manual on counterinsurgency[83] illustrated both changing attitudes and the immense gulf in experience in and understanding of counterinsurgency that had opened up since Vietnam. Its predecessor had been published in 1985;[84] in the interim the Army had gone through three different operational-level doctrines.[85] Indeed, some of FMI 3-07.22 *Counterinsurgency Operations* assumptions seemed at least partially to be relics of the Vietnam era. The authors described the archetypal insurgency as a Maoist three-stage strategy that would construct a mass movement and then go to eventually overwhelm the government in a final, strategic offensive.[86] The manual argued that virtually all insurgencies, from communist to Islamic, tended to adopt this model due to its simplicity, logic, and emphasis on mass mobilization. Similarly, it emphasized the importance of the insurgency setting up a clandestine infrastructure as an alternative to the state: a "counterstate."[87] At the same time, the manual's authors did not spend as much time exploring events in Iraq that indicated that contemporary insurgencies operated in more complex ways, with disparate groups alternatively cooperating and competing. While the reintroduction of counterinsurgency into Army doctrine, even in an interim form, was a major change, the manual did not move beyond Vietnam-era understandings of the concept.

The authors also critiqued the Army's way of war in a way that recalled similar complaints from dissident officers in Vietnam:

> The American way of war has been to substitute firepower for manpower. As a result, US forces have frequently resorted to firepower in the form of artillery or air any time they make contact. This creates two negatives in a counterinsurgency. First, massive firepower causes collateral damage, thereby frequently driving the locals into the arms of the insurgents. Second, it allows insurgents to break contact after having inflicted casualties on friendly forces. A more effective method is to attack with ground forces to gain and maintain contact, with the goal of completely destroying the insurgent force.[88]

Despite this emphasis on destroying insurgents, the authors also recognized that "in planning counterinsurgency operations, it is imperative that leaders and Soldiers understand that military force is not an end in itself, but is just one of the instruments of national power employed by the political leadership to achieve its broader objectives."[89] However, as David Ucko has pointed out, the manual very much focused on strictly military tasks, while assuming that the problems of governance and basic services would be the prerogative of other agencies.[90]

There were further models from Vietnam in the manual: Abrams-style "clear and hold" operations were discussed in some detail, and even population relocation was seen as a viable, if undesirable, method of combating the insurgency. Interestingly, the manual, unlike most post-Vietnam doctrine, was open to counterinsurgency campaigns conducted by conventional US forces. It stated:

> When supporting a counterinsurgency, the US and its multinational partners assist the H[ost] N[ation] in implementing a sustainable approach. To the extent the HN has its basic institutions and security forces intact, the burden upon US and multinational forces and resources is lessened. To the extent the HN is lacking basic institutions and functions, the burden upon the US and multinational forces is increased.[91]

The post-Vietnam emphasis on the Army's supporting role in any counterinsurgency had now disappeared. The weight of the "burden" on US forces now depended almost entirely on the existing strength of the host nation. The interim field manual, unlike earlier iterations, made no assumptions about the likelihood or otherwise of US intervention in counterinsurgencies. The caution that had characterized such doctrine in the post-Vietnam era was now gone. However, what remained was a characterization of insurgency and counterinsurgency that was firmly rooted in the 1960s or even the 1950s. The manual was the clearest doctrinal signal yet of the return of Vietnam and counterinsurgency to the Army's consciousness, something that would be built on in the years to come.

CONCLUSION

The Army's performance in Iraq from 2003 to 2006 remains difficult to characterize. While there were certainly some positive elements, such as the early, improvised adaption in terms of retasking artillery units for military police duty, the use of the Commander's Emergency Response Fund, and the innovation of SWET teams to help improve quality of life in urban slums, overall a catalogue of errors and problems undermined the Army's mission. Units found it extremely difficult to exert control over Iraqi cities, most notably Fallujah, Ramadi, and Samarra, but the list included many more urban centers and large swaths of Baghdad. Troops were restricted to missions from large FOBs that made them insensitive to local conditions and security, and the effort to train, equip, and advise Iraqi security forces met with patchy success, at best. The results of this failure were disturbing: an intensifying Sunni insurgency, a looming Sunni–Shia civil war, as well as numerous intra-Sunni and intra-Shia conflicts.

These difficulties stemmed in a large part from circumstance but also from a dearth of understanding about counterinsurgency in the Army. The Army was not ready to carry out counterinsurgency operations in Iraq in the summer of 2003, and the occupation was characterized by intense struggle with the imperatives of counterinsurgency. Similarly, the Army struggled with the lessons of Vietnam in this period. While initially, the relevance of the Vietnam analogy was rejected by Ambassador L. Paul Bremer and did not feature in Army discourse, the problems of Iraq led to a return of Vietnam as both analogy and lesson. Initially, the dominant lesson was that the sensitivity of public opinion created a need to tailor Army operations to minimize casualties; later there was an exploration of how Vietnam could provide lessons for the orderly withdrawal of the United States from Iraq. However, all the while, there was a certain tension between lessons that emphasized minimizing casualties and withdrawal and those that emphasized the importance of counterinsurgency in its most activist sense. Over the four years following the invasion of Iraq, there was a gradual but perceptible shift among the officer corps toward accepting the latter set of lessons. However, this understanding of Vietnam and counterinsurgency was not yet institutionalized. For that to happen, there would need to be a significant shift in fortunes in Iraq and strong sponsorship of these new lessons from within the Army's doctrinal and educational establishment.

7 THE RETURN TO COUNTERINSURGENCY:
FM 3-24 AND THE "SURGE"

THE EVENTS OF 2006 TO 2008 marked a profound shift in both how the Army understood Vietnam and how it approached counterinsurgency, although this shift had already begun in the earlier years of the war in Iraq. In many ways, the prospect of failure in Iraq had dislocated many of the Army's core assumptions about how war was fought and the pertinence of their previously agreed-on lessons of Vietnam. Now the Army's challenge was to make sense of Vietnam again in light of its experiences in Iraq and to reevaluate the place of counterinsurgency in its doctrine.

This reevaluation and reimagining took place in two arenas: on the ground in Iraq and in the United States as the Army attempted to formulate a new doctrine to deal with the unexpected challenges the Army faced. Much of the innovation on counterinsurgency came from relatively junior officers in the field. Their experience of insurgency in Iraq in 2003 through 2006 disabused them of respect for the Army's traditional focus on conventional operations. Vietnam also heavily influenced these officers' perceptions of counterinsurgency, in the sense that they were consciously struggling to avoid the mistakes of that war and were deeply aware of the relevance of the Vietnam analogy for Iraq. They felt an intense pressure neither to let Iraq become "another Vietnam" nor to follow the example of the Vietnam-era officer corps who had not only lost that war but almost lost their army with it.

THREE COLONELS

In many ways, the evolution of counterinsurgency in Iraq can be attributed not to doctrinal innovation from above but to ad-hoc action on the part of midranking officers, such as commanders of brigades and battalions. This is not to say that these actions contradicted higher strategy; these officers were as successful as they were because they received backing from higher head-quarters. Despite this support, it is clear that the imperative to change the Army's attitudes toward counterinsurgency came from the field in Iraq. As James Russell has argued, various units and leaders adapted to their environ-ment and introduced tactical innovations to cope with the demands of the insurgency.[1] As we saw in Chapter 6, discussing the Army of 2003 through 2006, the Army began to slowly reconsider its lessons of Vietnam and its focus on conventional warfare.

Dissident officers in Iraq accelerated this process by putting into practice their own understanding of counterinsurgency, which was inevitably influ-enced by their understanding of the lessons of Vietnam. These officers, in-cluding H. R. McMaster, Sean MacFarland, and Paul Yingling, were among the Army's brightest colonels: All three challenged or subverted prevailing assumptions about the war in Iraq. McMaster did so by conducting a deliber-ate, classic counterinsurgency campaign in Tal Afar; MacFarland by collabo-rating with local forces at the expense of central government; and Yingling by directly challenging the Army's senior leaders on their incompetence. All three were heavily influenced by lessons of Vietnam that stressed the need to be honest with superior officers and politicians, the need to stick with and cultivate local allies, and, above all, the need to follow classic precepts of counterinsurgency.

Col. H. R. McMaster, who led the 3rd Armored Cavalry Regiment into Tal Afar in the summer of 2005, was an unusual officer in that he was also a published, widely read historian. His 1997 book *Dereliction of Duty: Johnson, McNamara, the Joint Chiefs of Staff, and the Lies That Led to Vietnam* heavily criticized the Joint Chiefs for their failure to advise Johnson against interven-tion in Vietnam (see Chapter 4 for discussion of its contemporary impact). In many ways, McMaster's work had become the US Army's primer for les-sons from Vietnam in 2005 in a way that Harry Summers's *On Strategy* had been fifteen years earlier.[2] McMaster's argument centered on the importance of offering unflinchingly honest advice to civilian policy makers; the Joint Chiefs had failed in their duty because they had failed to demur as Johnson and McNamara committed grave errors in strategy. McMaster's historical training informed his preparations for deployment to Iraq; before deploy-ing, he drew up a counterinsurgency reading list for his officers that included

T. E. Lawrence's *Seven Pillars of Wisdom* and Nagl's *Learning to Eat Soup with a Knife*[3] and sent a number of his soldiers to a local community college for a basic Arabic course.[4] His actions on deployment to Tal Afar reflected this preparation, as his tactics largely reflected classic counterinsurgency precepts, with emphasis on methodically clearing an area of insurgents and then holding it by setting up platoon-sized security stations.

Tal Afar resembled the Fallujah of August through November 2004 in many ways: It was controlled by insurgents, and, as Fallujah had done for Baghdad, it served as a base of operations for insurgent attacks in Mosul; with 150,000 residents, it was only slightly smaller than the Anbar city. However, McMaster's retaking of the city was much less conventional than Operation "Phantom Fury," the Army–Marine assault on Fallujah in November 2004. First, he constructed a dirt barrier around the city in July 2005 to restrict the movement of the population and conducted reconnaissance to understand the tribal, ethnic, and sectarian dynamics of the city before US troops moved into the city methodically in September, setting up patrol bases in neighborhoods that they cleared. The 3rd ACR established twenty-nine such bases across Tal Afar, from which US and Iraqi troops patrolled the city. McMaster also attempted to differentiate between Sunni nationalists and Islamist extremists, a distinction that he felt "in the war's first year or two, American soldiers were rarely able to make; they were simply fighting 'bad guys.'"[5]

However, to characterize the 3rd Armored Cavalry Regiment's operations in Tal Afar as primarily focused on soft power would be incorrect. Violence formed a core part of the counterinsurgency tactics. McMaster later recalled:

> We had some initial actions against the enemy which were devastating to the enemy. [We] were killing 30, 40, 50 of the enemy at a time. I think that helped us; people thanked us for that. Intelligence came in at a much higher level after those very sharp engagements with the enemy within the city . . . With the intelligence we were receiving, we could conduct very precise offensive operations to capture them. We had people who were willing to come forward and tell us exactly what these people did and to testify against them in court, because people were really desperate to return to normalcy and to bring security to the city and to their children.[6]

This deliberate, population security–driven approach, combined with brutal and targeted force, had impressive results. McMaster's success at counterinsurgency was a result not of minimizing or obscuring the use of force but, rather, of restoring its utility. Tal Afar in many ways represented a breakthrough in that it showed that military operations, if couched in a broader cultural, political, and economic strategy, could in fact quell insurgent violence in Iraq. This breakthrough was not long in being publicized. The journalist George Packer published a piece in the *New Yorker* explaining the "lesson of Tal Afar" and arguing that "the Americans' achievement in Tal Afar showed that, in the war's third year, individuals and units within the Army could learn and adapt on their own." Packer also argued that "the soldiers who worked to secure Tal Afar were, in a sense, rebels against an incoherent strategy that has brought the American project in Iraq to the brink of defeat."[7] While the soldiers of Tal Afar may have rebelled against existing strategy, they quickly became its future. Secretary of State Condoleezza Rice presented it as an example of the "clear, hold, and build strategy" she was advocating,[8] while President George W. Bush dedicated an entire speech to it.[9] Most important, from the Army's point of view, the writers of the new counterinsurgency field manual used Tal Afar to demonstrate how to execute counterinsurgency operations. Consequently, Tal Afar became an important part of the counterinsurgency narrative. In many ways, the retaking of Tal Afar represented a contemporary version of the counterinsurgency lessons of Vietnam: partnering with local forces, deep and sophisticated understanding of local conditions, and a deliberate, methodical approach to clearing the city that was rooted in the need to protect the population rather than destroy the enemy.

If Tal Afar was central to the construction of a new counterinsurgency doctrine, events in Ramadi were central to the development of a new counterinsurgency *strategy* in Iraq. The 1st Brigade, 1st Armored Division, led by Col. Sean MacFarland, relieved McMaster's 3rd Armored Cavalry Regiment in Tal Afar in March 2006. MacFarland continued to follow McMaster's tactics in Tal Afar but was then ordered to retake Ramadi, the provincial capital of Anbar province in June 2006. Instructed by General Casey and Multi-National Corp-Iraq (MNC-I) commander, General Peter Chiarelli to "fix Ramadi, but don't do a Fallujah,"[10] MacFarland redeployed the bulk of his force, reinforced by Marines, to the city. MacFarland later recalled that, similarly to McMaster:

> We intended to take the city and its environs back one neighborhood at a time by establishing combat outposts and developing a police force in the secured neighborhoods. The plan called for simultaneously engaging local leaders in an attempt to find those who had influence, or "wasta," and to get their sup-

port. We recognized this as a critical part of the plan, because without their help, we would not be able to recruit enough police to take back the entire city.[11]

It was this engagement with local leaders that, through a combination of luck, local disaffection with al-Qaeda, and a willingness to take risks on the part of the US commanders, was the most revolutionary aspect of MacFarland's plan. In his planning, MacFarland distinguished between Al-Qaeda militants and local insurgents, aiming to co-opt rather than fight local insurgents.[12] With American help (in the form of weapons, money, and communications equipment), local sheikhs turned against al-Qaeda and turned the province from an insurgent stronghold to a remarkably peaceful region, albeit one barely under central government control. This "Anbar Awakening" later became a key part of US strategy in Iraq, with the success being duplicated throughout Sunni areas, in Baghdad in particular.[13] For MacFarland, the lesson of Ramadi was that "the tribes represent the people of Iraq, and the populace represents the 'key terrain' of the conflict," and any worries about the provenance of some of these forces would have to be put aside:

> That indigenous forces are the key to winning a counterinsurgency fight and you have to accept them for what they are and not be put off by the fact that they are not like us and don't operate just like us. You know, over there, a lot of their leaders are not necessarily the most savory characters; but, you can trust them for what it is that you are asking them to do as long as you understand and you don't ask them to do more than necessary and you are able to deliver on everything that you say that you are going to. You know, we always ask ourselves, "Well, are they worthy allies?" Well, you know, we need to ask ourselves that same question and I would argue that we had not been worthy allies up until that point and, certainly, our history requires a bit of a leap of faith for anybody who wants to align with the United States. Anybody who watched our experience in Vietnam kind of has to really swallow hard when we say, "Don't worry. We are not going to leave you behind."[14]

Evidently, some of his allies in Iraq shared that view; speaking of Sheikh Abdul al-Sattar, the leader of the "Anbar Awakening," MacFarland said, "The negative example he [al-Sattar] cites is Vietnam. He says, yeah, so, Vietnam beat the Americans, and what did it get them? You know, 30 years later, they're still living in poverty."[15] Despite the fact that the Vietnam War had ended more than three decades ago, its varying lessons still reverberated in a corner of Western Iraq in the summer of 2006.

For Lt. Col. Paul Yingling, who had served with McMaster's 3rd Armored Cavalry Regiment in Tal Afar, Vietnam was also relevant. An artillery officer, Yingling made his dissatisfaction with the way in which the Army was handling the war in Iraq known on his return from his tour with 3rd ACR. Yingling's target was the institutional Army, which had both failed to prepare its troops for counterinsurgency and refused to take responsibility for its failures. Interestingly, the Vietnam that animated Yingling's concern was the same as that described by his regimental commander, McMaster. In a May 2007 essay entitled "A Failure of Generalship" in *Armed Forces Journal*, Yingling was heavily critical of the Army's general officer corps. Yingling argued that "the intellectual and moral failures common to America's general officer corps in Vietnam and Iraq constitute a crisis in American generalship" and that "as matters stand now, a private who loses a rifle suffers far greater consequences than a general who loses a war." For Yingling, the lessons of Vietnam were a mix of those of H. R. McMaster and Andrew Krepinevich. Yingling charged that:

> America's generals have repeated the mistakes of Vietnam in Iraq. First, throughout the 1990s our generals failed to envision the conditions of future combat and prepare their forces accordingly. Second, America's generals failed to estimate correctly both the means and the ways necessary to achieve the aims of policy prior to beginning the war in Iraq. Finally, America's generals did not provide Congress and the public with an accurate assessment of the conflict in Iraq.[16]

To Yingling's mind, the senior officers of his era were just as culpable as the Joint Chiefs of Staff of 1965 in their dereliction of duty. By failing to learn from Vietnam, they were in danger of repeating it. Like many US Army officers who had served in Iraq, he was unimpressed with the training he received prior to deployment. In a postdeployment debriefing interview he argued:

> I've now had two combat tours where I was involved in developing ISF [Iraqi Security Forces] and I've been to every Army school you can go to as an officer, and no one has ever talked to me about that challenge. No one has ever given me any classes on how to do that . . . The institutional Army . . . has not caught up in either professional education or organizational design with the challenges of counterinsurgency.[17]

Yingling's central point was that this attitude toward counterinsurgency on the part of the institutional army was inadequate: "Waiting until we get there to understand that those are the problems we have to solve creates a lot of heartache. Our task as senior leaders is to anticipate those challenges and train for them before we have to go fight." In essence, this was a call to reform the Army to make it better equipped to conduct counterinsurgency campaigns, so that commanders like McMaster and MacFarland would not be reliant on their own readings of history to formulate a workable approach.

Yingling's criticisms provoked some reflection on the part of the institutional Army, with his article being widely distributed in the officer corps; Yingling was invited to speak at the Command and General Staff College.[18] While some generals reacted badly to Yingling's criticisms, others, such as Peter Chiarelli and David Petraeus, accepted the Vietnam analogy and the broader indictment of the Army's efforts. Yingling's invocation of Vietnam served to make these generals even more aware of their responsibility to the Army to avoid the fate of their predecessors in Vietnam and to preserve the Army from the destruction that followed defeat in Indochina.[19]

THE NEW LESSONS OF VIETNAM

As Vietnam influenced colonels in the field, it became increasingly important in the Army's public discourse about counterinsurgency. One of the primary early venues for this reevaluation of the lessons of Vietnam was the Army's Combined Arms Center, which held a series of annual conferences on subjects pertinent to contemporary challenges. At the 2006 conference, Richard Stewart of the Army's Center for Military History argued:

> Our involvement in pacification and counterinsurgency activities in Vietnam should . . . provide us a wealth of experience that we can use today as we face similar problems in Reconstruction and Stabilization activities, and yet, with a few notable exceptions, Vietnam is only slowly being examined for lessons, good or bad.[20]

Even as Stewart published those remarks, they were becoming redundant; in 2004 through 2006, the pages of *Military Review*, the Army's professional journal, saw a major upswing of articles about Vietnam,[21] and the Combat Studies Institute's annual military history symposium featured multiple presentations of lessons from Vietnam.[22] The discussion featured contributions from professional military historians and displayed a remarkably strong consensus on the lessons of Vietnam. The debate about whether to commit troops to counterinsurgency campaigns was at this point redundant, and so contributors emphasized the need for the Army to learn counterinsurgency and focus its efforts on the security of the population of the "host country." Authors used Vietnam to highlight the importance of interagency unity of effort (seen in such programs as CORDS), concepts of small unit tactics and mentoring of local forces based on the Marine Corps' Combined Action Platoons (CAPs), and, above all else, the importance of "clear and hold" operations. Writing in the Army War College's journal *Parameters*, Lt. Col. Robert Cassidy argued that "the lessons of these programs are relevant today. Improving the quantity and capabilities of indigenous forces, establishing an integrated and unified civil–military approach, and increasing the security of the population continue to be central goals in Afghanistan and Iraq." In *Military Review*, Kalev Sepp, offering some practices in Vietnam that might be useful in Iraq, wrote that "over time, the Americans improved their counterinsurgency practices in Vietnam, which resulted in viable combined and interagency efforts."[23]

The lessons also filtered outside the pages of military journals. Sepp was at that time serving as counterinsurgency advisor to General George Casey in Iraq[24] and was able to transmit his thoughts on the lessons of Vietnam directly to Casey. Cassidy had the chance to help apply these lessons of Vietnam when, through participation in lessons-learned conferences on Iraq, he helped draft Department of Defense (DoD) Directive 3000.5, "Stability Operations," which mandated that "it is DoD policy that stability operations are a core US military mission that the Department of Defense shall be prepared to conduct and support. They shall be given priority comparable to combat operations and be explicitly addressed and integrated across all DoD activities."[25] This directive, which went beyond anything seen during the 1980s interest in low-intensity conflict and the 1990s focus on peacekeeping, marked, in many ways, a return to the high point of the popularity of counterinsurgency in Vietnam. This time, however, the enthusiasm for counterinsurgency was not coming from outside the military, from the Kennedy White House, but from advocates within the Army.

If these new lessons of Vietnam meant a focus on the tactical, they also meant a reconstruction of the history of that war, a reimagining that made the past more useful for the purposes of the present. The argument that American tactics in Vietnam had improved as the war wore on, was a popular one, as many promoted the concept of "clear, hold, and build"—closely associated with the man who succeeded William Westmoreland in Vietnam, General Creighton Abrams.[26] Advocates of replicating Abrams-style counterinsurgency in Iraq, such as Lewis Sorley and Andrew Krepinevich, addressed the 2005 Combat Studies Institute Symposium. According to these historians, the lesson of Vietnam was that the war could have been won had the United States adopted such tactics earlier or had US public support held out post-1968 when—according to Sorley—the war was actually being won. If the acceptance of lessons that emphasized population security and counterinsurgency good practice was beginning to become more widespread, then the popularity Sorley's work was, in many ways, an indicator of just how well established those lessons were becoming. Robert Cassidy's writings on the lessons of Vietnam offer a succinct summary of the emerging new narrative:

> Abrams' unified strategy to clear and hold the countryside by pacifying and securing the population met with much success . . . The Special Forces' experiences in organizing Civilian Irregular Defense Groups (CIDG), the Combined Action Program (CAP), and Abrams' expansion of the Civil Operations and Revolutionary (later Rural) Development and Support (CORDS) pacification effort offer valuable lessons for current and future counterinsurgency operations.[27]

One of Secretary of State Condoleezza Rice's aides used Sorley's book *A Better War* as a source for drafting the White House's "National Strategy for Victory in Iraq."[28] General John Abizaid, head of CENTCOM, also read Sorley in his spare time.[29] General David Petraeus, then head of the Combined Arms Center in Fort Leavenworth, described Sorley "as probably, at this point in time, I think the leading scholar" of Vietnam military history.[30] Reacting to Sorley's talk at the CSI conference, Petraeus commented:

> I must say, I was sort of struck . . . you know, over time in Iraq, folks have continually asked, you know, "Is Iraq Vietnam?" And of course, the stock answer is, "Of course it's not Vietnam." . . . We all know that every case is unique and contextual and all the rest of that. Nonetheless . . . it is very, very interesting how many sort of key ideas are common to both situations.[31]

While it is important to contextualize these remarks in that they were those of a host thanking a guest speaker, and therefore more effusive than they might otherwise have been, they were still indicative of a broad acceptance of Lewis

Sorley's narrative of Vietnam as educational and worthy of note. Sorley's lessons offered the comforting thought that the Army *could* achieve victory, even in the most difficult circumstances, if only it approached the problem correctly.

Petraeus, however, who was instrumental both in the drafting of the new counterinsurgency field manual and in the shift in strategy in Iraq in 2007, had more than a passing acquaintance of the history and lessons of the Vietnam War. He had read much of the orthodox historiography on Vietnam, including David Halberstam's *The Best and the Brightest*, Bernard Fall's *Street without Joy*, and Neil Sheehan's *A Bright Shining Lie*, which, for him, "seemed to put a sort of punctuation mark on the whole scholarship."[32] Most importantly, he had written his 1987 doctoral thesis on "The American Military and the Lessons of Vietnam" and had closely studied the post-Vietnam military's aversion to intervention.[33] Petraeus broadly understood and supported such caution, but he worried about potential negative effects on counterinsurgency capabilities:

> Counterinsurgency operations, in particular, require close political–military integration. Unfortunately, this requirement runs counter to the traditional military desire, reaffirmed in the lessons of Vietnam, to operate autonomously and resist political meddling and micromanagement in operational concerns. Though most military officers quote flawlessly Clausewitz' dictum that war is a continuation of politics by other means—many do not appear to accept fully the implications of his logic.[34]

Furthermore, Petraeus recognized that this meant that "American involvement in counterinsurgencies is almost universally regarded as more likely than in most other types of combat—more likely, for example, than involvement in high intensity conflict on the plains of NATO's Central Region."[35] Petraeus was concerned the military's determination to ignore counterinsurgency obscured the fact that "Presidents may commit the United States to involvement in a conflict whether optimum forces exist or not." In many ways, this was the key flaw in the Army's adoption of the Powell Doctrine as its core lesson of Vietnam. When George W. Bush disregarded Powell's caution and invaded Iraq in 2003, the Army became entangled in counterinsurgency by default and lacked a backup plan. Petraeus saw the paradox this created for military leaders:

The senior military thus find themselves in a dilemma. The lessons taken from Vietnam would indicate that, in general, involvement in a counterinsurgency should be avoided. But prudent preparations for a likely contingency (and a general inclination against limiting a president's options) led the military to recognize that significant emphasis should be given to counterinsurgency forces, equipment, and doctrine. Military leaders are thereby in the difficult position of arguing for the creation of more forces suitable for such conflicts, while simultaneously realizing they may advise against the use of those forces unless very specific circumstances hold.[36]

As we have seen in earlier chapters, the paradox was essentially resolved in favor of not creating forces suitable for such conflicts and letting institutional memory on counterinsurgency lapse. The flurry of interest on Vietnam, however, represented a concerted attempt to reverse that trend. The prospect of failure in Iraq had led to a fundamental reexamination of many of the Army's core beliefs on Vietnam. The articles in *Military Review*, the presentations at the Combat Studies Institute, and the popularity of authors such as Lewis Sorley and John Nagl among Army officers indicated not only a new attempt to mine that war for lessons but an attempt to create a new narrative of Vietnam. If this new narrative was not always the "better war" that Sorley described, then it at least had something that had something to say about Iraq, not only in terms of the decision to intervene and the mistakes made, but in terms of how to fight the war on the ground. The rise of Petraeus stands as a remarkable example of how the Army's older lessons of Vietnam were losing their force. Petraeus was not an admirer of either Harry Summers or "transformation."[37] The institutionalization of Petraeus's lessons of Vietnam began during his time at Fort Leavenworth, with the writing of the Army's new manual on counterinsurgency in 2006.

A NEW COUNTERINSURGENCY DOCTRINE: THE DRAFTING OF FM 3-24

Petraeus took command of the Combined Arms Center at Fort Leavenworth in October 2005, after two tours in Iraq, one commanding the 101st Airborne Division and the other overseeing the training of Iraqi security forces. He saw the Combined Arms Center as an "engine of change" for the Army and used the scheduled update of the counterinsurgency field manual to radically shift the Army's attention back toward counterinsurgency. Even the serial number of the new manual—FM 3-24—underlined the importance he attached to counterinsurgency. The interim manual FMI 3-07.22 (2004) was defined as a subset of "stability operations," whereas Petraeus and Conrad Crane, the lead author of the new manual, agreed that counterinsurgency was too broad a theme to be subsumed under the rubric of "stability operations."[38] Unlike the interim manual, which focused largely on the tactics, techniques, and procedures of counterinsurgency, FM 3-24 would have a broad, often reflective focus, engaging with both strategy and political conditions. Indeed, breadth was apparent not only in the focus of the manual, but the authorship; FM 3-24 was initially meant to be a joint product with the US Marines and the British Army. The British had to pull out due to the pressure of the ambitious writing schedule, but the Marines, under Lt. Gen. James Mattis, made a full contribution.[39]

Petraeus had earlier outlined his views on counterinsurgency in a *Military Review* article entitled "Learning Counterinsurgency: Observations from Soldiering in Iraq."[40] These observations found their way into the counterinsurgency manual as part of the nine "paradoxes of counterinsurgency," an innovation of Conrad Crane. For Petraeus, T. E. Lawrence was a major influence, as he approvingly quoted Lawrence's admonition that "better the Arabs do it tolerably than that you do it perfectly" and offered "do not try to do too much with your own hands" as the first of his fourteen points about counterinsurgency in Iraq. Petraeus, though, shied away from imperialism by also noting that "in a situation like Iraq, the liberating force must act quickly, because every Army of liberation has a half-life beyond which it turns into an Army of occupation."[41] Later, when asked about the possible conjunction between counterinsurgency and imperialism, he replied, "It's a wonderful debate to have . . . But we are where we are . . . At a certain point . . . you have to say, with respect, 'Let's take the rear-view mirrors off this bus.'"[42] However, this attitude may have proven necessary in Iraq, where he was dealing with the irrevocable consequences of the Bush administration's decision to invade, but he took a different approach during his time as commander of the Combined Arms Center in Fort Leavenworth. In overseeing the production of a new field manual, Petraeus made frequent use of the "rearview mirror" to explicitly codify lessons from history that could be useful to the Army in Iraq and elsewhere.

Compared to other field manuals, the writing process for FM 3-24 was unusually broad and discursive. Petraeus hosted a "counterinsurgency workshop" in Fort Leavenworth to solicit comment on a first draft of the manual. Guests included representatives from other government agencies; foreign officers such as British Brigadier Nigel Alwyn-Foster, who had been fiercely critical of US counterinsurgency practice in Iraq; academics such as Eliot Cohen and Sarah Sewell (of Harvard's Carr Center for Human Rights); and journalists such as Thomas Ricks, Linda Robinson, James Fallows, and George Packer.[43] The inclusion of such media figures pointed not only to a unique openness about the formulation of the doctrine but to Petraeus's focus on the importance of public relations. With public support for the war in Iraq at a low ebb, he was in some way co-opting critics of the war effort by engaging them on how to improve the Army's counterinsurgency performance. All those figures, especially Ricks and Robinson, were later to write positive reviews of Petraeus's performance in Iraq, leading some critics of the manual to argue that the manual itself was essentially a public relations exercise.[44] Steve Coll of the *New Yorker* noted that "this was warfare for northeastern graduate students—complex, blended with politics, designed to build countries rather than destroy them, and fashioned to minimize violence. It was a doctrine with particular appeal to people who would never own a gun."[45] Certainly, the manual was unusually discursive in tone, which surely could not hurt its appeal for graduate students; it included not only historical vignettes (staple for most US Army field manuals) but a bibliography, footnotes, and a series of principles, imperatives, and paradoxes of counterinsurgency. However, while Petraeus may have had an eye on publicity when overseeing the production of the manual, there was a real need to produce a revised, broad doctrine if the Army was to fully refocus its attention on counterinsurgency after such a long absence. The uneven performance of Army units in Iraq betrayed the need to produce something that could provide guidance to commanders at all levels.

The manual certainly produced a broad doctrine, with its chapters revealing a sophisticated understanding of the tenets of counterinsurgency. The first chapter illustrated the complex, fundamentally political nature of counterinsurgency, while the chapter on intelligence (which relied heavily on concepts developed by the anthropologist Montgomery McFate)[46] described in detail the cultural, social, and human intelligence that counterinsurgents needed if they were to be successful. The chapter on executing counterinsurgency campaigns outlining five tasks, or logical lines of operations, that must be taken by counterinsurgents. These logical lines of operation were: combat operations and civil security operations, building host nation security forces, essential services, governance, and economic development, all of which would be linked and surrounded by a program of "information operations." The manual also strongly emphasized the importance of using the appropriate level of force, stating that "counterinsurgents should calculate carefully the type and amount of force to be applied and who wields it for any operation. An operation that kills five insurgents is counterproductive if collateral damage leads to the recruitment of fifty more insurgents," that "sometimes the more force is used, the less effective it is" and that "some of the best weapons for counterinsurgents do not shoot."

Indeed, the manual defined so many different roles and problems that some critics charged that the qualities needed in a counterinsurgent, as defined in FM 3-24, meant that the Army could never come up with enough qualified personnel to conduct these campaigns.[47] Certainly, the intention of the drafters of FM 3-24 was that the Army was to move beyond "three-block war" to an even more complex "mosaic war," and the "sociologist captain" now joined the "strategic corporal" of 1990s fame.[48] To enact the doctrine described by the manual, the Army would have to fundamentally rethink its culture. In that sense, the manual's heavy use of historical vignettes and a scholarly bibliography can be seen as an attempt to help reshape that culture by contesting the historical memory that forms such an important part of that culture.

In keeping with this challenge, the intellectual foundations of the manual were deeply rooted in the writings of the 1960s theorists who had attempted to reshape Western militaries then. Their lessons on counterinsurgency were at the core of the manual. The experiences of Robert Thompson in Malaya and Vietnam, Frank Kitson in Kenya, and (especially) David Galula in Algeria were all strong influences. Every member of the writing team, at Nagl's suggestion, read Galula. Distilled to its essence, Galula's primary lesson was the primacy of the political. The manual quoted his admonition that "essential though it is, the military action is secondary to the political one, its primary purpose being to afford the political power enough freedom to work safely with the population."[49] To that end, the manual devoted an entire chapter to the concept of "unity of effort" and how best to integrate military and civilian efforts. With Thompson, the authors focused on his message of the importance of patience in counterinsurgency:

> It is a persistently methodical approach and steady pressure which will gradually wear the insurgent down. The government must not allow itself to be di-

verted either by countermoves on the part of the insurgent or by the critics on its own side who will be seeking a simpler and quicker solution. There are no short-cuts and no gimmicks.[50]

Thompson, who had advocated continuing the war in Vietnam long after Nixon had begun withdrawal, was perhaps the archetypal 1960s counterinsurgency advocate, and his emphasis on committing to campaigns for the long haul was redolent of an era when Western governments could afford to commit forces to such missions for years without public outcry.

Given such a clear influence from the 1960s, it is understandable that critics argued the manual was too reliant on a characterization of insurgency as a Maoist phenomenon, focusing, Frank Hoffman worried, "perhaps myopically, on the glorious heyday of revolutionary warfare in the 1950s and 1960s."[51] Certainly, when outlining various types of insurgency, the authors dwelt on Mao's three-stage, protracted warfare model, while the oft-quoted Galula and Thompson both based their thinking on Maoist insurgency, and the case study picked to illustrate the importance of logical lines of operation was Chiang Kai Shek's failed campaign against Mao.[52] However, although the manual certainly did emphasize "classical insurgency" to the detriment of more recent, fragmented models of insurgencies (something that many of the authors subsequently acknowledged),[53] the enemy the authors had in mind was not Mao, but Giap. Conrad Crane considered FM 3-24's logical lines of operation as a way of beating Giap's *dau tranh* strategy (of protracted and multilinear warfare) that proved so successful in Vietnam.[54] The manual noted how *dau tranh* not only modified Mao's three phases but "delineated LLOs [Logical Lines of Operation] for achieving political objectives among the enemy population, enemy soldiers and friendly forces . . . It did not attack a single enemy centre of gravity, instead it put pressure on several."[55] Crane believed that the way to beat this strategy was for the counterinsurgents to pursue their own logical lines of operation to push against the insurgents' efforts in every area. Vietnam, then, was a central consideration for the drafters of the manual, but it was not a version of Vietnam where the only thing that could defeat the United States was the United States itself.[56] This was not an interpretation of the Vietnam War that held that American mistakes alone led to defeat but rather one that credited a challenging, flexible, and resilient foe and attempted to learn from that foe. The enemy the writing team considered was not just the caricature of some NLF cadre in the villages or a PAVN division in the highlands but a challenging, flexible, and dangerous foe. In that sense, FM 3-24 moved beyond some of the more simplistic assumptions of 1960s theorists, even if it did not move beyond the Vietnam experience.

The relevance of the Vietnam experience partially explains the choice of Crane to lead the writing team as his monograph *Avoiding Vietnam* argues that the Army had intentionally turned away from counterinsurgency in the post-Vietnam era.[57] The man Crane replaced as lead author, Lt. Col. John Nagl, was also a student of the American experience of Vietnam. Indeed, the writing team broadly shared the view that the post-Vietnam neglect of counterinsurgency had been a mistake. In an article in *Military Review* outlining an early draft of the manual they argued:

> After Vietnam, the US Army reacted to the threat of irregular warfare chiefly by saying "never again." The study of counter-guerrilla and COIN operations was leached from the various military college curricula, and the hard-won experience of a generation of officers was deliberately ignored. The Army told itself that the failure in Vietnam was the fault of an overweening civilian leadership, a timorous high command, a feeble domestic base of support, a hostile press, and the sheer impossibility of the task. These judgments were grounded in reality, but the Army's institutional failures deserved no less attention.[58]

In some ways, while the authors most certainly turned away from such interpretations of Vietnam, they turned toward Lewis Sorley's interpretation of that war, quoting Creighton Abrams's lament on the delay in implementing a policy of "Vietnamization" that "there's very clear evidence . . . in some things that we helped too much. And we *retarded* the Vietnamese by doing it . . . *We* can't run this thing . . . *They've* got to run it. The nearer we get to that the better off *they* are and the better off *we* are."[59] CORDS and Abrams's Accelerated Pacification Campaign were also included in the manual as a historical vignette that claimed that "by 1972, pacification had largely uprooted the insurgency from among the South Vietnamese population" and that "pacification, once it was integrated under CORDS, was generally led, planned and executed well."[60] However, despite this affirmation of CORDS, one of its centerpieces—the Hamlet Evaluation System—was left out, on the advice of Crane, and the manual noted that "numerical and statistical indicators have limits when measuring social environment."[61]

The importance of Abrams did not mean that the authors all subscribed to Lewis Sorley's narrative of Vietnam. Conrad Crane has said that Sorley's account did not inform the writing team's views, even if certain elements of his narrative were useful for illustrative purposes.[62] Instead, Crane preferred to emphasize the broader historiography of Vietnam, and, in many ways, his focus on the importance of *dau tranh* bears this out. Crane cited Phillip Davidson's history of the war, which strongly stresses the importance of Giap, as a significant intellectual underpinning.[63] If the logical lines of operation of FM 3-24 were based on an imperative to counter Giap's strategy, then the manual was informed by a narrative of Vietnam that was more complex and nuanced than that of some of the theorists the authors drew inspiration from. FM 3-24, however, was strongly influenced by Vietnam. In many ways, it offered a belated solution to the problems Westmoreland and Abrams faced in that war and further embedded lessons that emphasized how counterinsurgency could be done correctly, rather than those that questioned whether it should be done at all. The power of these lessons however, largely depended on events in Iraq.

PETRAEUS, ODIERNO, AND THE SURGE

While Petraeus's writing team worked on the new counterinsurgency manual, conditions in Iraq continued to worsen. According to the Iraq Body Count database, 3,164 civilians were killed in July 2006, the highest figure since the invasion, while fifty-six people a day were killed by execution or gunfire throughout the year. Much of this increase in violence took place in the aftermath of Al-Qaeda in Iraq's February 2006 bombing of al-Askaria mosque, a Shia shrine in Samarra, with the intention of fomenting sectarian conflict.[64] The bombing and the violence that followed certainly signaled that the ethnic conflicts of Iraq were on the verge of descending into all-out civil war. In what amounted to a last-ditch effort to avoid this, President Bush announced the deployment of five extra brigades to Iraq on January 10, 2007. In doing so, Bush disregarded the recommendations of the bipartisan Iraq Study Group (a ten-person panel set up by Congress to examine the situation in Iraq and offer policy recommendations), which had argued for a stronger emphasis on training the Iraqi military while accelerating withdrawal.[65] The Iraq Study Group's suggested strategy of disengagement was supported by General Casey in Iraq, Secretary of State Condoleezza Rice, Secretary of Defense Donald Rumsfeld, the Joint Chiefs of Staff, and, most important, by the bulk of US public opinion.[66] A December 2006 poll by CNN claimed that 54 percent of Americans wanted to withdraw from Iraq within a year and fully 70 percent disapproved of President Bush's handling of the war.[67] In sending extra troops to Iraq, Bush ignored the professional advice of his closest advisors in favor of National Security Advisor Steven J. Hadley, retired General Jack Keane, and Multi-National Corps-Iraq (MNC-I) commander Raymond Odierno—all considered key proponents of the new strategy.[68] Those who advocated what was later called "the surge" operated under the assumption that those troops that would be sent to Iraq would operate in a manner akin to that described in FM 3-24. Such assumptions were reinforced by the selection of General Petraeus to take over as commander of MNF-I. For what mattered in Iraq was not necessarily the "surge" itself, but the strategy.

On taking command, Petraeus commissioned a Joint Strategic Assessment (or JSAT) to examine strategy in Iraq. This team consisted of officers with PhDs, such as Cols. H. R. McMaster, Peter Mansoor, Michael Meese, and Lt. Col. Doug Ollivant, and civilian academics such as Montgomery McFate, Toby Dodge, and David Kilcullen.[69] At the time, Tom Ricks wrote that "essentially, the Army is turning the war over to its dissidents, who have criticized the way the service has operated there the past three years, and is letting them try to wage the war their way."[70] Certainly, many members of the JSAT shared broadly critical views of how the war had been conducted in its early stage—David Kilcullen, for instance, called the decision to invade "f- - - stupid."[71] These planners also recognized the complexity of the war. Kilcullen's model of the war in Iraq (and he was careful to note that it was a simplified model) defined the war as not simply an insurgency but a mixture of terrorism, insurgency, and communal conflict, all occurring within the framework of a nation-building operation.[72] Lt. Col. Doug Ollivant, who was not only a member of the JSAT but the chief architect of the plan to secure Baghdad, preferred the analogy of Bosnia, arguing that "while analogies are slippery, our current predicament somewhat echoes pre-Dayton Bosnia. The most notable difference, of course, is that in Iraq all parties involved are also shooting at us."[73] The fundamental problem in this situation, as Kilcullen defined it, was one of "control—of people, of terrain, of information."[74]

To help understand this complex environment, the members of the JSAT turned to the example of Vietnam. Kilcullen credited William Westmoreland in Vietnam with "getting" the problem of counterinsurgency but then noted that "understanding by leaders is not enough: everyone needs to understand, and we need a framework, doctrine, a system, processes and structures to *enact* [emphasis in the original] this understanding."[75] For Kilcullen, Robert Komer provided the most pertinent set of lessons from Vietnam, with the primary problem being one of institutional and bureaucratic constraints. Kilcullen's emphasis in this regard differed slightly from that of Conrad Crane and the FM 3-24 team (although Kilcullen did attend the February 2006 workshop that critiqued drafts of the manual) in that he seemed to discount the role of the enemy in Vietnam. In this version of events, the biggest problem was not the NLF or the PAVN but bureaucratic ineptitude. Indeed, there were echoes of revisionist Vietnam history throughout the planning process, with Steve Coll noting that those involved in the JSAT and in promoting counterinsurgency within the Army "developed a particular interest in the generalship of Creighton Abrams, who assumed command of US forces in Vietnam in 1968, after William Westmoreland." According to Coll, "The General's 1969 campaign plan for Vietnam, titled 'One War,' anticipated the Joint Campaign Plan that Petraeus would write in Iraq."[76] In Iraq as much as at Fort Leavenworth, the new interpretation of the Army's experience of Vietnam was taking hold.

Petraeus's campaign plan meant a radical overhaul of the strategy in Iraq. According to Kilcullen, the concept was "to knock over several insurgent safe havens simultaneously, in order to prevent terrorists relocating their infrastructure from one to another, and to create an operational synergy between what we're doing in Baghdad and what's happening outside."[77] Baghdad, as mandated in President Bush's speech announcing the troop surge, was to be the primary focus of the new strategy, and for Kilcullen, this was an obvious move as "about 50% of the war in Iraq happens inside Baghdad city limits. Improving security in the capital therefore makes a major difference."[78] "Clear, hold, and build" would again be the priority, only with a more explicit focus on the population. Kilcullen explained:

> When we speak of "clearing" an enemy safe haven, we are not talking about destroying the enemy in it; we are talking about rescuing the population in it from enemy intimidation. If we don't get every enemy cell in the initial operation, that's OK. The point of the operations is to lift the pall of fear from population groups that have been intimidated and exploited by terrorists to date, then win them over and work with them in partnership to clean out the cells that remain—as has happened in Al Anbar Province and can happen elsewhere in Iraq as well.[79]

This vision of operations in Baghdad closely matched the experience of Tal Afar and explicitly invoked MacFarland's lessons from Anbar, but it also took its cues from FM 3-24. Like the authors of FM 3-24, the planners on the JSAT responsible for drafting strategy in Iraq displayed a sophisticated understanding of counterinsurgency and optimism about its utility.

However, while the JSAT helped conceptualize a new type of strategy in Iraq, one much closer to classic counterinsurgency doctrine, such a concept was worthless without troops capable of carrying it out. One of the major criticisms of FM 3-24 was that the type of soldiers required to carry out counterinsurgency of the sort described in the field manual were rare. Not every soldier was a Special Forces advisor. Petraeus, to his credit, was adept at communicating the nuances of these operations in as simple and direct manner as possible. For instance, in a "counterinsurgency guidance" directive issued to all troops in June 2008, he listed the following imperatives for counterinsurgency in Iraq:

- Secure and serve the population. The Iraqi people are the decisive "terrain." Together with our Iraqi partners, work to provide the people security, to give them respect, to gain their support, and to facilitate establishment of local governance, restoration of basic services, and revival of local economies.
- Hold areas that have been secured. Once we clear an area, we must retain it. Develop the plan for holding an area before starting to clear it. The people need to know that we and our Iraqi partners will not abandon their neighborhoods. When reducing forces and presence, gradually thin the line rather than handing off or withdrawing completely. Ensure situational awareness even after transfer of responsibility to Iraqi forces.
- Walk. Move mounted, work dismounted. Stop by, don't drive by. Patrol on foot and engage the population. Situational awareness can only be gained by interacting with the people face-to-face, not separated by ballistic glass.[80]

The biggest difference, however, with previous strategy was contained in Petraeus's simplest point: "Live among the people. You can't commute to this fight . . . Living among the people is essential to securing them and defeating the insurgents."[81] These aphorisms, which first appeared in a March 2007 letter to the troops, displayed the same succinct style that typified much of FM 3-24 and were directly addressed at the junior and midgrade leaders who would have to move to these isolated combat outposts.

Petraeus's letter also advised troops to "position Joint Security Stations, Combat Outposts, and Patrol Bases in the neighborhoods we intend to secure." These combat outposts and joint security stations would be the centerpiece of the plan to secure Baghdad. The plan, Operation *Fardh al-Qanoon*

(Enforcing the Rule of Law), created an interlocking grid of US and Iraqi units across the city, with battalions living in combat outposts outside the big Forward Operating Bases and sending out smaller elements to the police station–sized Joint Security Stations. The plan, which was drafted under the direction of Lt. Col. Doug Ollivant, was heavily influenced by Galula's ideas on population control.[82] Previous efforts to secure Baghdad had fallen short, despite the best intentions. Lt. Gen. Peter Chiarelli, the advocate of nonkinetic means and a major influence on FM 3-24, had overseen the most recent and high-profile of these efforts, Operation Together Forward II, between August and October of 2006. The failure of this operation, despite the application of many classic principles of counterinsurgency (partnering with local forces, tending to the economic needs of locals) gave the Iraq Study Group pause when it considered its findings. The Study Group found that "the results of Operation *Together Forward II* are disheartening. Violence in Baghdad—already at high levels—jumped more than 43 percent between the summer and October 2006. US forces continue to suffer high casualties. Perpetrators of violence leave neighborhoods in advance of security sweeps, only to filter back later."[83] This time, however, there were sufficient troops to hold neighborhoods that had been cleared. By the time Petraeus attempted his operation to secure Baghdad, the Army had more fully bought into the concept of counterinsurgency, and the extra brigades meant that the plan had a much better chance at succeeding.

Operations in Baghdad were marked not only by an intensified attempt to secure the population but also by dividing the population: Barriers were erected between Sunni and Shia neighborhoods, and access between the two communities was often restricted, something Kilcullen characterized as an "urban tourniquet—the lesser of several evils."[84] Furthermore, the operation to secure Baghdad itself used only half the forces available. The other half went instead to the new Multinational Division-Center (MND-C), an innovation of Odierno's; this division was to sweep the towns surrounding Baghdad of insurgent forces, and it engaged in several large-scale sweep operations directed at insurgent "sanctuaries," such as Operation Phantom Phoenix and Operation Phantom Strike. Dale Andrade, who wrote a history of the surge south of Baghdad, characterized the operations of MND-C as "in essence a purely military push. Known as kinetic or lethal operations in current Army argot, the campaign was needed initially to halt insurgent movement from the belts, by attacking the enemy and maintaining a permanent presence in the insurgent sanctuaries."[85]

The fact that these sweeps often resulted in heavy firefights with insurgents would help explain why the number of bombs dropped on Iraq in 2007 was over five times the amount dropped in 2006, jumping from 229 to 1,447.[86] The *Washington Post* noted that, one morning during Operation Phantom Phoenix, "In Arab Jabour, southeast of Baghdad, the US military dropped 38 bombs with 40,000 pounds of explosives in 10 minutes, one of the largest strikes since the 2003 invasion. US forces north of Baghdad employed bombs totaling more than 16,500 pounds over just a few days."[87] The new strategy then was not entirely based on humanitarian impulses; violence—and coercion—had their place. Similarly, American and British Special Forces, operating under Lt. Gen. Stanley McChrystal's Joint Special Operations Command (JSOC), massively increased their targeting of both Al-Qaeda and insurgent leaders.[88] Aided by much-improved intelligence, JSOC increased the intensity of its operations to the point where it was launching raids every night, eventually killing or capturing thousands of high-level insurgents.[89] Counterinsurgency, as practiced in Iraq, was certainly not a less violent form of warfare than what had preceded it. The difference was that the violence was much more carefully targeted and more closely allied to strategic goals.

Despite the increased tonnage of high explosives dropped on Iraq during 2007, violence dropped drastically throughout Iraq in the aftermath of the surge. According to Petraeus's testimony before Congress in September 2007, civilian deaths of all categories (not including natural causes) across Iraq declined by over 45 percent from the height of sectarian violence in December 2006, while deaths in Baghdad declined 70 percent; ethnosectarian deaths declined by over 55 percent across Iraq and by 80 percent in Baghdad. In Anbar province, previously the heartland of the insurgency, monthly attack levels declined from 1,350 in October 2006 to just over 200 in August 2007.[90] The debate over the reasons for this drop in violence, which continued throughout 2008, has intensified in recent years. Dissenters from what Doug Ollivant called the "new orthodoxy" have emphasized Shia militant Moqtada al-Sadr's decision not to contest the surge, Iraqi animosity toward Al-Qaeda insurgents, general exhaustion among the population, and a contention that ethnic cleansing was effectively complete in Baghdad by the time Petraeus and Odierno deployed their extra forces.[91] Ollivant, who was instrumental in the Baghdad security plan, bluntly declared that "the fundamental truth of the Iraqi settlement is that the sectarian civil war ended—and the Sunni lost."[92] Nonetheless, while the debate over the strategic significance of the surge—and the role the US Army's counterinsurgency tactics played in the decrease in violence in Iraq—will continue until much more evidence is available, what is important is that the drop-off in violence coincided with Petraeus's increased emphasis on counterinsurgency. More than anything else, this correlation meant that FM 3-24 and its lessons of Vietnam would gain significant currency within the Army. It also meant that the lessons of Iraq would play a crucial role in deliberations over strategy in Afghanistan in the years to come.

CONCLUSION

Counterinsurgency was now firmly at the center of the Army's focus, and the new doctrine confirmed that it would remain so for some time to come. While FM 3-24 marked a significant shift and effectively reintroduced counterinsurgency to the Army's doctrine for the first time since Vietnam (the 1986 manual on counterguerrilla operations and the 2004 interim field manual notwithstanding), this shift was only confirmed with the publication of the next swath of doctrine in 2008 (see Chapter 8). Unsurprisingly, this shift was closely linked to events on the ground in Iraq. The events of 2007 through 2008 showed that counterinsurgency could succeed, at least in terms of reasserting control over the population and quelling violence, under the right conditions. Had the "surge" not succeeded in reducing violence in Iraq, it is likely that the fate of counterinsurgency doctrine within the Army would have taken a different turn.

The man responsible for that change of fortunes in Iraq, General David Petraeus, is—in many ways—representative not only of the new ascendency of counterinsurgency but also of the changing consensus in the Army on the lessons of Vietnam. No longer was Vietnam held up as an example of why the United States should not engage in counterinsurgency warfare, but it was mined for examples of *how* to conduct counterinsurgency. In the new doctrine—and in the minds of the soldiers (and civilians) in charge of strategy in Iraq—lessons like the importance of organizations such as CORDS, the need to restrict the use of firepower, and the efficacy of "clear and hold" operations were all given a prominent place. Related to these lessons was a partial consensus on a narrative that redeemed much of the US effort in Vietnam by focusing on the performance of General Creighton Abrams, even if not everyone subscribed to Lewis Sorley's "better war" thesis, which essentially declared victory in Vietnam on Abrams's behalf.

Fundamentally, the years from 2006 to 2008, from the drafting of FM 3-24 in 2006 to General Petraeus's testimony to Congress in September 2007 and April 2008, marked the biggest shift in the Army's identity since Vietnam. Counterinsurgency became engrained in that identity in a way it never had been in Vietnam, even at the height of President Kennedy's enthusiasm for the doctrine. The rise of General Petraeus and his cohort indicated a profound shift in focus. It is fitting, however, that Petraeus was a scholar of Vietnam and that this turn toward counterinsurgency necessitated, and was informed by, a thorough rethinking of what Vietnam meant and what lessons it had to offer the Army.

8 A NEVER-ENDING WAR?

The Renegotiation of "Vietnam" in Afghanistan

FOR ALL THE NARRATIVES OF SUCCESS built around the "surge," the lessons of Iraq would be mediated through those of another large conflict—Afghanistan (2001–)—in a way that the lessons of Vietnam were not. While conflicts like El Salvador, Nicaragua, Panama, the Gulf War, Somalia, Bosnia, and Kosovo all helped refract and reshape the lessons of Vietnam, the war in Indochina stood alone in significance until the war in Iraq. Even so, if a historical analogy was influential in the minds of US commanders in Afghanistan, it was the fate of the USSR's earlier efforts in that country. Avoiding the "Soviet Vietnam" was paramount even as the original Vietnam analogy was not influential in the early years of the conflict and Afghanistan was something of a "forgotten war" throughout much of the Bush presidency.[1] With Army resources overwhelmingly committed to Iraq, the growing Taliban insurgency registered as significant only to those outside Afghanistan following a series of pitched battles in places like Wanat and the Korengal Valley in eastern Afghanistan throughout 2007 and 2008.[2] In this context, lessons centered on the success of the "surge" in Iraq would carry little weight unless a similar surge of forces in Afghanistan brought success. The Obama administration's decision to dramatically increase troop numbers throughout 2009 and to commit to a strategy based on counterinsurgency saw both an application of Petraeus's lessons of Iraq and the reintroduction of the Vietnam analogy to the discourse on Afghanistan. While Vietnam was not as central as it was in the Army's imagination in Iraq, Afghanistan in 2009 through 2011 also pointed to an organization still struggling with the lessons of the Vietnam experience.

Those lessons were inextricably linked to the fortunes of counterinsurgency: General Stanley McChrystal's short-lived tenure as commander of International Security Assistance Force (ISAF) in Afghanistan saw a strong focus on the nonviolent aspects of counterinsurgency doctrine, and McChrystal's replacement, General David Petraeus, was the man responsible both for disseminating the lessons of Iraq and for reshaping the Army's lessons of Vietnam. The McChrystal-Petraeus era of the war in Afghanistan, then, offered a new proving ground to the Army's counterinsurgency doctrine. Not only that, but the McChrystal and Petraeus strategies in Afghanistan also illustrated the ways in which the lessons of Vietnam had been modified by the Iraq experience, for the strategies applied in Afghanistan were profoundly influenced by the experience of Iraq; the period between the Iraq "surge" and the similar infusion of troops into Afghanistan saw a widespread embedding of a certain set of lessons from Iraq.

INSTITUTIONALIZING COUNTERINSURGENCY

In an unusual departure from normal practice, Petraeus returned to the United States in the middle of his tour in Iraq to oversee a promotion board that would select the next slate of Army generals. The Petraeus-led board unsurprisingly selected counterinsurgency experts such as Col. Sean MacFarland and Col. H. R. McMaster (who had been passed over twice before by previous boards) for promotion, an indication of how much Army attitudes had changed. Seeing the promotion board as evidence of a realignment similar to the one initiated in the 1970s by William DePuy, retired Maj. Gen. Robert H. Scales argued that "we are in a very similar place now to the period after Vietnam in the 1970s, when a lot of officers returned and everyone was asking 'what is next?' . . . It's time now for the Army to think about the future and institutionally anticipate the changing nature of war."[3]

The Army's answer to the "what is next?" question appeared to come with the publication of new editions of two manuals: FM 3-07 *Stability Operations* and, especially, FM 3-0 *Operations*, the Army's capstone doctrinal publication.[4] The key development in the new edition of FM 3-0 was the elevation of "stability operations" as coequal with more conventional types of conflict, stating that "stability and civil support operations cannot be something that the Army conducts [only] in 'other than war' operations. Army forces must address the civil situation directly and continuously, combining tactical tasks directed at non-combatants with tactical tasks directed against the enemy."[5] There were still some holdovers from the previous doctrine, with the head of TRADOC, General William S. Wallace, acknowledging "that the Army's primary purpose remains deterrence. Should deterrence fail, the Army will fight as part of an interdependent joint team to decisively win the Nation's wars."[6] However, "winning decisively" had a new meaning. Lt. Gen. William B. Caldwell, Petraeus's successor at the Combined Arms Center and the officer responsible for overseeing the production of the manual, declared that the manual represented a "revolutionary shift in focus" and

> Where our capstone doctrine was once based upon a traditional approach to military operations that focused operations on seizing terrain and destroying enemy formations, this edition acknowledges that the current and future operating environments will be characterized by conflict against amorphous enemies that hide among and are supported by civilian populations. American dominance of the maritime, air, and space domains is no longer the effective deterrent it once was.[7]

Caldwell also argued that "the ability to engage, close with, and destroy our enemy on the ground remains indispensable. But it is the 'soft power,' constructive capabilities of the force—or as we prefer to say, 'smart power' skills— that we must increasingly promote as the tools required to make permanent the otherwise temporary effects of successful combat actions."[8] "Nonlethal actions" were given as much prominence, in all areas of conflict, as lethal actions. Caldwell's version of the *Operations* field manual was in many ways a direct rebuke to that of William DePuy's 1976 edition of FM 100-5. General Wallace called it a "revolutionary departure from past doctrine" and even put it on a par with DePuy's efforts, claiming:

> Just as the 1976 edition of FM 100-5 began to take the Army from the rice paddies of Vietnam to the battlefield of Western Europe, this edition will take us into the 21st century urban battlefields among the people without losing our capabilities to dominate the higher conventional end of the spectrum of conflict.[9]

The intellectual inspiration for much of FM 3-0 came from retired British General Sir Rupert Smith.[10] Smith's notion of "war among the people" was featured throughout, with the manual asserting:

Future conflicts are much more likely to be fought "among the people" instead of "around the people." . . . War remains a battle of wills—a contest for dominance over people. The essential struggle of the future conflict will take place in areas in which people are concentrated and will require US security dominance to extend across the population.[11]

For Smith, Vietnam represented a model of future war rather than the anomaly some US leaders thought it was. The actions of the PAVN and the NLF represented a formula for success against Western militaries, one that the United States needed to be prepared to deal with. The February 2008 FM 3-0 represented an affirmation not only of Smith's thesis but also of the idea that the US Army could not avoid future counterinsurgencies.

This was further reinforced with the October 2008 publication of the updated FM 3-07 *Stability Operations*.[12] Like FM 3-0, this manual was careful to emphasize the nonlethal aspects of power. It stated that "stability operations leverage the coercive and constructive capabilities of the military force to establish a safe and secure environment; facilitate reconciliation among local or regional adversaries; establish political, legal, social, and economic institutions; and facilitate the transition of responsibility to a legitimate civil authority." Furthermore, FM 3-07 downplayed the ability of the military to act alone. According to the manual, military forces would merely "help to set the conditions that enable the actions of the other instruments of national power to succeed in achieving the broad goals of conflict transformation."[13]

Produced by the same team that wrote the new edition of FM 3-0, FM 3-07 subscribed to the notion that "contrary to popular belief, the military history of the United States is one characterized by stability operations, interrupted by distinct episodes of major combat." The introductory chapter reproduced a brief history of American experience of small wars, noting that US military forces had fought only eleven wars considered conventional, whereas it had engaged in hundreds of other military operations, most of which "are now considered stability operations, where the majority of effort consisted of stability tasks. Contrary to popular belief, the military history of the United States is one characterized by stability operations, interrupted by distinct episodes of major combat."[14] FM 3-07 drew on a history that emphasized the experience in the Philippines more than the Civil War and Bosnia rather than the Gulf War. Vietnam, too, was present as something that earned the United States "an invaluable experience with the complexity of conducting operations among the people."[15] The manual again offered CORDS as an example of successful civil–military integration, a major theme of the manual.

The drafters of FM 3-07 gave some credit to William Westmoreland for implementing CORDS in the first place, although they also emphasized that a shift in emphasis took place under Abrams. Most importantly, though, they recognized that "CORDS was too little, too late" and that "even as the pacification effort achieved broad success across South Vietnam and, by all indications, brought the Viet Cong insurgency to its knees, American popular support for the war had evaporated. The national will necessary to maintain the momentum gained through CORDS could not be regained; the initiative was lost and so, eventually, was the war."[16] The primary lesson of Vietnam, though, was that counterinsurgency experience should not have been forgotten. The authors declared:

> In the years after the fall of South Vietnam, we failed to institutionalize perhaps the most important lesson learned: the need for broad unity of effort among all agencies of government in operations conducted among the people of a foreign nation. Instead, we turned away from the bitter experiences of that time, and in many respects abandoned the rich body of lessons learned and tactics, techniques, and procedures that we assumed we would never need again.[17]

Indeed, the writing team recognized the problems caused by forgetting Vietnam, noting "as the Iraq insurgency continued to evolve, haunting parallels from South Vietnam grew difficult to ignore." They also credited the FM 3-24 team with recognizing the important lessons of Vietnam and the need for change and applauded their "efforts to resuscitate a counterinsurgency doctrine relegated to obscurity for more than three decades."[18] FM 3-07 would further institutionalize those lessons and add the experiences of Iraq and Afghanistan to doctrine. In some ways, these two field manuals—FM 3-0 and FM 3-07—could potentially do for the Army of Iraq and Afghanistan what the *Active Defense* doctrine did for the post-Vietnam Army and set down how the Army would fight (and define itself) for the next generation.

The efforts of the writing team behind FM 3-0 and FM 3-07 mirrored a broader shift in the defense establishment. Speaking in November 2007, Secretary of Defense Robert Gates argued, "One of the most important lessons of the wars in Iraq and Afghanistan is that military success is not sufficient to win" and that future conflicts "will be fundamentally political in nature, and require the application of all elements of national power." Gates also reiter-ated the now-common lessons of Vietnam, stating, "However uncomfortable it may be to raise Vietnam all these years later, the history of that conflict is instructive." Gates saw the CORDS program as a great success story in the integration of military and civilian efforts and argued, "It had the effect of, in the words of General Creighton Abrams, putting 'all of *us* on one side and the enemy on the other.' By the time U.S. troops were pulled out, the CORDS program had helped pacify most of the hamlets in South Vietnam."[19]

The importance of CORDS as a lesson was reflected in the publication of new doctrine at higher levels, such as Joint Publication 3-24 *Counterinsur-gency Operations* (2009) and the US Government Counterinsurgency Guide, both of which presented counterinsurgency as a key element of any future US security doctrine and emphasized interagency unity of effort.[20] Similarly, strategy documents such as Department of Defense Directive 3000.7, "Irregu-lar Warfare," and the Army's "Capstone Concept" (drafted by the now-Brig. Gen. H. R. McMaster) spoke of the need to prepare the Army and the military to conduct counterinsurgency campaigns and to learn the "right" lessons of Iraq in a way they had not with those of Vietnam.[21] McMaster was highly criti-cal of the "Revolution in Military Affairs," and the Capstone Concept declared that "concepts that had relied mainly on the ability to target enemy forces with long range precision munitions separated war from its political, cultural, and psychological contexts." More bitingly, the authors argued that "some of this work focused on how U.S. forces might prefer to fight and then assumed that preference was relevant to the problem of future war."[22] Gates took a similar view and, in contrast to his predecessor Donald Rumsfeld, advocated cutting expensive high-technology programs and prioritizing the counterinsurgency campaigns in Iraq and Afghanistan. In a May 2010 speech, Gates argued, "We must always recognize the limits of technology—and be modest about what military force alone can accomplish . . . no one should ever neglect the psycho-logical, cultural, political, and human dimensions of war or succumb to the techno-optimism that has muddled strategic thinking in the past."[23] In effect, Gates was talking about the limits of American power as well as the limits of technology, even as he advocated the creation of capabilities for counterinsur-gency campaigns.

The Obama administration's 2010 Quadrennial Defense Review chose to highlight the need for such capabilities, arguing, "The United States must retain the capability to conduct large-scale counterinsurgency, stability, and counterterrorism operations in a wide range of environments."[24] The QDR envisioned a future where there would be "few cases in which the U.S. Armed Forces would engage in sustained large-scale combat operations without the associated need to assist in the transition to just and stable governance."[25] Given this future, it was vital that the armed forces institutionalize the lessons of Iraq and Afghanistan in a way they had not in the wake of Vietnam. "Military doctrine, training, capability development, and operational planning" would all need to reflect these lessons, and the Department of Defense would need to continue to "make substantial changes to personnel management practices, professional military education and training programs, and career development pathways."[26]

The assumptions built into this new doctrine, at both Army and DoD level, were very much at odds with Powell's lessons of Vietnam. The new field manuals, the speeches of senior leaders, and the Quadrennial Defense Review all envisioned a world in which the United States would constantly be involved in some form of military conflict. Given that the Powell Doctrine had nothing to say about such a world—indeed, it was formulated to avoid such an outcome—then the United States would need a new doctrine on intervention. Chairman of the Joint Chiefs of Staff Admiral Mike Mullen attempted to lay out his alternative to Powell. In a March 2010 speech at Kansas State University, Mullen laid out three key principles for the employment of US force in such a world. He argued for a much more flexible approach to the United States of military force, contending, "We must not look upon the use of military forces only as a last resort, but as potentially the best, first option when combined with other instruments of national and international power." If military force was no longer the last resort, then it followed that the United States "must not try to use force only in an overwhelming capacity, but in the proper capacity, and in a precise and principled manner." Powell's emphasis on overwhelming force no longer applied. Lastly, Mullen preferred not to emphasize Powell Doctrine tenets such as clearly defined objectives and preplanned exit strategies but instead talked about the need to embrace "the tug of war . . . that inevitably plays out between policymaking and strategy execution."[27] For Mullen, the interplay between policy and strategy as the latter adapted to mirror changes in the former was a healthy thing.

Mullen's speech, attempting as it did to enunciate a foreign policy doctrine on the use of force, was in many ways the culmination of the doctrinal embedding of counterinsurgency in the years directly after the "surge" in Iraq.

From Army tactical and operational doctrine to joint doctrine to Department of Defence policy to the pronouncements of senior leaders such as Gates and Mullen, counterinsurgency was as prevalent as it had been absent in the years leading up to the war in Iraq. However, the primacy of counterinsurgency—and its hold over the Army's imagination—would immediately be challenged in Afghanistan. How the concept fared there would do much to decide how deeply embedded Petraeus's—and Mullen's—lessons of Iraq would remain.

OBAMA'S DECISIONS

Mullen's lessons on the interplay between strategy and policy were clearly derived from the Obama administration's decision-making process on the war in Afghanistan. As a candidate, Obama had condemned the invasion of Iraq, while talking of Afghanistan as the "necessary war." On taking office, one of his first moves was to announce a drawdown of troops from Iraq, with all combat forces to depart by the summer of 2010 and all other troops to be gone by the end of 2011. Afghanistan, however, would receive a renewed focus. In a March 2009 strategy review, the administration committed itself to executing and resourcing a "civilian and military counterinsurgency campaign" by committing 17,000 more troops to Afghanistan.[28] Obama, who had been critical of counterinsurgency as a senator, now embraced the concept that had seemingly proven itself in Baghdad. However, when announcing the new policy he was careful to differentiate himself from Bush:

> Going forward, we will not blindly stay the course. Instead, we will set clear metrics to measure progress and hold ourselves accountable. We'll consistently assess our efforts to train Afghan security forces and our progress in combating insurgents. We will measure the growth of Afghanistan's economy, and its illicit narcotics production. And we will review whether we are using the right tools and tactics to make progress towards accomplishing our goals.[29]

General David Petraeus, now commanding CENTCOM, was eager to apply what he saw as the lessons of Iraq to the newly central war in Afghanistan. At a number of venues in Washington, D.C., and elsewhere, he gave speeches on the lessons of Iraq throughout the spring and summer of 2009. While he recognized that "if there is any overriding principal of counterinsurgency it is that context matters" and that "we certainly cannot perform a wholesale transplant of successful practices from Iraq and expect them to work in Afghanistan," Petraeus argued that "as was the case in Iraq, additional forces are needed in Afghanistan."[30] He argued that the most important element of the surge in Iraq was not the number of forces per se but rather that these additional forces began to focus on securing the population while living among them. At an address to an audience at the annual conference of the Center for a New American Security (CNAS) think tank in June 2009, Petraeus argued that this focus on population security was the key lesson that could be transferred from Iraq to Afghanistan. Other lessons that could be applied included:

- Assume a comprehensive approach and establish a "unity of effort" among the interagency participants;
- Pursue the enemy relentlessly and "hold" the cleared areas;
- Separate the "irreconcilables"—extremists incapable of reforming—from the "reconcilables" and promote reconciliation; and
- Exercise initiative, including being the first to disseminate the truth, and learn and adapt.[31]

In essence, these were Petraeus's lessons of Iraq. Counterinsurgency could succeed if properly resourced and applied relentlessly by the right commander. Ironically, these lessons did not acknowledge the importance of timing. In Iraq, Petraeus had been deeply conscious of the political clock and the danger of the American public and body politic growing weary of a slow and costly campaign.[32] Here, he was more concerned with promoting leadership that could execute counterinsurgency effectively.

Indeed, as Petraeus was addressing his audience at CNAS in Washington, a new commander was flying out to take over the war in Afghanistan. General Stanley McChyrstal, who had run the Special Forces campaign in Iraq under Petraeus, was to take over from General David McKiernan, who had both made insufficient progress in fighting the Taliban insurgency and shown insufficient understanding of the tenets of counterinsurgency in the eyes of the Obama administration. McKiernan's removal, however, was also at least partly due to the rapidly deteriorating situation in Afghanistan. A report from CNAS (issued shortly after McKiernan's dismissal) bluntly spelled out the problem. The authors declared, "In counterinsurgency campaigns, if you are not winning, then you are losing. By this standard, the United States and its allies are losing the war in Afghanistan."[33] Like Petraeus, they recommended pursuing a fully resourced counterinsurgency campaign, while worrying that "because population-centric counterinsurgency operations demand a high concentration of troops, there will still be a sizable gap between the coalition's stated objectives and its available resources, even with these significant new commitments of forces."[34] Foreshadowing later difficulties, they claimed that "one of the more worrying trends in Afghanistan has been the way in which the U.S. military—while claiming to faithfully execute population-centric counterinsurgency—has continued to articulate its aims in terms of terrain controlled and enemies killed or captured."[35]

McChrystal echoed the CNAS conclusions and even used some of the authors of the report to help him write his own strategic assessment of the campaign, which he began when he took over ISAF in June. McChrystal's report, leaked to the press before it was sent to the White House in September, was both pessimistic about the war's prospects and heavily critical of American efforts thus far. According to McChrystal, the operational culture of ISAF was a major problem; US forces had been "pre-occupied with protection of our own forces" and had "operated in a manner that distances us—physically and psychologically—from the people we seek to protect."[36] He criticized ISAF as a "conventional force that is poorly configured for COIN, inexperienced in local languages and culture, and struggling challenges inherent to coalition warfare."[37] McChrystal argued that "the status quo will lead to failure" and that "almost every aspect of our collective effort and associated resourcing has lagged a growing insurgency—historically a recipe for failure."[38]

For McChrystal, it was clear that "this is a different kind of fight. We must conduct classic counterinsurgency operations in an environment that is uniquely complex."[39] The strategy must be to secure the population. In a close parallel to FM 3-24's "paradoxes of counterinsurgency," he argued that "the insurgents cannot defeat us militarily; but we can defeat ourselves" and that "security may not come from the barrel of a gun. Better force protection may be counterintuitive; it might come from less armor and less distance from the population."[40] Under McChrystal, ISAF would focus on securing the Afghan population, increasing cooperation with Afghan security forces, and improving governance, and would no longer "run the risk of strategic defeat by pursuing tactical wins that cause civilian casualties or unnecessary collateral damage." For McChrystal, the central lesson of Iraq that could be applied to Afghanistan was that "a classic counterinsurgency campaign, well resourced, is going to be required."[41] Resourcing then, was the central issue. While much of the assessment focused on describing the reasons for deterioration in security in Afghanistan, and ISAF's planned counterinsurgency campaign, McChrystal was careful to point out that "resources will not win this war, but under-resourcing could lose it." Indeed, inadequate resources would "likely result in failure."[42] McChrystal was calling on Obama to provide him with enough troops to pursue a "properly resourced strategy" that could accomplish the mission with "appropriate and acceptable risk."[43]

McChrystal's strategic assessment and subsequent request for 40,000 additional troops led to extensive debate on Afghanistan throughout the autumn of 2009. That debate was largely—though not exclusively—framed by the contrasting lessons of Vietnam. While McChrystal had consulted historian Stanley Karnow on what lessons could be learned from Vietnam and applied to Afghanistan, the book on Vietnam that he read and reread was Sorley's *Better War*.[44] McChrystal received support for his assessment from CNAS, whose president, the now-retired Lt. Col. John Nagl, was a staunch advocate of counterinsurgency and of those lessons of Vietnam that emphasized population-centric counterinsurgency as a winning strategy. In September 2009, Nagl even submitted testimony entitled "A Better War for Afghanistan" to Congress at the height of the debate over strategy in Afghanistan.[45] Echoing Sorley, Nagl argued for a "clear, hold, and build" counterinsurgency campaign with more troops. If the "Better War" had not been possible in Vietnam, then the United States could still apply lessons learned from Abrams's experience in Afghanistan.

For the Obama administration, however, McChrystal's request opened up new questions about the war. While McChrystal and other Army leaders had read Sorley's work and sympathized with his "better war" thesis, the lessons of Vietnam did not resonate in quite the same way in the Obama White House. Obama had apparently declared in his first National Security Council meeting that "Afghanistan was not Vietnam," but the ghosts of that war still haunted the White House.[46] Even as early as January 2009, *Newsweek* put a story titled "Obama's Vietnam" on its front cover with the analogy making its way into *The New York Times* by August.[47] As McChrystal's report made clear, the war was not going well, and the strategy needed to be reassessed. This did not, however, necessarily mean increased support for population-centric counterinsurgency, despite the March 2009 strategy. Advisors such as National Security Advisor General James Jones, White House staffers such as White House Chief of Staff Rahm Emmanuel, National Security Advisor Jim Jones, Deputy National Security Advisor Tom Donilon, senior advisor David Axelrod, special advisor Lt. Gen. Douglas Lute, as well as Vice President Joe Biden and Vice Chairman of the Joint Chiefs of Staff General James Cartwright were all skeptical of the utility of counterinsurgency in Afghanistan.[48]

Some of those doubts came from a different reading of the lessons of Vietnam to that current in the military; Deputy National Security Advisor Tom Donilon had read Gordon Goldstein's *Lessons in Disaster*, which offered a very different set of lessons of Vietnam from those of Sorley and the revisionists.[49] The book, which offers lessons from the experience of McGeorge Bundy, the Johnson administration national security advisor, who helped lead the United States in Vietnam, was read by Donilon, Emmanuel, Axelrod, Jones, and President Obama himself.[50] Goldstein's lessons focused on how a dysfunctional national security bureaucracy and decision-making process had led the Johnson administration into an unwinnable war in Vietnam. Central to this critique was the fact that Johnson had used "military means to pursue indeterminate ends," something that White House staffers seem determined to avoid in Afghanistan. Obama's Special Envoy for Afghanistan and Pakistan, Ambassador Richard Holbrooke, had served in Vietnam for three years and was strikingly open about the comparisons between Afghanistan and Vietnam. Speaking of the comparisons made between Vietnam and Afghanistan at a State Department conference on the war in Vietnam, he said that "structurally there are obvious similarities. And leafing through these books here, they leap out at you. Many of the programs that are being followed, many of the basic doctrines are the same ones that we were trying to apply in Vietnam" and that "this is not Vietnam, but there's a lot to learn."[51]

Holbrooke and others in the State Department—such as Deputy Secretary of State Jim Steinberg, who worried that the United States was "on the path to another Vietnam"—were concerned about the seemingly open-ended nature of the commitment that McChrystal was calling for.[52] The most open critic of McChrystal's request was the US ambassador to Afghanistan, Karl Eikenberry. Eikenberry, a retired general who had previously commanded US forces in Afghanistan, sent a pair of highly critical diplomatic cables to Washington in November 2009, in which he outlined his "reservations about a counterinsurgency strategy that relies on a large infusion of US forces." Eikenberry was "concerned that we underestimate the risks of this expansion and that we have not fully studied every alternative. The proposed troop increase will bring vastly increased costs and an indefinite large-scale US military role in Afghanistan."[53] Eikenberry saw counterinsurgency not as a way out of Afghanistan but as a means of creating deeper dependence on the part of the Afghans, while US and NATO forces would do most of the fighting and take most of the casualties.

Obama's choice therefore was framed by different assessments of the utility of counterinsurgency and very different lessons from Vietnam. His decision-making process, however, sought in many ways to marry the two sets of lessons together. Even if Obama saw himself as "the first president who is young enough that the Vietnam War wasn't at the core of [his] development," the debate over that war and its lessons still framed his decision making in Afghanistan.[54] The debate on Afghanistan was extraordinarily lengthy and thorough, with meetings, chaired by Obama, ongoing from September right through to early December. Crucially, Obama also sought to clarify the goals in Afghanistan by revisiting them repeatedly in these meetings. This quest for clarity resulted in Obama eventually producing a six-page "terms sheet" for his commanders, which he had typed up himself, outlining a strategy centered on denying safe haven to Al-Qaeda and denying the Taliban the ability to overthrow the Afghan government.[55] Obama, then, was following Goldstein's lessons on Vietnam in terms of *process*, by emphasizing rigor, lengthy debate, and a clear articulation of goals and limits. Even so, he still largely acceded to McChrystal's demand for more forces, agreeing to send 30,000 additional troops in early 2010 and supporting his counterinsurgency campaign, even if the word was not mentioned in Obama's "terms sheet." Significantly, though, this support was tempered by a desire to begin withdrawing these forces in July 2011. If Obama was willing to let the military apply their lessons of Vietnam and Iraq in Afghanistan, then they had only a limited window in which to do so.

COUNTERINSURGENCY IN AFGHANISTAN

In Obama's speech to the cadets at West Point in December 2009 outlining this strategy, this tension between the lessons again emerged. The president rejected the arguments of "those who suggest that Afghanistan is another Vietnam" and therefore advocated cutting losses and withdrawing. For Obama, "this argument depends on a false reading of history," while he claimed that the United States now had broad international support and, crucially, was not facing a broad-based popular insurgency. If Obama rejected the Vietnam analogy for Afghanistan, he still shrank from maximalist ambitions there, saying that "as President, I refuse to set goals that go beyond our responsibility, our means, or our interests."[56] It was this calculus of means and interests that McChrystal would now have to address in Afghanistan.

McChrystal therefore had limited time, although virtually all the resources he had asked for, to revalidate the concept of counterinsurgency in Afghanistan. The experience of David Petraeus and the "surge" in Iraq still loomed large, but the deteriorating situation in Afghanistan called the utility of the concept into question. McChrystal argued that this deterioration was due to insufficient understanding of counterinsurgency on the part of prior ISAF commanders. In a speech in London in October 2009 he outlined the complexities of the environment in which he operated:

> If you build a well in the wrong place in a village, you may have shifted the basis of power in that village. If you tap into underground water, you give power to the owner of that well that they did not have before, because the traditional irrigation system was community-owned. If you dig a well and contract it to one person or group over another, you make a decision that, perhaps in your ignorance, tips the balance of power, or perception thereof, in that village.[57]

Crucially, McChrystal emphasized that, while protecting Afghan civilians from Taliban attacks was important, "we also need to protect them from our own actions. When we fight, if we become focused on destroying the enemy but end up killing Afghan civilians . . . we convince the Afghan people that we do not care about them."[58] This sentiment was operationalized in a tactical directive issued by McChrystal on July 2, 2009, an order that proscribed the use of air strikes and artillery unless "very limited and prescribed conditions" held.

This policy was further refined in a series of tactical directives throughout 2009 and 2010; a revised policy on escalation of force in April 2010 emphasized "tactical patience" and advised that "just because an engagement is permissible by the law of war and rules of engagement does not always mean that forces should engage" and that "in cases where units are determining positive identification . . . of perceived hostile intent, in the absence of an immediate threat to friendly forces, [commanders should] take time to develop a better understanding of the situation. When feasible, capture instead of kill."[59] A "tactical driving directive" issued in July 2009 banned overly aggressive driving by ISAF forces while noting that "aggressive driving practices anger local Afghans, fostering feelings of resentment and distrust toward ISAF forces" and that "these feelings can result in increased violence and reduced opportunities for partnering between ISAF military units, Afghan security forces, and government officials."[60] The culmination of this push for a less aggressive force was a revision of ISAF standard operating procedures on escalation of force in February 2010, which introduced the concept of "courageous restraint" and emphasized using nonlethal force at vehicle checkpoints wherever possible.[61] One US official told a reporter that "the most dangerous place to be in Afghanistan was in front of McChrystal after a 'civ cas' incident."[62]

These policies did apparently have an effect on Afghan civilian casualties. UN reports showed a 26 percent decrease in Afghan civilians killed by ISAF troops in 2010, while air strikes killed 171 civilians in 2010, half the 2009 figure.[63] ISAF's own civilian casualty reporting showed 11 percent fewer deaths. There were also subtler signs of progress in the data. Crucially, deaths due to escalation of force at checkpoints dropped 50 percent in the eight months after the February directive, compared to the same eight months in 2009.[64] However, while ISAF under McChrystal was becoming a safer force, overall civilian casualties continued to climb; UN reports showed a 15 percent increase in civilian casualties from 2009 to 2010, while ISAF's own reporting showed a 19 percent increase.[65] These increasing civilian deaths seemed to indicate that although McChrystal was able to control casualties caused by his own forces, protecting civilians from the Taliban—the core of his counterinsurgency campaign—would be much more difficult.

An indication of just how difficult this would be was the fate of Operation Moshtarak, the largest NATO offensive in Afghanistan since the US invasion in 2001. Aimed at securing the central Helmand River valley, it involved over 15,000 troops and was intended to break the Taliban insurgency in the south of Afghanistan. Although the operation was led by US Marines and British troops, it would be a showcase to validate the US Army's conception of counterinsurgency. Much of the press coverage of the upcoming operation explicitly talked of it as a test of Obama's war plan.[66] Speaking of an offensive to seize the town of Marja, a Taliban stronghold, McChrystal told reporters that Afghan government forces were ready to take over the town as soon as US Marines cleared the town of insurgents, claiming, "We've got a government in a box, ready to roll in."[67] While the operation was signaled well in advance to let civilians flee the area, it took months to clear the town of Taliban. Events in Marja showed that not only was it much more difficult to prevent the Taliban from inflicting civilian casualties than it was to curb ISAF-inflicted deaths, but providing governance in the town proved to be extremely difficult.

Apparently, planning for what would happen after the town was secure was vague, despite McChrystal's promise of "government in a box"; the Provincial Reconstruction Team complained that Marine planning for this "was very last minute."[68]

Indeed, when McChrystal visited the operation in May, he expressed frustration with the lack of progress, telling his commanders, "You don't feel it here . . . but I'll tell you, it's a bleeding ulcer outside."[69] One hundred days into the offensive, Marine patrols were still running into firefights on their patrols and were unable to hand over any of their sectors to Afghan forces, barring one outlying rural district, while the Afghan civilian administrators struggled to exert control over a population that was still subject to a campaign of beheadings and intimidation by the Taliban.[70] While Theo Farrell has argued that the British component of Operation Moshtarak, centered on North Nad-e Ali, was quite successful, the failure in Marja, where Afghan forces were unable to take over either security or governance despite a heavy investment of money and troops by ISAF, indicated the limitations of McChrystal's counterinsurgency plan.[71]

McChrystal, however, did not long remain in Kabul to oversee the war as he was fired by President Obama for critical remarks he and his staff made to a *Rolling Stone* reporter.[72] McChrystal's firing meant that General David Petraeus, in many ways the embodiment of the lessons of Iraq, would take over the war in Afghanistan. On taking command, Petraeus did not signal any shift in strategy, instead preferring to emphasize continuity with the existing plan that he had helped to shape. However, within weeks there had been a subtle shift in operations; while the contents of the counterinsurgency guidance that Petraeus issued to his troops in August 2010 would have been recognizable to anyone familiar with the similar guidance he issued in Iraq, emphasizing that "decisive terrain is the human terrain" and instructing troops to "live among the people," he also ordered them to "get [their] teeth into the insurgents and don't let go. When the extremists fight, make them pay. Seek out and eliminate those who threaten the population."[73] This was a much more aggressive approach than the one taken by McChrystal, and under Petraeus, air strikes— which had abated under McChrystal—significantly increased again. Indeed, air strikes doubled during Petraeus's tenure, with ISAF recording over twenty air strikes a day in July 2011, up from only ten a day in July 2010, the month Petraeus took over. October 2010 saw coalition aircraft use their weapons on 1,043 missions, up from 660 in 2009.[74]

Petraeus also drastically increased the use of Special Forces raids, target-ing midlevel Taliban commanders. The number of raids jumped from seventy-four in June 2010 to 144 in September 2010, with a concurrent increase in the number of detainees and deaths due to the raids. Under Petraeus, ISAF maintained a heavy tempo of night raids, with the monthly figure peaking in June 2011 with 215 raids carried out.[75] Critics argued that these raids were deeply counterproductive and indeed contrary to the larger goals of the coun-terinsurgency campaign; a report from the Open Societies Initiative argued:

> The costs of night raids have metastasized and the benefits (in the form of decreased insurgent attacks) have yet to materialize. The dramatic increase in the number of night raids, and evidence that night raids or other opera-tions may be more broadly targeting civilians to gather information and intel-ligence appear to have overwhelmed Afghan tolerance of the practice. Afghan attitudes toward night raids are as hostile as ever, if not more so . . . This issue has risen to a strategic level, seriously undermining long-term U.S. relations with the Afghan government.[76]

Petraeus himself pushed back on the idea that this focus on raiding and air strikes represented a shift away from counterinsurgency, arguing that coun-terterrorist raids were "absolutely part of a comprehensive civil–military counterinsurgency campaign. Not only are those [operations] not at odds with counterinsurgency, they're a very important element in the overall ap-proach."[77] Nonetheless, the effects of the night raids accumulated. By August 2010, in an echo of the Vietnam-era "body count," ISAF reported that their special forces had conducted 2,846 "kinetic" operations and killed or captured 365 insurgent leaders, captured 1,355 insurgents, and killed 1,031 lower-level Taliban.[78]

Perhaps the best example of the shift in Petraeus's emphasis was the con-troversy over the destruction of the village of Tarok Kalache. After an attempt to clear the abandoned village by an American unit failed due to a network of IEDs, the battalion commander decided to destroy the village rather than at-tempt to clear it again. On October 6, 2010, US aircraft and artillery dropped 49,200 pounds of explosives on the village to completely level it.[79] The com-mander who made the decision, Lt. Col. David Flynn, later said, "I literally cringed when we dropped bombs on these places—not because I cared about the enemy we were killing or the H[ome] M[ade] E[xplosives] destroyed, but I knew the reconstruction would consume the remainder of my deployed life."[80]

Petraeus approved $1 million in reconstruction projects,[81] and the village was rebuilt, but the controversy over the destruction seemed to crystallize discontent with the shift in strategy, providing as it did the uncomfortable echo of "destroying the village in order to save it." The destruction of Tarok Kolache may have been an extreme manifestation of this, but it fit a broader pattern, with the *New York Times* reporting in November 2010 that NATO troops had destroyed at least 174 booby-trapped homes in Kandahar since September of that year.[82]

This combination of increased air strikes, Special Forces raids, and demolitions seemed to belie Petraeus's prior focus on counterinsurgency. Indeed, retired Army Maj. Gen. Robert Scales described this development as "the slow gravitation of Afghanistan from a counterinsurgency-centered strategy to one tied more to direct action," with the objective being to kill as many Taliban as possible to drive the rest to the negotiating table, so that the US might find the space to leave.[83] Army officers saw that this shift toward withdrawal meant that the wisdom of applying counterinsurgency in Afghanistan was open to question. Writing of his experiences in as a brigade commander Afghanistan in *Military Review*, Col. John M. Spiszer argued:

> We in the military . . . define the decisive effort in counterinsurgency as winning hearts and minds. However, based on my experiences, I would argue that this is an improper mind-set around which to base operations . . . Our ultimate goal is to leave Afghanistan. We must maintain good enough relations with the people, the Afghan National Security Forces (ANSF), and the Government of the Islamic Republic of Afghanistan, but we don't have to win hearts and minds; we have to leave and turn the effort over to the Afghans.[84]

McChrystal's counterinsurgency campaign had failed to produce the tangible results it needed in Marja and Kandahar, and Petraeus, the foremost advocate of counterinsurgency, appeared to turn away from the central tenets of his own doctrine during his tenure at ISAF. The challenge of Afghanistan dented the newly formed Army consensus on counterinsurgency. As the Army prepared to draw down its forces in Afghanistan, the future of counterinsurgency within the institution was no longer clear.

LEAVING AFGHANISTAN, AND COUNTERINSURGENCY

Speaking in June 2011, President Obama announced that the surge would end and that US forces would leave Afghanistan by 2014. Although he defended the results of the surge, he also sounded a cautious note, declaring, "We won't try to make Afghanistan a perfect place. We will not police its streets or patrol its mountains indefinitely." Instead, it was "time to focus on nation building here at home," with Obama arguing that one of the lessons of the past decade of war was that the United States should respond with force when threatened, but that "when that force can be targeted, we need not deploy large armies overseas."[85] This echoed Secretary of Defense Robert Gates's acknowledgment that "the Army also must confront the reality that the most plausible, high-end scenarios for the U.S. military are primarily naval and air engagements—whether in Asia, the Persian Gulf, or elsewhere" and that any future secretary of defense who advised a president to send a large land army to the Middle East, Africa, or Asia "needed his head examined." Instead, while avoiding a repeat of the mistakes of the post-Vietnam years, the Army should acknowledge that the odds of repeating another Iraq or Afghanistan were low but still focus on retaining "unconventional abilities" to prevent problems from developing into full-blown crises that would require large-scale American military intervention. This, however, did not mean that the Army's future would be defined by counterinsurgency. Speaking to the cadets at West Point Gates made it clear that "by no means am I suggesting that the army will, or should, turn into a Victorian nation building constabulary, designed to chase guerrillas, build schools or sip tea."[86] Even some counterinsurgency advocates, such as retired Col. Peter Mansoor, claimed that "as we pull out of Afghanistan, there will be a shift back to training for conventional wars . . . counterinsurgency is going to slowly die out, just as it died out after Vietnam."[87]

What then of the lessons of Vietnam? The frustration of the ongoing counterinsurgency campaign in Afghanistan saw a reemergence of the ghosts of that war, in a way familiar to those who had studied the Army's reaction to the insurgency in Iraq. The pages of *Military Review* and other professional journals began to be filled with essays comparing Afghanistan with Vietnam, and again extracting lessons from the latter conflict. One of the most direct comparisons, Thomas Johnson and Christopher Mason's "The Vietnam Template in Afghanistan," appeared in *Military Review* in November 2009. They essentially doubled down on the Army's new consensus of the lessons of Vietnam, arguing that "since 2002, the prosecution of the war in Afghanistan—at all levels—has been based on an implied strategy of attrition via clearing operations virtually identical to those pursued in Vietnam" and that "as in Vietnam, the U.S. Army in Afghanistan is still subconsciously determined to fight the kind of war of maneuver it likes to fight, rather than adapt its tactics to the kind of war it is actually in."[88]

Unsurprisingly, the authors thought that this approach was bound to failure, but they believed that McChrystal was the first American commander since the war began to understand that a different approach was needed. The problem was that he was not pursuing counterinsurgency *enough*. "Clear, hold, and build" operations were not being properly resourced, and too few troops had reconstruction as their primary mission. In a sense, Johnson and Mason were resurrecting the Krepinevich/Nagl critique of the Army's institutional mentality. Indeed, counterinsurgency advisors such as Col. Robert Cassidy continued to find tactical lessons from Vietnam useful in Afghanistan. Cassidy provided ISAF headquarters with copies of a Center of Military History study of command and control in Vietnam in early 2009 and continued to advocate for a CORDS-like organization in Kabul.[89] In this reading, the tactical counterinsurgency lessons of Vietnam still applied in Afghanistan.

Long-time critics of the Army's turn toward counterinsurgency, however, applied a very different analysis of Vietnam to the situation in Afghanistan. Testifying before the Senate Foreign Relations Committee, Andrew Bacevich remarked that "once again, as in Vietnam, the enemy calls the tune, obliging us to fight on his terms. Decision has become elusive. As fighting drags on, its purpose becomes increasingly difficult to discern" and that the central of lesson of Vietnam was that "to embark upon an open-ended war lacking clearly defined and achievable objectives was to forfeit public support, thereby courting disaster."[90] Bacevich echoed Army critics, such as Col. Gian Gentile, who argued that the Army was now so committed to counterinsurgency that it did not know how to do anything else. For Gentile, the narrative of Vietnam as advanced by Krepinevich, Nagl, and Sorley was a false and dangerous one, as it led an army that had "difficulty thinking in historical context" to embrace a "strategy of tactics" that emphasized protecting the population to the detriment of all other goals.[91] Indeed, Gentile inverted Sorley, arguing that any success the United States had in countering the insurgency in Vietnam was based not on population security but on effectively pursuing and killing the enemy. Writing in *World Policy Journal*, Michael Cohen agreed, claiming that there was a "myth" of a "kinder, gentler war" that was being promoted by David Petraeus and FM 3-24. Like Gentile, he claimed that Vietnam taught that targeted killing could work, citing the Phoenix Program and a figure of 26,000 dead Viet Cong operatives as examples of how to effectively target an insurgency.[92] Given this renewed debate, it appeared as though the consensus around the lessons of Vietnam that Petraeus and other counterinsurgency advocates had established in 2006–2007 was already under threat.

That challenge to the procounterinsurgency consensus not only undermined the newly agreed-on lessons of Vietnam but led to a radical reassessment of a much more recent set of lessons: those from Iraq. While Petraeus strongly promoted lessons based on securing the population and had them embedded in broader Army doctrine, critics of counterinsurgency were much more skeptical about the results of the "surge." Writing in the *New York Times*, Celeste Ward Gventer—who had served in Iraq as a civilian advisor—warned against "an oversimplified and glamorized—and thus dangerously misleading—pop history about the 'surge' in Iraq and the role it played in the still-unfolding outcomes there" and said that the United States in fact had not defeated an insurgency there so much as taken sides in a civil war by picking "winners and losers" despite having only a limited understanding of the complex political environment in which they operated.[93]

An important indicator of the strength of this challenge to the accepted lessons of the surge was the publication of a critical piece in *Military Review*; Col. Craig Collier argued that the most effective way to protect the Iraqi population was combat operations to kill and capture criminals and insurgents. Further, erecting thousands of barriers to "separate the insurgents from the population" and conducting "relentless lethal operations" were the keys to success. Collier expressed surprise that "we seem reluctant to admit that killing the enemy actually worked" and argued that the supply of insurgent personnel was limited, claiming that killing key leaders was an effective way of making sure that insurgent recruiting dried up. For Collier, "killing or capturing an insurgent consistently and quantifiably had a more positive impact than anything else we did," a complete inversion of FM 3-24 and the lessons of Petraeus, and he argued that "in the final analysis, attrition matters. We should not feel ashamed that traditional combat operations worked in Iraq."[94] This focus on attrition was essentially a complete inversion of the accepted lessons of the "surge."

This dissent on the lessons of Iraq and the erosion of the consensus on counterinsurgency paralleled a fresh reconsideration of the lessons of Vietnam. If counterinsurgency proved to be fallible in Afghanistan, then the accepted lessons of Vietnam and Iraq would have to change. Again, the Army's understanding of the past was being remediated through contemporary circumstances. This backlash against counterinsurgency in the wake of Afghanistan, however, meant a reopening of the debate, not a closure. The consensus on counterinsurgency, which had seemed so deeply embedded in the Army's institutional culture in 2008 and 2009, was broken, but a new one has not yet emerged. The war in Afghanistan is still ongoing, and, although US troops may have withdrawn from Iraq, the final outcome there is still uncertain. Much will hinge on the way in which the United States departs Afghanistan; the lessons of Iraq and Afghanistan are still not clear. The only thing that is certain is that the experience of the US Army in Afghanistan from 2009 to 2011 shows that those lessons will be amended and reamended to suit contemporary circumstances, as with the lessons of Vietnam.

CONCLUSION

SUCH WAS THE IMPACT of the Vietnam War on the Army's culture that the lessons of the war reverberated all the way through to the war in Iraq and then on to Afghanistan. Nowhere were these echoes more clear than in the Army's counterinsurgency doctrine. Vietnam had a profound and continuing effect on Army attitudes toward counterinsurgency, and the Army's lessons of Vietnam were fluid, contested, and changeable. The fortunes of counterinsurgency within the US Army and the Army's lessons of Vietnam were inextricably linked throughout the post-Vietnam era; the relationship was not one way but rather symbiotic. Just as the Army's post-Vietnam distrust of counterinsurgency closely related to its lessons of Vietnam, similarly, the post-2005 revisiting of the lessons of Vietnam was tied to the reemergence of counterinsurgency within the Army. The nature of this relationship says much about the Army's organizational culture, its identity, its collective memory, the manner in which it learns lessons, and the way it adapts and innovates in response to crises.

THE FALL AND RESURRECTION OF COUNTERINSURGENCY

Although the Army has a long history of engaging in counterinsurgency campaigns, counterinsurgency has rarely been a core part of the Army's identity. Even during the Vietnam War, at the height of the Kennedy administration's enthusiasm for the concept, the Army's attitude toward counterinsurgency was lukewarm at best. This ambivalence contributed to the poor quality of both the Army's counterinsurgency doctrine and its strategy in Vietnam. Counterinsurgency was never at the heart of the campaigns prosecuted by either Westmoreland or Abrams, despite later triumphant narratives that claim the latter embraced pacification with great success. Furthermore, the experience of those units that did attempt to conduct counterinsurgency suggests that even an enthusiastic embrace of that strategy in Vietnam would not have been enough to overcome the systemic problems—such as a lack of leverage with the Saigon regime and the strength of the NLF and PAVN opposition—undermining the US effort. In the end, counterinsurgency might have been an effective tactic in Vietnam, but it could not compensate for overall strategic failings.

Given the Army's antipathy for counterinsurgency and the eventual ordeal of defeat in Vietnam, it is not surprising that Army leaders attempted to erase it from the institution's core doctrine by drastically reducing the relevant classes and courses and by downsizing or disbanding units specialized in counterinsurgency-type operations—such as the Special Forces. These actions reflected and reinforced the Army's institutional preference for conventional conflict, but the rapid and near-total elimination of counterinsurgency from Army doctrine suggests an almost-universal reaction to the traumas of Vietnam. The Army aggressively turned away from the doctrine it associated with the humiliating defeat in Vietnam, and Army leaders were almost uniformly cautious in advocating military intervention.[1] Not only that, but the Army's force structure and doctrine were amended with the intention of making policy makers more reluctant to call on the military to intervene. Army reticence was just as much a crucial constraint on interventionist impulses in the post-Vietnam era as the public reticence traditionally associated with the Vietnam syndrome.

The strength of this post-Vietnam reaction ensured the rejection of later attempts to reintroduce aspects of counterinsurgency doctrine to the Army by advocates of low-intensity conflict in the 1980s—such as the School for Advanced Military Studies's suggestion that "operations other than war" doctrine be made coequal with conventional doctrine. Where such proposals were not discarded outright, they were subverted, as with the rapid transformation of the new Light Infantry Divisions in the 1980s from LIC to supporting heavy forces on NATO's Northwest Europe theater of operations. Indeed, the profusion of phrases and concepts associated with counterinsurgency—Foreign Internal Defense, Internal Defense and Development, Low Intensity Conflict, Operations Other Than War, Stability Operations—reveals not only the inchoate (and occasionally incoherent) nature of counterinsurgency theory but the reluctance of even its supporters in the Army to call it by name, lest it conjure up the ghosts of Vietnam. Even those who saw El Salvador as representative of future Army operations considered counterinsurgency only as advice and support to foreign governments, not something that would include the commitment of American combat forces.

Reflecting the long-lasting opposition to counterinsurgency, 1990s supporters of both peacekeeping and operations other than war sought something less than a return of counterinsurgency. Even the label "operations other than war" suggested something divorced from the Army's core activities and mission. Rather than working to adapt itself for peacekeeping operations, the Army's distaste for such missions privileged an optimistic reliance on technology to provide quick, clean victories. This preference had deep roots in American strategic culture but was amplified by discourse on the "revolution in military affairs" and "transformation" in the wake of the Gulf War. Ironically, this "transformation" made intervention easier to contemplate, as it seemed to offer victory without the danger of prolonged war and heavy American casualties. This, in turn, influenced decision making on the question of whether to invade Iraq in 2003, where civilian policy makers (and their military allies) overrode the Army's reluctance to intervene. It took the shock of an increasingly successful Iraqi insurgency to dislocate such confidence in US military power.

The Army that invaded Iraq had been suffering from something of a crisis of identity, with "transformation" activists promoting a much lighter force and veterans of peacekeeping operations in the Balkans calling for a force better equipped to deal with "stability operations." That existing crisis of identity was exacerbated by the failures of the occupation of Iraq, which in turn were directly related to the Army's confusion over its role. When the chaos of spring 2003 in Iraq gave way to a growing insurgency, Army leaders were slow to recognize the situation and struggled to adapt to the changes. Yet, adapt they did, if slowly and haltingly. From the summer of 2003 to early 2007, at least some Army units tried to implement counterinsurgency-based plans, albeit with mixed levels of success. However, these efforts were isolated and not part of an overall strategy aimed at securing the Iraqi population. Instead, the emphasis was on training Iraqi forces and killing insurgents, which did not change until General David Petraeus took command in February 2007.

Built on tactical successes, such as the retaking of Tal Afar in 2005 and Ramadi in 2006, Petraeus's approach also incorporated an understanding of counterinsurgency codified in the 2006 field manual, FM 3-24 *Counterinsurgency*. This effort benefited from the Army's state of institutional and intellectual disarray to eventually elevate counterinsurgency in Army doctrine to a level not seen since Vietnam. However, the success of the manual relied heavily on Petraeus's implementation of the tenets of FM 3-24 during his tenure in Iraq; given the tenuous nature of the perceived success of Petraeus's 2007 to 2008 "surge" and the Army's long-held institutional distaste for counterinsurgency, the permanence of counterinsurgency's place in Army doctrine is still uncertain. Nonetheless, the Army of 2003 through 2008 certainly underwent a "transformation" very different from the one that Secretary of Defense Donald Rumsfeld envisioned. That Army now saw counterinsurgency as a central part of its organizational culture, even more so than it did during the Vietnam War.

The examples of the post-Vietnam era and Iraq suggest that major innovation and change *can* be driven from within military organizations but that such changes tend to be in reaction to major traumatic events. Only a major crisis such as the one the Army faced in Iraq presented an opening for counterinsurgency advocates to reshape the Army's identity, whereas previous efforts ended in failure. The refusal of the Army to shift toward counterinsurgency or similar types of operations despite the profusion of such conflicts throughout the 1980s and 1990s also indicates that the Army's perception of its identity as a "war-fighting" organization mattered as much as reality on the ground. The construction of the concept of "operations other than war" to contain unmilitary activities and the Army's failure (or even acquiescence in the failure of higher authorities) to rigorously plan for events after the end of "major combat operations" in Iraq are powerful examples of how institutional identity can obstruct organizational adaptation.

THE ARMY'S CHANGING LESSONS OF VIETNAM

It is impossible, however, to consider the fortunes of counterinsurgency within the Army without also considering the way in which the Army's consensus on the lessons of Vietnam shifted as circumstances dictated and the manner in which memories of that war were contested and reimagined in a way to make them useful for contemporary needs. The rebirth of counterinsurgency in Iraq grew out of a reconsideration of memories of Vietnam and the construction of lessons that emphasized the need to conduct population-centric counterinsurgency. While never quite universally accepted, the Army settled on a new consensus: a narrative of the war in Vietnam that privileged the experience of Creighton Abrams over that of William Westmoreland and the concept of pacification over that of "search and destroy."

This drawn-out construction of a usable narrative of the Vietnam War confirms Hugh Trevor-Roper's observation:

> Historians of every generation . . . see history against the background—the controlling background—of current events. They call upon it to explain the problems of their own time, to give to those problems a philosophical context, a continuum in which they may be reduced to proportion and perhaps made intelligible.[2]

In this light, one of the key difficulties in constructing lessons of Vietnam was that the lessons were contested even as the war was ongoing. The variety of experiences in Vietnam made it possible for Harry Summers to construct a narrative that focused on failure to prosecute conventional war in Vietnam, for Andrew Krepinevich to decry the Army's failure to understand counterinsurgency, and for Lewis Sorley to claim that the Army *had* understood and successfully prosecuted counterinsurgency in the latter stages of the war.[3] This profusion of competing narratives made it easier for Army leaders to construct lessons that suited their institutional imperatives at particular times and places and allowed competing groups within the Army to call on the "lessons of Vietnam" at will.

What is interesting about the way the Army selected its narratives of Vietnam is that these choices both shaped the Army's collective memory and identity and were themselves shaped by identity. This led to a self-reinforcing phenomenon, whereby the Army's institutional identity as it related to the "American way of war" led the Army to construct narratives and lessons from Vietnam that emphasized the need to not let the Army's focus stray from conventional operations, and those narratives and lessons in turn further reinforced the Army's "war-fighting" identity. This could help explain the profusion of a "warrior culture" in the Army that declared every clerk and quartermaster to be a "war-fighter first" and published field manuals on "warrior ethos."[4]

Certainly, in the immediate aftermath of the war, when the Army was at a low ebb, both in terms of morale and in terms of capabilities, it preferred institutional silence on Vietnam rather than engagement. Vietnam disappeared from the Army's professional military journals and education system; its field manuals, from the capstone FM 100-5 *Operations* on down, made no mention of the war, and no definitive "lessons learned" study emerged. Despite the long silence on Vietnam, implicit lessons worked their way through the Army. William DePuy and other reformers attempted to retrain the Army in conventional skills ostensibly lost in Vietnam. The lesson of Vietnam embodied by DePuy's reforms was that the Army should concern itself only with the high-technology, mechanized operations. That this lesson was not explicitly challenged within Army leadership ensured that the official "lessons" of Vietnam codified with the publication of Harry Summers's *On Strategy: The Vietnam War in Context* in 1982, closely mirrored DePuy's focus on conventional operations and created the doctrinal foundations for an Army determined to avoid similar situations in the future.

This "never again" school of thought thoroughly dominated the Army's thinking on Vietnam in the postwar era. It found its most powerful and succinct expression in the Weinberger-Powell Doctrine, which cautioned that the United States should not intervene unless the objectives were clear, congressional and public support could be assured, overwhelming force was available, and an exit strategy was at hand. With few exceptions, the Army organized its doctrine and its forces to conform to Powell's lessons of Vietnam. Nonetheless, these lessons were contested when first announced by Secretary of Defense Casper Weinberger. Indeed, for some, El Salvador offered a set of lessons that would allow the United States to avoid future Vietnams by limiting the use of combat troops and instead providing close military, political, and economic support to threatened friendly governments and ensuring that US advisors had a solid knowledge of all aspects of counterinsurgency campaigning.

While the lessons of El Salvador were mediated through those of Vietnam, they did not fundamentally change the Army's understanding of Vietnam as something that should never be repeated. However, the Army's experiences there made it more open to very specific kinds of intervention. The 1990–1991 Gulf War seemingly validated Weinberger and Powell's lessons as the Army triumphed through the use of overwhelming force and high-technology firepower, while eschewing ambitious or vague objectives, such as the overthrow of Saddam Hussein's regime. These lessons were reinforced by the failures of the mission in Somalia in 1993, where a two-day-long firefight in Mogadishu left eighteen Americans (and several hundred Somalis) dead. Even as the Army increased its involvement in peacekeeping operations in the 1990s, the lessons of Vietnam essentially became static, and challenges to the Powell Doctrine within the Army were minimal. Indeed, the overriding concern within the Army was to avoid creating another Vietnam in the Balkans, resulting in an essentially tentative and cautious approach to peacekeeping. At the same time, alternative lessons from Vietnam, such as the importance of civil–military integration (as seen with CORDS in Vietnam) also influenced the debate.

Given the extent to which Vietnam still dominated the Army's conscious-ness, it is no surprise to see that competing lessons of Vietnam played a large part in its understanding of the war in Iraq. After an initial inability to grasp the extent of the challenge they faced, a narrative evolved that cast "Iraqifi-cation" as a better version of Vietnamization. Army leaders such as General George Casey were anxious to use "Iraqification" as a way to help an over-stretched army withdraw from Iraq and avoid the sort of breakdown that oc-curred in the Vietnam-era Army. This Vietnam-influenced understanding of Iraq gradually evolved into the more counterinsurgency-oriented interpreta-tion of FM 3-24 promoted by General David Petraeus. This understanding fo-cused on the tactical lessons of Vietnam, on what could have been done better and therefore (partially) on Lewis Sorley's "Better War" thesis and the actions of General Creighton Abrams rather than the failures of the war. The Vietnam of David Petraeus and John Nagl bore little resemblance to that of William DePuy and Harry Summers, other than that both versions were constructed to serve didactic purposes.

In the context of a growing insurgency in Iraq, this effort to reshape the lessons of Vietnam succeeded where earlier attempts had failed and transfor-mation of the Army's "Vietnam" in 2005 through 2008 was remarkably swift. This transformation of the meaning of "Vietnam" was a crucial element in the rise of the Petraeus-led counterinsurgency advocates. That the institution changed its understanding of the war so quickly indicates a crisis on the same scale as the one that engulfed the Army of the post-Vietnam era, a shock that fatally undermined the prevailing consensus. This complete transformation of the Army's lessons of Vietnam also illustrates that its understanding of history was never fixed but always contingent on the need to be usable in con-temporary circumstances. The Powell Doctrine was useful for avoiding wars like Iraq, but it had nothing to contribute once the Army was engaged in such a war. Similarly, the Army's institutional and doctrinal focus on conventional war may have been of use in discouraging policy makers from committing the Army to lengthy occupations, but it left the force completely ill equipped, both in organization and mentality, after policy makers committed them to invasion and occupation anyway. In such circumstances, the lessons of Vietnam were constructed anew (as they had been to a lesser extent in El Salvador), and the narrative of the war was recast and made useful for the present.

Ultimately, what has been largely absent from the Army's discourse on counterinsurgency is a recognition that both caution toward intervention—the central insight of the Powell Doctrine—counterinsurgency's caution about the use of force at the tactical level can coexist. For one of the central truths of counterinsurgency experience, although one seldom recognized by its practitioners, is that there are limits to both the broader strategic utility of force and its tactical application. Those within the Army who have debated counterinsurgency since Vietnam have tended to recognize only one of these insights at a time. Either the utility of force was inherently limited and therefore had to be applied in massive, overwhelming doses to ensure success, or military intervention was usable in a much broader range of scenarios, as long as the application of force was tailored to acceptable and useful levels. Given that the Army's organizational culture seems to have shifted toward an acceptance of counterinsurgency in a way it had not earlier, during or after the Vietnam War, the lessons of Iraq and Afghanistan may well recognize restraint in both the utility and application of force. Doubtless, though, these lessons will be contested and reinterpreted anew as contemporary contingencies dictate.

What is clear is that the "lessons" of history are malleable and contingent on circumstances. The lessons influence events, but events also change the lessons. Perhaps the best formulation to explain the way the Army's lessons of Vietnam influenced its attitude toward counterinsurgency is Robert MacIver's statement,

> Wherever he goes, whatever he encounters, man spins about him his web of myth . . . The myth mediates between man and nature. From the shelter of his myth he perceives and experiences the world. Inside his myth he is at home in his world.[5]

The constructed narrative of Vietnam through which the Army perceived the world was destroyed by events in Iraq; the response was to construct a new, more usable narrative that highlighted counterinsurgency rather than ignored it. If the "history of the lesson" of the Army's lessons of Vietnam has demonstrated anything it is that these lessons and narratives are fluid and open to reconstruction. The lessons literature, however, ignores Michael Howard's paraphrase of Jakob Burckhardt that "the true use of history, whether military or civil, is . . . not to make men clever for next time; it is to make them wise forever."[6] In considering the lessons of Iraq, the US Army must do what it did not do with the lessons of Vietnam and move beyond a focus on "next time" to an understanding that approaches wisdom.

REFERENCE MATTER

NOTES

Introduction

1. Victor H. Krulak, "Address by Major General Victor H. Krulak, USMC, Special Assistant to Director, Joint Chiefs of Staff, for Counterinsurgency and Special Activities, to Army War College, Wednesday, 23 May 1962: Tactics and Techniques of Insurgency and Counterinsurgency," May 23, 1962, Army War College Lectures, box 1961–1962-6 lectures AY 1961–62, folder 6, Maj. Gen. Krulak (Carlisle, PA: U.S. Army Military History Institute).

2. Ibid.

3. In 1991, President George H. W. Bush claimed in the aftermath of the Persian Gulf War that "the specter of Vietnam has been buried forever in the desert sands of the Arabian Peninsula"; President George H. W. Bush, Radio Address to U.S. Armed Forces Stationed in the Persian Gulf Region, March 2, 1991, George H. W. Bush Presidential Library Website, available at http://bushlibrary.tamu.edu/research/papers/1991/91030200.html. President Barack Obama denied any validity in Vietnam–Afghanistan comparisons during his speech announcing that extra troops would be sent to Afghanistan; "Obama's Address on the War in Afghanistan," *The New York Times*, December 2, 2009, available at www.nytimes.com/2009/12/02/world/asia/02prexy.text.html.

4. For a full discussion of the literature on the Vietnam–Iraq analogy, see David Ryan and David Fitzgerald, "Iraq and Vietnam: Endless Recurrence or Stirrings Still?" *Critical Asian Studies* 41, no. 4 (December 2009), 621–653.

5. Mikkel Vedby Rasmussen, "The History of a Lesson: The Social Construction of the Past," *Review of International Studies* 29, no. 3 (2003), 499–519.

6. Russell Weigley, *A History of the Unites States Army* (New York: MacMillan, 1967), 161.

7. John Nagl, *Learning to Eat Soup with a Knife: Counterinsurgency Lessons from Malaya and Vietnam* (Chicago: University of Chicago Press, 2005). Nagl's work on the US Army in Vietnam was strongly influenced by earlier works such as Douglas Blaufarb, *The Counterinsurgency Era: US Doctrine and Performance 1950 to Present* (New York: The Free Press, 1977); Andrew Krepinevich, *The Army and Vietnam* (Baltimore, MD: The Johns Hopkins University Press, 1988); and Larry Cable, *Conflict of Myths: The Development of Counter-Insurgency Doctrine and the Vietnam War* (New York: New York University Press, 1986).

8. Richard D. Downie, *Learning from Conflict: The U.S. Military in Vietnam, El Salvador and the Drug War* (Westport, CT: Greenwood Press, 1998); Robert Cassidy, *Counterinsurgency and the Global War on Terror: Military Culture and Irregular War* (Stanford, CA: Stanford University Press, 2008); and Conrad C. Crane, *Avoiding Vietnam: The U.S. Army's Response to Defeat in Southeast Asia* (Carlisle Barracks, PA: Strategic Studies Institute, U.S. Army War College, 2002).

9. David Ucko, *The New Counterinsurgency Era: Transforming the U.S. Military for Modern Wars* (Washington, DC: Georgetown University Press, 2009).

10. Andrew J. Birtle, *U.S. Army Counterinsurgency and Contingency Operations Doctrine 1942–1976* (Washington, DC: US Army Center of Military History, 2006). See also: Andrew J. Birtle, *U.S. Army Counterinsurgency and Contingency Operations Doctrine 1860–1941* (Washington, DC: US Army Center of Military History, 1997).

11. Max Boot, *The Savage Wars of Peace: Small Wars and the Rise of American Power* (New York: Basic Books, 2003); and Robert D Kaplan, *Imperial Grunts: The American Military on the Ground* (New York: Random House, 2005).

12. D. Michael Shafer, *Deadly Paradigms: The Failure of U.S. Counterinsurgency Policy 1945–1965* (Princeton, NJ: Princeton University Press, 1988); and Michael McClintock, *Instruments of Statecraft: U.S. Guerrilla Warfare, Counterinsurgency, and Counter-terrorism, 1940–1990* (New York: Pantheon Books, 1992). Both the failures of modernization theory and the tendency to support repressive regimes are themes that have received considerable attention in the broader field of US foreign relations. See Michael Latham, *Modernization as Ideology: American Social Science and "Nation Building" in the Kennedy Era* (Chapel Hill: University of North Carolina Press, 2000); and David F. Schmitz, *Thank God They're on Our Side: The United States and Right-Wing Dictatorships, 1921–1945* (Chapel Hill: University of North Carolina Press, 1999).

13. Barry R. Posen, *The Sources of Military Doctrine: France, Britain and Germany between the World Wars* (Ithaca, NY: Cornell University Press, 1984); and Jack Snyder, *The Ideology of the Offensive: Military Decision-Making and the Disasters of 1914* (Ithaca, NY: Cornell University Press, 1984).

14. Graham T. Allison, *Essence of Decision* (Boston: Little, Brown, 1971).

15. Deborah Avant, *The Institutional Sources of Military Doctrine: The United States in Vietnam and Britain in the Boer War and Malaya* (PhD dissertation, Univer-

sity of California, San Diego, 1991); Stephen Rosen, *Winning the Next War: Innovation and the Modern Military* (Ithaca, NY: Cornell University Press, 1991); Samuel P. Huntington, *The Soldier and the State: The Theory and Politics of Civil–Military Relations* (Cambridge, MA: Belknap Press of Harvard University Press, 1981); Douglas A. Macgregor, *Breaking the Phalanx: A New Design for Land Power in the 21st Century* (New York: Praeger Paperback, 1997); and Douglas A. Macgregor, *Transformation under Fire: Revolutionizing How America Fights* (New York: Praeger Publishers, 2003).

16. Chad Serena, *A Revolution in Military Adaptation: The US Army in the Iraq War* (Washington, DC: Georgetown University Press, 2011); and James A. Russell, *Innovation and War: Counterinsurgency Operations in Anbar and Ninewa Provinces, Iraq, 2005–2007* (Stanford, CA: Stanford University Press, 2011).

17. Kimberley Marten Zisk, *Engaging the Enemy: Organization Theory and Soviet Military Innovation 1955–1991* (Princeton, NJ: Princeton University Press, 1993).

18. Elizabeth Kier, *Changes in Conventional Military Doctrines: The Cultural Roots of Doctrinal Change* (PhD dissertation, Cornell University, 1992), 62.

19. For work that emphasizes the importance of cultural constructs in military history, see Michael Hogan, *A Cross of Iron: Harry S. Truman and the Origins of the National Security State, 1945–1954* (Cambridge, UK: Cambridge University Press, 1998); John Dower, *War without Mercy: Race and Power in the Pacific War* (New York: Pantheon Books, 1986); Michael Sherry, *The Rise of American Air Power: The Creation of Armageddon* (New Haven, CT: Yale University Press, 1987); and Theo Farrell, "Transnational Norms and Military Development: Constructing Ireland's Professional Army," *European Journal of International Relations* 7, no. 1 (March 1, 2001), 63–102.

20. Colin S. Gray, "National Style in Strategy: The American Example," *International Security* 6, no. 2 (1981), 21–47.

21. Jeremy Black, *War and the Cultural Turn* (Cambridge, UK: Polity, 2011); *idem.*, "Determinisms and Other Issues," *The Journal of Military History*, 68 (October 2004), 1217–1232; Adrian R. Lewis, *The American Culture of War: A History of US Military Force from World War II to Operation Iraqi Freedom* (London: Routledge, 2006), 5; and Patrick Porter, "Good Anthropology, Bad History: The Cultural Turn in Studying War," *Parameters* 37, no. 2 (Summer 2007), 45–58.

22. Many studies of strategic culture examine comparative national experiences. As well the aforementioned work by Kier, Posen, and Avant, there is also Eitan Shamir, *Transforming Command: The Pursuit of Mission Command in the U.S., British and Israeli Armies* (Stanford, CA: Stanford University Press, 2011) and Dima Adamsky, *The Culture of Military Innovation: The Impact of Cultural Factors on the Revolution in Military Affairs in Russia, the US, and Israel* (Stanford, CA: Stanford University Press, 2010).

23. Michael Howard, *The Franco-Prussian War: The German Invasion of France, 1870–1871* (New York: Macmillan, 1961), 1.

24. Russell Weigley, *The American Way of War: A History of United States Military Strategy and Policy* (New York: Macmillan, 1973).

25. John Ellis, *Brute Force: Allied Strategy and Tactics during the Second World War* (London: Viking, 1990); and Michael H. Hunt, *The American Ascendancy* (Chapel Hill: University of North Carolina Press, 2007), 129–135.

26. Cited in Max Hastings, *Armageddon: The Battle for Germany 1944–45* (London: Macmillan, 2004), 90.

27. Richard Lock-Pullan, *U.S. Intervention Policy and Army Innovation: From Vietnam to Iraq* (London: Routledge, 2005).

28. Though still heavily dependent on technology, the emphasis on the operational art echoed the German *Wehrmacht* of World War II. See David Schoenbaum, "Review: The Wehrmacht and G.I. Joe: Learning What from History? A Review Essay," *International Security* 8, no. 1 (Summer 1983), 201–207.

29. Carl Builder, *The Masks of War: American Military Styles in Strategy and Analysis: A RAND Corporation Research Study* (Baltimore, MD: The Johns Hopkins University Press, 1989).

30. Lock-Pullan, *U.S. Intervention Policy and Army Innovation: From Vietnam to Iraq*, 9. This argument is also made in Lewis, *The American Culture of War*.

31. Stuart Kinross, *Clausewitz and America: Strategic Thought and Practice from Vietnam to Iraq* (London: Routledge, 2008); and Robert R. Tomes, *US Defence Strategy from Vietnam to Operation Iraqi Freedom: Military Innovation and the New American War of War, 1973–2003* (London: Routledge, 2006). See also: Keith L. Shimko, *The Iraq Wars and America's Military Revolution* (New York: Cambridge University Press, 2010).

32. Brian M. Linn, *The Echo of Battle: The Army's Way of War* (Cambridge, MA: Harvard University Press, 2007), 9.

33. Ibid., 4–5.

34. This is something that Linn had already set out to do in earlier correspondence with Weigley. See Brian M. Linn and Russell F. Weigley, "'The American Way of War' Revisited," *The Journal of Military History* 66, no. 2 (April 2002), 501–533.

35. For scholarship that addresses culture as a fluid process, see Mary A. Renda, *Taking Haiti: Military Occupation and the Culture of US Imperialism 1915–1940* (Chapel Hill: University of North Carolina Press, 2000).

36. Gabriel Kolko, *Anatomy of a War: Vietnam, the United States, and the Modern Historical Experience* (New York: Pantheon Books, 1985); Noam Chomsky, *Rethinking Camelot: JFK, the Vietnam War and US Political Culture* (London: Verso, 1993); and Marilyn B. Young, *Vietnam Wars, 1945–1990* (New York: Harper, 1991).

37. Cited in H. R. McMaster, "The Human Element: When Gadgetry Becomes Strategy," *World Affairs Journal*, Winter 2009, available at www.worldaffairsjournal .org/article/human-element-when-gadgetry-becomes-strategy.

38. Earl Ravenal, *Never Again: Learning from America's Foreign Policy Failures* (Philadelphia: Temple University Press, 1978).

39. W. Scott Thompson and Donaldson D. Frizzell, *The Lessons of Vietnam* (New York: Crane Russak, 1977).

40. Robert McNamara, *In Retrospect* (New York: Random House, 1996).

41. This set of lessons was very popular within the US military. See Kenneth J. Campbell, "The Crucial Constraint: Containment and the Post-Vietnam Military's Reluctance to Use Force" (PhD dissertation, Temple University, 1989); Kenneth J. Campbell, "Once Burned, Twice Cautious: Explaining the Weinberger-Powell Doctrine," *Armed Forces and Society* 24, no. 3 (1988); George Herring, "Preparing *Not* to Refight the Last War: The Impact of the Vietnam War on the US Military," in Charles E. Neu (ed.), *After Vietnam: Legacies of a Lost War* (Baltimore, MD: Johns Hopkins University Press, 2000), 56–84; Lock-Pullan, *U.S. Intervention Policy and Army Innovation: From Vietnam to Iraq*; and David H. Petraeus, "The American Military and the Lessons of Vietnam: A Study of Military Influence and Use of Force in the Post-Vietnam Era" (PhD dissertation, Woodrow Wilson School of Public and International Affairs, Princeton University, 1987).

42. Richard Melanson, *American Foreign Policy since the Vietnam War: The Search for Consensus from Nixon to Clinton* (London: M. E. Sharpe, 2000).

43. Arnold R. Isaacs, *Vietnam Shadows: The War, Its Ghosts and Its Legacies* (Baltimore, MD: Johns Hopkins University Press, 1997); Robert Schulzinger, *A Time for Peace: The Legacy of the Vietnam War* (Oxford, UK, and New York: Oxford University Press, 2006); Charles E. Neu, *After Vietnam: Legacies of a Lost War* (Baltimore, MD: Johns Hopkins University Press, 2000); Robert McMahon, "Contested Memory: The Vietnam War and American Society, 1975–2001," *Diplomatic History* 26, no. 2 (4, 2002), 159–184; and David Ryan, "Vietnam in the American Mind: Narratives of the Nation and the Sources of Collective Memory," in *Cultural Memory and Multiple Identities* (Berlin: Lit Verlag, 2008).

44. Ernest May, *"Lessons" of the Past: The Use and Misuse of History in American Foreign Policy* (New York: Oxford University Press, 1973).

45. Ibid., xi.

46. Alexander L. George, *Bridging the Gap: Theory and Practice in Foreign Policy* (Washington, DC: US Institute of Peace Press, 1993); Ernest May and Richard Neustadt, *Thinking in Time: The Uses of History for Decision Makers* (New York: The Free Press, 1986); Jeffrey Record, *Making War, Thinking History: Munich, Vietnam and the Presidential Use of Force from Korea to Kosovo* (Annapolis, MD: Naval Institute Press,

2002); and Theodor Schieder, *Historical Consciousness and Political Action* (Middleton, CT: Wesleyan University Press, 1978).

47. Robert Jervis, *Perception and Misperception in International Politics* (Princeton, NJ: Princeton University Press, 1976), 217.

48. Yueng Foong Khong, *Analogies at War: Korea, Munich, Dien Bien Phu and the Vietnam Decisions of 1965* (Princeton, NJ: Princeton University Press, 1992).

49. Barbara Tuchman, *The Guns of August* (New York: Macmillan, 1962).

50. Michael Howard, "The Use and Abuse of Military History: Lecture to the Royal United Services Institute, 18 October 1961," *Royal United Services Institute Journal* 107, no. 4 (February 1962).

51. Rasmussen, "The History of a Lesson: The Social Construction of the Past."

52. Ibid., 504.

53. Ibid., 500.

54. Ibid., 503.

55. David Lowenthal, *The Past Is a Foreign Country* (Cambridge, UK: Cambridge University Press, 1985); Jacques Le Goff, *History and Memory* (New York: Columbia University Press, 1992); Dominick LaCapra, *History and Memory after Auschwitz* (Ithaca, NY: Cornell University Press, 1998); Roy Rosenzweig, *How Americans Use and Understand the Past* (New York: Columbia University Press, 1998); Michael Hogan, *Hiroshima in History and Memory* (Cambridge, UK: Cambridge University Press, 1996); John Bodnar, *Remaking America: Public Memory, Commemoration, and Patriotism in the Twentieth Century* (Princeton, NJ: Princeton University Press, 1992); Paul Connerton, *How Societies Remember* (Cambridge, UK: Cambridge University Press, 1989); Theo Farrell, "Memory, Imagination and War," *History* 87, no. 285 (January 2002); and Patrick Finney, "On Memory, Identity and War," *Rethinking History* 6, no. 1 (2002), 1–13.

56. David Thelen, "Memory and American history," *The Journal of American History* 75, no. 4 (1989), 1117–1129.

57. Jay Winter, *Remembering War: The Great War between History and Memory in the Twentieth Century* (New Haven, CT: Yale University Press, 2006), 197.

58. Alon Confino, "Collective Memory and Cultural History: Problems of Method," *The American Historical* Review 102, no. 5 (Dec. 1997), 1398.

59. Jeffrey K. Olick, *The Politics of Regret: On Collective Memory and Historical Responsibility* (London: Routledge, 2007), 109.

60. Susan Sontag, *Regarding the Pain of Others* (New York: Farrar, Straus and Giroux, 2003), 85–86.

61. Jay Winter, "Thinking about Silence," in Efrat Ben Ze'ev, Ruth Gino, and Jay Winter (eds.), *Shadows of War: A Social History of Silence in the Twentieth Century* (Cambridge, UK: Cambridge University Press, 2010), 3–31.

62. Theo Farrell, "Constructivist Security Studies: Portrait of a Research Program," *International Studies Review* 4, no. 1 (Spring 2002), 49–72.

63. For perspectives on the social construction of knowledge, see Peter Berger, *The Social Construction of Reality: A Treatise in the Sociology of Knowledge* (Garden City, NY: Doubleday, 1966); Ian Hacking, *The Social Construction of What?* (Cambridge, MA: Harvard University Press, 1999); Alexander Wendt, *Social Theory of International Politics* (Cambridge, UK: Cambridge University Press, 1999); and Alexander Wendt, "Constructing International Politics," *International Security* 20, no. 1 (1995), 71.

64. Farrell, "Constructivist Security Studies," 60.

65. Larry E. Cable, *Conflict of Myths: The Development of Counterinsurgency Doctrine and the Vietnam War* (New York: New York University Press, 1986), 3.

66. Krepinevich, *The Army and Vietnam.*

67. Keith Bickel, "Mars Learning: The Marine Corps Development of Small Wars Doctrine 1915–1940" (PhD dissertation, Johns Hopkins University, 1998).

Chapter 1

1. Nancy Tucker, "Vietnam, the Never-Ending War," in *The Vietnam War as History*, ed. Elizabeth Errington and B. J. C. McKercher (New York: Praeger, 1990), 177.

2. John Prados, "Author's response to Roundtable Review: John Prados. Vietnam: The History of an Unwinnable War, 1945–1975," *H-Diplo Roundtable* X, no. 7 (November 30, 2009), available at www.h-net.org/~diplo/roundtables/PDF/Roundtable-XI-7.pdf. Those works that have attempted to present a single grand narrative of the war include John Prados, *Vietnam: The History of an Unwinnable War, 1945–1975* (Lawrence: University Press of Kansas, 2009); Stanley Karnow, *Vietnam, a History* (New York: Viking Press, 1983); George C. Herring, *America's Longest War: The United States and Vietnam, 1950–1975* (New York: McGraw Hill, 1979); Marilyn B. Young, *The Vietnam Wars, 1945–1990* (New York: Harper, 1991); and Gabriel Kolko, *Anatomy of a War: Vietnam, the United States, and the Modern Historical Experience* (New York: Pantheon Books, 1985).

3. David Elliott is strongly critical of such a limited, US-focused perspective. See David W. P. Elliott, "Official History, Revisionist History and Wild History," in Mark Bradley and Marilyn B. Young (eds.), *Making Sense of the Vietnam Wars: Local, National and Transnational Perspectives* (New York: Oxford University Press, 2008).

4. Larry Cable, *Conflict of Myths: The Development of American Counterinsurgency Doctrine and the Vietnam War* (New York: New York University Press, 1986); William Colby, *Lost Victory* (Chicago: Contemporary Books, 1989); Cecil B. Currey, *Edward Lansdale: The Unquiet American* (Boston: Houghton Mifflin, 1988); Robert Komer, *Bureaucracy at War: US Performance in the Vietnam Conflict* (Boulder, CO: Westview Press, 1986); Andrew Krepinevich, *The Army and Vietnam* (Baltimore, MD:

Johns Hopkins University Press, 1986); Guenter Lewy, *America and Vietnam: Illusion, Myth and Reality* (New York: Oxford University Press, 1978); and Lewis Sorley, *A Better War: The Unexamined Victories and Final Tragedy of America's Last Years in Vietnam* (New York: Harcourt Brace & Company, 1999).

5. Many detailed studies have pushed back against the "hearts and minds" argument that the United States could have won the war had it been more effective at counterinsurgency. See Zalin Grant, *Facing the Phoenix: The CIA and the Political Defeat of the United States in Vietnam* (New York: W. W. Norton, 1991); Neal Sheehan, *A Bright Shining Lie: John Paul Vann and America in Vietnam* (New York: Random House, 1988); Andrew J. Birtle, *US Army Counterinsurgency and Contingency Operations Doctrine 1942–1976* (Washington, DC: US Army Center of Military History, 2006); Jeffrey Clarke, *Advice and Support: The Final Years 1965–73* (Washington, DC: US Army Center of Military History, 1988); Richard Hunt, *Pacification: The American Struggle for Vietnam's Hearts and Minds* (Boulder, CO: Westview Press, 1995); Jefferson Marquis, "The Other Warriors: American Social Science and Nation Building in Vietnam," *Diplomatic History* 24, no. 1 (2000), 79–105; Michael E. Peterson, *The Combined Action Platoons: The US Marines' Other War in Vietnam* (New York: Praeger, 1989); and Ronald Spector, *After Tet: The Bloodiest Year in Vietnam* (New York: Maxwell Macmillan International, 1993). Province-level studies have been particularly effective in illustrating just how deep the problems with pacification efforts were. See David W. P. Elliott, *The Vietnamese War: Revolution and Social Change in the Mekong Delta 1930–75* (concise edition) (London: M. E. Sharpe, 2002); Jeffrey Race, *War Comes to Long An: Revolutionary Conflict in a Vietnam Province* (Berkeley: University of California Press, 1972); James Trullinger, *Village at War: An Account of Revolution in Vietnam* (New York: Longman, 1980); and Eric Bergerud, *The Dynamics of Defeat: The Vietnam War in Hau Nghia Province* (Boulder, CO: Westview Press, 1991).

6. For the "Clausewitzian" perspective on US strategy in the war, see U. S. Grant Sharp, *Strategy for Defeat: Vietnam in Retrospect* (San Rafael, CA: Presidio Press, 1978); Dave Richard Palmer, *Summons of the Trumpet: US-Vietnam in Perspective* (San Rafael, CA: Presidio Press, 1978); Bruce Palmer, *The 25 Year War: America's Military Role in Vietnam* (Lexington: Kentucky University Press, 1984); Harry G. Summers, *On Strategy: The Vietnam War in Context* (Honolulu: University of the Pacific Press, 1981); Shelby Stanton, *The Rise and Fall of an American Army: US Ground Forces in Vietnam 1965–73* (Novato, CA: Presidio Press, 2003); and Phillip B. Davidson, *Vietnam at War: The History: 1946–1975* (New York: Oxford University Press, 1991).

7. Gary R. Hess, "The Unending Debate: Historians and the Vietnam War," *Diplomatic History* 18, no. 2 (1994), 242–244.

8. Office of the Deputy Chief of Staff for Military Operations, *A Program for the Pacification and Long-Term Development of South Vietnam*, volume 1 (Washington DC: Department of the Army, March 1966).

9. Andrew Krepinevich, *The Army and Vietnam* (Baltimore, MD: Johns Hopkins University Press, 1988); John Nagl, *Learning to Eat Soup with a Knife: Counterinsurgency Lessons from Malaya and Vietnam* (Chicago: University of Chicago Press, 2005).

10. Dale Andrade, "Westmoreland Was Right: Learning the Wrong Lessons from the Vietnam War," *Small Wars and Insurgencies* 19, no. 2 (June 2008), 145–181; and Andrew J. Birtle, "PROVN, Westmoreland, and the Historians: A Reappraisal," *The Journal of Military History* 72, no. 4 (October 26, 2008), 1213–1247.

11. Sorley, *A Better War*, xiv.

12. Lewis Sorley (ed.), *Vietnam Chronicles: The Abrams Tapes 1968–72* (Lubbock: Texas Tech University Press, 2004) [hereafter referred to as *Abrams Tapes*], 152–153.

13. For the debate over the efficacy and morality of the Phoenix Program see Dale Andrade, *Ashes to Ashes: The Phoenix Program and the Vietnam War* (Lexington, MA: Lexington Books, 1990), Grant, *Facing the Phoenix*, and Mark Moyar, *Phoenix and the Birds of Prey: Counterinsurgency and Counterterrorism in Vietnam* (Lincoln: University of Nebraska Press, 2007).

14. See Bergerud, *Dynamics of Defeat*; Birtle, *US Army Counterinsurgency and Contingency Operations 1942–1972* (Washington, DC: US Army Center of Military History, 2006), ; David W. P. Elliott, *The Vietnamese War: Revolution and Social Change in the Mekong Delta, 1930–1975*, Concise edition (Armonk, NY: M. E. Sharpe, 2006); and Kolko, *Anatomy of a War* for critiques that come from both the right and the left ends of the political spectrum but effectively occupy the same space.

15. George D. Jacobson, assistant chief of staff for CORDS, *The Abrams Tapes*, 376.

16. The HES was a statistical method for measuring the relative control of the GVN over a hamlet.

17. Thomas Thayer, *A Systems Analysis View of the Vietnam War, vol. 9, Population Security*, (Washington, DC: OASD(SA)RP Southeast Asia Intelligence Division, 1975), 116–139.

18. James Embery, "Reorienting Pacification Support: The Accelerated Pacification Campaign of 1968," PhD dissertation, University of Kentucky, 1997, 64–67.

19. Thayer, *Systems Analysis, vol. 9, Population Security*, 250–257.

20. Hunt, *Pacification*, 186.

21. Colby, *Lost Victory*, 259.

22. Brian Jenkins, "The Unchangeable War," RAND Corporation, November 1970, RM-6278-2-ARPA, 1–2.

23. Craig Johnstone, "Memorandum for the Record: Status of Pacification, June 1969," June 4, 1969, Record Group 472 Records of US Military Forces in Southeast Asia, Records of the Office of Civil Operations and Rural Development Support, Plans, Policy and Programs Dir, CORDS Historical Working Group Files, 1967–1973, Box 9, Folder 1601-10A intensive pacification program, US National Archives, Modern Military Records, Archives II, College Park, MD.

24. Arthur S. Collins, "Memorandum for the Record: Observations after One Month in Command of 1 FFORCEV," March 24, 1970, Arthur S. Collins Papers, Box 5, I FFV MFR, US Army Military History Institute, Carlisle, PA.

25. Birtle, "PROVN, Westmoreland, and the Historians," 1227–1238. According to Birtle, Abrams made extensive use of large-unit operations, while spending priorities and artillery expenditure remained skewed towards offensive operations.

26. Jenkins, "The Unchangeable War," 5.

27. David Hackworth, *Steel My Soldier's Hearts: The Hopeless to Hardcore Transformation of the 4th Battalion, 39th Infantry, US Army, Vietnam* (New York: Touchstone, 2002), 370.

28. Kevin P. Buckley, "Pacification's Deadly Price," *Newsweek*, June 19, 1972, 42–43.

29. Julian J. Ewell, "Senior Officer Oral History Project," April 10, 1979, Julian J. Ewell papers oral history, US Army Military History Institute, Carlisle, PA.

30. Ibid.

31. Deborah Nelson, *The War Behind Me: Vietnam Veterans Confront the Truth about Vietnam War Crimes* (Philadelphia: Basic Books, 2008), 83.

32. Patricia J. Sullivan, "Julian J. Ewell, 93, Dies; Decorated General Led Forces in Vietnam," *The Washington Post*, August 5, 2009, available at www.washingtonpost .com/wp-dyn/content/article/2009/08/04/AR2009080403187.html.

33. Julian Ewell and Ira Hunt, *Sharpening the Combat Edge: The Use of Analysis to Reinforce Military Judgment* (Washington DC: Department of the Army, 1995), 227.

34. See *The Abrams Tapes*, 18, 22, 61–62.

35. "Remarks of General Creighton Abrams at the Change of Command Ceremony of the Ninth Infantry Division, Dong Tam, Vietnam, 2 April 1969," in Julian J. Ewell, "Senior Officer Oral History Project," April 10, 1979, Julian J. Ewell papers oral history, US Army Military History Institute, Carlisle, PA. A note from Ewell highlighting Abrams's praise accompanies the transcript.

36. *The Abrams Tapes*, 11, 16, 18, 112, 169–170, 357, 486–487.

37. Ibid., 28.

38. Robert A. Doughty, "The Evolution of US Army Tactical Doctrine 1946–76," The Leavenworth Papers (Fort Leavenworth, KS: Combat Studies Institute Press, 1979), 36.

39. See Julian Ewell and Ira Hunt, *Sharpening the Combat Edge: The Use of Analysis to Reinforce Military Judgment* (Washington, DC: Department of the Army: 1995) for Ewell's (semiofficial) analysis of counterinsurgency operations in Vietnam.

40. *The Abrams Tapes*, 213.

41. John W. Barnes, "CDC presentation on Operation WASHINGTON GREEN, Fort Belvoir, Virginia" (US Army Combat Developments Command, November 19,

1969), CDC Debriefings of Senior Officers, MACV Command Historians Collection, US Army Military History Institute, Carlisle, PA.

42. Combat Developments Command, *Debriefing of Brigadier General John W. Barnes*, USACDC Guest Debriefing Program, November 1969, MACV Command Historians Collection, CDC Debriefing of senior officers 1967–1971, US Army Military History Institute, Carlisle, PA.

43. Pacification Studies Group, "173rd Airborne Bde Participation in Pacification in Northern Binh Dinh Province," July 28, 1969, Record Group 472 Records of US Military Forces in Southeast Asia, Records of the Office of Civil Operations and Rural Development Support, Plans, Policy and Programs Dir, CORDS Historical Working Group Files, 1967–1973, Box 16 PSG Studies 1969 Book I, Folder II, US National Archives, Modern Military Records, Archives II, College Park, MD.

44. Ibid.

45. Kevin Boylan, "The Red Queen's Race: Operation Washington Green and Pacification in Binh Dinh Province, 1969–70," *The Journal of Military History* 73, no. 4 (October 14, 2009), 1207–1208.

46. Charles P. Brown, "Senior Officer Oral History Project," 1983, Charles P. Brown Papers box 1, US Army Military History Institute, Carlisle, PA.

47. John S. Figueira, "Contra-Productive activities of 173rd Airborne Brigade," July 10, 1969, Record Group 472 Records of US Military Forces in Southeast Asia, Records of the Office of Civil Operations and Rural Development Support, Plans, Policy and Programs Dir, CORDS Historical Working Group Files, 1967–1973, Box 9, Folder 1601-10A intensive pacification program, US National Archives, Modern Military Records, Archives II, College Park, MD.

48. Elias Townsend, "US Troop Conduct in Binh Dinh Province," September 1, 1969, Record Group 472 Records of US Military Forces in Southeast Asia, Records of the Office of Civil Operations and Rural Development Support, Plans, Policy and Programs Dir, CORDS Historical Working Group Files, 1967–1973, Box 16 PSG Studies 1969 Book I, Folder I, US National Archives, Modern Military Records Branch, Archives II, College Park, MD.

49. John S. Figueira, "The First Phase of the 1969 Pacification Program, Binh Dinh Province," July 8, 1969, Record Group 472 Records of US Military Forces in Southeast Asia, Records of the Office of Civil Operations and Rural Development Support, Plans, Policy and Programs Dir, CORDS Historical Working Group Files, 1967–1973, Box 16 PSG Studies 1969 Book I, Folder I, US National Archives, Modern Military Records, Archives II, College Park, MD.

50. Boylan, "The Red Queen's Race," 1210.

51. Henry Kissinger, "Memorandum for the President: Analysis for Vietnam," September 5, 1969, Folder 2, Vietnam Special Studies Group, 2 of 2, Box 118, National

Security Council Vietnam Subject Files, Richard Nixon Presidential Library and Museum, Yorba Linda, CA.

52. Vietnam Special Studies Group, "The Situation in the Countryside," January 10, 1969, Folder 2, Vietnam Special Studies Group, 2 of 2, Box 118, National Security Council Vietnam Subject Files, , Richard Nixon Presidential Library and Museum, Yorba Linda, CA.

53. Ibid.

54. Ibid.

55. Henry Kissinger, "Memorandum for the President: Situation in the Countryside in Vietnam," January 22, 1970, Folder 1 Vietnam Special Studies Group 1 of 2, Box 118, National Security Council Vietnam Subject Files, Richard Nixon Presidential Library and Museum, Yorba Linda, CA..

56. Ibid.

57. Minutes of Review Group Meeting, 10th July 1969, SRG Minutes, Box H–111, NSC Institutional Files (H-Files), NSC Files, , , Richard Nixon Presidential Library and Museum, Yorba Linda, CA.

58. National Security Study Memorandum 1, January 21, 1969, "The Situation in Vietnam," available on the Richard Nixon Presidential Library and Museum website at http://nixon.archives.gov/virtuallibrary/documents/nssm/nssm_001.pdf.

59. Summary of Interagency Responses to NSSM 1, March 28, 1969, NSSM Files, NSSM 1 Response, Box H–122, NSC Institutional Files (H-Files), NSC Files, . Richard Nixon Presidential Library and Museum, Yorba Linda, CA

60. Special National Intelligence Estimate, "Pacification in Vietnam," January 16, 1969, US Department of State, *Foreign Relations of the United States: Nixon-Ford Administrations, vol. vi. Vietnam, January 1969–July 1970*, 1.

61. See Robert Thompson, *Defeating Communist Insurgency: Lessons from Malaya and Vietnam* (New York: F. A. Praeger, 1966); and idem., *No Exit from Vietnam* (New York: D. McKay Co. 1969).

62. See reports from Thompson in, folders 3, 4, and 5, Box 92, and folders 5 and 6, Box 116, National Security Council Vietnam Subject Files, Richard Nixon Presidential Library and Museum, Yorba Linda, CA.

63. Memorandum from Henry Kissinger to President Nixon, 12 December 1969, NSC Files, Vietnam Subject Files, Box 92, Folder 4, Richard Nixon Presidential Library and Museum, Yorba Linda, CA.

64. Thompson appeared to recognize that political and strategic reality when he joked in a letter to Kissinger to "keep the home fires extinguished!" Letter from Robert Thompson to Henry Kissinger, October 22, 1969, Folder 4, Box 92, National Security Council Vietnam Subject Files, Richard Nixon Presidential Library and Museum, Yorba Linda, CA.

65. Memorandum from Secretary of Defense Laird to President Nixon, Folder: Secretary Laird's Trip to S. Vietnam, March 5–12, 1969, Box 70, March 13, 1969, National Security Council Vietnam Subject Files, , Richard Nixon Presidential Library and Museum, Yorba Linda, CA.

66. Richard Nixon, memorandum to Henry Kissinger, November 24, 1969, Folder 11/1969, Box 1 memos, White House Special Files: President's Personal File, , Richard Nixon Presidential Library and Museum, Yorba Linda, CA.

67. Notes by President Nixon of a Meeting, Paris, March 2, 1969, *FRUS, Nixon,* vol. vi, 83.

68. Richard Nixon, memorandum to Henry Kissinger and Al Haig, May 15, 1972, Folder: Presidential memos 11, Box 230, White House Special Files, Staff Member Office Files: H. R. Haldeman 1972, ,. Richard Nixon Presidential Library and Museum, Yorba Linda, CA.

69. Douglas Blaufarb, *The Counterinsurgency Era: US Doctrine and Performance* (New York: Free Press, 1977).

70. Richard Nixon, *Public Papers of the Presidents of the United States: Richard Nixon, Containing the Public Messages, Speeches, and Statements of the President* (Washington, DC: US Government Printing Office, 1971), vol. 1, 544–556.

71. *The Abrams Tapes,* 493.

Chapter 2

1. George S. Springsteen, "Memorandum for Lieutenant General Brent Scowcroft, Subject: Lessons of Viet-Nam," May 9, 1975, Presidential Country Files for East Asia and Pacific. Country File: Vietnam (20), Box 20, folder 23, Vietnam (23), Gerald R. Ford Presidential Library, Ann Arbor, MI.

2. For more on this caution, see Kenneth J. Campbell, "The Crucial Constraint: Containment and the Post-Vietnam Military's Reluctance to Use Force" (PhD dissertation, Temple University, 1989); Richard Lock-Pullan, *U.S. Intervention Policy and Army Innovation; From Vietnam to Iraq* (London: Routledge, 2005); and David H. Petraeus, "The American Military and the Lessons of Vietnam: A Study of Military Influence and Use of Force in the Post-Vietnam Era" (PhD dissertation, Woodrow Wilson School of Public and International Affairs, Princeton University, 1987).

3. US Army War College, *Study on Military Professionalism* (Carlisle Barracks, PA: US Army War College, June 30, 1970).

4. Ronald H. Spector, "The Vietnam War and the Army's Self-image," n.d. Historical Resource Collection 2 (Washington, DC: US Army Center of Military History), 5.

5. US Army War College, *Study on Military Professionalism,* B-1-10.

6. Ibid., 15.

7. See Rick Atkinson, *The Long Gray Line* (Boston: Houghton Mifflin, 1989), an account of the experiences of some of those graduates in Vietnam and its aftermath.

8. A. Gabriel Richard and P. L Savage, *Crisis in Command: Mismanagement in the Army* (New York: Hill and Wang, 1978); Richard Boyle, *The Flower of the Dragon: The Breakdown of the US Army in Vietnam* (San Francisco: Ramparts Press, 1972); Stuart H. Loory, *Defeated: Inside America's Military Machine* (New York: Random House, 1973); Cecil Currey, *Self-Destruction: The Disintegration and Decay of the United States Army during the Vietnam era* (New York: Norton, 1981); and Edward L. King, *The Death of the Army: A Pre-Mortem* (New York: Saturday Review Press, 1972).

9. Spector, "The Vietnam War and the Army's Self-Image," 20.

10. See Lock-Pullan, "An Inward Looking Time," and Richard Lock-Pullan, *US Intervention Policy and Army Innovation*, for detailed accounts of the structural changes the Army made at this time.

11. Lewis Sorley, *Thunderbolt: General Creighton Abrams and the Army of His Times* (New York: Simon & Schuster, 1992), 365. However, there is no evidence in available archival sources (the Creighton Abrams papers are still classified) that indicates that Abrams intentionally set out to restrict presidential decision making.

12. Fred C. Weyand, "America and Its Army: A Bicentennial Look at Posture and Goals, an Address by General Fred C. Weyand, Chief of Staff, United States Army, before the National Security Seminar, US Army War College, Carlisle Barracks, Pennsylvania," June 4, 1976, Historical Manuscripts Collection 2. Washington DC: US Army Center of Military History.

13. Fred C. Weyand and Harry G. Summers, "Serving the People: The Need for Military Power," *Military Review* 56 (December 1976), 17.

14. William Gardner Bell, *Department of the Army Historical Summary: FY 71* (Washington, DC: US Army Center of Military History., 1973), 11.

15. Donn A. Starry, "Welcome to the Counterinsurgency Century," *The Armor and Cavalry Journal*, September–October 2008, in Lewis Sorley (ed.), *Press On! Selected Works of Donn A. Starry*, vol. 1 (Fort Leavenworth, KS: Combat Studies Institute Press, 2009), 454.

16. Donn A. Starry, "Army of the Future," US Army Materiel Development and Readiness Command Executive Seminar, Atlanta, GA, February 14, 1980, in *Press On!*, 669.

17. Starry, "Welcome to the Counterinsurgency Century," in *Press On!*, 455.

18. For an example of strategic planning that focused on Europe and Japan, see the Astarita Report, which was extensively briefed throughout the Pentagon in the 1970s. Harry G. Summers Jr., *The Astarita Report: A Military Strategy for the Multipolar World* (Carlisle Barracks, PA: Strategic Studies Institute, US Army War College, 1981).

19. Weyand and Summers, "Serving the People: The Need for Military Power," 10.

20. Richard Lock-Pullan, "'An Inward Looking Time': The United States Army, 1973–1976", *The Journal of Military History* 67, no. 2 (April 2003), 483–511.

21. This was not a solely Vietnam-driven change. The imperatives of the all-volunteer force meant that such changes would have to occur anyway. Some argue that therefore the end of the draft was far more consequential for the Army than Vietnam. However, this is to miss the fact that the end of conscription and the founding of the volunteer military themselves directly stemmed from the Vietnam experience.

22. See the following for a full account of DePuy's time at TRADOC: Henry G. Gole, *General William E. DePuy* (Lexington: University Press of Kentucky, 2008); Paul H. Herbert, *Deciding What Has to Be Done: General William E. DePuy and the 1976 Edition of FM 100-5, Operations* (Fort Leavenworth, KS: Combat Studies Institute, US Army Command and General Staff College, 1988); and John L. Romjue, *From Active Defense to AirLand Battle: The Development of Army Doctrine from 1973 to 1982*, TRADOC historical monograph series (Fort Monroe, VA: Historical Office, US Army Training and Doctrine Command, 1984).

23. William E. DePuy (compiled by Richard M. Swain), *Selected Papers of General William E. DePuy* (Fort Leavenworth, KS: Combat Studies Institute, 1994), 194.

24. Wiliam E. DePuy, interview by Michael Pearlman, September 23, 1986, 23, William E DePuy Papers, Oral Histories Box 2, US Army Military History Institute, Carlisle, PA.

25. Ibid., 9.

26. US Army, *FM 100-5 Operations*, (Washington, DC: Department of the Army, 1976). 1–2.

27. Don A. Starry, "A Tactical Evolution—FM 100-5," *Military Review* 58 (August 1978), 4.

28. DePuy, interview by Pearlman, 25.

29. Michael J. Brady, "The Army and the Strategic Military Legacy of Vietnam" (Masters of Military Art and Science, Command and General Staff College, 1990), 129, available at http://cgsc.cdmhost.com/cdm4/item_viewer.php?CISOROOT=/p4013coll2&CISOPTR=1407.

30. DePuy served first in a staff position as MACV J-3 in 1964 (operations officer for the US military command in Vietnam) and then as commander of the First Infantry Division in 1966. He also served as special assistant for counterinsurgency and Special Activities in the Office of the Joint Chiefs of Staff from 1967 to 1969.

31. DePuy, interview by Pearlman, 15.

32. Wiliam E. DePuy, "Senior Officer Debriefing Program," interview by Bill Mullen and Les Brownlee, March 19, 1979, William E. DePuy Papers, Oral Histories Box 2, US Army Military History Institute, Carlisle, PA.

33. Ibid.

34. DePuy, interview by Pearlman, 9.

35. DePuy, *Selected Papers of General William E. DePuy*, 267.

36. DePuy, "Senior Officer Debriefing Program," 7.

37. William E. DePuy, "Implications of the Middle East War on US Army Tactics, Doctrine and Systems", n.d., DePuy, *Selected Papers of General William E. DePuy*, 75–111.

38. D. J. Vetock, *Lessons Learned: A History of US Army Lesson Learning* (Carlisle, PA: US Army Military History Institute, 1988), 120–121.

39. US Army, *FM 31-16, Counter-Guerrilla operations* (Washington, DC: Department of the Army, 1967). A replacement, *FM 90-8 Counter-Guerrilla Operations*, was issued in 1985, following involvement in counterinsurgency in Central America.

40. US Army, *FM 31-23 Stability Operations* (Washington, DC: Department of the Army, 1972).

41. US Army, *FM 100-20 Internal Defense and Development* (Washington, DC: Department of the Army, 1974).

42. Headquarters, U.S, Army John F, Kennedy School of Military Assistance, *Annual Historical Supplement* (Fort Bragg, NC: US Army JFK Center for Military Assistance, 1972), Washington, DC: Annual History Collection, US Army Center of Military History, 1972.

43. Andrew J. Birtle, *U.S. Army Counterinsurgency and Contingency Operations Doctrine 1942–1976* (Washington DC: US Army Center of Military History, 2006); Headquarters, U.S. Army John F Kennedy School of Military Assistance, *Annual Historical Supplement*, 1972.

44. David C. Schlacter and Fred J. Stubbs, "Special Operations Forces: Not Applicable?" *Military Review* 58 (February 1978), 15–26.

45. Conrad C. Crane, *Avoiding Vietnam: The US Army's Response to Defeat in Southeast Asia* (Carlisle Barracks, PA: Strategic Studies Institute, US Army War College, 2002), 12. Confirmed by author via interview with Dr. Steve Metz at the Army War College, Carlisle, PA, October 31, 2008. Metz was a colleague of the officer in question at the Command and General Staff College at the time.

46. Brady, "The Army and the Strategic Military Legacy of Vietnam," 186.

47. Donald B. Vought, "Preparing for the Wrong War?" *Military Review* 57, no. 5 (May 1977), 30.

48. CAC History Office, *US Army Combined Arms Center Annual Historical Review* (Fort Leavenworth, KS: US Army Combined Arms Center, December 1, 1982. and. Washington, DC: Annual History Collection, US Army Center of Military History).

49. US Army War College Conference on Strategy, *Final Report, Course 4 "Internal Defense and Development Operations" AY 1971* (Carlisle Barracks, PA: US Army War College), Curriculum Development Final Reports, Box 1971-2, Folder 7, US Army Military History Institute, Carlisle, PA. Interestingly, the course report also noted that students felt that, that prior to the Internal Defense and Development course, they had a limited understanding of the politicomilitary aspects of counterinsurgency, despite Vietnam service, which demonstrates the inadequacy of both the Army's counterin-

surgency approach in Vietnam and its broader efforts to ensure that officers understood this form of warfare.

50. Ibid.

51. DePuy, *Selected Papers of General William E. DePuy*, 197.

52. Ibid., 221.

53. Brady, "The Army and the Strategic Military Legacy of Vietnam," 211.

54. W. R. Smyser and W. L. Stearman, "Memorandum for Secretary Kissinger, Subject: Lessons of Vietnam," May 10, 1975, Presidential Country Files for East Asia and Pacific. Country File: Vietnam (20), Box 20, folder 23, Vietnam (23). Ann Arbor, MI: Gerald R. Ford Presidential Library.

55. Ibid.

56. Ibid.

57. Prior to BDM study, the US Army Center of Military History had published its *Vietnam Studies Series*, historical monographs on particular aspects of the war. The studies, largely written by senior officers, tended to focus on narrow topics. See Donn Starry, *Mounted Combat in Vietnam* (Washington, DC: Department of the Army, 1979); William Fulton, *Riverine Operations, 1966–1969* (Washington, DC: Department of the Army, 1985); and Charles Myer, *Division-Level Communications, 1962–1973* (Washington, DC: Department of the Army, 1982). Some studies, however, took a broader approach, such as Francis J. Kelly, *US Army Special Forces 1961–1971*, Vietnam Studies (Washington, DC: US Army Center of Military History, 1973); and Julian J. Ewell and Ira A. Hunt, *Sharpening the Combat Edge: The Use of Analysis to Reinforce Military Judgment*, Vietnam Studies (Washington, DC: US Army Center of Military History, 1974). Kelly was strongly critical of the US counterinsurgency effort, while Ewell and Hunt, controversially, offered an endorsement of "search and destroy" operations and the "body count" criteria for success.

58. Harry P. Ball, *Of Responsible Command: A History of the US Army War College, The School That Shaped the Military Leaders of the Free World*, Revised (Carlisle, PA: Alumni Association of the U.S. Army War College, 1994), 451–452.

59. Ibid., 452.

60. BDM Corporation, Defense Technical Information Center (US), and Scholarly Resources, Inc., *A Study of Strategic Lessons Learned in Vietnam* (McLean, VA: BDM Corp, 1979).

61. Ibid., EX-6.

62. Russell Weigley, *The American Way of War: A History of United States Military Strategy and Policy* (New York: Macmillan, 1973).

63. BDM Corporation, Defense Technical Information Center (US), and Scholarly Resources, Inc., *A Study of Strategic Lessons Learned in Vietnam*, VI-9.

64. See Chapter 1 for a discussion of Vietnam War historiography.

65. BDM Corporation, Defense Technical Information Center (US), and Scholarly Resources, Inc., *A Study of Strategic Lessons Learned in Vietnam*, VIII-11.

66. Ibid., EX-10.

67. Ibid., V-15.

68. Ibid., VI-7.

69. Ibid., II-16.

70. Robert Cassidy, *Counterinsurgency and the Global War on Terror: Military Culture and Irregular War* (Stanford, CA: Stanford University Press, 2008), 117.

71. Harry G. Summers, *On Strategy: The Vietnam War in Context* (Honolulu: University of the Pacific Press, 1981).

72. Ibid., 54.

73. Harry G. Summers, "The United States Army Institutional Response to Vietnam," in *Session IV: Vietnam* (presented at The Impact of Unsuccessful Military Campaigns on Military Institutions 1860–1980, US Army War College, Carlisle Barracks, PA, 1982), 296.

74. In fact, some scholars have disputed Summers's characterization of the trinity as consisting of the state, the people, and the military. The Clausewitz scholar Christopher Bassford instead argues that the trinity consists of reason, violence, and chance. See E. J. Villacres and C. Bassford, "Reclaiming the Clausewitzian Trinity," *Parameters* 25, no. 3 (1995), 9.

75. Summers, *On Strategy: The Vietnam War in Context*, 27.

76. Later scholarship has focused on that fact that these issues *were* considered, especially by President Lyndon B. Johnson, who feared widening the war. See Fredrik Logevall, *Choosing War: The Lost Chance for Peace and the Escalation of War in Vietnam* (Berkeley: University of California Press, 1999); H. R. McMaster, *Dereliction of Duty: Lyndon Johnson, Robert McNamara, the Joint Chiefs of Staff and the Lies That Led to Vietnam* (New York: HarperCollins, 1997).

77. Summers, *On Strategy*, 76.

78. Summers, "The United States Army Institutional Response to Vietnam," 298.

79. Ibid.

80. Summers, *On Strategy*, 46.

81. Ibid., 57.

82. Ibid., vii.

83. Brady, "The Army and the Strategic Military Legacy of Vietnam," 66.

84. Thomas F. Healy, preface to Harry G. Summers, *On Strategy: The Vietnam War in Context*, 4th ed. (Carlisle, PA: Strategic Studies Institute, 1993).

85. "Syllabus, Advanced Courses Program: Vietnam War Strategy," June 28, 1983, Army War College curriculum files, Box 1983-16 folder 11, Carlisle, PA: US Army Military History Institute.

86. Ibid.

87. Vought, "Preparing for the Wrong War?"

88. Brady, "The Army and the Strategic Military Legacy of Vietnam," 211.

89. William Westmoreland, *A Soldier Reports* (Garden City, NY: Doubleday, 1976); U. S. Grant Sharp, *Strategy for Defeat: Vietnam in Retrospect* (Novatio, CA: Presidio Press, 1978); and General Bruce Palmer, *The 25-Year War: America's Military Role in Vietnam*, 4th ed. (Lexington: University Press of Kentucky, 2002).

90. Arthur S. Collins, "Senior Officer Oral History Project," Box 1 Oral History, Arthur S. Collins Papers, US Army Military History Institute, Carlisle, PA.

91. Charles P. Brown, "Senior Office Oral History Program," interview by John C. Burlingame, 1983, Box 1. Charles P. Brown Papers, US Army Military History Institute, Carlisle, PA.

92. Douglas Kinnard, *The War Managers* (Hanover, NH: Published for the University of Vermont by the University Press of New England, 1977), 25, 45.

93. Ibid., 45.

94. Ibid., 74–75.

95. Brady, "The Army and the Strategic Military Legacy of Vietnam."

96. Ibid., 164.

97. Ibid., 167.

Chapter 3

1. Ronald Reagan, "Peace: Restoring the Margin of Safety" (presented at the Veterans of Foreign Wars Convention, Chicago, August 18, 1980), available at www .reagan.utexas.edu/archives/reference/8.18.80.html. Reagan's invocation of the "noble cause" coincided with the cultural evolution of Vietnam revisionism in literature, film, and political speeches. The archetypal character in this revisionist depiction of Vietnam was John Rambo, the wronged Vietnam veteran who simply wanted the chance to "win this time." See David Ryan, "Vietnam in the American Mind: Narratives of the Nation and the Sources of Collective Memory," in Rudiger Kunow and Wilfried Raussert (eds.), *Cultural Memory and Multiple Identities* (Berlin: Lit Verlag, 2008), 117; and Robert Schulzinger, *A Time for Peace: The Legacy of the Vietnam War* (Oxford, UK: Oxford University Press, 2006), 162–164.

2. For overviews of the Reagan Doctrine, see Mark P. Lagon, *The Reagan Doctrine: Sources of American Conduct in the Cold War's Last Chapter* (New York: Praeger, 1994); James M. Scott, *Deciding to Intervene: The Reagan Doctrine and American Foreign Policy* (Durham, NC: Duke University Press, 1996); Ted Galen Carpenter, "US Aid to Anti-Communist Rebels: The 'Reagan Doctrine' and Its Pitfalls," *Cato Policy Analysis # 74*, Cato Institute, June 24, 1986; and David Ryan, *US–Sandinista Diplomatic Relations: Voice of Intolerance* (London: Palgrave Macmillan, 1995).

3. Constantine Menges, who served on the National Security Council from 1983 to 1986 as a special advisor to the president on counterinsurgency, had worked for the

RAND Corporation as a counterinsurgency analyst during the Vietnam era. Menges was one of the original advocates of the Reagan Doctrine, urging US support for anticommunist insurgencies as early as 1968. See Constantine C. Menges, *Democratic Revolutionary Insurgency as an Alternative Strategy* (Santa Monica, CA: RAND Corp., 1968); and Constantine C. Menges, *Inside the National Security Council: The True Story of the Making and Unmaking of Reagan's Foreign Policy* (New York: Simon and Schuster, 1989).

4. Ronald Reagan, "Address to the Nation on United States Policy in Central America," May 9, 1984, Ronald Reagan Presidential Library website, available at www .reagan.utexas.edu/archives/speeches/1984/50984h.htm.

5. For FY (financial year) 1985, Reagan had secured $146.25 million in military aid and $433.9 million in economic aid for the Salvadoran regime. See William Leo-Grande, *Our Own Backyard: The United States in Central America, 1977–1992* (Chapel Hill: University of North Carolina Press, 1998), 258, 273.

6. Greg Grandin, *Empire's Workshop: Latin America, the United States, and the Rise of the New Imperialism* (New York: Holt Paperbacks, 2007), 72.

7. Richard Nixon, "Don't Let Salvador Become Another Vietnam," *Wall Street Journal*, May 2, 1983.

8. Francis X. Clines, "US May Increase Salvador Advisers," *The New York Times*, March 5, 1983.

9. William Tuohy, "War Similarities: El Salvador Faces the Ghosts of Vietnam," *The Los Angeles Times*, March 20, 1983.

10. Charles J. Hanley, "Memories of Vietnam Linger in El Salvador," *The Times-News* (Hendersonville, NC), September 22, 1983.

11. Walter S. Mossberg, "The Army Resists a Salvadoran Vietnam," *Wall Street Journal*, June 6, 1983.

12. Milt Freudenheim and Henry Giniger, "The World in Summary: General Sounds Cautionary Note on El Salvador," *The New York Times*, June 12, 1983.

13. Mossberg, "The Army Resists a Salvadoran Vietnam."

14. Courtney E. Prisk and Max G. Manwaring, "The Need for Strategic Perspective: Insights from El Salvador," in Max Manwaring (ed.), *Uncomfortable Wars: Toward a New Paradigm of Low Intensity Conflict* (Boulder, CO: Westview Press, 1991), 115. The Fulda Gap is a corridor of lowlands near Frankfurt, through which any Soviet armored invasion of Western Europe was expected. The "Choluteca Gap" appears to largely be an invention of Manwaring's.

15. Oddly enough, despite its heavy emphasis on the classic principles of counterinsurgency, Woerner confessed in his acknowledgments that he owed an intellectual debt to none other than Harry Summers. He wrote,

Thank you, Karl Von Clausewitz and Colonel Harry Summers. Harry Summers' book, *On Strategy: The Vietnam War in Context*, resurrected Clausewitz from the forgotten hours of Military History-I. It is a superb book. Brilliantly measuring US strategy in Vietnam against the Principles of War and the writings of Clausewitz, this book, more than any other source contributed to my understanding of the mission. Thank you, Harry, and you, too, Karl.

Fred F. Woerner, *Report of the El Salvador Military Strategy Assistance Team (Draft)* (U.S. Department of Defense, November 16, 1981), El Salvador, 1980–1994 collection, Digital National Security Archive, George Washington University, 107.

16. Ibid., 90.

17. Paul F. Gorman, "Cardinal Point: An Oral History—Training Soldiers and Becoming a Strategist in Peace and War," in *Strategy and Tactics for Learning: The Papers of General Paul F. Gorman (USA), Ret.* (Fort Leavenworth, KS: US Army Combined Arms Center, 2011), 106; available at http://usacac.army.mil/CAC2/CSI/docs/Gorman/00_ImportantDocs_ReadFirst/03_OralHistory_CPWeb.pdf.

18. Ronald Reagan, "Central America: Defending Our Vital Interests," Current Policy 482 (Washington, DC: Department of State, Bureau of Public Affairs, 1983).

19. Henry A. Kissinger, *Report of the National Bipartisan Commission on Central America* (Washington, DC: The White House, January 1984). However, elsewhere, there was deep concern over these linkages between US aid to the Salvadoran regime and human rights abuses. See David Carleton and Michael Stohl, "The Role of Human Rights in US Foreign Assistance Policy: A Critique and Reappraisal," *American Journal of Political Science* 31, no. 4, (November 1987), 1002–1018; Leigh Binford, *The El Mozote Massacre: Anthropology and Human Rights* (Phoenix: University of Arizona Press, 1996); James McCormick and Neill Mitchell, "Is US Aid Really Linked to Human Rights in Latin America?" *American Journal of Political Science* 32, no. 1 (1988), 231–239; James Dunkerley, *The Long War: Dictatorship and Revolution in El Salvador* (London: Verso, 1985); Raymond Bonner, *Weakness and Deceit: US Policy and El Salvador* (New York: Times Books, 1984); and David L. Cingranelli and Thomas E Pasquarello, "Human Rights Practices and the Distribution of US Foreign Aid to Latin American Countries." *American Journal of Political Science* 29, no. 3 (1985), 539–563.

20. John T. Fishel and Max G. Manwaring, "The SWORD Model of Counterinsurgency: A Summary and Update," *Small Wars Journal*, available at http://smallwarsjournal.com/mag/docs-temp/152-fishel.pdf.

21. Prisk and Manwaring, "Uncomfortable Wars," 116.

22. James Steele, quoted in Courtney E. Prisk and Max G. Manwaring (eds.), *El Salvador at War: An Oral History of Conflict from the 1979 Insurrection* (Washington, DC: National Defense University Press, 1988), 407.

23. Much of the patronage in El Salvador flowed through the *Tanda* system, which Andrew Bacevich memorably described as "a sort of West Point Protective Association gone berserk." A *Tanda* was a graduating class of the Salvadoran Military Academy, and members of the *Tanda* were expected to be fiercely loyal to one another. Many of those responsible for right-wing violence came from the *Tanda* of 1966, which took over the top ranks of the Salvadoran military in 1988 and was particularly extremist and even more loyal to each other than normal. See Andrew Bacevich et al., *American Military Policy in Small Wars: The Case of El Salvador* (Washington, DC: Pergamon-Brassey's, 1988); and Tom Barry, *Central America Inside Out* (New York: Grove Press, 1991), 164.

24. Woerner, *Report of the El Salvador Military Strategy Assistance Team (Draft)*, 48.

25. Ibid.

26. Frank del Olmo, "Bush Warns Salvador on Death Squads," *The Los Angeles Times*, December 12, 1983. Not a single Salvadoran Army officer was prosecuted for his role in the killings. One church official complained that "the problem is that the people running the death squads are also running the country . . . removing a few infamous offenders does nothing to dismantle the structure." Cited in LeoGrande, *Our Own Backyard*, 235.

27. Hanley, "Memories of Vietnam linger in El Salvador."

28. Benjamin Schwarz, *American Counterinsurgency Doctrine and El Salvador: The Frustrations of Reform and the Illusions of Nation Building* (Santa Monica, CA: RAND, 1991), 8.

29. Shockingly, the UN "Commission on the Truth in El Salvador," which investigated the killings, concluded that almost 85 percent of the acts of violence were carried out by "agents of the state, paramilitary groups allied to them, and the death squads," while the FMLN was responsible for only 5 percent of cases. Belisario Bentancur, Reinaldo Planchart, and Thomas Buergenthal, *From Madness to Hope: The 12-Year War in El Salvador: Report of the Commission on the Truth for El Salvador* (New York: United Nations, 1993), 43.

30. Cynthia Arnson and David Holiday, *El Salvador and Human Rights* (New York: Human Rights Watch, 1991); and Lawrence Michael Ladutke, *Freedom of Expression in El Salvador: The Struggle for Human Rights and Democracy* (Jefferson, NC: MacFarland, 2004).

31. Schwarz, *American Counterinsurgency Doctrine and El Salvador*, 60.

32. The White House, *National Security Strategy of the United States* (Washington, DC: The White House, 1987), 32–34.

33. Ibid.

34. The CIA were not as restricted as the military, and they encouraged deception and assassination in Central American. See Joanne Omang, *Psychological Operations in Guerrilla Warfare: The CIA's Nicaragua Manual* (New York: Random House, 1985).

35. LeoGrande, *Our Own Backyard*, 199–218.

36. Don Oberdorfer, "Inouye's Switch: Memories of Vietnam Lead Hawaiian to Break with Reagan on El Salvador," *The Washington Post*, March 16, 1983.

37. US National Security Council, *Report to the Congress on US Capabilities to Engage in Low Intensity Conflict and Conduct Special Operations* (Washington, DC: The White House, 1987), Terrorism and US Policy, 1968–2002, Digital National Security Archive, George Washington University, 13.

38. Michael W. Symanski, "Hoist with the LIC petard," *Military Review* 68, no. 9 (September 1988), 20.

39. While much of the literature on LIC mirrored discussion in the White House and Pentagon, some were critical of the concept from an anti-interventionist, anti-imperialist perspective. See Michael McClintock, *Instruments of Statecraft: US Guerrilla Warfare, Counterinsurgency, and Counter-Terrorism, 1940–1990* (New York: Pantheon Books, 1992); and Michael T. Klare and Peter Kornbluh (eds.), *Low Intensity Warfare: Counterinsurgency, Proinsurgency and Antiterrorism in the Eighties* (New York: Pantheon Books, 1988).

40. US National Security Council, *Report to the Congress on US Capabilities to Engage in Low Intensity Conflict and Conduct Special Operations*, 2.

41. US Army and US Air Force, *FM 100-20/AFP 3-20 Military Operations in Low Intensity Conflict* (Washington, DC: Department of the Army, 1991), sec. 1-8.

42. Albert M. Barnes, "After Action Report—Secretary of the Army visit" (Army–Air Force Center for Low Intensity Conflict, February 5, 1988), frame 583, reel 47670, microfilm collection, records of the Army–Air Force Center for Low Intensity Conflict, US Air Force Historical Research Agency, Maxwell Air Force Base, Alabama.

43. John S. Fulton, "The Debate on Low Intensity Conflict," *Military Review* 66, no. 1 (February 1986), 61.

44. Ibid., 63.

45. Symanski, "Hoist with the LIC petard," 19. Symanski's essay was the winner of the 1988 *Military Review* writing contest, suggesting at least some level of editorial support for his arguments.

46. Bacevich, *American Military Policy in Small Wars*.

47. This claim was supported by the comments of Dr. Laurence Cline at a 2005 Combat Studies Institute Symposium:

Everybody in 7th Special Forces Group was fighting to get down there. Having said that, though, at least one officer I was with in 7th Special Forces Group, the 18 branch suggested to him that he not go down there [El Salvador]. He'd not pulled the tour as an advisor. He was a Major. Because he was due up for Battalion S-3, and they considered Battalion S-3 to be more important than to be an advisor in El Salvador. So even within SF branch, there was a certain amount of that.

Laurence E. Cline, "The US Advisory Effort in El Salvador," *Security Assistance: US and International Historical Perspectives*. (Fort Leavenworth, KA: Combat Studies Institute Press, 2006), 440.

48. Bacevich, *American Military Policy in Small Wars*, 49.

49. Ironically, Gorman had earlier been a DePuy acolyte and had overseen the overhaul of TRADOC's education system that moved officer education away from the social sciences and back toward the study of conventional war.

50. David Cloud and Greg Jaffe, *The Fourth Star: Four Generals and the Epic Struggle for the Future of the United States Army* (New York: Crown Publishers, 2009), 65–66. Galvin was an early mentor of Petraeus's and was influential in getting him to attend Princeton and write his PhD on the US military and the lessons of Vietnam. See Chapter 7.

51. John R. Galvin, "Uncomfortable Wars: Toward a New Paradigm" in Max G. Manwaring (ed.), *Uncomfortable Wars: Toward a New Paradigm of Low Intensity Conflict* (Boulder, CO: Westview Press, 1991).

52. US Army, *FM 100-5, Operations* (Washington, DC: Department of the Army, 1986), secs 1-1, 1-4.

53. John L. Romjue, *A History of Army 86: Vol. II: The Development of the Light Division, the Corps and Echelons above Corps (Nov. 1979–Dec. 1980)* (Fort Leavenworth, KS: Historical Office, US Army Training and Doctrine Command, December 1981), 25, Historical Manuscripts Collection 2. Washington, DC: US Army Center of Military History, 25.

54. Romjue, *A History of Army 86: Vol. II*, 27.

55. John A. Wickham and Department of the Army, *Light Infantry Divisions*, White Paper (Washington, DC: Department of the Army, 1984), 1.

56. John L. Romjue, *The Army of Excellence: The Development of the 1980s Army* (Fort Monroe, VA: Office of the Command Historian, US Army Training and Doctrine Command, 1993), 68.

57. US Army Command and General Staff College, *FC 100-20 Low Intensity Conflict* (Fort Leavenworth, KS: Command and General Staff College, 1981); US Army and US Air Force, *FM 100-20/AFP 3-20 Military Operations in Low Intensity Conflict*.

58. *FC 100-20 Low Intensity Conflict*, vi.

59. Ibid., sec. 5-34.

60. Ibid., sec. 5-4.

61. On military reticence toward intervention in this period, see Kenneth J. Campbell, "The Crucial Constraint: Containment and the Post-Vietnam Military's Reluctance to Use Force" (PhD dissertation,Temple University, 1989); Kenneth J. Campbell, "Once Burned, Twice Cautious: Explaining the Weinberger-Powell Doctrine," *Armed Forces and Society* 24, no. 3 (1988); David H. Petraeus, "The American Military and the Lessons of Vietnam: A Study of Military Influence and Use of Force

in the Post-Vietnam Era" (PhD dissertation, Woodrow Wilson School of Public and International Affairs, Princeton University, 1987); and Richard Lock-Pullan, *US Intervention Policy and Army Innovation; From Vietnam to Iraq* (London: Routledge, 2005).

62. Cecil B. Currey, "Preparing for the Past," *Military Review* 69, no. 1 (January 1989), 3.

63. Rudolph C. Barnes, "The Politics of Low Intensity Conflict," *Military Review* 68, no. 2 (February 1988), 5.

64. John D. Waghelstein, "Post-Vietnam Counterinsurgency Doctrine," *Military Review* 65, no. 5 (May 1985), 42.

65. See also Michael Brown, "Vietnam: Learning from the Debate," *Military Review* 67, no.2 (February 1987).

66. Andrew Krepinevich, *The Army and Vietnam* (Baltimore, MD: Johns Hopkins University Press, 1988).

67. Unsurprisingly, the heaviest critics and harshest reviewers of Krepinevich had been senior officers in Vietnam. See Wiliam E. DePuy, "The Army War and the Proper Way in Vietnam: Review of The Army and Vietnam," *Army* 36, no. 9, 77–78; and Bruce Palmer, "Review: The Army and Vietnam," *Parameters* XVI, no. 3 (Autumn 1988), 83–85.

68. Gordon Sullivan, "Memorandum for MG Ostott; Subject: Close Combat" (US Army Command and General Staff College, February 29, 1988), frame 589, reel 47670, microfilm collection, records of the Army–Air Force Center for Low Intensity Conflict, US Air Force Historical Research Agency, Maxwell Air Force Base, AL.

69. CAC History Office, *US Army Combined Arms Center Annual Historical Review 1982* (Fort Leavenworth, KS: US Army Combined Arms Center, December 1, 1982), Annual History Collection. Washington, DC: US Army Center of Military History.

70. CAC History Office, *US Army Combined Arms Center Annual Historical Review 1986* (Fort Leavenworth, KS: US Army Combined Arms Center, 1986), Annual History Collection. Washington, DC: US Army Center of Military History.

71. "AirLand Battle" was largely the brainchild of General Don Starry and replaced DePuy's "Active Defense" doctrine after the latter concept was subjected to much debate after the release of the 1976 edition of FM 100-5. AirLand Battle emphasized close coordination between land forces acting as an aggressively maneuvering defense and air forces attacking rear-echelon forces feeding those front line enemy forces. See John L. Romjue, "The Evolution of the AirLand Battle Concept," *Air University Review* 35, no. 4 (1984), 4–15.

72. CAC History Office, *US Army Combined Arms Center Annual Historical Review 1987* (Fort Leavenworth, KS: US Army Combined Arms Center, 1987), Annual History Collection. Washington, DC: US Army Center of Military History.

73. CAC History Office, *US Army Combined Arms Center Annual Historical Review 1987*.

74. US Army Training and Doctrine Command, TRADOC PAM 525-44 *US Operational Concept for Low Intensity Conflict* (Fort Monroe, VA: TRADOC, 1986).

75. Thomas E. Swain, "Review of AirLand Battle Future (ALB-F) Briefing (draft)" (Army–Air Force Center for Low Intensity Conflict, n.d.), frame 742, reel 47672, microfilm collection, records of the Army–Air Force Center for Low Intensity Conflict, US Air Force Historical Research Agency, Maxwell Air Force Base, AL.

76. CAC History Office, *US Army Combined Arms Center Annual Historical Review 1987*, 103.

77. Ibid., 104.

78. CAC History Office, *US Army Combined Arms Center Annual Historical Review 1987*.

79. Maxwell Thurman, "Backchannel memorandum from General Thurman, Commanding General TRADOC to General Vuono, Chief of Staff, US Army; Subject: Doctrine for Low Intensity Conflict" (TRADOC, n.d.), frame 1108, reel 47670, microfilm collection, records of the Army–Air Force Center for Low Intensity Conflict, US Air Force Historical Research Agency, Maxwell Air Force Base, AL.

80. William F. Furr, "FM 100-20/AFM 2-20 (AFP 3-20) Chronology of Events" (Army–Air Force Center for Low Intensity Conflict, January 12, 1990), frame 978, reel 47671, microfilm collection, records of the Army–Air Force Center for Low Intensity Conflict, US Air Force Historical Research Agency, Maxwell Air Force Base, AL.

81. In a sense, he was arguing for a future where the United States would continue to back regimes like that of El Salvador. The fundamental lessons of Vietnam, which stressed that the United States should stop backing repressive regimes, had little influence on the debate at this point.

82. Fred F. Woerner, "The Strategic Imperatives for the United States in Latin America," *Military Review* 69 no. 2 (February 1989), 22.

83. Edward M. Kennedy et al., "Letter to Lt Gen Brent Scowcroft, Assistant to the President for National Security Affairs" (US Senate, January 25, 1989), frame 99, reel 47671, microfilm collection, records of the Army–Air Force Center for Low Intensity Conflict, US Air Force Historical Research Agency, Maxwell Air Force Base, AL.

84. US Congress, Senate, Public Law 99-661, S. 2638, 99th Congress, 2d Session (November 14, 1986).

85. David B. Ottoway, "Delay on Guerrilla Command Irks Hill," *The Washington Post*, March 10, 1987.

86. Paul F. Gorman, "Presentation: Low Intensity Conflict and the Central American Question.' Presented in a forum at the White Burkett Miller Center, Forum and Conversation Series, University of Virginia, Kenneth W. Thompson, ed., on April 13, 1987, in Folder A: Retired 1985–1990, *Strategy and Tactics for Learning: The Papers*

of General Paul F. Gorman (USA), Ret. (Fort Leavenworth, KS: US Army Combined Arms Center, 2011), available at http://usacac.army.mil/CAC2/CSI/docs/Gorman/06_ Retired/01_Retired_1985_90/23_87_LowIntensityConflict_CENTAMQuestion_Apr .pdf.

87. William C. Ohl, "Fixing Special Operations: Rational Actors Not Allowed" (Essay, National War College, 1993). *Defense Technical Information Center*, available at http://handle.dtic.mil/100.2/ADA441771.

88. Barnes, "The Politics of Low Intensity Conflict," 5.

89. Stephen D. Goose, "The Warriors and Their Weapons," in *Low-Intensity Warfare*, 82–83.

90. Headquarters, US Army John F. Kennedy Special Warfare Center and School, *Annual Historical Review* (Fort Bragg, NC: US Army JFK Special Warfare Center, 1987), Annual History Collection. Washington, DC: US Army Center of Military History.

91. Ibid.

92. Glenn M. Harned, "Special Operations and the AirLand Battle," *Military Review* 65, no. 9 (September 1985), 74.

93. Headquarters, US Army John F. Kennedy Special Warfare Center and School, *Annual Historical Review* (Fort Bragg, NC: US Army JFK Special Warfare Center, 1991), Annual History Collection. Washington, DC: US Army Center of Military History.

94. Eventually this was expanded to eighteen active duty divisions under Reagan.

95. William E. DePuy (compiled by Richard M. Swain), *Selected Papers of General William E. DePuy* (Fort Leavenworth, KS: Combat Studies Institute, 1994), 369.

96. Peter N. Kafkalas, "The Light Infantry Division and Low Intensity Conflict: Are They Losing Sight of Each Other?" *Military Review* 66, no. 1 (January 1986), 24.

97. William J. Olson, "The Light Force Initiative," *Military Review* 65, no. 6 (June 1985), 7.

98. Kafkalas, "The Light Infantry Division and Low Intensity Conflict: Are They Losing Sight of Each Other?," 22.

99. Operation URGENT FURY was the 1983 US invasion of Grenada. The invasion was carried out by Marines, Army Light Infantry, and Special Forces and was largely successful, given the very light opposition. However, command and control problems throughout the operation demonstrated serious flaws in the services' ability to operate jointly, which led to the Goldwater-Nichols Defense Reorganization Act of 1986.

100. Wickham and Department of the Army, *Light Infantry Divisions*, 1.

101. Louis D. Huddleston, "The Light Infantry Division: Azimuth Check," *Military Review* 65, no. 9 (September 1985), 16.

102. David H. Petraeus, "Light Infantry in Europe: Strategic Flexibility and Conventional Deterrence," *Military Review* 64, no. 12 (December 1984), 53.

103. "Notes for Chief of Staff of the Army, meeting with Representative Les Aspin, Roles and Missions Subcommittee, Armed Services Committee, US House of Representatives (draft)," January 21, 1992, Historical Manuscripts Collection 2. Washington, DC: US Army Center of Military History.

Chapter 4

1. George H. W. Bush, "Towards a New World Order: Address before a Joint Session of the Congress on the Persian Gulf Crisis and the Federal Budget Deficit," September 11, 1990; Francis Fukuyama, "The End of History," *The National Interest* no. 16 (Summer 1989); Samuel Huntington, *The Clash of Civilizations and the Remaking of World Order* (New York: Simon & Schuster, 1996); Bill Clinton, *National Security Strategy of the United States, 1994–1995: Engagement and Enlargement* (Washington, DC: The White House, 1995); and Dale A. Vesser to Secretaries of the Military Departments, Chairman of the Joint Chiefs of Staff, Under Secretary of Defense for Acquisition, Assistant Secretary of Defense for Program Analysis and Evaluation, and Comptroller of the Department of Defense, "FY 94-98 Defense Planning Guidance Sections for Comment," February 18, 1992, "The Nuclear Vault: Materials from the National Security Archive's Nuclear Documentation Project." The National Security Archive, available at www.gwu.edu/~nsarchiv/nukevault/ebb245/doc03_full.pdf.

2. President George H. W. Bush, Inaugural Address, Washington, DC, January 20, 1991 (College Station, TX: George H. W. Bush Presidential Library), available at http://bushlibrary.tamu.edu/research/public_papers.php?id=1&year=1989&month=01.

3. President George H. W. Bush, Radio Address to US Armed Forces Stationed in the Persian Gulf Region, March 2, 1991 (College Station, TX: George H. W. Bush Presidential Library), available at http://bushlibrary.tamu.edu/research/papers/1991/91030200.html.

4. For the historiography of the war, see Rick Atkinson, *Crusade: The Untold Story of the Persian Gulf War* (New York: Houghton Mifflin, 1994); Bob Woodward, *The Commanders* (New York: Simon & Schuster, 2002); Michael R. Gordon and General Bernard E. Trainor, *The Generals' War: The Inside Story of the Conflict in the Gulf* (Boston: Little, Brown, 1995); Stephen Bourque, *Jayhawk!: The VII Corps in the Persian Gulf War* (Washington, DC: Department of the Army, 2002); Norman Schwarzkopf, *It Doesn't Take a Hero: The Autobiography of General H. Norman Schwarzkopf* (New York: Bantam, 1993); Tom Clancy and Fred Franks, *Into the Storm: A Study in Command* (New York: Putnam, 1998); Lawrence Freedman and Efraim Karsh, *The Gulf Conflict 1990–1991: Diplomacy and War in the New World Order* (London: Faber, 1993); Robert Scales, *Certain Victory: The US Army in the Gulf War* (Washington, DC:

Potomac Books, 1998); and Robert A. Divine, "Historians and the Gulf War: A Critique," *Diplomatic History* 19, no. 1 (1995), 117–134.

5. Of course, the US Air Force came out of the conflict with its reputation even more enhanced than the Army's. See Richard Hallion, *Storm over Iraq* (Washington, DC: Smithsonian Institution Press, 1992); Eliot A. Cohen and Paul H. Nitze, *Gulf War Air Power Survey* (Washington, DC: GPO, 1993); and John Andreas Olsen, *Strategic Air Power in DESERT STORM* (London: Frank Cass, 2003).

6. Cited in Scales, *Certain Victory*, 35.

7. *Clancy and Franks, Into the Storm*, 65–127. One of the coauthors of *Into the Storm*, General Fred Franks, commanded VII Corps during the Gulf War. Franks had lost a leg in Vietnam, and the narrative in many ways presents his story as a metaphor for the Army's renaissance. A wounded Vietnam veteran in the 1970s, Franks recovered and helped rebuild his army, culminating in the triumph of US forces in Operation Desert Storm.

8. Donn A. Starry, "TRADOC's Analysis of the Yom Kippur War, the Jaffee Center Military Doctrine Joint Conference, Casarea, Israel, 16 March 1999," in Lewis Sorley (ed.), *Press On! Selected Works of General Donn A. Starry*, vol. I (Fort Leavenworth, KS: Combat Studies Institute Press, 2009), 224.

9. Colin Powell, "US Forces: The Challenges Ahead," *Foreign Affairs* 72 no. 5 (1992), 40.

10. Caspar Weinberger, "The Uses of Military Power,'" speech to National Press Club, Washington, DC, 28th November 1984," PBS transcript, available at www.pbs.org/wgbh/pages/frontline/shows/military/force/weinberger.html.

11. George Shultz, *Turmoil and Triumph: My Years as Secretary of State* (New York: Scribner's, 1993), 646.

12. Arnold R. Isaacs, *Vietnam Shadows: The War, Its Ghosts and Its Legacies* (Baltimore, MD: Johns Hopkins University Press, 1997), 74. Reagan's Secretary of State Alexander Haig argues that this lack of consensus was at least partly due to the manner in which the White House was run. He described it to be "mysterious as a ghost ship . . . You could hear the creak of the rigging and the groan of the timbers and sometimes even glimpse the crew on deck, but which of the crew had the helm? Was it Meese, was it Baker, was it someone else? It was impossible to know for sure." Alexander Haig, *Caveat: Realism, Reagan, and Foreign Policy* (New York: Macmillan, 1984), 85, 94.

13. Richard Melanson, *American Foreign Policy since the Vietnam War: The Search for Consensus from Nixon to Clinton* (London: M. E. Sharpe, 2000), 19–23.

14. Powell, "US Forces: The Challenges Ahead," 40.

15. Department of Defense, news conference on the DoD Bottom-Up Review, September 1, 1993. Cited in William J. Durch, *UN Peacekeeping, American Politics, and the Uncivil Wars of the 1990s* (Basingstoke, UK: Palgrave Macmillan, 1996), 41.

16. Powell later recounted in his memoirs that his reaction was, "*I thought I would have an aneurysm* [emphasis in the original]. American GIs were not toy soldiers to be moved around on some sort of global game board." Colin Powell with Joseph E. Persico, *My American Journey* (New York: Ballantine Books, 2003), 576.

17. Cited in Michael G. MacKinnon, *The Evolution of US Peacekeeping Policy under Clinton* (London: Frank Cass, 2000), 47.

18. In some ways, Clinton was a culturally polarizing figure to an increasingly conservative military. The fact that he did not serve in Vietnam made him something of a symbol of antiwar protest to many in the Army. He was even booed at a ceremony at the Vietnam Veterans Memorial in 1993. For the debate on civil–military relations during the Clinton era, see D. M. Snider and M. A. Carlton-Carew, *US Civil–Military Relations: In Crisis or Transition?* (Washington, DC: Center for Strategic & Intl studies, 1995); and John McLaughlin, *Re-Examining the Crisis: Civil–Military Relations during the Clinton Administration* (Fort Belvoir, VA: Defense Technical Information Center, 2008).

19. Dover Air Force Base, Delaware, is where the bodies of American military service members killed overseas are returned to US soil. The "Dover test" refers to whether public support for intervention drops at the sight of the bodies returning to the United States at Dover.

20. Henry H. Shelton, "Beyond Joint Vision 2010," *Keynote Address* (presented at the Fletcher Conference, Washington, DC, November 2, 1999) (Washington, DC: US Army Center of Military History), available at www.history.army.mil/documents/ Fletcher/Fletcher-99/F99-Key-T.htm.

21. H. R. McMaster, *Dereliction of Duty: Lyndon Johnson, Robert McNamara, the Joint Chiefs of Staff and the Lies that Led to Vietnam* (New York: HarperCollins, 1997).

22. Anthony Zinni, "Q&A," *The San Diego Union Tribune*, April 25, 2004, available at http://legacy.signonsandiego.com/uniontrib/20040425/news_mz1e25zinni.html.

23. John Barry, Richard Wolffe, and Evan Thomas, "Politicians vs. Generals: The Truth about War," *Newsweek*, July 4, 2006, available at www.msnbc.msn.com/id/8359694/ site/newsweek/print/1/displaymode/1098/.

24. For more on McMaster's interpretation of the lessons of Vietnam, see Rick Young, "The Lessons of Vietnam: A Conversation with Major H. R. McMaster," *Frontline: Give War a Chance* (PBS, May 11, 1999), available at www.pbs.org/wgbh/pages/ frontline/shows/military/etc/lessons.html.

25. There is then, some irony in the fact that Powell presided over the demise of his own doctrine in his role as George W. Bush's secretary of state during the 2003 invasion of Iraq.

26. Powell with Persico, *My American Journey*, 148.

27. Donn A. Starry, "Dedication of Vietnam War Memorial, Valley Station, Kentucky, May 1975," in Lewis Sorley (ed.), *Press On! Selected Works of General Donn A. Starry*, vol. II (Fort Leavenworth, KS: Combat Studies Institute Press, 2009), 974.

28. Donn A. Starry, "Mounted Combat in Vietnam: Letter to Michael J. Donahue, Houston, Texas, 10 October 1979," in ibid., 978.

29. Francis M. Doyle, Karen J. Lewis, and Leslie A. Williams, "Named Military Operations from January 1989 to December 1993" (HQ TRADOC, April 1994), Historical Resources Collection 2 (Washington, DC: US Army Center of Military History).

30. US Arny, *FM 100-5, Operations* (Washington, DC: Department of the Army, 1993).

31. John Romjue, *American Army Doctrine for the Post–Cold War* (Fort Monroe, VA: Military History Office, US Army Training and Doctrine Command, 1997), 29.

32. US Army, *FM 100-5, Operations*, sec. 2-0.

33. Ibid., v.

34. Ibid., sec. 1-2.

35. Ibid., sec. 13-3.

36. The Center for Low Intensity Conflict pushed hard for "low-intensity conflict" to be preserved in the 1991 edition of FM 100-5, but to no avail. See Clifton J. Everton and Arba Williamson, "Trip Report: School of Advanced Military Studies FM 100-5 'Operations,' Working Group meeting, 10–12 Dec 1991" (Army–Air Force Center for Low Intensity Conflict, December 24, 1991), frame 143, reel 47672, microfilm collection, records of the Army–Air Force Center for Low Intensity Conflict (Maxwell Air Force Base, AL: US Air Force Historical Research Agency).

37. Sam Deford, "Memorandum for Colonel Swain, Subject: Peacetime Engagement/Special Operations in the 1990s" (Army–Air Force Center for Low Intensity Conflict, January 24, 1990), frame 1881, reel 47671, microfilm collection, records of the Army-Air Force Center for Low Intensity Conflict (Maxwell Air Force Base, AL: US Air Force Historical Research Agency).

38. John B. Hunt, "Emerging Doctrine for LIC," *Military Review* 71, no. 6 (June 1991), 54.

39. George Bush, *National Security Strategy of the United States: 1990–1991* (Washington, DC: White House, 1990); Steven C. Sifers, *Peacetime Engagement: Beating Swords into Plowshares* (Fort Leavenworth, KS: School of Advanced Military Studies, Command and General Staff College, May 1992), Defense Technical Information Center, available at http://stinet.dtic.mil/oai/oai?&verb=getRecord&metadataPrefix=html&identifier=ADA256620; *National Military Strategy of the United States* (Washington, DC: Department of Defense, January 1992), Defense Technical Information Center, available at http://stinet.dtic.mil/oai/oai?&verb=getRecord&metadataPrefix=html&identifier=ADA338837; and B. J. Ohlinger, *Peacetime Engagement—A Search for Relevance?* (Carlisle, PA: US Army War College, 1992).

40. George H. W. Bush, "Address before the General Assembly of the United Nations," September 21, 1992 (College Station, TX: George H. W. Bush Presidential Library and Museum), available at http://bushlibrary.tamu.edu/research/public_papers .php?id=4820&year=1992&month=9.

41. Barton Gellman, "Wider UN Police Role Supported," *The Washington Post*, August 5, 1993; and R. Jeffrey Smith and Julia Preston, "US Plans Wider Role In U.N. Peace Keeping; Administration Drafting New Criteria," *The Washington Post*, June 18, 1993.

42. US Army, *FM 100-23 Peace Operations* (Washington, DC: Department of the Army, 1994).

43. Ibid., 17.

44. Ibid., v.

45. Donald Gregory Rose, "Peace Operations and Counterinsurgency: The US Military and Change" (PhD dissertation, University of Pittsburgh, 2000), 284.

46. Ibid., 279.

47. Gordon Sullivan and US Army Command and General Staff College Press, *Envisioning Future Warfare* (Fort Leavenworth, KS: US Army Command and General Staff College Press, 1995), 52, 35.

48. TRADOC Pamphlet 525-5 *Force XXI Operations* (Fort Monroe, VA: TRADOC, 1995), sec. 2-4.

49. Ibid., sec. 3-1.

50. Horwig, "525-5 'R+C' working paper" (Army–Air Force Center for Low Intensity Conflict, August 14, 1995), frame 1055, reel 47674, microfilm collection, records of the Army–Air Force Center for Low Intensity Conflict (Maxwell Air Force Base, AL: US Air Force Historical Research Agency).

51. "Historical Report: Army–Air Force Center for Low Intensity Conflict (A-AF CLIC) 1st July 1995–30th June 1996" (Army–Air Force Center for Low Intensity Conflict, 1996), frame 895, reel 47674, microfilm collection, records of the Army–Air Force Center for Low Intensity Conflict (Maxwell Air Force Base, AL: US Air Force Historical Research Agency).

52. Cited in Wray R. Johnson, "Warriors without a War: Defending OOTW," *Military Review* 78, no. 6 (December 1998–February 1999), 70.

53. Institute for Foreign Policy Analysis, *Summary Report of a Conference on Operations Other Than War, sponsored by HQ TRADOC* (Fort Monroe, VA: HQ TRADOC, April 11, 1995), 7. Historical Resources Collection 2 (Washington, DC: US Army Center of Military History).

54. "Historical Report: Army–Air Force Center for Low Intensity Conflict (A–AF CLIC) 1st July 1995–30th June 1996" (Army–Air Force Center for Low Intensity Conflict, 1996), frame 895, reel 47674, microfilm collection, records of the Army–Air

Force Center for Low Intensity Conflict (Maxwell Air Force Base, AL: US Air Force Historical Research Agency).

55. David A. Fastabend, "Checking the Doctrinal Map: Can We Get There from Here with FM 100-5?,"*Parameters* 25 (Summer 1995), 39–40.

56. Geoffrey B. Demarest, "Redefining the School of the Americas," *Military Review* 74 no. 10 (October 1994), 49.

57. PBS, interview with William Cohen, "Frontline: War in Europe," (PBS, February 22, 2000) available at www.pbs.org/wgbh/pages/frontline/shows/kosovo/interviews/cohen.html.

58. Henry H. Shelton, "Peace Operations: The Forces Required," *National Security Studies Quarterly* 6 (Summer 2000), 105.

59. General Barry McCaffrey, "Situation in Bosnia and Appropriate US and Western Responses," Hearing before the Committee on Armed Services, US Senate, 102nd Congress, Second Session, August 11, 1992.

60. Harry G. Summers, "US participation in United Nations Peacekeeping Activities," Hearing before the Subcommittee on International Security, International Organizations, and Human Rights, Committee on Foreign Affairs, US House of Representatives, 103rd Congress, 2nd Session, June 24, 1994.

61. Ibid.

62. Mark Bowden, *Black Hawk Down: A Story of Modern War* (New York: Atlantic Monthly Press, 1999).

63. Richard Holbrooke, "Annals of Diplomacy: Why Are We in Bosnia?" *The New Yorker,* May 18, 1998, 39, available at www.newyorker.com/archive/1998/05/18/1998_05_18_039_TNY_LIBRY_000015558.

64. S. L. Arnold, "Somalia: An Operation Other Than War," *Military* Review, 73, no. 12 (1993), 26.

65. PBS, interview with Richard Lugar, "Frontline: Ambush in Mogadishu," (PBS, November 1, 2001) available at www.pbs.org/wgbh/pages/frontline/shows/ambush/interviews/lugar.html.

66. Clinton, *National Security Strategy of the United States, 1994–1995.*

67. Ibid., 12.

68. Ibid., 13.

69. Ibid., 16.

70. "Reforming Multilateral Peace Operations (PDD 25)," Federation of American Scientists, available at www.fas.org/irp/offdocs/pdd25.htm. Bullet points in original.

71. "Historical Report: Army–Air Force Center for Low Intensity Conflict (A-AF CLIC), 1st January–30th June 1995" (Army–Air Force Center for Low Intensity Conflict), frame 422, reel 47674, microfilm collection, records of the Army–Air Force Center for Low Intensity Conflict (Maxwell Air Force Base, AL: US Air Force Historical Research Agency).

72. Kenneth Allard, *Somalia Operations: Lessons Learned* (Washington, DC: National Defense University, January 1995), 57.

73. US Army Center for Lessons Learned, Fort Leavenworth, KS, "US Army Operations in Support of UNISOM II: Operations Other Than War," October 1994, sec. I-4-7, Historical Resources Collection 2 (Washington, DC: US Army Center of Military History).

74. Ibid., I-1-11.

75. Peter Riehm, "The USS *Harlan County* Affair," *Military Review* 77, no. 4 (April 1997), 31.

76. Robert Baumann and US Army Command and General Staff College, *My Clan against the World: US and Coalition Forces in Somalia, 1992–1994* (Fort Leavenworth, KS: Combat Studies Institute Press, 2004), 3.

77. Robert Baumann, *Armed Peacekeepers in Bosnia* (Fort Leavenworth, KS: Combat Studies Institute Press, 2004), 128; and Stanley F. Cherrie, "Task Force Eagle," *Military Review* 77, no. 4 (April 1997), 63–72.

78. Richard R. Caniglia, "US and British Approaches to Force Protection," *Military Review* 81 no. 4 (April 2001), 73–81.

79. Baumann, *Armed Peacekeepers in Bosnia*, 134.

80. Ibid., 103.

81. Caniglia, "US and British Approaches to Force Protection," 76.

82. Anderson would later command a brigade of the 101st Airborne Division during Gen. David Petraeus's occupation of Mosul.

83. Joseph Anderson, "Military Operational Measures of Effectiveness for Peacekeeping Operations," *Military Review* 81, no. 5 (September–October 2001), 36.

84. Baumann, *Armed Peacekeepers in Bosnia*, 101. It should be noted that when the US established similar markets in Baghdad years later, the purpose was often to *prevent* groups from intermingling, that is, to secure a Shia market from Sunni suicide bombers and vice versa.

85. Ibid., 131.

86. See Michael Stewart, *Protecting the Force in Operations Other Than War* (Fort Leavenworth, KS: School of Advanced Military Studies, Command and General Staff College, 1995) for a critique of then-current Army doctrine that seeks to include force protection in a much more central role.

87. Caniglia, "US and British Approaches to Force Protection," 78.

88. Anthony Lake, *Confronting Backlash States* (Washington, DC: Executive Office of the President, 1994).

Chapter 5

1. This was Operation Enduring Freedom, the US-led effort to overthrow the Taliban government of Afghanistan and to kill or capture their Al-Qaeda allies. Combat Operations in Afghanistan started on October 7, 2001.

2. "Secretary Rumsfeld Speaks on '21st Century Transformation' of US Armed Forces" (transcript of remarks and question and answer period), *Remarks as Delivered by Secretary of Defense Donald Rumsfeld* (Washington, DC: National Defense University, Fort McNair, Thursday, January 31, 2002), available at www.Defencelink.mil/speeches/speech.aspx?speechid=183.

3. The German Army of World War II was the other model that Rumsfeld explicitly evoked during the speech, noting that despite a "German military that was only 10% or 15% transformed . . . the Germans saw that the future of war lay not with massive armies and protracted trench warfare, but rather in small, high-quality mobile shock forces—supported by air power—capable of pulling off 'lightning strikes' against the enemy." (Rumsfeld, ibid.).

4. William Westmoreland, "Address to the Association of the United States Army," October 14, 1969, cited in Antoine Bousquet, *The Scientific Way of Warfare: Order and Chaos on the Battlefields of Modernity* (New York: Columbia University Press, 2009), 126.

5. Seymour J. Deitchman, "The 'Electronic Battlefield' in the Vietnam War," *The Journal of Military History* 72, no. 3 (July 2008), 869–887.

6. James William Gibson, *The Perfect War: Technowar in Vietnam* (New York: Atlantic Monthly Press, 2000).

7. Harlan Ullman and James Wade Jr., *Shock and Awe: Achieving Rapid Dominance* (Washington, DC: National Defense University, 1996).

8. Ibid., xxv.

9. Ibid., xxvi.

10. "Iraq Faces Massive US Missile Barrage—CBS Evening News—CBS News," January 24, 2003, available at www.cbsnews.com/stories/2003/01/24/eveningnews/main537928.shtml.

11. Ullman and Wade, *Shock and Awe*, xviii–xix.

12. Ibid., 26.

13. *Joint Vision 2020: America's Military: Preparing for Tomorrow* (Washington, DC: US Government Printing Office, 2000).

14. "Information Operations," broadly defined, could certainly apply to insurgencies; however, discussion in JV 2020 sometimes seemed to define information operations as a new sphere of operations, analogous to cyberspace, rather than as something that could be integrated into a counterinsurgency effort: "Operations within the information domain will become as important as those conducted in the domains of sea, land, air, and space" (*JV 2020*, 30).

15. However, compared to its predecessor Joint Vision 2010 (published in 1996), JV 2020 was less technocentric. The former document not only contained comparatively little reference to information operations (which only became a key concept with JV 2020) but was replete with diagram after diagram demonstrating the use of high-tech forces on a "clean" battlefield.

16. Nor did the work of more pessimistic commentators, such as Mary Kaldor—whose *New and Old Wars* focused on the security challenges posed by transnational nonstate actors involved in versions of "low-intensity conflict"—impinge much on the publication. See Mary Kaldor, *New and Old Wars: Organized Violence in a Global Era* (Cambridge, UK: Polity Press, 1999).

17. Ibid., 5.

18. President George W. Bush, *Remarks by the President to the Troops and Personnel*, Norfolk Naval Air Station, Norfolk, VA (Washington, DC: The White House, February 13, 2001), available at www.whitehouse.gov/news/releases/20010213-1.html.

19. Marshall, a veteran of RAND, was a contemporary of the prominent early neoconservative Albert Wohlstetter. See Nicholas Lemann, "Dreaming about War," *The New Yorker*, July 16, 2001; and Ken Silverstein, "The Man from ONA," *The Nation*, October 25, 1999, available at www.thenation.com/doc/19991025/19991025 silversteininside.

20. Thomas E. Ricks, "Bush Review of Pentagon Sets Stage for a Shake-Up," *The Washington Post*, February 10, 2001.

21. Donald Rumsfeld, "DOD Acquisition and Logistics Excellence Week Kickoff—Bureaucracy to Battlefield," *Remarks as Delivered by Secretary of Defense Donald H. Rumsfeld* (Washington, DC: The Pentagon, September 10, 2001), available at www .Defencelink.mil/speeches/speech.aspx?speechid=430.

22. Thomas E. Ricks, "Rumsfeld, Joint Chiefs Spar over Roles in Retooling Military," *The Washington Post*, May 25, 2001.

23. Donald Rumsfeld, introduction to *Quadrennial Defense Review* (Washington, DC: US Department of Defense, September 2001).

24. *Quadrennial Defense Review 2001*, 6.

25. Dale A. Vesser to Secretaries of the Military Departments, Chairman of the Joint Chiefs of Staff, Under Secretary of Defense for Acquisition, Assistant Secretary of Defense for Program Analysis and Evaluation, and Comptroller of the Department of Defense, "FY 94-98 Defense Planning Guidance Sections for Comment," February 18, 1992, "The Nuclear Vault: Materials from the National Security Archive's Nuclear Documentation Project." The National Security Archive, available at www.gwu .edu/~nsarchiv/nukevault/ebb245/doc03_full.pdf.

26. Gary J. Dorrien, *Imperial Designs: Neoconservatism and the New Pax Americana* (New York: Routledge, 2004), 39.

27. Cited in Paul Wolfowitz, *Transcript of Deputy Secretary Wolfowitz, Interview with the New Yorker*, DoD press release (Washington, DC: The Pentagon, June 18, 2002), available at www.defense.gov/transcripts/transcript.aspx?transcriptid=3527.

28. John Sloan Brown, *Kevlar Legions: The Transformation of the US Army, 1989–2005* (Washington, DC: US Army Center of Military History, 2011), 192.

29. US Army, *Army Vision 2010* (Washington, DC: Department of the Army, 1996), available at www.army.mil/2010/.

30. Steven Metz, "America's Defense Transformation: A Conceptual and Political History," *Defence Studies* 6, no. 1 (2006), 1.

31. Ibid.

32. Sloan Brown, *Kevlar Legions*, 236.

33. James Kitfield, "An Army of One Feeling: Angst," *National Journal* 33, no. 23 (June 9, 2001), 1748.

34. Ibid.

35. General Eric Shinseki, "Army Transformation," Testimony before AirLand Subcommittee, Armed Services Committee, US Senate, 106th Congress, Second Session, March 8, 2000.

36. US Army, *FM 1 The Army* (Washington, DC: Department of the Army, 2001), sec 1-1.

37. US Army, *FM 3-0 Operations* (Washington, DC: Department of the Army, 2001), sec 1-31.

38. Ibid., sec 3-0.

39. Michael Burke, "Emerging Doctrine—FM 3-0: Doctrine for a Transforming Force," *Military Review* 82, no. 2 (2002), 92.

40. US Army, *FM 3-0*, sec 1-15.

41. Ibid., sec 1-16.

42. Ibid., sec 9-16.

43. Donald Gregory Rose, "FM 3-0 Operations: The Effects of Humanitarian Operations on US Army Doctrine," *Small Wars and Insurgencies* 13, no. 1 (Spring 2002), 60.

44. US Army, *FM 3-0*, sec. 9-27.

45. Ibid., sec 1-10.

46. Ibid., sec 9-51.

47. Ibid., sec 9-56.

48. Ibid., sec 6-89.

49. US Army, *FM 3-07 Stability and Support Operations* (Washington, DC: Department of the Army, 2003).

50. Ibid., sec 1-74.

51. Ibid., sec 1-86.

52. Ibid., sec 3-23.

53. Shinseki, "Army Transformation."

54. Governor George W. Bush, comments at Presidential Debate, October 12, 2001, available at www.pbs.org/newshour/bb/politics/july-dec00/for-policy_10-12.html.

55. Condoleezza Rice, "Promoting the National Interest," *Foreign Affairs* 79, no. 1 (January/February 2000), 53.

56. Michael R. Gordon, "The 2000 Campaign: The Military; Bush Would Stop US Peacekeeping in Balkan Fights," *The New York Times*, October 21, 2000, available at http://query.nytimes.com/gst/fullpage.html?res=9C07E4DE1E3EF932A15753C1A9669 C8B63&sec=&spon=&pagewanted=1.

57. Bill Gertz, "Rumsfeld Takes Dim View of US Peacekeeping Role," *The Washington Times*, February 27, 2002.

58. Douglas Holt, "Army Institute to Be Shut Down: Critics Hit Loss of Training Center for Peacekeeping," *Chicago Tribune*, April 15, 2003, available at www .chicagotribune.com/news/nationworld/chi-0304150249apr15,0,3402046.story.

59. Donald Rumsfeld, "Beyond Nation Building," *Remarks as Prepared for Delivery by Secretary of Defense Donald H. Rumsfeld, 11th Annual Salute to Freedom*, Intrepid Sea-Air-Space Museum, New York City, Friday, February 14, 2003, available at www.Defencelink.mil/speeches/speech.aspx?speechid=331.

60. General Eric Shinseki, "Memorandum for Secretary of Defense, Subject: End of Tour Memorandum," June 10, 2003, available at http://media.washingtonpost.com/wp-srv/opinions/documents/shinseki.pdf.

61. Studies that do discuss the Army's planning for the occupation include James Fallows, *Blind into Baghdad: America's War in Iraq* (New York: Vintage, 2006); Michael R. Gordon, *Cobra II: The Inside Story of the Invasion and Occupation of Iraq* (New York: Pantheon Books, 2006); and George Packer, *The Assassins' Gate: America in Iraq* (New York: Farar, Straus and Giroux, 2005).

62. Packer, *The Assassins' Gate*, 120.

63. Eric Schmitt, "Threats and Responses: Military Spending; Pentagon Contradicts General on Iraq Occupation Force's Size," *New York Times*, February 28, 2003, available at http://query.nytimes.com/gst/fullpage.html?res=9F06E2DA133CF93 BA15751C0A9659C8B63&sec=&spon=&pagewanted=al.

64. *Post-Saddam Iraq: The War Game—"Desert Crossing" 1999 Assumed 400,000 Troops and Still a Mess* (Washington, DC: National Security Archive, November 4, 2006), available at www.gwu.edu/~nsarchiv/NSAEBB/NSAEBB207/index.htm.

65. However, Gen. Anthony Zinni, commander of CENTCOM at the time, later found that the findings of Desert Crossing had been completely disregarded: "When it looked like we were going in [to Iraq], I called back down to CENTCOM and said, 'You need to dust off Desert Crossing.' They said, 'What's that? Never heard of it.' So in a matter of just a few years it was gone. The corporate memory. And in addition I was told, 'We've been told not to do any of the planning. It would all be done in the Pentagon.'" Leslie Evans, "Straight Talk from General Anthony Zinni," *UCLA International Institute*, May 14, 2004, available at www.international.ucla.edu/article .asp?parentid=11162.

66. Michael R. Gordon, "The Conflict in Iraq: Road to War; The Strategy to Secure Iraq Did Not Foresee a 2nd War," *New York Times*, October 19, 2004, available

at http://query.nytimes.com/gst/fullpage.html?res=9B07E2DD133AF93AA25753C1 A9629C8B63&sec=&spon=&pagewanted=2.

67. Gordon and Trainor, *Cobra II*, 50–54.

68. Ibid., 35.

69. *New State Department Releases on the "Future of Iraq" Project* (Washington, DC: National Security Archive, September 1, 2006), available at www.gwu.edu/~nsarchiv/NSAEBB/NSAEBB198/index.htm.

70. United States, *Hard lessons the Iraq Reconstruction Experience* (Arlington, VA: Office of the Special Inspector General for Iraq Reconstruction, 2009), 50.

71. Ibid., 49.

72. Seymour M. Hersh, "Annals of National Security: Offense and Defense: The Battle between Donald Rumsfeld and the Pentagon," *The New Yorker*, April 7, 2003, available at www.newyorker.com/archive/2003/04/07/030407fa_fact1.

73. Conrad C. Crane and Andrew Terrill, *Reconstructing Iraq: Insights, Challenges, and Missions for Military Forces in a Post-Conflict Scenario* (Carlisle Barracks, PA: Strategic Studies Institute, US Army War College, February 2003).

74. Ibid., 1.

75. Tommy Franks, *American Soldier* (New York: Regan Books, 2004), 441.

76. Andrew Bacevich, "A Modern Major General: Review of Tommy Franks, American Soldier," *New Left Review* 29 (October 2004); available at www.newleftreview.org/?view=2529.

77. General Jack Keane, quoted in *On Point II: Transition to the New Campaign: The United States Army in Operation Iraqi Freedom, May 2003–January 2005* (Fort Leavenworth, KS: Defense Department, US Army Combined Arms Center, Combat Studies Institute, 2008), 68.

78. Col. Kevin Benson, "Operational Leadership Experiences in the Global War on Terror," October 6, 2006, Combined Arms Research Library, available at http://cgsc.cdmhost.com/cdm4/item_viewer.php?CISOROOT=/p4013coll13&CISOPTR=270&CISOBOX=1&REC=7.

79. Ibid., 8.

80. Conrad C. Crane, "Phase IV Operations: Where Wars Are Really Won," presented at *Turning Victory into Success: Military Operations after the Campaign* (Fort Monroe, VA: US Army Training and Doctrine Command; and Fort Leavenworth, KS: Combat Studies Institute, US Army Command and General Staff College, 2004).

81. Jay Garner, "Iraq Revisited," presented at *Turning Victory into Success: Military Operations after the Campaign* (Fort Monroe, VA: US Army Training and Doctrine Command; and Fort Leavenworth, KS: Combat Studies Institute US Army Command and General Staff College, 2004).

82. Benson, "Operational Leadership Experiences in the Global War on Terror," 14.

83. *On Point II: Transition to the New Campaign: The United States Army in Operation Iraqi Freedom, May 2003–January 2005*, 78.

84. Col. Kevin Benson, "Phase IV CFLCC Stability Operations Planning," presented at *Turning Victory into Success: Military Operations after the Campaign* (Fort Monroe, VA: US Army Training and Doctrine Command; and Fort Leavenworth, KS: Combat Studies Institute, US Army Command and General Staff College, 2004).

85. Gordon, "The Conflict In Iraq: Road to War; The Strategy to Secure Iraq Did Not Foresee a 2nd War."

86. PBS, interview with Lt. Gen. William Scott Wallace, "Frontline: the Invasion of Iraq," February 26, 2004; available at www.pbs.org/wgbh/pages/frontline/shows/invasion/interviews/wallace.html.

87. Wallace, "The Invasion of Iraq."

88. Donald Rumsfeld and General Tommy Franks, "Testimony on 'Lessons Learned' during Operation Enduring Freedom in Afghanistan and Operation Iraqi Freedom, and Ongoing Operations in the United States Central Command Region," Armed Services Committee, US Senate, 108th Congress, First Session, July 9, 2003.

89. Gregory Fontenot, E. J. Degen, and David Tohn, *On Point: The United States Army in Operation Iraqi Freedom* (Washington, DC: Department of the Army, 2007), 47–52.

90. Antulio Echevarria, *Toward an American Way of War* (Carlisle Barracks, PA: Strategic Studies Institute, US Army War College, March 2004), vii.

91. Ibid., 16.

92. Fontenot, Degen, and Tohn, *On Point*, 390.

93. Thomas E. Ricks, *Fiasco: The American Military Adventure in Iraq* (London: Allen Lane, 2006), 152.

Chapter 6

1. There is large and growing literature documenting the failures of the occupation: Thomas E. Ricks, *Fiasco: The American Military Adventure in Iraq* (London: Allen Lane, 2006); Larry Jay Diamond, *Squandered Victory: The American Occupation and the Bungled Effort to Bring Democracy to Iraq* (New York: Times Books, 2005); Michael Gordon and Bernard Trainor, *Cobra II: The Inside Story of the Invasion and Occupation of Iraq* (London: Atlantic Books, 2006); Nora Bensahel et al., *After Saddam: Pre-War Planning and the Occupation of Iraq* (Santa Monica, CA: Rand Arroyo Center, 2008); Eric Herring and Glen Rangwala, *Iraq in Fragments: The Occupation and Its Legacy* (Ithaca, NY: Cornell University Press, 2006); Peter R. Mansoor, *Baghdad at Sunrise: A Brigade Commander's War in Iraq* (New Haven, CT: Yale University Press, 2008); James Fallows, *Blind into Baghdad: America's War in Iraq* (New York: Vintage, 2006); U.S. Office of the Special Inspector General for Iraq Reconstruction., *Hard Lessons: the Iraq Reconstruction Experience.* (Arlington, VA: Office of the Special

Inspector General for Iraq Reconstruction, 2009); Richard Downes, *In Search of Iraq: Baghdad to Babylon* (Dublin: New Island, 2006); Rick Atkinson, *In the Company of Soldiers: A Chronicle of Combat in Iraq* (New York: Henry Holt, 2004); David L. Phillips, *Losing Iraq: Inside the Postwar Reconstruction Fiasco* (Boulder, CO: Westview Press, 2005); George Packer, *The Assassins' Gate: America in Iraq* (New York: Farrar, Straus and Giroux, 2005); Peter Galbraith, *The End of Iraq: How American Incompetence Created a War without End* (London: Simon & Schuster, 2006); and Patrick Cockburn, *The Occupation: War and Resistance in Iraq* (London: Verso, 2006).

2. L. Paul Bremer III, *My Year in Iraq: The Struggle to Build a Future of Hope* (New York: Simon & Schuster, 2005), 36–39.

3. Ibid.

4. Thomas E. Ricks, "In Iraq, Military Forgot Lessons of Vietnam," *The Washington Post*, July 23, 2006.

5. James Dobbins, *Occupying Iraq: A History of the Coalition Provisional Authority* (Santa Monica, CA: RAND, 2009), 20.

6. Contemporary Operations Studies Team interview with Mark T. Kimmitt, January 12, 2006 (Fort Leavenworth, KS: Combined Arms Research Library); and Dobbins, *Occupying Iraq: A History of the Coalition Provisional Authority*, 53, 57.

7. *On Point II: Transition to the New Campaign: The United States Army in Operation Iraqi Freedom, May 2003–January 2005* (Fort Leavenworth, KS: Defense Department, US Army Combined Arms Center, Combat Studies Institute, 2008), 96.

8. Contemporary Operations Studies Team, interview with Michael Tucker, January 20, 2006 (Fort Leavenworth, KS: Combined Arms Research Library).

9. *On Point II*, 30.

10. Ricardo S. Sanchez and Donald T. Phillips, *Wiser in Battle: A Soldier's Story* (New York: Harper, 2008), 103–116.

11. Ibid., 231.

12. Contemporary Operations Studies Team, interview with Steven R. Whitcomb, June 7, 2006 (Fort Leavenworth, KS: Combined Arms Research Library).

13. *On Point II*, 162.

14. Ibid.

15. Ibid., 163.

16. Darryl Rupp. Interview by Operational Leadership Experiences Project team with Combat Studies Institute, digital recording, January 11, 2006 (Fort Leavenworth, KS: Combined Arms Research Library).

17. *On Point II*, 64.

18. Contemporary Operations Studies Team, interview with David C. Martino, December 8, 2005 (Fort Leavenworth, KS: Combined Arms Research Library).

19. *On Point II*, 374.

20. Paul Watson, "Ballots, Not Bullets, for Iraqi City; A US General Wins over Skeptics, and Now Mosul Prepares for Its First Post-War Election," *The Los Angeles Times*, May 4, 2003, available at http://pqasb.pqarchiver.com/latimes/access/332302371.html?dids=332302371:332302371&FMT=ABS&FMTS=ABS:FT&type=current&date=May+04%2C+2003&author=Paul+Watson&pub=Los+Angeles+Times&desc=AFTER+THE+WAR%3B+Ballots%2C+Not+Bullets%2C+for+Iraqi+City%3B+A+US+general+wins+over+skeptics%2C+and+now+Mosul+prepares+for+its+first+postwar+election.&pqatl=google; and Michael R. Gordon, "101st Airborne Scores Success in Reconstruction of Northern Iraq," *The New York Times*, September 4, 2003, available at www.nytimes.com/2003/09/04/international/worldspecial/04NORT.html?ex=1063252800&en=c4ad9f531f9b62f6&ei=5062&partner=GOOGLE.

21. Dexter Filkins, "Tough New Tactics by US Tighten Grip on Iraqi Towns," *The New York Times*, December 7, 2003; available at www.nytimes.com/2003/12/07/international/middleeast/07TACT.html?pagewanted=1.

22. Ibid.

23. Thomas E. Ricks, "'It Looked Weird and Felt Wrong,' " *The Washington Post*, July 24, 2006.

24. Gerry J. Gilmore, "Defense.gov News Article: US Iraq Operation Snags Pro-Saddam Suspects, Weapons, Ammo," June 12, 2003, available at www.defense.gov/news/newsarticle.aspx?id=28881; and "Defense.gov News Transcript: Video teleconference from Iraq with Maj. Gen. Odierno," July 25, 2003, available at www.defense.gov/Transcripts/Transcript.aspx?TranscriptID=2897.

25. Dexter Filkins, "The Fall of the Warrior King," *The New York Times Magazine*, October 23, 2005; available at www.nytimes.com/2005/10/23/magazine/23sassaman.html?_r=1&pagewanted=2.

26. *Ricks, Fiasco*, 251.

27. Michael Killian, "US Rocketing Down a Road That Leads to Victory, Vietnam-Style," *The Chicago Tribune*, August 10, 2003, available at http://articles.chicagotribune.com/2003-08-10/news/0308100237_1_vietnam-syndrome-saddam-hussein-iraq-operations/5; and Frank Rich, "Why Are We Back in Vietnam?" *The New York Times*, October 26, 2003, available at www.nytimes.com/2003/10/26/arts/26RICH.html?pagewanted=all.

28. Douglas McGregor, cited in Ahmed S. Hashim, *Insurgency and Counterinsurgency in Iraq* (Ithaca, NY: Cornell University Press, 2006), 326.

29. Filkins, "The Fall of the Warrior King."

30. Todd S. Brown, *Battleground Iraq: Diary of a Company Commander* (Washington, DC: Department of the Army, 2007), 153.

31. Nathan Sassaman and Joe Layden, *Warrior King: The Triumph and Betrayal of an American Commander in Iraq* (New York: St. Martin's Press, 2008), 117–119.

32. Kalev Sepp, cited in George Packer, "The Lesson of Tal Afar—The Pentagon Ignores Its Own Success Story," *The New Yorker* (April 10, 2006), 48.

33. William Hix, "Frontline: Endgame," interview by PBS, June 19, 2007, available at www.pbs.org/wgbh/pages/frontline/endgame/interviews/hix.html; and Kalev Sepp, "Frontline: Endgame," interview by PBS, June 19, 2007, available at www.pbs .org/wgbh/pages/frontline/endgame/interviews/sepp.html.

34. Bing West, *The Strongest Tribe: War, Politics, and the Endgame in Iraq* (New York: Random House, 2008), 45.

35. Thomas E. Ricks, "US Counterinsurgency Academy Giving Officers a New Mind-Set," *The Washington Post*, February 21, 2006.

36. Nancy Montgomery, "Counter-Insurgency Training Now at Heart of Iraq Effort: Academy Teaches Techniques, Theory to Newly Arriving Officers," *Stars and Stripes*, February 15, 2006, Mideast Edition.

37. *On Point II*, 178.

38. Quoted in Lawrence F. Kaplan, "Clear and Fold: Forgetting the Lessons of Vietnam," *The New Republic*, December 19, 2005.

39. *On Point II*, 178.

40. Ibid., 175.

41. CNN, "Iraq Insurgency in 'Last Throes,' Cheney Says," June 20, 2005, available at http://edition.cnn.com/2005/US/05/30/cheney.iraq/.

42. Bob Woodward, *State of Denial* (New York: Simon & Schuster, 2006), 477.

43. Derek J. Harvey, "A 'Red Team' Perspective on the Insurgency in Iraq," in *An Army at War: Change in the Midst of Conflict* (presented at the Combat Studies Institute, 2005 Military History Symposium, Fort Leavenworth, KS; Fort Monroe, VA: Combat Studies Institute Press; US Army Training and Doctrine Command, 2005).

44. George W. Bush, "President Addresses the Nation in Prime Time Press Conference" (The White House, April 13, 2004), available at http://georgewbush-whitehouse.archives.gov/news/releases/2004/04/20040413-20.html.

45. For more on the troop withdrawals in Vietnam and Iraq, see "Special Forum: The Politics of Troop Withdrawal" in *Diplomatic History* 34, no. 3 (June 2010), 459–600.

46. Melvin R. Laird, "Iraq: Learning the Lessons of Vietnam," *Foreign Affairs* 84, no. 6 (December 2005), 23.

47. The National Security Council, *National Strategy for Victory in Iraq* (Washington, DC: The White House, November 2005), 12.

48. West, *The Strongest Tribe*, 80–81.

49. See Leonard Wong, *CU @ the FOB: How the Forward Operating Base Is Changing the Life of Combat Soldiers* (Carlisle, PA: Strategic Studies Institute, US Army War College, 2006), for a detailed description of how operating from FOBs affected every aspect of the soldier's day-to-day routine.

50. *Mansoor, Baghdad at Sunrise*, 50.

51. *On Point II*, 580.

52. Col. Kevin P. Reynolds (ret.), "Insurgency/Counterinsurgency: Does the Army 'Get It?'" Paper for Presentation at the International Studies Association Annual Convention, February 28–March 3, 2007, Chicago.

53. Ibid.

54. See Steven E. Clay, *Iroquois Warriors in Iraq* (Fort Leavenworth, KS: Combat Studies Institute Press, 2007), for the Army's official history of the deployment of reservists to Iraq as advisors.

55. Interview with Jeffrey Terhune, "Operational Leadership Experiences in the Global War on Terrorism," March 22, 2007 (Fort Leavenworth, KS: Combined Arms Research Library).

56. Ross Brown, "Commander's Assessment: South Baghdad—A Former Squadron Commander Discusses His Unit's Year in Iraq and Lists His 11 Commandants for Winning the COIN War in South Baghdad," *Military Review* 87, no. 1 (January–February 2007), 27.

57. Ralph O. Baker, "The Decisive Weapon: A Brigade Combat Team Commander's Perspective on Information Operations," *Military Review* vol. 86, no. 3 (May–June 2006), 19.

58. Brown, "Commander's Assessment," 30.

59. Interview with Joseph DiSalvo, "Operational Leadership Experiences in the Global War on Terrorism," March 27, 2006 (Fort Leavenworth, KS: Combined Arms Research Library).

60. Dexter Filkins, "A Skeptical Vietnam Voice Still Echoes in the Fog of Iraq," *The New York Times*, April 25, 2007, available at www.nytimes.com/2007/04/25/world/middleeast/25halberstam.html?ref=media; Ricks, "In Iraq, Military Forgot Lessons of Vietnam"; Peter Spiegel, "Iraq Reopens Debate on Vietnam," *The Seattle Times*, November 25, 2006, available at http://seattletimes.nwsource.com/html/nationworld/2003446915_iraqnam25.html; and Alex Spillius, "George Bush: Iraq Must Not Become Vietnam," *The Telegraph* (London), August 24, 2007, available at www.telegraph.co.uk/news/worldnews/1561123/George-Bush-Iraq-must-not-become-Vietnam.html.

61. Gian Gentile, "A (Slightly) Better War: A Narrative and Its Defects," *World Affairs* (Summer 2008), available at www.worldaffairsjournal.org/2008%20-%20Summer/full-Gentile.html.

62. Gian P. Gentile, "Eating Soup with a Spoon," *Armed Forces Journal*, September 2007, available at www.armedforcesjournal.com/2007/09/2786780.

63. Brig. Gen. Ricky Rife, "AR 15-6 Investigating Officer's Findings and Recommendations Regarding the Command Climate and Use of Force by 3rd BCT during

OIF 05-07" (Washington, DC: Department of the Army, Office of the Deputy Chief of Staff, G 3/5/7, February 11, 2008).

64. Brian Bennett and Al Jallam, "On Scene: How Operation Swarmer Fizzled," *Time*, March 17, 2006, available at www.time.com/time/world/article/0,8599,1174448,00.html; and Edward Wong, "US Forces in Big Assault Near Samarra," *The New York Times*, March 17, 2006, available at http://query.nytimes.com/gst/fullpage.html?res=9506E6DE1E31F934A25750C0A9609C8B63.

65. Paul Von Zielbauer, "Army Says Improper Orders by Colonel Led to 4 Deaths," *The New York Times*, January 21, 2007, available at http://query.nytimes.com/gst/fullpage.html?res=9F06E2D61E30F932A15752C0A9619C8B63.

66. PBS, interview with Andrew Krepinevich, *Frontline: End Game*, June 19, 2007, available at www.pbs.org/wgbh/pages/frontline/endgame/interviews/krepinevich.html.

67. Andrew F. Krepinevich, "How to Win in Iraq," *Foreign Affairs* 84, no. 5 (October 2005), 87–104.

68. James H. Willbanks, "Vietnamization: An Incomplete Exit Strategy," presented at *Turning Victory into Success: Military Operations after the Campaign* (Fort Leavenworth, KS: US Army Training and Doctrine Command; and Fort Monroe, VA: Combat Studies Institute, US Army Command and General Staff College, 2004).

69. David Cloud and Greg Jaffe, *The Fourth Star: Four Generals and the Epic Struggle for the Future of the United States Army* (New York: Crown Publishers, 2009), 203.

70. John Nagl, *Learning to Eat Soup with a Knife: Counterinsurgency Lessons from Malaya and Vietnam* (Chicago: University of Chicago Press, 2005).

71. Peter Schoomaker, foreword to Nagl, *Learning to Eat Soup with a Knife*, x.

72. See Chapter 1 for a deeper description of Vietnam revisionism.

73. Apparently, *Eating Soup with a Knife* was the first book Casey had ever read on counterinsurgency; Cloud and Jaffe, *The Fourth Star*, 168.

74. United States, *Hard Lessons: The Iraq Reconstruction Experience*, 101.

75. Peter W. Chiarelli and Patrick R. Michealis, "Winning the Peace: The Requirement for Full-Spectrum Operations," *Military Review* 85, no. 4 (July–August 2005), 15.

76. Contemporary Operations Studies Team, interview with Robert Abrams, November 2005 (Fort Leavenworth, KS: Combined Arms Research Library).

77. David H. Petraeus, "Keynote Address," in *Security Assistance: US and International Historical Perspectives* (presented at the 2006 TRADOC/Combat Studies Institute Military History Symposium, Fort Leavenworth, KS: Combat Studies Institute Press, 2006).

78. Robert Cone, "The Changing National Training Center—The Days of Large-Formation Battle in the Mojave Aren't Quite Over, but the NTC Has Definitely Moved Toward Scenarios More Attuned to Current Combat Operations," *Military Review* 86, no. 3 (2006), 70.

79. Ibid.

80. Andrew J. Birtle, *US Army Counterinsurgency and Contingency Operations Doctrine 1942–1976* (Washington, DC: US Army Center of Military History, United States Army, 2006), 455–466.

81. Reynolds, "COIN: Does the Army Get It?"

82. Ibid.

83. US Army, *FMI 3-07.22 Counterinsurgency Operations* (Washington, DC: Department of the Army, 2004).

84. US Army, *FM 90-8 Counter-Guerrilla Operations* (Washington, DC: Department of the Army, 1985).

85. US Army, *FM 100-5 Operations* (Washington, DC: Department of the Army, 1986); US Army, *FM 100-5 Operations* (Washington, DC: Department of the Army, 1993); US Army, *FM 3-0 Operations* (Washington, DC: Department of the Army, 2001).

86. US Army, *FMI 3-07.22 Counterinsurgency Operations*, 1–30.

87. Ibid., 1–3.

88. Ibid., 3–40.

89. Ibid., 2–67.

90. David H. Ucko, *The New Counterinsurgency Era: Transforming the US Military for Modern Wars* (Washington, DC: Georgetown University Press, 2009), 68.

91. Ibid., 1–40.

Chapter 7

For an earlier version of this chapter, see David Fitzgerald, "Vietnam, Iraq and the Re-birth of Counterinsurgency," *Irish Studies in International Affairs*, 21 (2010), 149–159.

1. James A. Russell, *Innovation, Transformation, and War: Counterinsurgency Operations in Anbar and Ninewa Provinces, Iraq, 2005–2007* (Stanford, CA: Stanford University Press, 2011).

2. H. R. McMaster, *Dereliction of Duty: Lyndon Johnson, Robert McNamara, the Joint Chiefs of Staff and the Lies that Led to Vietnam* (New York: HarperCollins, 1997); and Harry G. Summers, *On Strategy: The Vietnam War in Context* (Honolulu: University of the Pacific Press, 1981).

3. George Packer, "The Lesson of Tal Afar: The Pentagon Ignores Its Own Success Story." *The New Yorker* (April 10, 2006), 48.

4. David McCone et al., *The 3rd ACR in Tal'Afar: Challenges and Adaptations* (Carlisle Barracks, PA: Strategic Studies Institute, 2007), 7.

5. Packer, "The Lesson of Tal Afar."

6. PBS, interview with H. R. McMaster, *Frontline: The Insurgency*, February 21, 2006, available at www.pbs.org/wgbh/pages/frontline/insurgency/interviews/mcmaster.html.

7. Packer, "The Lesson of Tal Afar."

8. Secretary of State Condoleezza Rice, "Iraq and US Policy," testimony before the US Senate Committee on Foreign Relations, 109th Congress, Second Session, October 19, 2005, available at foreign.senate.gov/testimony/2005/RiceTestimony051019.pdf.

9. George W. Bush, "President Discusses War on Terror and Operation Iraqi Freedom," Renaissance Hotel, Cleveland, OH, March 20, 2006, George W. Bush Presidential Website (archived), available at http://georgewbush-whitehouse.archives.gov/news/releases/2006/03/20060320-7.html. See also White House Press Office, "Fact Sheet: Strategy for Victory: Clear, Hold, and Build," March 20, 2006, available at http://georgewbush-whitehouse.archives.gov/news/releases/2006/03/20060320-6.html.

10. Contemporary Operations Studies Team, interview with Sean MacFarland, January 17, 2008 (Fort Leavenworth, KS: Combined Arms Research Library).

11. Niel Smith and Sean MacFarland, "Anbar Awakens: The Tipping Point," *Military Review* 88 no. 2 (March–April 2008), 43.

12. Captain Travis Patriquin was central to this effort to engage with local tribes. Patriquin, who was later killed in action in Ramadi, was instrumental both in responding to the Albu Soda tribe's request for help when they got into a major firefight with Al-Qaeda and in briefing senior leaders on the need to distinguish between different types of insurgents, for which he used a Powerpoint briefing based on stick figures. See Thomas E. Ricks, *The Gamble: General David Petraeus and the American Military Adventure in Iraq, 2006–2008* (New York: Penguin Press HC, 2009), 68; and Bing West, *The Strongest Tribe: War, Politics, and the Endgame in Iraq* (New York: Random House, 2008), 211. Patriquin's "stick figure" briefing is available at http://abcnews.go.com/images/US/how_to_win_in_anbar_v4.pdf.

13. See Austin Long, "The Anbar Awakening," *Survival: Global Politics and Strategy* 50, no. 2 (2008), 67.

14. Contemporary Operations Studies Team, interview with MacFarland.

15. Matt Millham, "1st BCT Soldiers Return from 14-Month Iraq Tour: Anxious Wives Welcome Soldiers Back from Battles in Ramadi," *Stars and Stripes*, February 22, 2007, available at www.stripes.com/article.asp?section=104&article=43759.

16. Paul Yingling, "A Failure in Generalship," *Armed Forces Journal* (May 2007), available at www.afji.com/2007/05/2635198.

17. John McCool, interview with Paul Yingling, "Operational Leadership Experiences in the Global War on Terrorism," September 22, 2006 (Fort Leavenworth, KS: Combined Arms Research Library).

18. Paul Yingling, "Irregular Warfare and Adaptive Leadership" (Fort Leavenworth, KS: US Army Command and General Staff College, [videoconference], April 2, 2009), available at http://smallwarsjournal.com/blog/2009/04/irregular-warfare-and-adaptive/.

19. Ironically, General George Casey, on taking over as chief of staff of the Army, also attempted to save the Army from repeating its post-Vietnam experience, but he did so by seeking withdrawal of troops from Iraq, lest the Army crack under the strain. David Cloud and Greg Jaffe, *The Fourth Star: Four Generals and the Epic Struggle for the Future of the United States Army* (New York: Crown Publishers, 2009), 269.

20. Richard W. Stewart, "CORDS and the Vietnam Experience: An Interagency Organization for Counterinsurgency and Pacification," in *Security Assistance: US and International Historical Perspectives*, presented at the 2006 TRADOC/Combat Studies Institute Military History Symposium (Fort Leavenworth, KS: Combat Studies Institute Press, 2006).

21. Kalev Sepp, "Best Practice in Counterinsurgency," *Military Review* 85 no. 3 (May–June 2005), 8; Dale Andrade and James H. Willbanks, "CORDS/Phoenix: Counterinsurgency Lessons from Vietnam for the Future," *Military Review* 86, no. 2 (March–April 2006), 9; M. Sullivan, "Leadership in Counterinsurgency: A Tale of Two Leaders," *Military Review* 87, no. 5 (September–October 2007), 119–123; Ross Coffey, "Revisiting CORDS: The Need for Unity of Effort to Secure Victory in Iraq," *Military Review* 86, no. 2 (March–April 2006), 24; and Robert M. Cassidy, "Winning the War of the Flea: Lessons from Guerrilla Warfare," *Military Review* 84, no. 5 (September–October 2004), 41.

22. Stewart, "CORDS and the Vietnam Experience"; Lewis Sorley, "Security Assistance in the Vietnam War," in *Security Assistance: US and International Historical Perspectives*, presented at the 2006 TRADOC/Combat Studies Institute Military History Symposium (Fort Leavenworth, KS: Combat Studies Institute Press 2006); James H. Willbanks, "Vietnamization: An Incomplete Exit Strategy," presented at *Turning Victory into Success: Military Operations after the Campaign* (Fort Leavenworth, KS: US Army Training and Doctrine Command and Fort Monroe, VA: Combat Studies Institute, US Army Command and General Staff College, 2004); and Andrew Krepinevich, "Vietnam and Iraq: Why Everything Old Isn't New Again," in *Security Assistance: US and International Historical Perspectives*, presented at the 2006 TRADOC/Combat Studies Institute Military History Symposium (Fort Leavenworth, KS: Combat Studies Institute Press, 2006).

23. Sepp, "Best Practice in Counterinsurgency," 12.

24. Sepp was serving as part of a counterinsurgency advisory group, the "doctors without orders," a group of soldiers with PhDs who were given a wide remit by Casey to examine the war effort. In many ways, this was a precursor of the similar group that David Petraeus set up when he took over command in 2007.

25. Department of Defense Directive 3000.05, "Military Support for Stability, Security, Transition, and Reconstruction (SSTR) Operations" (Fort Belvoir, VA: Defense Technical Information Center, November 8, 2005), available at www.dtic.mil/whs/directives/corres/html/300005.htm. Unsurprisingly, the directive was signed by

Undersecretary Gordon England rather than Secretary of Defense Donald Rumsfeld, who, at that time, was still objecting to soldiers providing security for the newly established Provincial Reconstruction Teams. Rumsfeld's 2006 Quadrennial Defense Review (QDR) essentially reinforced the policy of the 2001 QDR and still emphasized "network-centric warfare" and defense transformation, even though it also marked the debut of the phrase "the long war," under the influence of David Kilcullen.

26. See Chapter 1 for a discussion of Abrams's strategy versus that of Westmoreland.

27. Cassidy, "Winning the War of the Flea: Lessons from Guerrilla Warfare," 44.

28. Bob Woodward, *State of Denial* (New York: Simon & Schuster, 2006), 418.

29. Rick Perlstein, "The Best Wars of Their Lives," *The Nation*, September 27, 2007, available at www.thenation.com/doc/20071015/perlstein/4.

30. David Petraeus, comments during Sorley, "Security Assistance and the Vietnam War."

31. Ibid.

32. Steve Coll, "The General's Dilemma—David Petraeus and the Lessons of the Surge," *The New Yorker* (September 8, 2008), 34; David Halberstam, *The Best and the Brightest* (New York: Random House, 1972); Bernard Fall, *Street without Joy: The French Debacle in Indochina*, Rev. ed. (London: Stackpole, 2005); and Neil Sheehan, *A Bright Shining Lie: John Paul Vann and America in Vietnam* (New York: Random House, 1988).

33. David H. Petraeus, "The American Military and the Lessons of Vietnam: A Study of Military Influence and Use of Force in the Post-Vietnam Era" (PhD dissertation, Woodrow Wilson School of Public and International Affairs, Princeton University, 1987).

34. Ibid., 303.

35. Ibid., 307.

36. Ibid., 308.

37. However, it should be made clear that he had no problem with the "American way of war" in other circumstances; in 1997 he published an article in *Field Artillery* entitled "Never Send a Man When You Can Send a Bullet," thus invoking the phrase most favored by advocates of firepower since at least Patton. See David H. Petraeus, Damian P. Carr, and John C. Abercrombie, "Why We Need FISTs—Never Send a Man When You Can Send a Bullet," *Field Artillery* (Fort Sill, OK: US Army Field Artillery School) 1997 (3), 3–5.

38. Conrad Crane, "Minting New COIN: The Development and Content of Contemporary American Counterinsurgency Doctrine" (Draft paper in the author's possession), 2.

39. Ibid., 4.

40. David H. Petraeus, "Learning Counterinsurgency: Observations from Soldiering in Iraq," *Military Review* 86, no. 1 (January–February 2006).

41. Ibid., 3.

42. Coll, "The General's Dilemma."

43. Ibid., 10.

44. Ricks, *The Gamble*; and Linda Robinson, *Tell Me How This Ends: General David Petraeus and the Search for a Way Out of Iraq* (New York: Public Affairs, 2008). For critical perspectives, see Gian Gentile, "A (Slightly) Better War: A Narrative and Its Defects," *World Affairs* (Summer 2008), available at www.worldaffairsjournal. org/2008%20-%20Summer/full-Gentile.html; and Michael A. Cohen, "The Myth of a Kinder, Gentler War," *World Policy Journal* 27, no. 1 (April 1, 2010), 75–86.

45. Coll, "The General's Dilemma."

46. Crane, "Minting New COIN," 10.

47. Dunlap, *Making Revolutionary Change: Airpower in COIN Today* (Fort Belvoir, VA: Defense Technical Information Center, 2008).

48. The "strategic corporal" and the "three-block war" were concepts introduced by Marine Corps Commandant, General Charles Krulak (son of the Vietnam-era counterinsurgency advocate, Maj. Gen. Victor Krulak). These concepts illustrated the complexity of the situations that would confront soldiers on the modern battlefield—describing a situation where soldiers conducted a full-scale fire-fight, peacekeeping, and humanitarian aid within the space of three contiguous blocks—and that advocated for allowing junior leaders leeway to take major decisions, as their actions were likely to have strategic repercussions in such an environment. See Charles Krulak, "The Strategic Corporal: Leadership in the Three-Block War," *Marines Magazine*, January 1999.

49. David Galula, quoted in US Marine Corps and US Army, *FM 3-24 Counterinsurgency* (Washington, DC: Headquarters, Dept. of the Army Headquarters, Marine Corps Combat Development Command, Department. of the Navy, Headquarters, US Marine Corps, 2006), 53.

50. Robert Thompson, quoted in ibid., 151.

51. Frank Hoffman, "Neo-Classical Counterinsurgency?" *Parameters* 37, no. 2 (2007), 71–87.

52. US Army, *FM 3-24 Counterinsurgency*, secs. 1-31–1-35.

53. Brian Burton and John Nagl, "Learning as We Go: The US Army Adapts to Counterinsurgency in Iraq, July 2004–December 2006," *Small Wars and Insurgencies* 19, no. 3 (September 2008), 303–327.

54. Conrad Crane, interview with author, Carlisle, PA, October 24, 2008.

55. *US Army, FM 3-24 Counterinsurgency*, sec. 1-36.

56. Elements of the Vietnam War historiography that argue that the US defeat was largely self-inflicted include William Colby, *Lost Victory* (Chicago: Contemporary Books, 1989); Lewis Sorley, *A Better War: The Unexamined Victories and the Final Tragedy of America's Last Years in Vietnam* (New York: Harcourt Brace, 1999); David

R. Palmer, *Summons of the Trumpet* (Novato, CA: Presidio Press, 1978); and Phillip B. Davidson, *Vietnam at War: The History: 1946–1975* (New York: Oxford University Press, 1991).

57. Conrad C. Crane, *Avoiding Vietnam: The US Army's Response to Defeat in Southeast Asia* (Carlisle Barracks, PA: Strategic Studies Institute, US Army War College).

58. Eliot Cohen et al., "Principles, Imperatives, and Paradoxes of Counterinsurgency," *Military Review* 86, no. 2 (2006), 49.

59. US Army, *FM 3-24 Counterinsurgency*, sec 1-154.

60. Ibid., 73–75.

61. Crane, interview with author. *Op. Cit.*

62. Conrad Crane, e-mail to author, March 14, 2008.

63. Conrad Crane, "The Emergence of New American Counterinsurgency Doctrine," presentation at Columbia University, New York, March 12, 2008.

64. In fact, Al-Qaeda in Iraq's campaign against the Shia was so strong that Al-Qaeda's second-in-command, Ayman al-Zawahiri, wrote to Abu Musab al-Zarqawi, leader of al-Qaeda in Iraq, to urge him to moderate his attacks. Douglas Jehl, "Document Provides Glimpses Into Qaeda's Intentions," *The New York Times*, October 11, 2005, available at www.nytimes.com/2005/10/11/politics/11cnd-intel.html?hp&ex=1129089600&en=9383738d0ee1cb61&ei=5094&partner=homepage.

65. President George W. Bush, "President's Address to the Nation: The New Way Forward in Iraq," Office of the Press Secretary, January 10, 2007, available at http://georgewbush-whitehouse.archives.gov/news/releases/2007/01/20070110-7.html.

66. Ricks, *The Gamble*, 74–124; and Bob Woodward, *The War Within: A Secret White House History 2006–2008* (New York: Simon & Schuster, 2008), 244–290.

67. "Poll: Approval for Iraq Handling Drops to New Low," CNN.com, December 18, 2006, available at http://edition.cnn.com/2006/POLITICS/12/18/bush.poll/index.html.

68. Bob Woodward credits Hadley with authoring the surge. See Woodward, *The War Within*, 320–321. But Tom Ricks, Bing West, and Linda Robinson all argue that Jack Keane and Raymond Odierno were the key proponents. See Ricks, *The Gamble*, 74–124; West, *The Strongest Tribe*, 216–223; and Robinson, *Tell Me How This Ends*, 25–37.

69. *Robinson, Tell Me How This Ends*, 98–100.

70. Thomas E. Ricks, "Officers with PhDs Advising War Effort," *The Washington Post*, February 5, 2007.

71. Spencer Ackerman, "A Counterinsurgency Guide for Politicos," *The Washington Independent*, available at http://washingtonindependent.com/427/a-counterinsurgency-guide-for-politicos.

72. David Kilcullen, "Counterinsurgency in Iraq: Theory and Practice" (Seminar, Quantico, VA, September 26, 2007), available at smallwarsjournal.com/documents/kilcullencoinbrief26sep07.ppt.

73. Douglas Ollivant, "Producing Victory: A 2007 Postscript for Implementation," *Military Review* 87, no. 2 (2007): 109.

74. Kilcullen, "Counterinsurgency in Iraq: Theory and Practice," available at smallwarsjournal.com/documents/kilcullencoinbrief26sep07.ppt.

75. Ibid.

76. Coll, "The General's Dilemma."

77. David Kilcullen, "Understanding Current Operations in Iraq," *Small Wars Journal Blog*, June 26, 2007, available at http://smallwarsjournal.com/blog/2007/06/understanding-current-operatio/.

78. David Kilcullen, "Don't Confuse the 'Surge' with the Strategy," *Small Wars Journal Blog*, January 19, 2007, available at http://smallwarsjournal.com/blog/2007/01/dont-confuse-the-surge-with-th/.

79. Kilcullen, "Understanding Current Operations in Iraq."

80. David H. Petraeus, "Multi-National Force-Iraq Commander's Counterinsurgency Guidance" (Headquarters Multi-National Force Iraq, June 21, 2008), available at www.mnf-iraq.com/images/CGs_Messages/080621_coin_%20guidance.pdf.

81. Ibid.

82. Robinson, *Tell Me How This Ends*, 119–140.

83. James Baker, Lee Hamilton, et al., *The Iraq Study Group Report: The Way Forward, a New Approach* (New York: Vintage Books, 2006), 15.

84. David Kilcullen, "The Urban Tourniquet—'Gated Communities' in Baghdad," *Small Wars Journal Blog*, April 27, 2007, available at http://smallwarsjournal.com/blog/2007/04/the-urban-tourniquet-gated-com/.

85. Dale Andrade, *Surging South of Baghdad: The 3rd Infantry Division and Task Force Marne in Iraq, 2007–2008* (Washington, DC: US Army Center of Military History, 2010), 21.

86. Josh White, "US Boosts Its Use of Airstrikes in Iraq," *The Washington Post*, January 17, 2008, available at www.washingtonpost.com/wp-dyn/content/article/2008/01/16/AR2008011604148.html.

87. Ibid.

88. Woodward, *The War Within*, 380.

89. Stephen Grey, "Task Force Black: A Review," *The Sunday Times* (London, February 28, 2010).

90. David Petraeus, "Report to Congress on the situation in Iraq," Committee on Foreign Relations, US Senate, 110th Congress, First Session, September 11, 2007.

91. The argument that ethnic cleansing had a part to play in the decline in violence is certainly convincing. See Karen DeYoung, "Balkanized Homecoming:

As Iraqi Refugees Start to Trickle Back, Authorities Worry about How They Will Fit into the New Baghdad," *The Washington Post*, December 16, 2007, available at www .washingtonpost.com/wp-dyn/content/article/2007/12/15/AR2007121501921_pf.html; Maggie Fox, "Satellite Images Show Ethnic Cleanout in Iraq," *Reuters* (Washington, DC, September 19, 2008), available at www.reuters.com/article/idUSN1953066020080919; and Steven Simon, "The Price of the Surge," *Foreign Affairs* 87, no. 3 (May 2008), 57–76.

92. Douglas A. Ollivant, "Countering the New Orthodoxy: Reinterpreting Counterinsurgency in Iraq" (Washington, DC: The New America Foundation, June 2011), 3, available at www.newamerica.net/sites/newamerica.net/files/policydocs/Ollivant_Reinterpreting_Counterinsurgency.pdf.

Chapter 8

1. The Army's own official history documents the underresourcing of the war very well. See Donald P. Wright with the Contemporary Operations Studies Team, *A Different Kind of War: The United States Army in Operation Enduring Freedom, October 2001–September 2005* (Fort Leavenworth, KS: Combat Studies Institute Press, 2010).

2. The operations in the Korengal and Wanat have been extensively covered. See Elizabeth Rubin, "Battle Company Is Out There," *The New York Times*, February 24, 2008; Sebastian Junger, *War* (New York: Twelve, 2010); *Restrepo*, dir. Tim Hetherington and Sebastian Junger (Outpost Films, National Geographic Channel, 2010); and Staff of Combat Studies Institute, *Wanat: Combat Action in Afghanistan, 2008* (Fort Leavenworth, KS: Combat Studies Institute Press, 2010).

3. Ann Scott Tyson, "Army's Next Crop of Generals Forged in Counterinsurgency," *The Washington Post*, May 15, 2008, available at www.washingtonpost.com/wp-dyn/content/article/2008/05/14/AR2008051403366.html.

4. US Army, *FM 3-0 Operations* (Washington, DC: Department of the Army, 2008).

5. Ibid., viii.

6. Lt. Gen. William Scott Wallace, "FM 3-0 Operations: The Army's Blueprint," *Military Review* 88, no. 2 (March–April 2008), 4.

7. William B. Caldwell, *The Impact of Field Manual 3-0, Operations on the United States Army*, Armed Services Committee, AirLand Subcommittee, US Senate, 110th Congress, Second Session, April 1, 2008, available at http://armed-services.senate.gov/statemnt/2008/April/Caldwell%2004-01-08.pdf.

8. Ibid.

9. William Wallace, foreword to *FM 3-0 Operations*.

10. Rupert Smith, *The Utility of Force: The Art of War in the Modern World* (London: Allen Lane, 2005).

11. *FM 3-0 Operations*, sec. 1-20.

12. US Army, *FM 3-07 Stability Operations* (Washington, DC: Department of the Army, 2008).

13. Ibid., sec. 2-6.

14. Ibid., sec. 1-1.

15. Ibid., sec. 1-8.

16. William Caldwell IV, "Field Manual 3-07, Stability Operations: Upshifting the Engine of Change," *Military Review* 88, no. 4 (2008), 6.

17. Ibid.

18. Ibid.

19. Robert M. Gates, *Remarks as Delivered by Secretary of Defense Robert M. Gates, Manhattan, Kansas, Monday, November 26, 2007* (Manhattan, KS: Kansas State University, November 26, 2007), available at www.defense.gov/speeches/speech .aspx?speechid=1199.

20. Joint Chiefs of Staff, *Joint Pub 3-24: Counterinsurgency Operations* (Washington, DC: Department of Defense, 2009); and Interagency Counterinsurgency Initiative, *US Government Counterinsurgency Guide* (Washington, DC: Department of State, 2009).

21. "TRADOC Pam 525-3-0: The Army Capstone Concept: Operational Adaptability: Operating under Conditions of Uncertainty and Complexity in an Era of Persistent Conflict 2016–2028" (Fort Monroe, VA: HQ TRADOC, December 21, 2009); and Department of Defense, "Directive 3000.7: Irregular Warfare" (Washington, DC: Department of Defense, December 1, 2008).

22. "Army Capstone Concept," 6.

23. Robert M. Gates, "Remarks as Delivered by Secretary of Defense Robert M. Gates, Fort Leavenworth, KS, Friday, May 07, 2010" (Fort Leavenworth, KS: Command and General Staff College, May 7, 2010), available at www.defense.gov/speeches/ speech.aspx?speechid=1465.

24. Department of Defense, *Quadrennial Defense Review Report* (Washington, DC: Department of Defense, 2010), viii.

25. Ibid., 20.

26. Ibid., 21.

27. Mike Mullen, *Landon Lecture Series Remarks: As Delivered by Adm. Mike Mullen, Chairman of the Joint Chiefs of Staff, Kansas State University, Manhattan, Kansas, Wednesday, March 3, 2010* (Manhattan: Kansas State University, 2010), available at www.jcs.mil/speech.aspx?id=1336.

28. White House, "White Paper of the Interagency Policy Group's Report on US Policy Towards Afghanistan and Pakistan" (Washington, DC: The White House, 2009), available at www.whitehouse.gov/assets/documents/afghanistan_pakistan_ white_paper_final.pdf.

29. Barack Obama, "Remarks by the President on a New Strategy for Afghanistan and Pakistan," March 27, 2009, available at www.whitehouse.gov/the_press_office/ Remarks-by-the-President-on-a-New-Strategy-for-Afghanistan-and-Pakistan/.

30. David Petraeus, Landon Lecture, Kansas State University, Manhattan, KS, April 27, 2009, available at www.k-state.edu/media/newsreleases/landonlect/ petraeustext409.html.

31. David Petraeus, "Striking a Balance: A New American Security," Keynote Address, Center for a New American Security Conference, Washington, DC, June 11, 2009, available at www.cnas.org/files/multimedia/documents/Petraeus_transcript_ Complete.pdf.

32. Lolita C. Baldor, "Petraeus: Iraq Needs Enormous Commitment," *USA Today*, April 27, 2007, available at www.usatoday.com/news/washington/2007-04-26-2006341827_x.htm.

33. Andrew M. Exum, Nathaniel C. Fick, Ahmed A. Humayun, and David Kilcullen, *Triage: The Next Twelve Months in Afghanistan and Pakistan* (Washington, DC: Center for a New American Security, 2009), 7.

34. Ibid., 8.

35. Ibid., 15.

36. Stanley McChrystal to Robert M. Gates, *Commander's Initial Assessment* (Kabul, Afghanistan: Headquarters, NATO International Security Assistance Force, Afghanistan), August 30, 2009, sec. 1-2, available at http://media.washingtonpost.com/ wp-srv/politics/documents/Assessment_Redacted_092109.pdf.

37. Ibid.

38. Ibid., sec. 1-4.

39. Ibid., sec. 1-1.

40. Ibid., sec. 1-3.

41. Stanley McChrystal, remarks at "Hearing to Consider the Nominations of Admiral James G. Stavridis, USN, for Reappointment to the Grade of Admiral and to Be Commander, US European Command and Supreme Allied Commander, Europe; Lieutenant Douglas M. Fraser, USAF to be General and Commander, US Southern Command; and Lieutenant General Stanley A. McChrystal, USA to be General and Commander, International Security Assistance Force, Afghanistan," Armed Services Committee, US Senate, 111th Congress, 1st Session June 2, 2009, 19.

42. McChrystal, "Commander's Initial Assessment," sec. 1-4.

43. Ibid.

44. Evan Thomas and John Barry, "The Surprising Lessons of Vietnam: Unraveling the Mysteries of Vietnam May Prevent Us from Repeating Its Mistakes," *Newsweek*, November 6, 2009.

45. John A. Nagl, "A 'Better War' in Afghanistan," prepared statement before the Committee on Foreign Relations, US Senate, 111th Congress, 1st Session, September 16, 2009.

46. Marvin Kalb, "The Other War Haunting Obama," *The New York Times*, October 8, 2011, available at www.nytimes.com/2011/10/09/opinion/sunday/the-vietnam-war-still-haunting-obama.html?pagewanted=all. See also Marvin Kalb and Deborah Kalb, *Haunting Legacy: Vietnam and the American Presidency from Ford to Obama* (Washington, DC: Brookings Institution Press, 2011), 241–306.

47. John Barry, "Obama's Vietnam," January 30, 2009.

48. Bob Woodward recorded the White House debate extensively. See Bob Woodward, *Obama's Wars: The Inside Story* (New York: Simon and Schuster, 2010).

49. Gordon M. Goldstein, *Lessons in Disaster: McGeorge Bundy and the Path to War in Vietnam* (New York: Times Books, 2008).

50. Peter Spiegel and Jonathon Weisman, "Behind Afghan War Debate, a Battle of Two Books Rages," *The Wall Street Journal*, October 7, 2009.

51. Richard Holbrooke, remarks at conference on "The American Experience in Southeast Asia," Office of the Historian, US State Department, September 29, 2010.

52. Woodward, *Obama's Wars*, 250.

53. Karl Eikenberry, cable to Hillary Clinton, subject: "COIN Strategy, Civilian Concerns," November 6, 2009, 1, available at http://documents.nytimes.com/eikenberry-s-memos-on-the-strategy-in-afghanistan.

54. Woodward, *Obama's Wars*, 377.

55. Ibid., 385–390.

56. Barack Obama, "Remarks by the President in Address to the Nation on the Way Forward in Afghanistan and Pakistan," US Military Academy at West Point, NY, December 1, 2009, available at www.whitehouse.gov/the-press-office/remarks-president-address-nation-way-forward-afghanistan-and-pakistan.

57. Stanley McChrystal, remarks at the International Institute of Strategic Studies, London, October 1, 2009, available at www.iiss.org/recent-key-addresses/general-stanley-mcchrystal-address/.

58. Ibid.

59. Publically available version at Counterinsurgency Advisory and Assistance Team, "COIN Advisory: Tactical Patience" (Kabul: Headquarters, International Security Assistance Force Afghanistan, May 12, 2010), available at https://ronna-afghan.harmonieweb.org/CAAT/Shared%20Documents/COIN%20Advisory%2020100512-001%20(Tactical%20Patience).pdf; summary also released by Headquarters, ISAF on July 6, 2009, available at www.nato.int/isaf/docu/official_texts/Tactical_Directive_090706.pdf.

60. Publically available version at Counterinsurgency Advisory and Assistance Team, "COIN Advisory: Documenting, Reporting and Stopping Aggressive Driv-

ing Practices" (Kabul: Headquarters, International Security Assistance Force Afghanistan, May 11, 2010), available at: https://ronna-afghan.harmonieweb.org/CAAT/Shared%20Documents/COIN%20Advisory%2020100511-001%20(Tactical%20Driving%20Directive).pdf.

61. Discussion of revised ISAF SOP 373, "Escalation of Force" in *COIN Common Sense*, vol. 1, issue 1 (Kabul: Headquarters, ISAF, February 2010), available at www.isaf.nato.int/COIN-publication/feb10.pdf.

62. Michael Hastings, "The Runaway General," *Rolling Stone*, June 22, 2010.

63. International Security Assistance Force (ISAF), CIVCAS, January 13, 2011; as referred to in J. Bohannon, *Science* 331, 1256 (2011); UN Assistance Mission in Afghanistan (UNAMA), Civilian Casualty Data, February 24, 2011; as referred to in J. Bohannon, *Science* 331, 1256 (2011).

64. Ibid.

65. Ibid.

66. Mark Thompson, "US Troops Prepare to Test Obama's Afghan War Plan," *Time*, February 9, 2010; Gordon Lubold, "Marjah Offensive a Test of Obama's Broader Afghanistan Strategy," *The Christian Science Monitor*, February 14, 2010; and Saeed Shah, "US-Led Offensive Underway in Southern Afghanistan," *McClatchy Newspapers*, February 12, 2010.

67. David Sanger, "A Test for the Meaning of Victory in Afghanistan,"` *The New York Times*, February 13, 2010.

68. Theo Farrell, "Appraising Moshtarak: The Campaign in Nad-e-Ali District, Helmand," *RUSI Briefing Note* (London: Royal United Services Institute, June 23, 2010), 8–9, available at www.rusi.org/downloads/assets/Appraising_Moshtarak.pdf. Further, the choice of Marja and Helmand for the showcase offensive of the surge was a curious one. According to Rajiv Chandrasekaran, the decision to surge forces into Helmand rather than concentrate on the more strategically important districts around Kandahar was dictated by a desire on the part of the US Marines to have a contiguous area of operations. See Rajiv Chandrasekaran, *Little America: The War within the War for Afghanistan* (London: Bloomsbury, 2012), 57–77.

69. Dion Nissenbaum, "McChrystal Calls Marjah a 'Bleeding Ulcer' in Afghan Campaign," *McClatchy Newspapers*, May 24, 2010.

70. Ibid.

71. Farrell, "Appraising Moshtarak."

72. Hastings, "The Runaway General."

73. David Petraeus, *COMISAF's Counterinsurgency Guidance* (Kabul: Headquarters, International Security Assistance Force, Afghanistan, August 1, 2010), available at www.isaf.nato.int/article/caat-anaysis-news/comisaf-coin-guidance.html.

74. US Air Force Central Command Air and Space Operations Center statistics, cited in Noah Schactman, "Bombs Away: Afghan Air War Peaks with 1,000 Strikes

in October," *Danger Room Blog, Wired.com*, November 10, 2010, available at www.wired.com/dangerroom/2010/11/bombs-away-afghan-air-war-peaks-with-1000-strikes-in-october/.

75. Alex Strick van Linschoten and Felix Kuehn, *A Knock on the Door: 22 Months of ISAF Press Releases* (Kandahar: Afghan Analysts Network, October 12, 2011), 12, 20; data visualized by Simon Rogers, "Every NATO Kill-Capture Mission in Afghanistan Detailed and Visualised," *Data blog*, guardian.co.uk, October 12, 2011, available at www.guardian.co.uk/news/datablog/2011/oct/12/afghanistan-nato-kill-capture-raids-isaf-petraeus.

76. Open Societies Foundations Regional Policy Initiative on Afghanistan and Pakistan, *The Cost of Kill/Capture: Impact of the Night Raid Surge on Afghan Civilians* (Kabul: Open Societies Foundation and the Liaison Office, September 19, 2011), 28–29.

77. Spencer Ackerman, "David Petraeus: The Danger Room Interview," *Danger Room blog, Wired.com*, August 18, 2010, available at www.wired.com/dangerroom/2010/08/petraeus-interview/.

78. ISAF briefing slide, cited in Spencer Ackerman, "Drones Surge, Special Ops Strike in Petraeus Campaign Plan," *Danger Room blog, Wired.com*, August 18, 2010, available at www.wired.com/dangerroom/2010/08/petraeus-campaign-plan/. The emphasis on the body count was also criticized in Lawrence F. Kaplan, "Vietnamization: Enemy Body Count Makes a Grim Return," *The New Republic*, March 3, 2011; Spencer Ackerman, "Team Petraeus Brings Body Counts Back," *Danger Room blog, Wired.com*, March 8, 2011, available at www.wired.com/dangerroom/2011/03/team-petraeus-brings-body-counts-back; and Carlotta Gall, "Night Raids Curbing Taliban, but Afghans Cite Civilian Toll," *The New York Times*, July 8, 2011.

79. Josh Foust, "How Short-Term Thinking Is Causing Long-Term Failure in Afghanistan," *The Atlantic*, January 24, 2011, available at www.theatlantic.com/international/archive/2011/01/how-short-term-thinking-is-causing-long-term-failure-in-afghanistan/70048/.

80. Paula Broadwell, "Travels with Paula (I): A Time to Build," *The Best Defense, foreignpolicy.com*, January 13, 2011, available at http://ricks.foreignpolicy.com/posts/2011/01/13/travels_with_paula_i_a_time_to_build.

81. Megan McCloskey, "Petraeus Promises Villagers US Will Rebuild What It Has Knocked Down," *Stars and Stripes*, December 21, 2010.

82. Taimoor Shah and Rod Nordland, "NATO Is Razing Booby-Trapped Afghan Homes," *The New York Times*, November 16, 2010.

83. Michael Hirsh and Jamie Tarabay, "Washington Losing Patience with Counterinsurgency in Afghanistan," *The Atlantic*, June 2, 2011.

84. John M. Spiszer, "Counterinsurgency in Afghanistan: Lessons Learned by a Brigade Combat Team," *Military Review* 91, no. 1 (2011), 74.

85. Barack Obama, "Remarks by the President on the Way Forward in Afghanistan" (Washington, DC: The White House, June 22, 2011), available at www.whitehouse.gov/the-press-office/2011/06/22/remarks-president-way-forward-afghanistan.

86. Robert M. Gates, remarks at US Military Academy at West Point, February 25, 2011, available at www.defense.gov/speeches/speech.aspx?speechid=1539.

87. Peter Mansoor, cited in Hirsh and Tarabay, "Washington Losing Patience with Counterinsurgency in Afghanistan."

88. Thomas H. Johnson and M. Chris Mason, "Refighting the Last War: Afghanistan and the Vietnam Template," *Military Review* 89, no. 6 (2009), 9.

89. Robert Cassidy, *War, Will and Warlords: Counterinsurgency in Afghanistan and Pakistan, 2001–2011* (Quantico, VA: Marine Corps University Press, 2012), 45.

90. Andrew J. Bacevich, "Inverting the Lessons of Vietnam," testimony before the Committee on Foreign Relations, US Senate, April 23, 2009, 111th Congress, 1st Session.

91. Gian P. Gentile, "A Strategy of Tactics: Population-Centric COIN and the Army," *Parameters*, Autumn 2009, 11.

92. Michael A. Cohen, "The Myth of a Kindler, Gentler War," *World Policy Journal*, spring 2010, 81.

93. Celeste Ward Gventer, "A False Promise of Counterinsurgency," *Room for Debate: Obama's Surge Strategy in Afghanistan*, NYTimes.com, December 1, 2009, available at http://roomfordebate.blogs.nytimes.com/2009/11/30/obamas-surge-strategy-in-afghanistan/.

94. Craig A. Collier, "Now That We're Leaving Iraq, What Did We Learn?" *Military Review* 90, no. 5 (2010), 93.

Conclusion

1. For more on this caution, see Kenneth J. Campbell, "The Crucial Constraint: Containment and the Post-Vietnam Military's Reluctance to Use Force" (PhD dissertation, Temple University, 1989); Richard Lock-Pullan, *U.S. Intervention Policy and Army Innovation: From Vietnam to Iraq* (London: Routledge, 2005); and David H. Petraeus, "The American Military and the Lessons of Vietnam: A Study of Military Influence and Use of Force in the Post-Vietnam Era" (PhD dissertation, Woodrow Wilson School of Public and International Affairs, Princeton University, 1987).

2. Hugh Trevor-Roper, "History and Imagination: A Valedictory Lecture Delivered before the University of Oxford on 20 May, 1980," in Hugh Lloyd-Jones, Valerie Pearl, and Blair Worden (eds.), *History & Imagination: Essays in Honor of H. R. Trevor-Roper* (New York: Holmes & Meier Publishers, 1982), 358.

3. Harry G. Summers, *On Strategy: The Vietnam War in Context* (Honolulu: University of the Pacific Press, 1981); Andrew Krepinevich, *The Army and Vietnam* (Baltimore, MD: Johns Hopkins University Press, 1988); and Lewis Sorley, *A Better War:*

The Unexamined Victories and the Final Tragedy of America's Last Years in Vietnam (New York: Harcourt Brace, 1999).

4. US Army, *FM 3-21.75: The Warrior Ethos and Soldier Combat Skills* (Washington, DC: Department of the Army, 2008).

5. Robert M. MacIver, *The Web of Government* (New York: Macmillan, 1947), 4–5.

6. Michael Howard, "The Use and Abuse of Military History: Lecture to the Royal United Services Institute, October 18, 1961," *Royal United Services Institute Journal* 107, no. 4 (February 1962), 8.

INDEX

Abizaid, John, 137–38, 145, 165
Abrams, Creighton, 22–29, 35–36, 38, 41, 42, 56, 150, 152, 165, 172, 175, 179, 185, 186, 191, 204, 207, 209
Abrams, Robert, 152
Abu Ghraib prison, 140
Accelerated Pacification Campaign (APC), 23–27, 32, 38, 172
Active Defense, 43–46, 239n71
Adid, Mohammed Farrah, 101
Advanced sensors, 110–11
Afghanistan, 18, 121; conditions in, 189; counterinsurgency in, 181, 188–98, 201–2; intervention in, 109, 181, 248n1; Iraq compared to, 123, 124; leaving, 198–202; Obama and, 188–93; Soviet Union in, 181; Vietnam compared to, 191–93, 199–200
AirLand battle doctrine, 8, 77, 79, 81, 83, 87, 91, 93, 98–99, 111–12, 152, 239n71
Albright, Madeline, 90
Allison, Graham, 5
Alwyn-Foster, Nigel, 169
American Embassy, Saigon, 34
American view of war, 93–94
American Way of War, 7, 9, 29, 51, 58, 94, 141, 154, 207
Analogies, in historical analysis, 11–13, 135
Anbar Awakening, 161
Anderson, Gary, 135
Anderson, Joseph, 106, 139

Andrade, Dale, 20–22, 177
Angola, 44
Annihilation strategy, 7
Anticommunism, 61–62
Antiwar movement, 54
APC. *See* Accelerated Pacification Campaign
Armed Forces Journal, 162
Armor and Artillery Schools, 48
Arms Export Act (1976), 44
Army–Air Force Center for Low Intensity Conflict, 70, 72
Army 86, 73
Army of Excellence, 73
Army Special Forces, 22
Army War College, 48, 55, 153; Peacekeeping Institute, 97, 99–100, 121–22; Strategic Studies Institute, 51, 53, 124
Arnold, S. L., 101
ARVN. *See* Republic of Vietnam Armed Forces
Aspin, Lee, 90
Asymmetric warfare, 113
Attrition strategy, 20, 22–24, 56, 201
Automated battlefield, 110, 111, 113
Avant, Deborah, 5
Axelrod, David, 191–92

Baath Party, 135–36
Bacevich, Andrew, 71–72, 127, 200, 236n23
Baghdad, Iraq, 128–31, 136, 148, 156, 159, 161, 174–78
Baker, Ralph O., 147–48

Balkans, 89, 101, 102, 106, 108, 110, 113, 118,
139, 152, 205, 209
Banana wars, 52
Barnes, Albert M., 70
Barnes, John W., 30–31
Barnes, Rudolph C., 75
BDM Corporation, Vietnam War study by,
51–53, 57–58
Beirut, Marine barracks bombing in (1983),
89
Benson, Kevin, 127–29
Bergerud, Eric, 21
"Better war" thesis, 19–28, 38, 165, 167, 179,
191, 209
B-52 bombers, 29
Bickel, Keith, 15
Biden, Joe, 192
Birtle, Andrew J., 4, 20–22, 26
Black, Jeremy, 7
Blaufarb, Douglas, 37, 216n7
Body armor, 105–6
Body counts, 25, 27–30, 40, 56–57, 140, 173,
197
Boot, Max, 4
Bosnia, 90, 92, 99, 100, 105–7, 112, 119, 121,
123, 139, 142, 174
Boylan, Kevin, 32
Brady, Michael, 57
Bremer, L. Paul, 135–36, 156
Brigades, 116
Britain, 150
British Army, 3, 168, 195
Brown, Charles P., 31, 56
Brown, John Sloan, 117
Brown, Ross, 147
Brown, Todd S., 141
Buckley, Kevin, 27
Builder, Carl, 8
Bundy, McGeorge, 192
Burckhardt, Jakob, 211
Burke, Michael D., 118
Bush, George H. W., 12, 66, 86, 87, 95
Bush, George W., 114, 116, 121, 124, 126, 130,
137, 144–45, 160, 166, 173–74, 181, 188

Cable, Larry, 14, 20, 216n7
Caldwell, William B., 183
CALL. See Center for Army Lessons Learned
Calley, William, 28
Cambodia, 26, 45, 55
Cao Van Vien, 38
Capabilities-based approach, 113, 115–16, 118

Capstone Concept, 186
Carland, John M., 20
Carter, Jimmy, 51, 62
Cartwright, James, 192
Casey, George, 106, 142–43, 145, 149–51, 160,
164, 173, 209, 262n24
Cassidy, Robert, 4, 164, 165, 200
Casualties, concern with prevention of,
17, 101, 104–8, 146, 156. See also Body
counts; Civilian casualties
Cebrowski, Art, 115
CENTCOM. See US Central Command
Center for a New American Security (CNAS),
189–90
Center for Army Lessons Learned (CALL),
15, 104
Center for Low Intensity Conflict, 98, 103
Central America, 17, 47, 60–68
Central Intelligence Agency (CIA), 22,
236n34
Central Pacification and Development
Council (Vietnam), 24, 34
CGSC. See Command and General Staff
College
Cheney, Dick, 144
Chiang Kai Shek, 171
Chiarelli, Peter, 151, 160, 163, 177
Chieu Hoi (Open Arms) program, 23–24
Civilian casualties, 27–28, 173, 178, 195
Civilian policy makers, 5, 54, 90, 115, 126. See
also Intervention: civilian desire for
Civil Operations and Revolutionary
Development Support (CORDS), 16, 22,
32, 52, 150, 172, 179, 185–86; Pacification
Studies Group, 25, 30
Civil War (US), 7
CJTF-7. See Combined Joint Task Force-7
Clark Amendment, Arms Export Act (1976),
44
Clausewitz, Carl von, 20, 53, 55, 110, 166,
234n15
"Clear, hold, and build" strategy, 147, 160,
164–65, 179, 191, 200
Clemenceau, Georges, 5
Clinton, William J. (Bill), 86, 90, 95–96, 99,
101–3, 108, 244n18
Coalition Land Forces Component
Command (CFLCC), 126–28, 136–37
Coalition Provisional Authority (CPA),
135–38
Cody, Richard A., 152
Cognitive psychology, 11–13

Cohen, Eliot, 169
Cohen, Michael, 200
Cohen, William, 99
Colby, William, 25
Cold War, 62
Coll, Steve, 169, 175
Collective memory, 13–14
Collier, Craig, 201
Collins, Arthur S. (Art), 25–26, 56
Comanche attack helicopter, 121
Combat Studies Institute (CSI), 15, 104, 163, 165, 167
Combined Action Platoons (CAPs), 164
Combined Arms Center (CAC), 15, 163, 167–68, 183
Combined Campaign Plan, 24
Combined Joint Task Force-7 (CJTF-7), 137–38, 142
Command and General Staff College (CGSC), 47–48, 55, 57, 77–78, 97–98
Commander in Chief, Pacific Command (CINCPAC), 34
Commander's Emergency Response Program (CERP), 151
Communism, 62
Cone, Robert W., 152–53
Confino, Alon, 13
Constructivism, 14
Contras, 69
Conventional warfare, 17, 22, 30, 33, 39, 48–50, 52, 58–59, 65, 75, 77, 81, 86, 113, 118, 126, 131, 141, 149, 209
CORDS. See Civil Operations and Revolutionary Development Support
Cosmas, Graham, 20, 26
Counterinsurgency: in Afghanistan, 181, 188–98, 201–2; aversion/skepticism concerning, 2, 53–58, 71, 103, 148–49, 153–54, 203–5; in Central America, 47, 60–68; declining interest in, 42, 45–47, 52–53, 108; defining, 1, 84–85; doctrinal neglect of, 5, 45–47, 109, 128, 134, 142, 162–63, 167, 185, 204–5; doctrine of, 21, 30, 35, 37–38, 51, 54, 66, 87, 148, 152–55, 167–73, 176, 179; educational neglect of, 47–49, 153–55, 162–63, 167; in El Salvador, 61–68, 71–72; failure of, 36–38; innovations in, 142–44, 148–52, 158–63; institutionalization of, 182–88; in Iraq, 134–80; limitations of, 32–33; low-intensity conflict and, 73–74; Nixon and, 33–37; peace operations compared to,

96, 108; renewed interest in, 73–78, 164, 167–73, 179; training in, 152–53; in 2001 manual, 120–21; US Army and, 3–5, 39–40, 180, 182, 199, 206; in Vietnam, 19–38, 53–57, 179. See also Low-intensity conflict
Crane, Conrad, 4, 168, 171–73, 175; Avoiding Vietnam, 172; Reconstructing Iraq, 124–25, 128
Crusader artillery system, 121
Cuba, 62
Cuban Missile Crisis, 12
Currey, Cecil B., 75

Dau tranh strategy, 171, 173
Davidson, Phillip, 173
Death squads, 65–66, 71, 236n26, 236n29
Decision making, 11–12
Demilitarized zone (DMZ), 54
Department of Defense (DoD) Directive 3000.5 "Stability Operations," 164
Department of Defense (DoD) Directive 3000.7 "Irregular Warfare," 186
Department of Joint and Combined Operations, 77
DePuy, William E., 43–46, 49–51, 58, 80, 82, 85, 87, 154, 183, 208, 209, 229n30, 239n71
Desert Crossing, 123, 124, 252n65
DiSalvo, Joseph, 148
"Doctors without orders," 142, 262n24
Doctrine: AirLand, 8, 77, 79, 81, 83, 87, 91, 93, 98–99, 111–12, 152, 239n71; assumptions vs. in Iraq planning, 126–32; counterinsurgency, 21, 30, 35, 37–38, 51, 54, 66, 87, 148, 152–55, 167–73, 176, 179; formal, 15; history in relation to, 110; informal, 15; on low-intensity conflict, 77–78; Nixon, 37, 42, 46, 48, 60, 61, 78; peacekeeping, 92–100, 132; peacekeeping aims in tension with, 87, 90, 93, 100, 107–8, 130, 133, 166, 210; post-Iraq, 182–83; post-Vietnam, 43–47; Powell, 17, 87–93, 101, 105, 107, 114, 124, 166, 187, 208–10, 244n25; Reagan, 61, 65, 69–70, 233n3; role of, 14–15; Rumsfeld, 116, 124; "transformation" not apparent in, 117; Weinberger, 88–89, 208. See also Training and Doctrine Command
Dodge, Toby, 174
Dominance, 111–13, 116, 129
Donilon, Tom, 191–92
Dover test, 90, 99, 244n19

Downie, Richard, 4
Draft, end of, 41, 229n21
Draft Defense Planning Guidance, 116

Echevarria, Antulio, 131–32
Education, 43–50, 55, 97, 152–53
Egypt, 46
Eikenberry, Karl, 192–93
Eisenhower, Dwight, 9
Eliot, T. S., 42
Elliott, David, 21, 29
Ellis, John, 7
El Salvador, 47, 57, 60–69, 71–72, 74–75, 79,
    113, 205, 208, 236n23, 236n26
Emmanuel, Rahm, 191–92
Europe: planning for war in, 83–84; as US
    Army's post-Vietnam focus, 42–45, 60
Ewell, Julian J., 27–29, 231n57
Exit strategy, 90, 107, 124, 125

Falkland Islands, 83
Fall, Bernard, 166
Fallows, James, 169
Fallujah, Iraq, 144, 156, 159
Farrell, Theo, 14, 196
Fastabend, David A., 98, 132
Feith, Douglas, 129
Field Circular (FC) 71-101 *Light Infantry
    Division Operations*, 82–83
Field Circular (FC) 100-20, 73–74
Field Manual (FM) 1 *The Army*, 117–18
Field Manual (FM) 3-0 *Operations*, 117–20,
    182–85
Field Manual (FM) 3-07 *Stability Operations*,
    120, 132, 182, 184–85
Field Manual (FM) 3-07.22
    Counterinsurgency Operations, 154
Field Manual (FM) 3-24 *Counterinsurgency*,
    167–73, 175–77, 179–80, 185, 190, 200,
    201, 206, 209
Field Manual (FM) 31-16, 46
Field Manual (FM) 31-23 *Stability
    Operations*, 46–47
Field Manual (FM) 90-8 *Counter-Guerrilla
    Operations*, 120
Field Manual (FM) 100-5 *Operations*, 15,
    43–45, 49, 54, 58, 72, 77, 82–83, 93–94,
    99–100, 108, 118, 208, 239n71
Field Manual (FM) 100-20 *Low Intensity
    Conflict*, 47, 70, 73, 77–78, 83
Field Manual (FM) 100-23 *Peace Operations*,
    96, 99–100, 108

Field manuals, 15
Figueira, John S., 31
Filkins, Dexter, 140
Firepower orientation, 27–30, 51, 68, 140–41,
    150, 154
1st Brigade, 1st Armored Division, 160–61
I Field Force Vietnam, 31
Flynn, David, 197
FMLN. *See* Frente Farabundo Martí para la
    Liberación Nacional
Force protection, 104, 105–8, 141
Force XXI, 97–98
Ford, Gerald, 51, 114
Foreign Affairs (journal), 88, 89, 121, 145,
    150
Foreign internal defense (FID), 81, 119,
    204. *See also* Internal defense and
    development
Forgetting war lessons, 5; silence and, 14,
    49–50, 58; Vietnam, 43–47, 49–50, 55–56,
    58, 113
Formal doctrine, 15
Forward Operating Bases (FOBs), 145, 177
Foss, John W., 78–79
4th Infantry Division, 139–41
Franks, Fred, 243n7
Franks, Tommy, 123–24, 126–27, 129–30,
    136–37
Frente Farabundo Martí para la Liberación
    Nacional (FMLN), 61–63, 67, 74–75,
    236n29
Fukuyama, Francis, 86
Full spectrum operations, 132
Fulton, John S., 70–71
"The Future of Iraq" project, 124

Galula, David, 170–71, 177
Galvin, John R., 72, 238n50
Gardner, Lloyd, 22
Garner, Jay, 128
Garret (major general), 97–98
Gates, Robert, 185–86, 199
Gaza, 140
Gentile, Gian, 148–49, 200
George, Alexander, 11
Germany, as analogy for Iraq, 135–36
Giap, Vo Nguyen, 171, 173
Gibson, James, 111
Gingrich, Newt, 55
Goldstein, Gordon, 192, 193
Goldwater-Nichols Defense Reorganization
    Act (1986), 80, 241n99

Gorman, Paul, 49, 64–65, 72, 80, 238*n*49
Government of Vietnam (GVN), 22–26, 29, 32–35
Gradualism, 89
Grant, Ulysses S., 7
Gray, Colin, 6
Grenada, 83, 241*n*99
"Guardian" approach to war and defense, 9
Guatemala, 60
Guerrilla warfare, 3, 63, 83
Gulf War (1991), 86–88, 90, 99, 111, 208
Gventer, Celeste Ward, 201
GVN. *See* Government of Vietnam

Hadley, Stephen, 123, 174, 265*n*68
Haig, Alexander, 36, 62, 243*n*12
Haiti, 90, 92, 107, 125, 139
Halberstam, David, 166
Hamburger Hill, battle of, 26
Hamlet Evaluation Survey (HES), 24–25, 30, 32, 34, 172
USS *Harlan County*, 104
Harned, Glenn M., 81
Harvey, Derek, 144
Hearts and minds approach, 4, 20–22, 24, 27, 37, 106, 143, 147, 149
"Heroes" approach to war and defense, 9
HES. *See* Hamlet Evaluation Survey
Hess, Gary, 19–20
Historical narrative: analogies in, 11–13; collective memory and, 13–14; construction of, 2, 10–16, 206–11; lessons of war and, 15–16, 210–11
Hitler, Adolf, 12
Ho Chi Minh Trail, 45
Hoffman, Frank, 171
Holbrooke, Richard, 101, 192
House Armed Services Committee (HASC), 64–65
Howard, Michael, 7, 12, 211
Huddleston, Louis D., 83
Hunt, Ira A., 231*n*57
Hunt, Richard, 25
Huntington, Samuel, 5, 86
Hussein, Saddam, 12, 87, 135, 151, 208

Infantry in Battle, 46
Informal doctrine, 15
Information operations, 112, 170, 249*n*14
Inouye, Daniel K., 69
Intelligence School, 48
Interagency cooperation, 81, 96, 120, 164

Internal defense and development (IDD), 47, 48, 204. *See also* Foreign internal defense
International Security Assistance Force (ISAF), 182, 190, 194–97
Intervention: civilian desire for, 87, 90, 93, 102–3, 107–8, 126; post-Vietnam caution about, 19, 39, 41, 44, 46–47, 51–52, 58–61, 69–70, 87, 89–90, 92–93, 102–3, 107–8, 119, 122 (*see also* Prevention of Vietnam, desire for); public opinion on, 41, 63, 69–70, 88–89, 96, 99, 105, 116, 244*n*19
Iraq Body Count database, 173
Iraqification, 144–48, 209
Iraqi Security Forces (ISF), 143, 145–48
Iraq Study Group, 173, 177
Iraq War and aftermath (2003–2011), 17–18, 205; Afghanistan compared to, 123, 124; counterinsurgency in, 134–80; dissident officers in, 158–63; innovation related to, 6, 142; innovations in, 142–44, 148–52, 158–63; insurgency in, 134–35, 137–38, 143–44, 149, 161, 177–78; Iraqi Army and, 136; Iraqification, 144–48, 209; lessons of, 181–82, 188–90; postwar conditions in, 130, 135–42, 173; public opinion on, 143, 145–46, 173; "the surge" in, 173–79, 181–82, 189, 201, 265*n*68; troop drawdown, 188; Vietnam compared to, 2, 17–18, 23, 108, 134–57, 161–67, 174–75, 209. *See also* Gulf War (1991); Northern Iraq; Planning for Iraq
Isaacs, Arnold, 10, 89
ISAF. *See* International Security Assistance Force
Israel, 46, 83, 140

Jenkins, Brian, 25, 27
Jervis, Robert, 11
John F. Kennedy School for Special Warfare, 47, 81
Johnson, Harold K., 21
Johnson, Lyndon B., 41, 54, 158, 192, 232*n*76
Johnson, Thomas, 199–200
Johnstone, Craig, 25
Joint Chiefs of Staff, 34, 91, 103, 112, 115, 158, 173
Joint Publications 3-24 *Counterinsurgency Operations*, 186
Joint Readiness Training Center, 83
Joint Special Operations Command (JSOC), 178
Joint Strategic Assessment (JSAT), 174–76

Joint Vision 2010 (JV 2010), 249*n*15
Joint Vision 2020 (JV 2020), 112–13, 249*n*15
Jones, James, 191–92
Joulwan, George, 106
JSAT. *See* Joint Strategic Assessment

Kafkalas, Peter N., 82
Kaldor, Mary, 250*n*16
Kandahar, Afghanistan, 198
Kaplan, Robert, 4
Karnow, Stanley, 191
Keane, Jack, 127, 174, 265*n*68
Kelly, Francis J., 231*n*57
Kennan, George, 86
Kennedy, John F., 12, 37, 48, 54, 75
Kennedy, Ted, 80
Khalilzad, Zalmay, 150
Khong, Yueng Foong, 11–12
Kier, Elizabeth, 6
Kilcullen, David, 174–75, 177
Kill ratios, 57. *See also* Body counts
Kinetic operations, 143, 151–53, 177, 197
Kinnard, Douglas, 56
Kinross, Stuart, 8
Kissinger, Henry, 33–34, 36, 50
Kissinger Commission, 65
Kitson, Frank, 170
Komer, Robert W., 22, 24, 174
Korean War, 12, 54, 88, 92
Kosovo, 90, 92, 121, 123, 139
Krepinevich, Andrew, 15, 20, 21, 37, 147, 150,
    162, 165, 200, 207, 216*n*7; *The Army in
    Vietnam*, 75–76
Krulak, Charles, 264*n*48
Krulak, Victor, 1
Kuwait, 12

Laird, Melvyn, 31, 35–36, 145
Lake, Anthony, 108
Landry, John, 78
Laos, 45
Lawrence, T. E., 168; *Seven Pillars of Wisdom*,
    159
Lebanon, 83
Lee, Robert E., 7
"Lessons learned" literature, 15–16
Lessons of war: analogies in, 11–13;
    Balkans, 118; CALL, 104; changes
    and developments in, 8, 12–13, 50–57,
    206–11; construction of, 14; El Salvador,
    72, 74–75; and historical narrative,
    15–16, 210–11; Iraq, 181–82, 188–90;

Somalia, 103, 118; Vietnam, 1–2, 9–10,
    15, 39, 50–57, 61, 64–65, 68, 72, 75–76, 85,
    87–92, 100, 102, 118, 119, 122, 125–26,
    134–36, 143, 151, 156–58, 163–67, 173,
    181–82, 184–85, 191–93, 199–201, 206–11;
    Weinberger/Powell version of, 87–92;
    Yom Kippur War, 46. *See also* Forgetting
    war lessons
Lethality, 97, 140–41
Lewis, Adrian, 7
Lewy, Guenter, 20
LIC. *See* Low-intensity conflict
Light footprint, 123, 124, 126, 130
Light Infantry Divisions, 72–73, 82–84
Linn, Brian McAllister, *The Echo of Battle*,
    8–9
Local military forces, 30, 32, 54
Local populations, 32, 87, 105, 106, 143, 161
Lock-Pullan, Richard, 8, 42
Logical lines of operation, 171
Low-intensity conflict (LIC), 17, 60–85, 204;
    defining, 60–61, 68–74; in El Salvador,
    61–68; end of concept of, 94–95, 98;
    institutionalization of, 74–79; Light
    Infantry Divisions and, 72–73, 82–84;
    remodeling Army for, 79–84; types of, 60
Lugar, Richard, 101
Lute, Douglas, 192

MacFarland, Sean, 158, 160–61, 175, 182
MacIver, Robert, 210
MACV. *See* Military Assistance Command,
    Vietnam
Malaya, 35, 150
"Managerial" approach to war and defense, 9
Mansoor, Peter, 145, 174, 199
Manwaring, Max, 63, 65
Mao Zedong, 171
Marja, Afghanistan, 195–96
Marshall, Andrew, 114–16, 250*n*19
Marshall, George, 9
Mason, Christopher, 199–200
Mattis, James, 168
May, Ernest, 11
McCaffrey, Barry, 87, 100
McChrystal, Stanley, 18, 178, 182, 189–91,
    194–96, 198, 200
McClintock, Michael, 4
McFate, Montgomery, 169, 174
McGregor, Douglas, 140–41
McKiernan, David, 189
McMahon, Robert, 10

McManaway, Clayton, 136
McMaster, H. R., 158–60, 162, 174, 182, 186; *Dereliction of Duty*, 91, 158
McNamara, Robert, 158
McNamara Line, 111
Meese, Michael, 174
Melanson, Richard, 10
Menges, Constantine, 233*n*3
Merritt, Jack N., 55
Metrics. *See* Statistics, use and value of
Metz, Steven, 117
Metz, Thomas, 143
Meyer, Edward C., 63, 73
Military advisors, 47, 62–64, 66–68, 152
Military Assistance Command, Vietnam (MACV), 22, 33–34, 36
Military doctrine. *See* Doctrine
Military operations other than war (MOOTW), 97–98, 119
Military Review (journal), 15, 47, 55–56, 70–71, 75, 81, 82, 83, 94, 106, 163, 164, 167, 168, 172, 198, 199, 201
Military strategy, 7–8
Military training, 49. *See also* Education
Mission, clarity of, 56, 88–89, 94, 99, 101–2, 105
Mission creep, 101, 102, 120
Modernization theory, 4
Mogadishu incident, 101, 104, 149, 208
Montaigne, Michel de, 13
Montgomery, Thomas, 103
Mosul, Iraq, 139
Mullen, Mike, 187–88
Multinational Division-Center (MND-C), 177
Multi-National Force Iraq (MNF-I), 142, 174
Multi-National Security Transition Command-Iraq (MNSTC-I), 146

Nagl, John, 20, 21, 37, 167, 170, 172, 191, 200, 209, 216*n*7; *Learning to Eat Soup with a Knife*, 3–4, 150–51, 159
Narrative. *See* Historical narrative
National Defense University, 55, 103, 111
National Liberation Front (NLF), 20–22, 26, 34
National Military Strategy, 93
National Security Council, 33, 69, 80, 101–3, 124, 126, 145
National Security Presidential Directive (NSPD) 24 *Post-War Iraq Reconstruction*, 124

National Security Strategy, 93, 101–2, 116
National Security Strategy (NSS, 1987), 68–69
National Strategy for Victory in Iraq, 165
National Strategy for Victory in Iraq (National Security Council), 145
National Training Center, 152–53
Nation building, 101, 121–22, 139
NATO. *See* North Atlantic Treaty Organization
Naval War College, 55
Negroponte, John, 144, 150
Neoconservatism, 116, 129
Network-centric warfare, 115
Neu, Charles, 10
Neustadt, Richard, 11
Newsweek (magazine), 191
New World Order, 86, 95
New York Times (newspaper), 22–23, 191, 198, 201
Nicaragua, 60, 62, 69, 79
9/11 terrorist attacks, 115
9th Infantry Division, 27–30, 33–34
Nixon, Richard, 31, 33–37, 62, 120
Nixon Doctrine, 37, 42, 46, 48, 60, 61, 78
NLF. *See* National Liberation Front
North Atlantic Treaty Organization (NATO), 17, 58, 99, 106, 193, 195, 198
Northern Iraq, 90, 93, 96, 110
North Vietnamese Army. *See* People's Army of Vietnam
Nunn-Cohen Amendment, Goldwater-Nichols Defense Reorganization Act (1987), 80
NVA. *See* People's Army of Vietnam (PAVN)

Obama, Barack, 181, 186, 188–89, 191–94, 196, 198–99
Objectives, clarity of. *See* Mission, clarity of
Odierno, Raymond, 139–40, 142, 174, 178, 265*n*68
Office of Force Transformation, 115
Office of Net Assessment, 114
Office of Reconstruction and Humanitarian Assistance, 126
Office of the Secretary for Defense, 34
Olick, Jeffrey, 13
Ollivant, Doug, 174, 177, 178
101st Airborne Division, 139, 141, 149–50
173rd Airborne Brigade, 27, 30–33
"One War" strategy, 23
OOTW. *See* Operations other than war
Open Societies Initiative, 197

Operation Cobra Gold, 81
Operation Desert Shield, 92
Operation Desert Storm, 88, 91, 92
Operation Eclipse II, 127–28
Operation Enduring Freedom, 109, 248n1
Operation *Fardh al-Qanoon* (Enforcing the Rule of Law), 176–77
Operation Ivy Serpent, 140
Operation Moshtarak, 195–96
Operation Peninsula Strike, 140
Operation Phantom Fury, 159
Operation Phantom Phoenix, 177–78
Operation Phantom Strike, 177
Operation Provide Comfort, 93
Operation Restore Hope, 93, 125
Operations other than war (OOTW), 17, 94–108, 112, 118, 182, 204, 205
Operation Speedy Express, 27–30, 33–34
Operation Swarmer, 149
Operation Together Forward II, 177
Operation Urgent Fury, 241n99
Operation Washington Green, 30–33, 38
Optimism, in war doctrines, 112–13
Organizational culture, 5–10, 40–41
Overwhelming force, 7, 79, 89–90, 105, 111, 124, 130–31, 150, 187

Pacification, 20–30, 31, 33–36
Packer, George, 160, 169
Palmer, Bruce, 56
PAM 525-44 *US Operational Concept for Low Intensity Conflict*, 77
Pamphlet 525-5 *Force XXI Operations*, 97–98
Panama, 139
Parameters (journal), 15, 164
Patriquin, Travis, 261n12
Patton, George S., 7–8, 9
PAVN. *See* People's Army of Vietnam
Peacekeeping, 17; Army doctrine for, 92–100, 132; counterinsurgency compared to, 96, 108; in 1990s, 100–108; skepticism about, 99, 101, 121, 147–48; tensions between military doctrine and, 87, 90, 93, 100, 107–8, 130, 133, 166, 210
Peacekeeping Institute, 97, 99–100, 121–22
Peacetime engagement, 95–96
Pentagon. *See* US Defense Department
People's Army of Vietnam (PAVN), 20, 23–24, 26, 30, 54–55
People's Self-Defense Force (PSDF), 23
Perry, William J., 105

Petraeus, David, 18, 72, 83–84, 106, 139, 141–42, 150, 152, 163, 165–69, 173–83, 188–89, 194, 196–98, 200–201, 205–6, 209, 238n50
Philippines, 184
Phoenix Program, 22, 23, 200
Phuong Hoang program. *See* Phoenix Program
Planning for Iraq: Army errors in, 127, 129, 136; external warnings on, 123–26; Phase IV, 126–31; roots of, 108; Rumsfeld and, 123–26; shock-and-awe doctrine and, 111–13; and transformation of Army, 124–27, 131–32
Policy makers, history as used by, 11–12
Popkins, Samuel, 32
Popular Forces (PF), 23, 25, 30–31
Popular support. *See* Public opinion
Population security, 24, 26–27, 30, 32, 65, 175–77, 189–90
Powell, Colin, 9, 87, 87–93, 100, 102, 111, 118, 122, 124, 143, 187, 208, 244n25
Powell Doctrine, 17, 87–93, 101, 105, 107, 114, 124, 166, 187, 208–10, 244n25
Prados, John, 19
Precision-guided munitions, 110–11
Presidential Decision Directive (PDD) 25, 102, 108
Presidential Review Directive (PRD) 13, 95
President's National Bipartisan Commission on Central America (Kissinger Commission), 65
Prevention of Vietnam, desire for, 17, 39, 41, 50–51, 62–63, 65, 69, 91, 192, 208–9. *See also* Intervention
Professionalism, 106
Program for the Pacification and Long-Term Development of South Vietnam (PROVN), 21–22
Public opinion: on Iraq, 143, 145–46, 173; on military intervention, 41, 63, 69–70, 88–89, 96, 99, 105, 116, 244n19; on Vietnam War, 19, 41, 165

Al-Qaeda, 161, 173, 178, 193, 265n64
Quadrennial Defense Review (QDR 2001), 115, 116
Quadrennial Defense Review (QDR 2010), 186–87

Race, Jeffrey, 21
Raids, 47–48

Ramadi, Iraq, 156, 160–61, 205
Rambo (film), 233*n*1
RAND Corporation, 67
Rasmussen, Mikkel Vedby, 2, 12–14
Ravenal, Earl, 10
Reagan, Ronald, 60–62, 65, 68–69, 120, 243*n*12
Reagan Doctrine, 61, 65, 69–70, 233*n*3
Record, Jeffrey, 11
Regional Forces (RF), 23, 25, 30–31
Report of the El Salvador Military Strategy Assistance Team (Woerner Report), 64
Repressive regimes, US support for, 4, 240*n*81
Republic of Vietnam Armed Forces (RVNAF), 21, 24, 25, 32–34, 40
Reserve forces, 41, 54
Revolution in military affairs, 7, 17–18, 86, 110, 111, 114, 117, 186, 205. *See also* Transformation of Army
Reynolds, Kevin P., 146–47, 153
Rice, Condoleezza, 121, 123, 130, 160, 165, 173
Ricks, Thomas, 135, 169, 174; *Fiasco*, 132
Risk assessment, 122
Robinson, Linda, 169
Rogers, Bernard, 49
Rolling Stone (magazine), 196
Rose, Donald, 118
Rosen, Stephen Peter, 5
Rumsfeld, Donald, 109, 114–33, 138, 146, 173, 186, 206
Rumsfeld Doctrine, 116, 124
Rupp, Daryl, 139
Russell, James, 6, 158
RVNAF. *See* Republic of Vietnam Armed Forces
Rwanda, 103
Ryan, David, 10

Al-Sadr, Moqtada, 178
Sadr City, Iraq, 151
Samarra, Iraq, 149, 156
Sanchez, Ricardo, 106, 137–38, 142
Sassaman, Nathan, 141, 149
Al-Sattar, Abdul, 161
Scales, Robert H., 182, 198
School of Advanced Military Studies (SAMS), 76–77, 204
School of the Americas, 98–99
Schoomaker, Peter, 150–51
Schulzinger, Robert D., 10

Scowcroft, Brent, 80
Search and destroy tactics, 26, 54, 56, 65
Security Assistance Programs, 48
Senate Armed Services Committee, 130
Sepp, Kalev, 122, 142, 150, 164, 262*n*24
Serena, Chad, 6
Sewell, Sarah, 169
Shadow wars, 48
Shafer, D. Michael, 4
Sharp, Grant, 56
Sheehan, Neil, 166
Shelton, Hugh, 90–91, 99
Shia, 156, 177, 265*n*64
Shinseki, Eric, 116–17, 121–23, 125, 128–29
Shock-and-awe approach, 111–13, 124, 126, 130–31
Shultz, George, 89
Smith, DeWitt, 51, 55
Smith, Rupert, 183
Smyser, W. R., 50–52
Somalia, 90, 92, 93, 96, 101–4, 108, 110, 113, 118
Sontag, Susan, 13
Sorley, Lewis, 22, 165–67, 172–73, 179, 191–92, 200, 207, 209
SOUTHCOM. *See* US Southern Command
South Vietnam. *See* Government of Vietnam; Pacification
Soviet Union, 44–45, 62, 77, 181
Special Forces, 47–50, 80–82, 109, 178, 197
Special National Intelligence Estimate (NIE), 34–35
Special Operations Command (SOCOM), 80
Spector, Ronald, 41
Spiszer, John M., 198
Stability operations, 46–47, 97, 106, 108, 109, 118–21, 123, 132, 138, 149, 164, 182–85, 204, 205
Starry, Donn, 42, 44, 80, 88, 91–92, 112, 239*n*71
Statistics, use and value of, 25, 28, 172
Stearman, W. L., 50–52
Steele, James, 66
Steele, Michael D., 149–50
Steinberg, Jim, 192
Stewart, Richard, 163
Strategic corporal, 170, 264*n*48
Strategic culture, 6–9
Strategists, history as used by, 11–12
Strategy. *See* Military strategy
Stryker Brigade, 116–17
Sullivan, Gordon R., 76–77, 97, 117

Summers, Harry, 41, 45, 71, 75, 85, 92, 100–101, 167, 207, 209, 234n15; *On Strategy: The Vietnam War in Context*, 53–58, 158, 208
Sunni, 156, 159, 177, 178
Support operations, 118, 149
"Surge," in Iraq War aftermath, 173–79, 181–82, 189, 201, 265n68
Swain, Thomas E., 77
Symanski, Michael W., 71
Syria, 46

Tal Afar, Iraq, 158–60, 205
Talbott, Orwin C., 28
Taliban, 181, 189, 193, 195–98
Tanda system, 236n23
Tarok Kalache, Afghanistan, 197–98
Task Force Eagle, 119
Task Force Hurricane Andrew, 92
Technology: determinism linked to, 7; emphasis on, 31, 39, 51, 77, 97; insufficiencies in, 46; limitations of, 186; and transformation of Army, 86, 88, 110–16, 122, 249n15
Terrill, Andrew, *Reconstructing Iraq*, 124–25, 128
Tet Offensive (1968), 16, 111, 143
Thailand, 81
Thelen, David, 13
3rd Armored Cavalry Regiment, 158–59
3rd Infantry Division, 139
Third World, 45–46, 61–62
Thompson, Robert, 35, 37, 170–71
Three-block war, 170, 264n48
Thurman, Maxwell R., 65, 78
Tilford, Earl, 9–10
Time-phased forces-deployment list (TPFDL), 124
Tomes, Robert, 8
Torrance, Thomas, 129
Total Force Concept, 41
TRADOC. *See* Training and Doctrine Command
Training and Doctrine Command (TRADOC), 43, 44, 49, 77, 92–93, 97–98
Transformation of Army, 109–22, 205; criticisms of, 167; intellectual origins of, 110–14; and Iraq planning, 124–27, 131–32; limitations of, 117; Rumsfeld and, 114–22; technology and, 86, 88, 110–16, 122, 249n15. *See also* Revolution in military affairs

Trevor-Roper, Hugh, 207
Trinity, Clausewitzian, 53, 232n74
Trullinger, James, 21
Truman, Harry, 12
Tuchman, Barbara, 12
Tucker, Michael, 136
Tucker, Nancy, 19
Turse, Nick, 28
25th Infantry Division, 21

Ucko, David, 4, 155
Ullman, Harold, *Shock and Awe*, 111–13, 124, 126
Unconventional warfare, 47
Uniforms, 106
United Nations, 95, 102
Unity of effort, 94, 120, 164, 170
US Air Force, 117
US Army: change in, 5–6; and counterinsurgency, 3–5, 39–40, 180, 182, 199, 206; and counterinsurgency in Iraq, 134–80; criticisms of, 40–41, 49–54, 57, 75–76, 154, 158–63, 200; doctrine in (*see* Doctrine); educational system and curriculum of, 43–50, 55, 97; in El Salvador, 62–68, 71–72; force structure remodeling, 79–84, 97–98; identity of, 4, 8, 41, 43, 45, 58–59, 87, 94, 180, 205–7; institutional structure of, 40–42, 56; intellectual traditions in, 9; learning culture in, 3–4; limits of, 42, 45–46, 52–53, 60; modernization of, 46, 97; morale and discipline in, 40–41, 45; organizational culture of, 5–10, 40–41; and peace operations, 94–108; and planning for Iraq, 127, 129, 136; post–Cold War, 86–108; post-Vietnam, 39–59; strategy of, 7–8; tensions in, 8–9; transformation of (21st century), 109–22, 131–32, 167, 205
US Army Center of Military History, 150, 231n57
US Central Command (CENTCOM), 123, 124, 126, 137–38, 140, 145, 146, 188, 252n65
US Congress: and Central America policy, 64–65, 68–69; and force structure remodeling, 80; on US intervention, 44, 62
US Defense Department (Pentagon), 54, 64, 72, 80, 90, 124, 126, 135, 164, 187
US Government Counterinsurgency Guide, 186

US Marine Corps, 117, 160, 164, 168, 195–96; Combined Action Program, 20, 30–33
US Navy, 117
US Southern Command (SOUTHCOM), 63–64, 72, 137
USSR. *See* Soviet Union
US State Department, 34, 39, 124, 126, 148

Vann, John Paul, 27
Van Tien Dung, 54
VC. *See* Vietcong
V Corps, 126, 131, 136–37
Vietcong (VC), 26, 27, 30
Vietmalia syndrome, 101, 108
Vietnamese People's Army. *See* People's Army of Vietnam
Vietnamization, 30–31, 144–46, 148, 172
Vietnam Special Studies Group (VSSG), 33–34
Vietnam Studies Series, 231n57
Vietnam syndrome, 19, 59, 61, 89, 122, 136. *See also* Vietnam War: persistence of, in public memory
Vietnam War: Afghanistan compared to, 191–93, 199–200; conflicting theories of, 9–10, 20–22, 31, 37–38, 85, 207; counterinsurgency in, 19–38, 53–57, 179; El Salvador and, 62–68; failure/success of, 3–4; forgetting/ignoring of, 43–47, 49–50, 55–56, 58, 207–8; historiography of, 19–23, 52, 173; Iraq compared to, 2, 17–18, 23, 108, 134–57, 161–67, 174–75, 209; lessons of, 1–2, 9–10, 15, 39, 50–57, 61, 64–65, 68, 72, 75–76, 85, 87–92, 100, 102, 113, 118, 119, 122, 125–26, 134–36, 143, 151, 156–58, 163–67, 173, 181–82, 184–85, 191–93, 199–201, 206–11; moral response to, 40; persistence of, in public memory, 2, 61, 87, 233n1 (*see also* Vietnam syndrome); prevention of involvement similar to, 17, 39, 41, 50–51, 62–63, 65, 69, 91, 192, 208–9; public opinion on, 19, 41, 165; stability operations in, 119 (*see also* Population security); tactics in, 29; technology in, 31, 39, 46, 51, 111; US Army after, 39–59; winnability of, 19–27, 36–38, 53, 165
Vought, Donald, 56
VSSG. *See* Vietnam Special Studies Group
Vuono, Carl, 78

Wade, James, Jr., *Shock and Awe*, 111–13, 124, 126
Waghelstein, John, 75
Wallace, Scott, 130, 137
Wallace, William S., 183
Warsaw Pact, 17, 43, 44
Washington Post (newspaper), 178
Weigley, Russell, 3, 8–9, 51; *The American Way of War*, 7
Weinberger, Caspar, 80, 87–89, 102, 208
Weinberger Doctrine, 88–89, 208
West Bank, 140
Westmoreland, William, 20–24, 38, 54, 56, 110, 150, 174, 185, 204, 207
Weyand, Frederick C. (Fred), 41–43, 56, 80
Whitcomb, Steve, 137
Whole man concept, 49
Wickham, John C., 73, 82, 83
Winter, Jay, 13–15
Woerner, Fred, 64, 66, 72, 79, 234n15
Woerner Report, 64
Wohlstetter, Albert, 250n19
Wolfowitz, Paul, 116
Woods, George, 128
Woodward, Bob, 144
World Policy Journal, 200
World War II, 7

Yingling, Paul, 158, 162–63; "A Failure of Generalship," 162
Yom Kippur War (1973), 46

Zinni, Anthony, 252n65
Zisk, Kimberly Marten, 6

Milton Keynes UK
Ingram Content Group UK Ltd.
UKHW050023210624
444428UK00005B/239

9 780804 793377